Leading to Occupational Health and Safety

How Leadership Behaviours Impact Organizational Safety and Well-Being

Edited by

E. Kevin Kelloway, Karina Nielsen and Jennifer K. Dimoff

WILEY Blackwell

This edition first published 2017

Registered Office
John Wiley & Sons Ltd, The Atrium, Southern Gate, Chichester, West Sussex, PO19 8SQ, UK

Editorial Offices
350 Main Street, Malden, MA 02148-5020, USA
9600 Garsington Road, Oxford, OX4 2DQ, UK
The Atrium, Southern Gate, Chichester, West Sussex, PO19 8SQ, UK

For details of our global editorial offices, for customer services, and for information about how to apply for permission to reuse the copyright material in this book please see our website at www.wiley.com/wiley-blackwell.

Library of Congress Cataloging-in-Publication Data

Names: Kelloway, E. Kevin, editor. | Nielsen, Karina, 1973– editor. | Dimoff, Jennifer K., 1989– editor.
Title: Leading to occupational health and safety : how leadership behaviours impact organizational safety and well-being / edited by E. Kevin Kelloway, Karina Nielsen and Jennifer K. Dimoff.
Description: Chichester, West Sussex, UK : John Wiley & Sons, 2017. | Includes bibliographical references and index.
Identifiers: LCCN 2016036897| ISBN 9781118973707 (cloth) | ISBN 9781118973745 (pbk.) | ISBN 9781118973714 (epub) | ISBN 9781118973738 (pdf)
Subjects: LCSH: Industrial hygiene–Management. | Industrial safety–Management. | Organizational behavior. | Leadership.
Classification: LCC HD7261 .L39 2017 | DDC 658.3/82–dc23
LC record available at https://lccn.loc.gov/2016036897

A catalogue record for this book is available from the British Library.

Cover image: 7postman/Gettyimages
Cover design: Wiley

Set in 10/12pt Warnock by SPi Global, Pondicherry, India

10 9 8 7 6 5 4 3 2 1

Leading to Occupational Health and Safety

Contents

Notes on Contributors

Kara A. Arnold is Professor of Organizational Behaviour and Human Resource Management at the Faculty of Business Administration at Memorial University in St. John's, NL, Canada. Her research focuses on transformational leadership, employee and leader well-being, and gender issues in organizations. Her work has been published in the *Journal of Occupational Health Psychology, Work & Stress,* the *Journal of Applied Psychology, Human Resource Management,* and the *Leadership & Organization Development Journal,* as various book chapters, and has been presented at leading international conferences.

Julian Barling is the Borden Chair of Leadership at the Queen's School of Business, Canada, and author of *The Science of Leadership: Lessons from Research for Organizational Leaders* (Oxford University Press, 2014). His research focuses on the effects of leaders' psychological well-being on the quality of their leadership behaviours, and the development of leadership behaviours. He is co-editor (with Christopher Barnes, Erica Carleton and David Wagner) of *Sleep and Work: Research Insights for the Workplace* (Oxford University Press, 2016).

Andrea Bishop is a Postdoctoral Fellow at the IWK Health Centre/School of Nursing, Dalhousie University, Canada. She completed her Interdisciplinary PhD at Dalhousie University, exploring patient engagement in patient safety. She went on to complete a postdoctoral fellowship in the Department of Psychology at Saint Mary's University, Canada, with a focus on organizational safety culture. She is currently developing expertise in knowledge translation research methods during her two-year postdoctoral work with the Strengthening Transitions in Pediatric Care Research Program. Her research interests include transitions of care, patient safety, and patient engagement.

Kate C. Bowers completed a Bachelor of Arts (Hons.) degree in Psychology at Grenfell Campus, Memorial University of Newfoundland, before pursuing graduate studies at Saint Mary's University, Canada. Under the direction of Mark Fleming, Kate completed a Master's of Science in Applied Psychology (Industrial/Organizational specialization) where she focused on safety culture and understanding how management practices inform organizational safety outcomes. Kate is a recipient of numerous academic awards including the Joseph-Armand Bombardier Master's Scholarship. At present, Kate is employed as a Human and

Organizational Factors Specialist with the National Energy Board of Canada where she combines her specialized training with research and innovation to advance industry safety.

Julie Dyrdek Broad is completing her doctoral studies at George Washington University, US, where she studies organizational sciences, focusing her research on the emergence of collective Psychological Capital (*c*PsyCap) for intact groups and teams. She has more than 24 years of global executive experience, and is currently working at Booz Allen Hamilton, where she has supported the DoD, to include the Army Resiliency Directorate, Comprehensive Soldier & Family Fitness program. Ms Broad's research stream also includes work on serious gaming solutions to build PsyCap in the workplace, and on how PsyCap can be leveraged in the treatment of traumatic brain injuries (TBIs).

Erica L. Carleton is Assistant Professor of Organizational Behavior at Edwards School of Business, University of Saskatchewan. She was formerly a Postdoctoral Research Fellow at Ivey Business School, Western University, Canada. She completed her PhD in Organizational Behavior at the Smith School of Business, Queen's University, under the supervision of Julian Barling. Her research interests include leadership, sleep and well-being. She conducted her dissertation research on sleep, well-being and leadership. She is a co-editor (with Julian Barling, Christopher Barnes and David Wagner) of *Sleep and Work: Research Insights for the Workplace* (Oxford University Press, 2016).

Sharon Clarke is a full Professor of Organizational Psychology at Alliance Manchester Business School, University of Manchester, UK. She has research interests in safety culture, safety climate, leadership, well-being and health. Her work has been widely published in leading academic and practitioner journals and in co-authored books, including *Human Safety and Risk Management*, now in its third edition (CRC Press, 2015). She is currently Editor-in-Chief of the *Journal of Occupational and Organizational Psychology* and has served on the editorial boards of the *Journal of Occupational Health Psychology* and the *International Journal of Stress Management*.

Jennifer K. Dimoff is an Assistant Professor of Industrial/Organizational (I/O) Psychology at Portland State University (PSU). She completed her Ph.D. in I/O Psychology from Saint Mary's University, Canada, in 2016, where she also received her MSc. in Applied Psychology. Dr. Dimoff received her Honors BSc. in the Biological Sciences at Queen's University, where she was also a research assistant in Organizational Behavior at the Smith School of Business. Her key research interests include workplace mental health, leadership training, and psychological resilience. Dr. Dimoff's most recent work has focused primarily on the development and evaluation of manager-focused workplace mental health training programs, notably the Mental Health Awareness Training (MHAT) for workplace leaders.

Emma Donaldson-Feilder is a Chartered Occupational Psychologist and Director of both Affinity Health at Work and Affinity Coaching and Supervision,

UK. She specializes in supporting organizations to achieve sustainable performance through positive employee health, well-being and engagement, with a particular emphasis on people management and leadership. In order to have the best possible evidence base for her work, she is actively involved in research; conversely, her consultancy and coaching with a range of organizations ensure that the research is of genuine practical use in real-world settings. She is also involved in public policy, writing and presenting on health and work issues.

Philippe Dubreuil is an Industrial/Organizational Psychologist and Professor at the Université du Québec à Trois-Rivières, Canada. He completed his doctoral studies at the Université de Sherbrooke, Canada, where his work mainly focused on the psychological processes involved in the relation between strengths use and work performance. His research topics concern strengths, passion, engagement and well-being at work and his contributions are published in academic journals such as *The Journal of Positive Psychology* and *Human Relations*. As a consultant, he also works with leaders, teams and organizations, helping them increase their engagement and performance through better awareness and use of their strengths.

Ståle Einarsen is Professor in Work and Organizational Psychology at the Faculty of Psychology, University of Bergen, Norway, where he is head of Bergen Bullying Research Group. Professor Einarsen has published extensively in issues related to workplace bullying, sexual harassment, whistle-blowing, destructive leadership, innovation and creativity in organizations, and health and well-being at work. He is a co-founder of the International Association on Workplace Bullying and Harassment and has co-edited three international volumes on this subject.

Mark Fleming is the CN Professor of Safety Culture in the Department of Psychology at Saint Mary's University, Canada. Mark is an applied psychologist with over 20 years of experience in health and safety research in offshore oil and gas, patient safety, nuclear power, petrochemical and construction. His research includes investigating methods for measuring and improving safety culture, safety motivation, safety leadership and rail safety. He is dedicated to developing practical and valid tools to assist organizations to prevent harm.

Jacques Forest is a professor-researcher, organizational psychologist and CHRP in the organization and human resources department at the École des sciences de la gestion de l'Université du Québec à Montréal (ESG UQAM), the biggest French-speaking business school in Canada. His research and interventions specialize in human motivation and optimal functioning using strengths management and self-determination theory. The underlying concern of his work is to activate, develop and sustain high-quality motivation so that performance and well-being can be experienced on a daily basis for long periods of time.

Annilee M. Game is a Lecturer in Organizational Behaviour and Business Ethics at the University of East Anglia, UK. Her research focuses on how individual experiences of work and careers can be enhanced through healthy, respectful and effective relationships. She conducts both quantitative and qualitative research. Specific topics of interest include ethics in leadership and decision-making, workplace incivility, emotions and well-being, adult attachment in organizations, and skilled migrant careers.

Sara Guediri is a Lecturer in Organizational Psychology at Alliance Manchester Business School, University of Manchester, UK. Her research explores issues of occupational safety and well-being, with a focus on leadership in high-risk contexts.

E. Kevin Kelloway is the Canada Research Chair in Occupational Health Psychology and Professor of Psychology at Saint Mary's University, Canada. A prolific researcher, he is a Fellow of the Association for Psychological Science, the Canadian Psychological Association, the Society for Industrial and Organizational Psychology and the International Association of Applied Psychology. His research interests include leadership, occupational safety and workplace mental health. He is a recipient of the Distinguished Psychologist in Management Award from the Society for Psychologists in Management and currently serves as President of the Canadian Psychological Association.

Allan Lee is an academic working at the University of Manchester, UK. Before joining Alliance Manchester Business School, Allan studied Psychology and Organizational Psychology at Cardiff University, before moving to Aston Business School, UK to complete his PhD. He has conducted research on leadership in a variety of settings. His research focuses mainly on the premise that leadership is largely determined by the quality of the relationship between leaders and followers.

Rachel Lewis is a Registered Occupational Psychologist, an Associate Professor in Occupational and Business Psychology at Kingston Business School, UK, and a Director of Affinity Health at Work (a niche occupational health psychology consultancy). She regularly publishes in both academic and practitioner publications in the areas of leadership, management and employee well-being and engagement (along with speaking and providing consultancy in these areas).

Fred Luthans received his PhD from the University of Iowa. He is University and Distinguished Professor of Management Emeritus at the University of Nebraska, US. He is a former President of the Academy of Management. He was or is editor or co-editor of three top journals. He is the author of several well-known books and over 200 articles. In total, his work has been cited over 43,000 times and his current H-Index is 85. His research at first focused on behavioural management, but in recent years he has given attention to what he has termed 'positive organizational behavior (POB)' and 'psychological capital (PsyCap)', which he founded.

Jane Mullen is an Associate Professor in the Department of Commerce, Ron Joyce Center for Business Studies at Mount Allison University, Canada. She received her PhD in Business Administration (Management) from the Sobey School of Business, Saint Mary's University, Canada. In the Commerce Department, which she joined in 2004, she teaches organizational behaviour and human resource management courses. Her research interests are in the area of occupational health and safety.

Karina Nielsen is the Chair of Work Psychology at the Institute of Work Psychology, University of Sheffield, UK, and a research affiliate at the Center for the Promotion of Health in the New England Workplace (CPH-NEW), US, and the Karolinska Institutet, Sweden. Her research interests lie within the area of the evaluation of organizational interventions and ways to develop methods to understand how and why such interventions succeed or fail. She has published more than 100 books, chapters and articles. She is currently on the editorial boards of *Human Relations, The Leadership Quarterly* and the *Journal of Business and Psychology*, and is an Associate Editor of *Work & Stress*.

Morten Birkeland Nielsen is a senior researcher at the Norwegian National Institute of Occupational Health and Professor in Work and Organizational Psychology at the University of Bergen, Norway. His research interests include occupational health and safety, workplace bullying and harassment, leadership, personality, and research methodology. Nielsen is an Associate Editor of *Work & Stress* and an editorial board member of *Scandinavian Psychologist*. He has authored over 50 refereed journal articles.

Timur Ozbilir is a PhD candidate in the Industrial/Organizational Psychology programme at Saint Mary's University, Canada. His research activities have focused on occupational health and safety, specifically on scale development for safety leadership and safety culture, and on safety leadership training. In addition to his academic research, he has been involved in consulting projects for a number of organizations, including the Workers' Compensation Board of Nova Scotia, Encana Corporation, and Soteria Strains. His other research interests include corporate social responsibility and personality. He has received research grants from the Social Sciences and Humanities Research Council of Canada and the Nova Scotia Health Research Foundation.

Samantha A. Penney is a doctoral candidate in Industrial/Organizational Psychology at Saint Mary's University, Canada. Her research focuses on promoting psychologically healthy workplaces and employees through training and individualized interventions. She has presented this work at national and international conferences. She has acted as an internal leadership and organizational development consultant for a large national organization. She is a member of the Nova Scotia Psychologically Healthy Workplace committee and the CN Centre for Occupational Health and Safety. Before her doctoral studies, Samantha received an MSc from Saint Mary's University in Industrial/Organizational Psychology and a BA (Hons.) in Psychology from Lakehead University, Canada.

Alfredo Rodríguez-Muñoz is Associate Professor at the Department of Social Psychology at Complutense University of Madrid, Spain. His current research interests focus on organizational and health psychology, bullying at work, and employee well-being. His work has been published in journals such as *Work & Stress*, the *Journal of Occupational and Organizational Psychology* and the *European Journal of Work and Organizational Psychology*.

Ana Isabel Sanz-Vergel is a Senior Lecturer in Organizational Behaviour at Norwich Business School, University of East Anglia, UK. Her research interests are related to the fields of work and organizational psychology, occupational health, and employee well-being, including topics such as daily recovery from stress, work–family conflict and crossover of work-related experiences. Her research has been published in such journals as *Human Relations*, the *Journal of Occupational and Organizational Psychology* and the *Journal of Occupational Health Psychology*.

Anders Skogstad is Professor in Work and Organizational Psychology at the Faculty of Psychology, University of Bergen, Norway, and a licensed specialist in organizational psychology. His research interests include role stressors, personality, leadership styles, bullying, organizational justice, counterproductive behaviour and organizational climate, with a primary focus on active and passive forms of destructive leadership. He has published extensively in various journals such as *The Leadership Quarterly, Journal of Occupational Health Psychology* and *Work & Stress*, and edited various books in work and organizational psychology.

Susanne Tafvelin is a Senior Lecturer in the Department of Psychology, Umeå University, Sweden. She has a background as an occupational health psychologist, and her thesis focused on the transformational leadership process in public organizations. Her present research interests include the relationship between leadership and employee health, leadership training as an occupational health intervention, and transfer of leadership training.

Megan M. Walsh is a PhD candidate in Management (Organizational Behaviour and Human Resource Management) at the Faculty of Business Administration at Memorial University, Canada. Her main research interests are mindfulness at work, leadership, stress, and employee well-being. She has presented research at national and international conferences, and has published in journals such as *Work & Stress* and the *Journal of Occupational Health Psychology*.

Jennifer Wong is pursuing her PhD in Industrial/Organizational Psychology at Saint Mary's University, Canada. Her core research interests are occupational health psychology, occupational safety, leadership and training, and the roles of emotions and cognition at work. She has expertise in experience sampling method, longitudinal field research, and using objective measurements of well-being and performance in her research designs. Her current work explores the role of different types of attention in human errors.

Introduction

E. Kevin Kelloway, Karina Nielsen and Jennifer K. Dimoff

This book began with our collective recognition that leaders play a pervasive role in determining the health and safety of organizations. Our own individual research has shown the effect of leaders on employee safety (e.g., Mullen & Kelloway, 2009) and employee well-being (Arnold, Turner, Barling, Kelloway & McKee, 2007; Nielsen & Daniels, 2012), and has pointed to the role leaders play as mental health resources in organizations (e.g., Dimoff, Kelloway & Burnstein, 2016) and as key determinants in the success of organizational interventions (Nielsen, 2013; Nielsen & Randall, 2009). Indeed, enough data have now accumulated that we thought it worthwhile to invite the leading researchers in this area to review the work they have been doing related to leadership and occupational health and safety.

Doing so, of course, requires a common understanding of what constitutes organizational 'leadership'. Offering a single authoritative definition of leadership is a daunting task that goes well beyond our scope. Indeed, there are likely to be as many definitions of leadership as there are researchers interested in the topic (Kelloway & Barling, 2010). For the most part, however, these definitions fall within one of two broad categories. First, some researchers have focused on the notion of role occupancy – being concerned with who occupies the formal leadership roles (e.g., supervisors, managers) in organizations (Barling, Christie & Hoption, 2011). A second definition has focused on how individuals influence others. This is the question of leadership style (Barling et al., 2011) that, in its modern manifestation, focuses on the specific behaviours in which leaders engage. Kelloway and Barling (2010) combined these two definitions, suggesting that when we talk about organizational leadership we are talking about the effectiveness and behaviours of those who hold formal leadership roles in organizations. Broadly speaking, this is the approach adopted by the authors who have contributed to this book. Through these contributions, we have aimed to capture both the theoretical underpinnings of effective leadership styles and the implications for the specific leadership styles and behaviours that may influence occupational health and safety in the twenty-first-century workplace.

Leading to Occupational Health and Safety: How Leadership Behaviours Impact Organizational Safety and Well-Being, First Edition.
Edited by E. Kevin Kelloway, Karina Nielsen and Jennifer K. Dimoff.

Theories of Effective Leadership

Early attempts to understand organizational leadership focused on studying the lives of influential people in order to identify the traits and qualities associated with leadership emergence and effectiveness (Carlyle, 1907). The focus on individual qualities or traits dominated the early twentieth century, but was subsequently supplanted by a focus on the behaviours enacted by successful leaders. In essence, the research question progressed from a focus on '*who* is a leader' to '*what* do effective leaders do' (Kelloway & Gilbert, in press). Although there have been many behavioural theories, relatively few continue to dominate most of the research literature. In our review, we focus on the specific theories that are referenced in the current volume in order to provide a common basis of understanding.

Transformational Leadership

Several reviewers have noted that Bass's (1985) transformational leadership theory is the focus of more research than all other leadership theories combined (Barling et al., 2011; Judge & Bono, 2000). The theory makes a fundamental distinction between transactional and transformational leadership behaviours (Bass, 1985). Transactional behaviours constitute an exchange between the leader and the follower: the leaders' behaviour is seen as a response to employee behaviours. Both negative and positive transactions are possible.

First, *laissez-faire* leadership occurs when the leader has no response to the behaviour of followers. In a sense this is the absence of transactions and such leaders do not take actions in the workplace and avoid getting involved in workplace decisions or activities. In the *management by exception* style, the leader responds to mistakes and failures to meet standards on the part of the employee. Two forms of management by exception are possible. In passive management by exception, managers act as laissez-faire leaders until a mistake is made and then they respond with criticism and punishment. In active management by exception, the leader actively looks for employee mistakes and then responds with criticism and punishment. *Contingent reward* behaviours are based on positive, rather than negative, transactions. Sometimes thought of as good management, leaders using this style set clear expectations for employee behaviour and respond with immediate and contingent feedback – either critiquing or praising performance depending on the nature of the employee behaviours. Judge and Piccolo's (2004) meta-analysis found that laissez-faire and management by exception behaviours were associated with employee dissatisfaction. In contrast, when leaders displayed contingent reward behaviours, employee satisfaction and individual and organizational performance were enhanced.

Transformational leadership is posited to result in performance above and beyond those attributable to transactions. Indeed, Bass (1985) entitled his book

Leadership and Performance Beyond Expectations, in recognition of the hypothesized effects of transformational leadership behaviours. In essence, these transformational behaviours comprise four behaviours (Bass & Riggio, 2006) that constitute the 'four I's' of transformational leadership. *Inspirational motivation* occurs when leaders set high but achievable standards and encourage followers to achieve more than they thought they could. Leaders show *idealized influence* when they create a sense of shared mission and build trust and respect among their followers because they can be counted on to go beyond self-interest to do what is right. Leaders display *individualized consideration* when they get involved in coaching, mentoring and providing support to employees. Finally, when leaders challenge employees' beliefs and encourage independent and creative thought they are engaging in *intellectual stimulation*.

There is a great deal of evidence supporting the effectiveness of transformational leadership behaviours. Transformational leadership is associated with increased individual, team, and organizational performance, as well as employee satisfaction and a variety of positive organizational outcomes (Judge & Piccolo, 2004). Importantly, leaders can be taught transformational behaviours, and when they are, employees demonstrate improved attitudes and performance in a variety of contexts (Barling et al., 1996; Mullen & Kelloway, 2009).

Leader–Member Exchange (LMX)

LMX can be thought of as the second most researched theory of leadership. Barling et al. (2011) reported that 63 per cent of the studies they reviewed were based on either transformational leadership theory or LMX, with the former being more researched. Essentially, LMX theory is premised on the idea that leaders and followers influence each other and that it is the quality of the relationship between the two that is most important (Gerstner & Day, 1997). The theory is explicitly rooted in social exchange theory (Blau, 1964) in that it focuses on the nature of the exchange between leaders and their followers. Meta-analyses (e.g., Gerstner & Day, 1997) largely support the hypothesized associations between high-quality relationships and employee attitudes and performance.

Authentic and Ethical Leadership

More recent theories of leadership that have garnered less research attention are theories about authentic (e.g., Avolio & Gardner, 2005) and ethical leadership. Although researchers have articulated slightly different views of authenticity, most draw on Kernis (2003), who identified four elements of authenticity: self-awareness, unbiased processing, relational authenticity, and authentic behaviour/action. Ethical leadership shares a similar concern with authentic and transformational leadership, in that all consider the moral dimension of leader behaviour (Brown & Treviño, 2006). Ethical leadership is more than just an individual leader having personal integrity. Rather, ethical leadership considers the leader's proactive attempts to encourage ethical, and discourage unethical, behaviour in organizations.

Theories of Negative Leadership

Although most of the extant research has focused on identifying the behaviours characteristic of effective leadership, more recently many researchers have focused on the dark side of leadership (see for example, Kelloway, Sivanathan, Francis & Barling, 2005; Kelloway, Teed and Prosser, 2007), identifying behaviours that might be considered destructive (see Chapter 9) forms of leadership.

Abusive Supervision

Abusive supervision happens when individuals in a formal leadership role engage in aggressive or punishing behaviour towards their employees (Tepper, 2000, 2007). Yelling at or ridiculing subordinates, name-calling, or threatening employees with punishment or job loss are all examples of abusive supervision in the workplace. Not surprisingly, employees who experience such behaviours from their supervisors report lower levels of job and life satisfaction, lower levels of affective commitment, increased work–family conflict, and psychological distress (Tepper, 2000). Wong and Kelloway (2016) provided data on how negative interactions with supervisors might affect physical health. Their study documented increased blood pressure as a result of negative supervisory interactions and this increase in blood pressure was maintained into the after-work evening period.

Supervisory Injustice

More broadly, a great deal of research has focused on the consequences of being treated unfairly by supervisors. In the well-known Whitehall II studies, data have also emerged that suggests the importance of supervisory injustice as a predictor of psychiatric illness (Ferrie et al., 2006). Kivimaki and colleagues (Kivimaki, Elovainio, Vahtera & Ferrie, 2003; Kivimaki et al., 2005) have shown that both procedural (whether the organization follows fair policies) and relational (how my supervisor treats me) injustice were predictors of sickness-related absence and minor psychiatric illness. A variety of physical health outcomes, such as heavy drinking (Kouvonen et al., 2008), impaired cardiac regulation (Elovainio, Leino-Arjas, Vahtera & Kivimaki, 2006), and use of sick time (Kivimaki et al., 2003) are linked to supervisory injustice.

Passive Leadership

Kelloway et al. (2005) suggested that one way in which leaders can be ineffective is through their own inaction. Drawing heavily on Bass's (1985) conceptualization of laissez-faire and passive management by exception, Kelloway, Mullen & Francis (2006) showed that passive leadership was not merely the absence of transformational leadership. In their study, passive leadership was associated with lower safety attitudes among employees even after controlling for the positive effects of transformational leadership. Similarly, Skogstad,

Einarsen, Torsheim, Aasland & Hetland (2007) argued that passive leadership is not just the absence of good leadership, but actively exerts a destructive force in organizations.

About This Book

Mirroring the evolution of occupational health and safety as a field, we begin with a consideration of the role of the leader in promoting or developing safe workplaces. Thus, Sharon Clarke, Sara Guediri and Allan Lee focus on safety leadership in organizations, while Bowers, Fleming and Bishop focus more intently on the role of senior leaders and their influence on safety within the organization. Wong, Ozbilir and Mullen round out the focus on safety by considering how safety leadership can be developed in the organization.

We then move to a consideration of employee health and the contributions leaders make to employee wellbeing. Tafvelin draws on conservation of resource and self-determination theory to explain how transformational leadership is linked to employee wellbeing. Game broadens this focus by examining the contribution leaders make to creating respectful workplaces. Similarly, Kelloway, Penney and Dimoff suggest that the creation of a psychologically healthy workplace is linked to the behaviour of leaders in organizations. Sanz-Vergel and Rodriguez-Muñoz consider how leaders affect the experience of work and family balance among their employees, and Dimoff and Kelloway discuss the role of organizational leaders as sources of social support for employees. Skogstad, Morten Birkeland Nielsen and Einarsen consider the nature and effects of destructive leadership on employee well-being. Karina Nielsen discusses the role of leaders in making or breaking organizational interventions aimed at improving employee well-being. Paralleling our earlier structure, Donaldson-Feilder and Lewis round off our focus on health by considering how positive leadership can be developed in organizations.

In the last chapters of the book, we move beyond the traditional divides of health and safety to consider myriad ways in which leadership and wellbeing are intertwined. Many of these focus on newly developed concepts that the authors integrate into existing literature. Walsh and Arnold introduce the notion of mindfulness and mindful leadership as an antecedent to leadership behaviours that result in employee wellbeing. Broad and Luthans consider the burgeoning literature on psychological capital (PsyCap) to suggest how leaders might develop collective psychological capital to enhance well-being. Dubreuil and Forest adopt a strengths-based approach to leadership development.

The last chapter in the book, by Carleton and Barling, makes a fitting end note for the book by reversing the link between leadership and wellbeing. These authors focus on the psychological wellbeing of leaders and the consequences that might have for leadership and organizations. In doing so, they introduce a novel, and thus far overlooked, perspective.

Conclusion

The observation that 'the way our leaders treat us has implications for our well-being' would come as no surprise to any working individual. However, we suggest that the range of topics addressed in this volume make the case that these effects are more diverse, and more far-reaching, than many of us would have guessed. We hope that in assembling this collection we have advanced both research and practice and that the result of our collective endeavours will be better leadership and healthier, safer organizations

References

Avolio, B. J. & Gardner, W. L. (2005). Authentic leadership development: Getting to the root of positive forms of leadership. *Leadership Quarterly*, 16, 315–38.

Arnold, K., Turner, N., Barling, J., Kelloway, E. K. & McKee, M. (2007). Transformational leadership and psychological well-being: The mediating role of meaningful work. *Journal of Occupational Health Psychology*, 12, 193–203.

Barling, J., Christie, A., & Hoption, A. (2011). Leadership. In S. Zedeck (editor-in-chief) Handbook of Industrial and Organizational Psychology. Washington, DC: American Psychological Association.

Barling, J., Weber, T. & Kelloway, E. K. (1996). Effects of transformational leadership training on attitudinal and financial outcomes: A field experiment. *Journal of Applied Psychology*, 81, 827–32.

Bass, B. M. (1985). Leadership and Performance Beyond Expectations. New York: Free Press.

Bass, B. M. & Riggio, R. E. (2006). Transformational Leadership (2nd edn). Mahwah, NJ: Lawrence Erlbaum Associates.

Blau, P. M. (1964). Exchange and Power in Social Life. New York: Wiley.

Brown, M. W & Treviño, L. K. (2006). Ethical leadership: A review and future directions. *Leadership Quarterly*, 17, 595–616.

Carlyle, T. (1907). Heroes and Hero Worship. Boston, MA: Houghton Mifflin.

Dimoff, J. K., Kelloway, E. K. & Burnstein, M. (2016). Mental health awareness training (MHAT): The development and evaluation of an intervention for workplace leaders. *International Journal of Stress Management*, 23(2): 167–89.

Elovainio, M., Leino-Arjas, P., Vahtera, J. & Kivimaki, M. (2006). Justice at work and cardiovascular mortality: A prospective cohort study. *Journal of Psychosomatic Research*, 61, 271–4.

Ferrie, J. E., Head, J. A., Shipley, M. J., Vahtera, J., Marmot, M. G. & Kivimaki, M. (2006). Injustice at work and incidence of psychiatric morbidity: The Whitehall II study. *Occupational and Environmental Medicine*, 63, 443–50.

Gerstner, C. R. & Day, D. V. (1997). Meta-analytic review of leader–member exchange theory: Correlates and construct issues. *Journal of Applied Psychology*, 82, 827–44.

Judge, T. A. & Bono, J. E. (2000). Five-factor model of personality and transformational leadership. *Journal of Applied Psychology*, 85, 751–65.

Judge, T. A. & Piccolo, R. F. (2004). Transformational and transactional leadership: A meta-analytic test of their relative validity. *Journal of Applied Psychology*, 89(5), 755–68.

Kelloway, E. K. & Barling, J. (2010). Leadership development as an intervention in occupational health psychology. *Work & Stress*, 24, 260–79.

Kelloway, E. K. & Gilbert, S. (in press). Does it matter who leads us? In N. Chmiel, M. Sverke & F. Fraccaroli, Introduction to Work and Organizational Psychology. Chichester, UK: Wiley.

Kelloway, E. K., Mullen, J. & Francis, L. (2006). Divergent effects of passive and transformational leadership on safety outcomes. *Journal of Occupational Health Psychology*, 11(1), 76–86.

Kelloway, E. K., Sivanathan, N., Francis, L. & Barling, J. (2005). Poor leadership. In J. Barling, E. K. Kelloway & M. Frone, Handbook of Work Stress, Thousand Oaks, CA: SAGE Publications, pp. 89–142.

Kelloway, E. K., Teed, M. & Prosser, M (2008). Leading to a healthy workplace. In A. Kinder, R. Hughes & C. Cooper (eds), Employee Well-being Support: A Workplace Resource. Chichester: John Wiley & Sons.

Kernis, M. H. (2003). Toward a conceptualization of optimal self-esteem. *Psychological Inquiry*, 14, 1–26.

Kivimaki, M., Elovainio, M., Vahtera, J. & Ferrie, J. E. (2003). Organisational justice and health of employees: Prospective cohort study. *Occupational and Environmental Medicine*, 60, 27–34.

Kivimaki, M., Ferrie, J. E., Brunner, E., Head., J., Shipley, M. J., Vahtera, K. & Marmot, M. (2005). Justice at work and reduced risk of coronary heart disease among employees: The Whitehall II Study. *Archives of Internal Medicine* 165, 2245–51.

Kouvonen, A., Kivimaki, M., Elovainio, M., Vaananen, A., De Vogli, R., Heponiemi, T., Linna, A., Pentti, J. & Vahtera, J. (2008). Low organisational justice and heavy drinking: A prospective cohort study. *Occupational and Environmental Medicine*, 65(1), 44–50.

Mullen, J. & Kelloway, E. K. (2009). Safety leadership: A longitudinal study of the effects of transformational leadership on safety outcomes. *Journal of Occupational and Organizational Psychology*, 20, 253–72.

Nielsen, K. (2013). How can we make organizational interventions work? Employees and line managers as actively crafting interventions. *Human Relations*, 66, 1029–50.

Nielsen, K. & Daniels, K. (2012). Does shared and differentiated transformational leadership predict followers' working conditions and well-being? *Leadership Quarterly*, 23, 388–97.

Nielsen, K. & Randall, R. (2009). Managers' active support when implementing teams: The impact on employee well-being. *Applied Psychology: Health and Well-Being*, 1, 374–90.

Skogstad, A. Einarsen, S., Torsheim, T. Aasland, M.S. & Hetland, H. (2007). The destructiveness of laissez-faire leadership behavior. *Work & Stress*, 12, 80–92.

Tepper, B. J. (2000). Consequences of abusive supervision. *Academy of Management Journal*, 43, 178–90.

Tepper, B. J. (2007). Abusive supervision in work organizations: Review synthesis, and research agenda. *Journal of Management*, 33, 261–89.

Wong, J. H. & Kelloway, E. K. (2016). What happens at work stays at work? Workplace supervisory social interactions and blood pressure outcomes. *Journal of Occupational Health Psychology*, 21(2), 13–41.

1

Leadership and Safety

A Self-Regulation and Social Learning Perspective

Sharon Clarke, Sara Guediri and Allan Lee

Leadership has long been established as a critical element in relation to workplace safety. We will consider the role of leadership in safety, with a focus on recent theoretical and practical developments in the area. Our chapter is organized into three parts that cover: (1) established, existing research on the role of leadership for safety; (2) emerging strands of research that approach safety leadership from a self-regulation and social learning perspective; (3) implications for safety leadership interventions. The chapter reviews established research as well as new thinking about leadership and safety to help drive novel research directions in the area of safety leadership.

Safety Leadership: The Current State of Knowledge

In this initial section, we discuss the current state of knowledge regarding safety leadership, in particular traditional leadership theories, such as Bass's (1985) full-range leadership theory (including transformational and transactional leadership) and the implications for workplace safety. We consider the importance of leadership in relation to the organization's safety culture and as an antecedent to safety climate, before turning our attention to the underlying psychological mechanisms linking leadership to safety outcomes.

Within organizations, leadership at the most senior levels has direct effects on organizational safety: senior management decisions (for example regarding resource allocation, investment in training, maintenance and updating of equipment) will determine how safety risks are managed at an operational level. Such decisions are fundamentally shaped by (and consequently shape) the organization's safety culture. The failure of leaders to adequately factor safety considerations into their business decisions has been repeatedly highlighted by investigations into major disasters, where the adverse effects of poor safety leadership can be measured in terms of their considerable human, societal and environmental costs. Reason (1993, 1997) argued that the majority of

Leading to Occupational Health and Safety: How Leadership Behaviours Impact Organizational Safety and Well-Being, First Edition.
Edited by E. Kevin Kelloway, Karina Nielsen and Jennifer K. Dimoff.

organizational accidents have their origins within the managerial sphere; but the deleterious effects of poor safety leadership permeate throughout the organization, affecting attitudes and behaviours at every level. For example, in 2010 a major accident at BP's Macondo offshore drilling rig in the Gulf of Mexico resulted in the deaths of 11 oil workers, and, subsequently, in an extensive oil spill with devastating and wide-ranging environmental effects. The National Commission on the BP Deepwater Horizon Oil Spill and Offshore Drilling (2011) report into the accident concluded that: 'most of the mistakes and oversights at Macondo can be traced back to a single overarching failure – a failure of management. Better management by BP, Halliburton, and Transocean would almost certainly have prevented the blowout by improving the ability of individuals involved to identify the risks they faced, and to properly evaluate, communicate, and address them' (p. 90). This conclusion is not unusual, and highlights the critical role that leaders play in setting the context within which individuals evaluate and manage risks on a day-to-day basis. Similar conclusions have been drawn from the analysis of earlier incidents in the oil and gas industry, such as the Texas City oil refinery explosion in 2005 (Hopkins, 2008), and the Piper Alpha disaster in 1988 (Cullen, 1990), and across various other industrial sectors.

As suggested by the above quote, failures of management affect the cognitions, perceptions and behaviours of individuals working at an operational level. Leaders may directly influence the level of hazards within working environments, but they may also affect risk evaluations and safety attitudes through employees' perceptions of the safety climate (i.e., perceptions of the priority that safety is given in relation to other organizational goals, such as productivity; Zohar, 1980, 2010). Leaders' actions and attitudes towards safety, which reflect the strength of their commitment to safety, are recognized as a key aspect of safety climate (Flin, Mearns, O'Connor & Bryden, 2000). Substantial research has investigated the role of safety climate and established that safety climate acts as an antecedent of a range of safety outcomes (such as injuries and accidents) and safety-related behaviours (such as safety compliance and safety participation). This body of work comprises both meta-analyses (e.g., Beus, Payne, Bergman & Arthur, 2010; Christian, Bradley, Wallace & Burke, 2009; Clarke, 2006, 2010; Nahrgang, Morgeson & Hofmann, 2011) and longitudinal studies (e.g., Johnson, 2007; Neal & Griffin, 2006; Zohar, 2000).

Safety leadership acts as an antecedent of safety climate, which in turn mediates the effects on safety outcomes (Clarke, 2013; Mullen & Kelloway, 2009; Zohar, 2002a), as well as having direct effects on behaviour (Clarke, 2010). Zohar (2002a) argued that the value-based and individualized interactions characteristic of transformational leadership underpin the positive impact of this leadership style on safety outcomes. Indeed, there is a well-established link between leaders who demonstrate genuine care for the well-being and safety of their workforce, and higher levels of workplace safety (Cohen, 1977; Dunbar, 1975; Hofmann, Jacobs & Landy, 1995; Mullen, 2005; Parker, Axtell & Turner, 2001). In a longitudinal study, Parker et al. (2001) demonstrated that having supportive, coaching-oriented supervisors led to safer working over an 18-month period. Furthermore, supportive leadership had a significant positive association with safety compliance, and also with employee engagement and satisfaction, as shown by the meta-analysis conducted by Nahrgang and colleagues (2011). Such relationships would suggest that supportive leaders encourage employees to follow safety rules and regulations, but also that they create a positive working environment, which enhances work-related attitudes, such as job satisfaction. Supportive leaders are more willing to listen to safety concerns and discuss safety issues with their team (Hofmann & Morgeson, 1999; Mullen, 2005). Such safety interactions not only will encourage further safety participation from employees, but should also raise managerial awareness of safety issues, leading to reduced hazards in the workplace. Evidence gathered from interventions involving enhanced interactions between supervisors and employees around safety supports a positive impact on employees' behaviour and safety outcomes (Kines, Andersen, Spangenberg, Mikkelsen, Dyreborg & Zohar, 2010; Zohar, 2002b; Zohar & Polachek, 2014).

Discussion concerning the most effective leadership style for promoting workplace safety has centred on the positive influence of transformational leadership on employees' safety perceptions, attitudes and behaviour (Barling, Loughlin & Kelloway, 2002; Conchie & Donald, 2009; Inness, Turner, Barling & Stride, 2010; Kelloway, Mullen & Francis, 2006; Zohar & Luria, 2004), and its association with fewer accidents and injuries (Yule, 2002; Zohar, 2002b). One mechanism through which transformational leaders influence their employees is based on the types of relationship that form between leaders and their subordinates over time. Transformational leaders are better able to build with their employees high leader–member exchange (LMX) relationships, which are based on trust, loyalty and integrity (Dulebohn, Bommer, Liden, Brouer & Ferris, 2012). Leader behaviours in these high-quality relationships are reciprocated by employees through safe working and safety citizenship behaviours (Hofmann, Morgeson & Gerras, 2003; Kath, Marks & Ranney, 2010). Because of the trust-based relationship with supervisors, high LMX has been associated with employees feeling comfortable speaking up and raising safety concerns in the workplace (Kath et al., 2010). However, while Hofmann et al. (2003) showed a strong positive association between high LMX and safety citizenship role definitions, suggesting that employees reciprocated high LMX through performing such behaviours, they also found that this relationship was moderated by safety climate. Thus, this relationship was strong in work groups with a positive safety climate, but much weaker in those exhibiting poorer safety climates. As high LMX relationships only lead to increased engagement in safety citizenship behaviours when safety climate is positive, this would suggest that safety-related behaviour is only viewed as a legitimate means of reciprocating a high LMX relationship with the leader when safety is perceived as having high priority. Similarly, Clark, Zickar and Jex (2014) showed that narrowly defined role definitions (i.e., those characterized by the belief that organizational citizenship behaviours (OCBs) are dependent on the quality of social exchange) moderated the positive relationship between safety climate and nurses' safety citizenship behaviours.

Transformational leaders, through a better understanding of safety issues and improved communications (Conchie, Taylor & Donald, 2012), may directly influence decisions about the management of safety hazards. In addition, there will be indirect influence through their capacity to build consensus amongst employees about the priority given to safety (Luria, 2008; Zohar & Tenne-Gazit, 2008). At a group level, Zohar and Tenne-Gazit (2008) found that transformational leaders encouraged team members to develop shared perceptions of safety through the promotion of shared values, the setting of collective goals, and teamwork. The study, which focused on group interactions within military platoons, using social network analysis, demonstrated that communication density (extent of platoon members' interactions) mediated the effect of transformational platoon leaders on the subsequent development of group safety climate. In contrast, it has been argued that passive leaders, who demonstrate no interest in safety and avoid safety problems, disrupt the formation of shared views regarding the importance of safety (Luria, 2008). Supporting research has shown that passive leadership results in significant negative effects on safety, including increased incidence of occupational injuries and adverse safety events (Kelloway et al., 2006; Mullen, Kelloway & Teed, 2011) and reduced safety-related behaviours, especially safety participation (Jiang & Probst, 2016; Smith, Eldridge & DeJoy, 2016). Furthermore, even transformational leaders who sometimes engage in passive safety leader behaviours risk damaging workplace safety: this inconsistent leadership style has been associated with negative safety outcomes. Mullen et al. (2011) found that, for those leaders who demonstrated both transformational and passive styles, the use of passive behaviours (e.g., avoiding safety issues) attenuated the positive effects of transformational behaviours (e.g., motivating employees to act safely). The importance of transformational leadership for activating those employees who are motivated to actively participate in safety was emphasized by Jiang and Probst (2016). They found that the relationship between safety motivation and safety participation was moderated by transformational leadership, so that the relationship only existed under high transformational conditions. The authors also found that passive leadership had a significant negative effect on safety participation: employees with passive leaders were less likely to actively engage in safety activities.

Although passive leadership has negative effects on workplace safety, active forms of transactional leadership (which involve proactive monitoring of employees' behaviour, taking corrective actions and anticipating problems) facilitate the development of a work environment in which opportunities for error recovery are increased and learning from mistakes is encouraged. This type of active leadership style enables leaders to learn how to anticipate potential adverse events, better preparing them to intervene and prevent safety incidents (Griffin & Hu, 2013; Rodriguez & Griffin, 2009). In addition to improving leaders' own capabilities, the proactive monitoring associated with active transactional leadership has been associated with employee safety behaviour, especially safety compliance (Clarke, 2013; Griffin & Hu, 2013). Thus, the emphasis on monitoring and correcting employees' behaviour increases awareness of the importance of safety regulations, and encourages rule-following. Research has shown that there are differential effects of leader behaviours in relation to employee safety behaviours.

For example, Griffin and Hu (2013) found that safety-inspiring leader behaviours were significantly associated with safety participation: motivating behaviour encouraged active involvement in safety activities, safety citizenship behaviours and speaking up about safety. On the other hand, safety-monitoring leader behaviours were aligned with safety compliance: close supervision encouraged adherence to safety rules and regulations. Similarly, Clarke (2013) supported a model of safety leadership in which transformational leadership was directly related to safety participation, and active transactional leadership was directly related to safety compliance. Such studies suggest that safety leaders might use a combination of transformational and active transactional behaviours to influence workplace safety effectively. Indeed, Clarke and Ward (2006) found that influence tactics associated with both leadership styles were effective in promoting employee safety participation.

Theoretical Perspectives Linking Leadership to Safety Performance

As highlighted in the previous section, a sizeable body of research demonstrates the link between leadership and various aspects of safety performance. While establishing this link is important, it is imperative to elucidate the underlying processes that explain how leaders, and different leadership styles, influence followers' safety performance. The theoretical frameworks described below demonstrate the reasons why certain leadership styles predict safety performance and can help establish the boundary conditions that may accentuate or attenuate such effects. Specifically, this section will review emerging approaches to studying leadership and safety. To provide a theoretical framework, we will integrate these emerging approaches within the wider conceptual perspectives of social learning, social exchange and self-regulation. Such theoretical perspectives have been prominent in recent research investigating the leadership–safety link.

Safety Leadership from a Social Learning and Social Exchange Perspective

The impact of leaders on employee safety attitudes and behaviour has been explained through the principles of social exchange and social learning. Social exchange theory posits that if a party acts favourably towards another party, this gives rise to a sense of obligation to reciprocate the beneficial behaviour (Blau, 1964). In an early study, Hofmann and Morgeson (1999) referred to social exchange theory as a theoretical foundation for a better understanding of the effect of leaders on workplace safety. If a leader provides resources for safety and invests in safety training for employees, this will create a sense of obligation amongst followers to reciprocate through engagement in positive safety behaviour (Hofmann & Morgeson, 1999; Hofmann et al., 2003). Social learning theory has been utilized as a second conceptual foundation for investigating the role of leaders in employee safety behaviour. Social learning theory proposes that learning occurs in a social context through the observation of and interactions with others (Bandura, 1977). Applying a social learning perspective to safety leadership, it is suggested that as leaders interact with their employees, they transmit messages about what is expected with regard to safety (Dragoni, 2005; Zohar & Tenne-Gazit, 2008). Consistent with a social learning perspective, numerous studies have shown that leaders influence their followers' safety behaviours through safety climate, as discussed previously. For example, meta-analytic evidence shows that safety climate mediates the relationship between transformational-transactional leadership styles and individuals' safety behaviour (Clarke, 2013). Thus, employees learn the value of safety, as well as what behaviours are accepted and rewarded, through observing and interacting with their leader. The following section will use the principles of social exchange and social learning to review research on the effects of different leadership approaches on employee safety behaviour and attitudes.

As discussed in the first section of this chapter, support for a positive relationship between transformational leadership and employee safety behaviours has been reported by several studies (e.g., Barling et al., 2002; Conchie & Donald, 2009; Inness et al., 2010; Kelloway et al., 2006; Zohar & Luria, 2004). Within transformational leadership, the dimension of idealized influence directly recognizes the importance of role modelling as part of effective leadership (Bass, 1985). Idealized influence is the extent to which a leader displays exemplary conduct and is regarded by their followers as a role model. Within the dimension, a behavioural and an attributional component can be distinguished (Bass & Riggio, 2006). The behavioural element is the extent to which the leader exhibits behaviours that result in their being viewed as a role model, and the attributional element is the extent to which followers attribute 'idealized' characteristics to the leader (e.g., being worthy of trust and respect). Barling et al. (2002) conceptualize that safety leaders who are high in idealized influence impart safety as a core value through their personal commitment and behaviour. Hoffmeister, Gibbons, Johnson, Cigularov, Chen and Rosecrance (2014) tested the relationship of individual facets of transformational leadership with each of safety climate, safety compliance and safety participation in a sample of construction workers. Using relative weights analysis, the authors revealed a pattern whereby idealized influence (attributes) and idealized influence (behaviours) explained greater amounts of variance in the safety outcomes than the other dimensions of transformational leadership. More precisely, idealized influence (attributes) was the most important predictor of safety climate and idealized influence (behaviours) was the most important predictor of safety participation. The finding suggests that transformational leaders predominately influence employees' attitudes towards safety and safety performance through a role-modelling process, while other leader actions associated with transformational leadership might carry less weight in the effect on safety outcomes. Hoffmeister et al. (2014) discuss the possibility that idealized influence is a prerequisite for other leadership tactics to be effective. For example, challenging existing assumptions about safety (Intellectual Stimulation) or getting employees to buy into a vision (Inspirational Motivation) is difficult to accomplish unless the leader is viewed as a role model. Consequently, a primary focus for safety leaders should be on establishing themselves as a role figure that employees endeavour to emulate. An important part of being considered as a role model involves building trusting and authentic relations with followers. Authentic leaders foster a social identification process through awareness of their own strength and limitations, acting in ways that are consistent with their own true self and placing moral conduct at the core of their actions (Eid, Mearns, Larsson, Laberg & Johnsen, 2012; Gardner, Avolio, Luthans, May & Walumbwa, 2005). Thus, it can be expected that, for effective role modelling, leaders need to deploy transformational practices as part of authentic relations where concern for well-being and safety are inherent to leader–follower exchanges. Within the wider leadership literature, it has been recognized that leaders can engage in pseudo-transformational leadership, where transformational behaviour is decoupled from ethical principles and aimed at maximizing self-interest (Bass & Steidlmeier, 1999; Christie, Barling & Turner, 2011). In the safety leadership literature, studies so far have demonstrated a positive association between authentic leadership and safety climate (Borgersen, Hystad, Larsson & Eid, 2014; Nielsen, Eid, Mearns & Larsson, 2013), but more research is needed on how transformational leadership style and authentic leadership interact with each other in their influence on safety outcomes.

The importance of role modelling for good safety leaders can be related to the concept of behavioural integrity. Zohar (2003, 2010) shows that the extent to which safety values are *espoused* is not necessarily aligned with the extent to which safety values are *enacted* during work operations. Safety can be proclaimed as a high priority through organizational policies, but in the face of budget or production pressures safety procedures might be compromised. The true priority of safety emanates from the degree of congruence between the espoused and enacted values of safety (Zohar, 2010). Behavioural integrity is the (mis)alignment between leaders' words and deeds, or the extent to which leaders 'walk the talk' (Simons, 2002, 2008). Research has demonstrated the importance of leader behavioural integrity in establishing and reinforcing the value of safety (Halbesleben, Leroy, Dierynck et al., 2013; Leroy, Dierynck, Anseel et al., 2012). The findings from these studies suggest that behavioural integrity influences employees' safety behaviour through two mechanisms. By putting words into practice, leaders clearly signal that adherence to safety protocols is desirable and constitutes behaviour that will be rewarded (this constitutes a social learning mechanism). In a second, complementary mechanism, behavioural integrity creates a predictable environment through consistent prioritization of safety, which consequently lets followers feel safe to speak up about safety concerns and report errors. This dual mechanism is important, as achieving excellent levels of safety performance involves following safety procedures to prevent errors as well as learning from failure through investigation of errors (Rodriguez & Griffin, 2009; Weick & Sutcliffe, 2007). Leroy et al. (2012) studied leader behavioural integrity as a predictor of reported treatment errors in a sample of hospital nurses. If head nurses displayed high levels of behavioural integrity with regard to safety issues, their teams rated the priority of safety as higher, which in turn was associated with fewer treatment errors. At the same time, head nurses' behavioural integrity was linked to higher psychological safety within the team, which in turn was related to more reporting of treatment errors. Thus, if leaders' actions live up to their words, they influence follower safety behaviour through role modelling, and the consistency in their support for safety delineates safety as a genuine concern, with the result that followers feel confident to report errors or breaches of safety protocol (Halbesleben et al., 2013; Leroy et al., 2012). Other studies (Blumer, 1969; Weick, 1995) have highlighted the relevance of social sensemaking in high-risk environments, where employees are typically confronted with multiple demands, such as ensuring safety while keeping a project on schedule and reducing cost (Zohar, 2010). Therefore, the priority of safety is not absolute, but relative to other demands and targets (Shannon & Norman, 2009; Zohar, 2008, 2010; Zohar & Tenne-Gazit, 2008). Moreover, dangerous work contexts or crisis situations might place increased cognitive demands on the individuals who operate within them (Dóci & Hofmans, 2015). Hence, it can be argued that a core function of safety leadership is to aid employees to make sense of the complexity and ambiguity that characterize their work environment (Baran & Scott, 2010; Mumford, Friedrich, Caughron & Byrne, 2007). Dahl and Olsen (2013) showed in a sample of offshore petroleum workers that if leaders were involved in daily work operations employees had greater levels of role clarity, which in turn improved safety compliance. The relevance of sensemaking for effective safety leadership is that good safety leaders need to engage in practices that can reduce ambiguity and demarcate accepted and expected behaviours from those that are not. This sensemaking approach would suggest that transactional leadership practices, which create structure and clarity, will be of importance to safety leadership (despite the focus of extant research on transformational leadership). As noted earlier, transformational leadership behaviours predict safety participation, while transactional leadership behaviours are associated with safety compliance (Clarke, 2013; Griffin & Hu, 2013). Probst (2015) found that supervisors' encouragement of safe working practices (e.g., through reward and praise) was related to a reduction in underreporting of accidents, and that this relationship was moderated by the organizational-level safety climate. If the organization's safety climate does not provide a clear frame of reference for safe working (because of a lack of systematic safety procedures and policies, for example), followers are dependent on the guidance of their leader through strict enforcement of safe working behaviours. This is in line with earlier research that has identified safety climate as a moderator of the leadership–safety outcome relationship (Hofmann et al., 2003).

Social exchange theory has also been drawn upon to explain the role of trust in safety leadership. Research evidence from several studies lends support to the idea that followers' trust in their leader assists that leader to exert influence on employee safety behaviour (Conchie, 2013; Conchie & Donald, 2009; Conchie, Taylor & Donald, 2012). In contrast to economic exchanges, where stakes can be clearly offset against each other, the equivalence of contributions in social interactions cannot be managed to the same level of precision (Blau, 1964). Therefore, if followers are to respond to their leaders' actions, they need to hold a certain level of trust that their behaviour will be valued and rewarded in some form (Conchie, Woodcock & Taylor, 2015). With regard to the effect of leadership on safety outcomes, empirical support exists for trust as mediator (e.g., Conchie et al., 2012) as well as moderator (e.g., Conchie, 2013; Conchie & Donald, 2009). As a moderator, trust in one's leader can be viewed as a factor that reinforces followers' willingness to look to their leader as a role figure. Because of the very nature of a leadership position – its associated status and visibility within a team or organization – employees might be likely to model their own behaviour on that of their leader. Yet, certain factors such as trust are likely to enhance this role model position. Honesty, and to a lesser extent competence and benevolence, have been identified as important qualities that help safety leaders to promote trust and avoid issues of distrust (Conchie, Taylor & Charlton, 2011). Moreover, ethical leadership has also been noted as a predictor of subordinates' trust in their supervisor (Chughtai, Byrne & Flood, 2015).

While empirical research has provided evidence on the importance of followers' trust in their leader for workplace safety, it can be argued that followers' feeling of being trusted by their management is also of relevance (Conchie et al., 2015). If employees perceive that their managers and the wider organization hold trust in them, they are likely to have a greater sense of obligation to reciprocate this trust (Conchie et al., 2015). Employees who feel that their manager trusts them with regard to safety matters will feel greater levels of responsibility for safety and reciprocate with higher levels of safety performance (Törner, 2011). This line of argument can be related to research on empowering leadership, which is aimed at enhancing follower autonomy and a team's potential for self-management (Arnold, Arad, Rhoades & Drasgow, 2000). In a series of studies in nuclear power plants, Martinez and colleagues demonstrated that empowering leadership has a positive impact on safety climate (Martínez-Corcóles, Gracia, Tomás & Peiró, 2011), safety compliance (Martínez-Corcóles, Gracia, Tomás & Peiró, 2014) and safety participation (Martínez-Corcóles, Schnöbel, Gracia, Tomás & Peiró, 2012), and is linked to a reduction in risk-taking behaviour (Martínez-Corcóles, Gracia, Tomás, Peiró & Schöbel, 2013). More specifically, collaborative learning and enhanced role clarity have been identified as the mechanisms through which empowering leaders positively influence followers' safety behaviour (Martínez-Corcóles et al., 2012; Martínez-Corcóles et al., 2014). Thus, through practices such as participative decision-making, the creation of opportunities for independent problem solving, and the facilitation of the dissemination of information, leaders can provide employees with more meaning in their job roles and work environment, which enhances followers' impetus to deploy safety protocols and enables them to become more engaged in safety matters. While there is conceptual overlap across transformational, authentic and empowering leadership approaches, they complement each other in the practical information they provide for safety leaders. Transformational leadership and authentic leadership emphasize the importance of role-modelling processes and communicating genuine concern; empowering leadership supplements this guidance for safety leaders by highlighting the power of delegation practices and participative decision-making to enhance employee safety performance.

While social learning theory has been used to explain the positive effects of constructive leadership styles on followers' safety behaviour, the same processes can be drawn upon to explain how non-leadership and destructive leadership negatively influence employee safety. As outlined earlier, there is empirical evidence that passive forms of leadership, as well as inconsistent leadership, which is characterized by active and passive leadership, have detrimental effects on safety (Kelloway et al., 2006; Mullen et al., 2011). Through an absence of attention to safety matters in leader–follower exchanges, leaders not only pass by the opportunity to reward positive safety behaviours or share safety knowledge, but convey the message that safety is a less important objective (Kelloway et al., 2006). Thus, safety leaders must recognize that social learning processes still take place when they take a passive stance towards safety, and that this passivity reinforces safety as something of lesser concern. Within the leadership literature, it is noted that destructive leadership can take a passive or an active form (Aasland, Skogstad, Notelaers, Nielsen & Einarsen, 2010; Einarsen, Aasland & Skogstad, 2007), and some argue further that passive, non-leadership should be considered separately from the concept of destructive leadership (Schyns & Schilling, 2013). Abusive supervision and tyrannical leadership, where a leader abuses their formal power and engages in behaviour that is targeted at influencing followers in a hindering or harmful way, are examples of active destructive leadership (Einarsen et al., 2007; Schyns & Schilling, 2013). There is robust evidence that active destructive leadership behaviour has negative effects on an employee's well-being, stress and performance (Krasikova, Green & LeBreton, 2013; Schyns & Schilling, 2013; Tepper, 2000). The effects of active destructive leadership forms on safety performance and perceptions of safety have been studied less (Kelloway & Barling, 2010), but Nielsen, Skogstad, Matthiesen, and Einarsen (2016) explain that, as the harmful effects on employee well-being have been established, similar effects can be expected for workplace safety. In a time-lagged study over six months, Nielsen et al. (2016) found a negative relationship between tyrannical leadership and subsequent safety climate, although tyrannical leadership was less strongly associated with safety climate than constructive leadership. Schyns and Schilling (2013) suggest that the effects of destructive leadership can work through the same social learning mechanisms as those of constructive leadership. By repeatedly engaging in negative behaviours, leaders role-model these as appropriate, and contribute towards a climate where destructive behaviour is tolerated. Thus, from observations of their leaders' tyrannical behaviour, followers learn that neglect of the welfare of others, including disregard of their physical safety, is acceptable. From a social exchange perspective, it can be argued that leaders' destructive behaviour is repaid by employees trying to 'restore justice' through equally negative behaviours (Schyns & Schilling, 2013). With regard to safety, such attempts to get even could involve disregard of formal policies, including safety regulations, or withdrawal of voluntary efforts for enhancing safety at work. Destructive leadership is also likely to prevent an atmosphere where followers feel safe to speak up about safety issues and might therefore suppress the sharing of safety knowledge and prevent safety learning. However, empirical research on these effects is still needed. Interestingly, Nielsen et al.'s (2016) results also indicated a reciprocal relationship between safety climate and tyrannical leadership. Thus, social interaction processes between leaders, followers and the wider work environment are not one-directional, but are likely to occur in a more dynamic form. The authors discuss how, under poor safety climate conditions, leaders might resort to becoming more authoritarian and even tyrannical in an attempt to assert safety practices. This could potentially lead to a downwards spiral, where such misguided efforts of destructive leadership produce the opposite effect, and instead of enforcing safety lead to the further deterioration of safety climate.

So far the focus of safety leadership research has largely been on understanding how individual, single leaders influence safety outcomes. Yet social learning and social exchange processes are not restricted to leader–follower exchanges, but can also occur in interactions with peers. Positive, high-quality relationships between co-workers are likely to facilitate similar role-modelling and behavioural imitation processes as occur within leader–follower interactions. Moreover, from a social exchange perspective, it can be argued that if a co-worker displays favourable behaviour towards a colleague (e.g., looking out for their safety during a job), this will create a sense of obligation in that colleague to reciprocate through similar concern for their peers' safety, and consequently create a work climate where colleagues expect positive safety behaviour from each other. For example, Zohar and Tenne-Gazit (2008) reported that friendship ties between co-workers are linked to a more positive safety climate. Nahrgang et al. (2011) provided meta-analytic evidence that a high level of social support amongst co-workers is related to reduced accident and injury rates. Turner, Chmiel, Hershcovis and Walls (2010) tested the role of co-worker social support in a sample of rail trackside workers. Their findings show that under demanding job conditions where employees experience high levels of role overload, co-worker social support for safety was related to reduced frequency of hazardous work events. Drawing on social information-processing theory (Salancik & Pfeffer, 1978), Turner et al. (2010) explain that employees rely on their co-workers' behaviour as social cues to understand what is expected under certain circumstances, such as safety-critical situations. Moreover, results from Turner et al. (2010) showed that perceptions about co-worker social support were more prominent in reducing hazardous work events than perceptions of supervisor and managerial social support. The authors base this finding on social impact theory (Latané, 1981), which proposes that the significance of sources for support will be larger for sources that exist in closer proximity and greater numbers. Within the wider organizational literature, a growing body of literature is devoted to understanding the effects of shared leadership for team effectiveness (e.g., Carson, Tesluk & Marrone, 2007; Nicolaides, LaPort, Chen et al., 2014; Pearce & Sims, 2002; Wang, Waldman & Zhang, 2014). The concept of shared leadership extends beyond social interactions between colleagues and suggests that co-workers can informally adopt leadership responsibilities to provide direction and influence (Carson et al., 2007). Several studies have demonstrated that shared leadership is more strongly linked to team effectiveness than formal, vertical leadership is (Carson et al., 2007; Ensley, Hmielski & Pearce, 2006; Nicolaides et al., 2014; Wang et al., 2014). Within the safety literature these potential benefits of shared leadership have been less explored. Evidence from Guediri and Fruhen (2015) indicates that shared leadership is positively related to safety performance if formal leaders have a low tendency to be concerned about safety. Given the growing evidence for positive effects of shared leadership with regard to non-safety outcomes, this presents a promising research stream for occupational safety research to explore how shared leadership can be utilized to further improve workplace safety.

Safety Leadership and Self-Regulation Theory

Like social learning theory, Self-Regulation Theory (SRT) is a stalwart of social psychology. In general, SRT is concerned with the conscious process of managing one's cognitions, behaviours and feelings to achieve a goal (e.g., Lord, Diefendorff, Schmidt & Hall, 2010). The theory emphasizes that individuals guide their own goal-directed activities and performance by setting their own standards and monitoring their progress towards these standards (e.g., Carver & Scheier, 1981). SRT has been posited as a mechanism that can explain safety leadership in two ways.

First, scholars have argued that SRT can be used as a framework to better understand the processes through which leaders avoid major errors or manage everyday safety requirements (e.g., Rodriguez & Griffin, 2009). Although transformational leadership specifies that managing activities, such as detection of errors, is a vital part of transformational change (Bass & Avolio, 1993), the theory largely fails to specify how this process actually occurs in leaders. To rectify this limitation researchers have proposed an integration between transformational-transactional leadership and situational regulatory focus theory. Higgins's (1997, 1998) Regulatory Focus Theory describes promotion focus and prevention focus as two distinct self-regulatory mindsets. Promotion focus is a mindset that stresses an individual's need for growth, attention to gains, and the attainment of aspirational goals. Prevention focus, on the other hand, is a mindset emphasizing the need for security, attention to losses, and the completion of obligations (Higgins, 1998). According to Rodriguez and Griffin (2009) regulatory focus can be used to explain why, in certain circumstances, monitoring subordinates and providing contingent feedback (i.e., Management by Exception) might be the most effective safety leadership style. Specifically, the authors suggest that when the goals of the leader, such as ensuring reliability or improving safety records, relate to safety, the leader will be prompted to assess the context as one of avoiding failure, thus exhibiting a prevention-focused mindset. Conversely, when the leader assesses the situation as one of approaching success (e.g., achieving a bonus), a promotion-focused mindset is likely to be prompted. In fact, a number of researchers have linked transformational and transactional leadership styles to promotion and prevention focus (e.g., Brockner & Higgins, 2001; Kark & van Dijk, 2007). Such arguments are predicated on the notion that transformational leadership style is motivated by a promotion focus, while transactional leadership is motivated by prevention focus because of the concern with deviations, safety and security. Further attesting to the importance of SRT to an understanding of safety leadership is the fact that authentic leadership theory suggests that both greater self-awareness and self-regulated positive behaviours on the part of leaders foster positive self-development (Luthans & Avolio, 2003). Indeed several distinguishing features associated with authentic self-regulation processes have been identified, including internalized regulation, balanced processing of information, relational transparency, and authentic behaviour (Gardner et al., 2005). As mentioned in the previous section authentic leadership has been linked to safety perceptions (Borgersen et al., 2014; Nielsen et al., 2013).

Second, despite the fact that SRT is conceived in terms of within-person processes, research has demonstrated that leaders can influence this process in their followers through providing impetus for the pursuit of certain goals. Again using Higgins's (1997, 1998) delineation of promotion focus and prevention focus as two distinct self-regulatory mindsets, researchers have attempted to better understand how leadership relates to safety performance. Although an individual may have a disposition towards a particular regulatory focus, situational triggers can elicit either a prevention or a promotion focus. For instance, Brockner and Higgins (2001) suggested that leaders influence followers' regulatory focus through the use of language and symbols. Accordingly, the more leaders employ rhetoric that focuses on ideals, the more chance they will have to evoke in followers a mindset that is promotion-focused. Indeed, research supports the claim that leaders can evoke different self-regulatory mindsets in their followers, leading to differential effects on outcomes such as performance, deviant behaviour and creativity (e.g., Neubert, Kacmar, Carlson, Chonko & Roberts, 2008). Applying this logic to the context of safety performance, scholars have argued that leaders can influence followers' self-regulation in a way that can explain effects on safety-related outcomes. In this context, employees are theorized to engage in safety performance as motivated by their safety goals. Accordingly, safety leadership can be understood as a leadership style that provokes followers to focus on, and achieve, their safety goals.

Using this framework, Griffin and Hu (2013) investigated how specific leader behaviours predicted two distinct employee safety behaviours: safety participation and safety compliance. The authors proposed that different leader behaviours, related to safety inspiration and safety monitoring, would differentially evoke safety-related goals, in accordance with SRT. Safety-inspiring leader behaviour involved the presentation of a positive vision of safety, deemed to be appealing and inspiring to the followers, whereas safety-monitoring leader behaviour involved the observation of whether employees are working safely. It was hypothesized that safety-inspiring leader behaviour would promote safety participation, as it would enable followers to see the meaning and value of safety activities, thus motivating the investment of time and effort to engage in safety activities in order to realize that vision (Griffin & Hu, 2013). Furthermore, the authors argued that the leader's engagement in safety-monitoring behaviour would motivate employee safety compliance. Specifically, in line with SRT, it was suggested that safety monitoring, a concept similar to the management-by-exception element of transactional leadership (Bass, 1985), would increase followers' awareness of the discrepancy between their current state and their desired state. In fact, within SRT, monitoring is considered as a crucial mechanism to motivate individuals to allocate resources towards a desired state. Thus, leader safety monitoring was hypothesized to evoke followers' awareness of unsafe actions or behaviours that did not comply with the current safety procedures. Consequently it was argued that followers would know where they need to focus and improve, thereby increasing their safety compliance behaviours. The empirical results of Griffin and Hu (2013), in accordance with the aforementioned rationale, demonstrated that while safety-inspiring leader behaviour was positively related to safety participation, safety monitoring was positively related to safety compliance.

Building on this research, a study by Kark, Katz-Navon and Delegach (2015) provided a more explicit test of the tenets of SRT in relation to safety leadership. While Griffin and Hu (2013) provided a theoretical link between leadership behaviour and follower safety performance, Kark et al. (2015) examined the mediators of the relationship. The authors examined the role of promotion and prevention self-regulations in explaining the dual effects of leadership on safety-initiative and safety-compliance behaviours. Predicating their claims on SRT, the authors argued that transactional and transformational leadership would differentially affect followers' safety-initiative and safety-compliance behaviours. More specifically, it was argued that a transactional style, whereby leaders closely monitor followers' behaviour and highlight their obligations and responsibilities, would evoke a prevention focus among followers. Self-regulation via a prevention focus involves paying attention to security needs and the fulfilment of duties and obligations (e.g., Lanaj, Chang & Johnson, 2012), and was therefore predicted to yield higher safety compliance in followers (Kark et al., 2015). On the other hand, the authors predicted that a transformational style, whereby leaders focus on followers' growth and development and encourage followers to examine problems from a new perspective (Bass, 1999), would elicit a promotion focus among followers. As a promotion focus facilitates motivation towards ideals through advancement and accomplishment, it should create a mindset that allows followers to think about safety in new and innovative ways rather than simply adhering to the set regulations. Thus, promotion focus was predicted to be positively related to safety initiative. The results of this study confirmed that followers' situational promotion focus mediated the positive relationship between transformational leadership and safety-initiative behaviours. The authors also showed, across three studies, that transactional leadership was positively associated with followers' situational prevention focus. However, mixed support was found for the link between prevention focus and safety-compliance behaviours, with expected mediation relationships shown in an experimental setting, but not in the field studies.

Recently, the concept of self-regulation has been studied in relation to safety performance within a mindfulness framework. Originally espoused within Buddhist traditions, mindfulness is a concept that can be defined as a mental state with the characteristics of present-focused awareness and attention (e.g., Brown, Ryan & Creswell, 2007). Interest in the topic has recently extended to the organization context, as witnessed by a proliferation of recent studies investigating the effects of mindfulness on various outcomes, such as employee performance and well-being (e.g., Dane & Brummel, 2014; Hülsheger, Alberts, Feinholdt & Lang, 2013). Furthermore, a number of studies have investigated the role of dispositional levels of mindfulness on various aspects of safety performance. For instance, higher levels of mindfulness in a sample of nuclear power plant control room operators were positively associated with both safety-compliance and safety-participation behaviours (Zhang & Wu, 2014). Using a similar sample, Zhang, Ding, Li and Wu (2013) showed that for highly complex tasks present-focused awareness and attention (facets of mindfulness) were positively related to safety performance. To understand the aforementioned effects of mindfulness, scholars draw on self-regulation theory to outline how this trait explains various outcomes. Put simply, it is suggested that mindfulness leads to better regulation of thoughts, emotions and behaviours. Brown and Ryan (2003), for instance, posit that mindfulness may increase self-endorsed behavioural regulation as individuals disengage from automatic thoughts, habits, and unhealthy behaviour patterns. For instance, in relation to safety performance, it is suggested that more mindful individuals are better equipped to avoid cognitive failures, involuntary lapses or errors because they are more aware of the external environment and internal processes (Herndon, 2008; Reason, Manstead, Stradling, Baxter & Campbell, 1990). Although research, to date, has not focused on leader mindfulness in relation to safety leadership, we suggest that this is a topic that holds great potential to explicate both leader and follower safety performance. Specifically, there are at least two ways in which mindfulness is relevant for safety leadership.

Firstly, as described above, leaders' self-regulation can be an extremely useful framework for explaining how safety goals are pursued (e.g., Rodriguez & Griffin, 2009). Reb, Narayanan and Chaturvedi (2014) found that leaders' trait mindfulness had a number of positive associations, for example with follower performance. The authors suggested that through increased emotional regulation, mindful leaders are able to develop better-quality relationships with followers, which in turn lead to increased performance and well-being. Mindfulness research draws on different self-regulatory mechanisms to explain the relationship between mindfulness and outcomes (e.g., Brown & Ryan, 2003). Leaders higher in trait mindfulness are thus predicted to be better at cognitive, behavioural and emotional regulation. Such self-regulatory process, as described earlier, should be positively related to the achievement of safety-related goals. Secondly, recent research has suggested that followers' level of trait mindfulness can influence their response to certain types of leadership. Specifically, Eisenbeiss and van Knippenberg (2015) found individuals high in mindfulness responded more positively to ethical leadership through the exhibition of discretionary work behaviour than those low in mindfulness. The authors posited that mindfulness can alter the way in which followers perceive and process the information conveyed by leaders. The awareness associated with being mindful should, theoretically, make followers especially aware of, and receptive to, information in the environment, conveyed by leaders, and this awareness should trigger the conscious processing of such information. The findings of Eisenbeiss and van Knippenberg (2015) may be applicable to safety leadership as they suggest that mindful followers will be more receptive to their leader's safety messages and as a result exhibit greater levels of safety performance. Overall, we believe mindfulness is a concept that holds great potential for our understanding of safety leadership and safety performance more generally.

Practical Implications for Safety Interventions

In this final section we consider the implications of safety leadership research for organizations, in particular regarding the design and implementation of safety interventions. Existing work suggests that leadership interventions are generally successful in changing leader behaviours (Avolio, Reichard, Hannah, Walumbwa & Chan, 2009) and that, while safety interventions targeted at leadership behaviour are used relatively infrequently, they are effective in improving workplace safety (Kelloway & Barling, 2010). Evaluation studies, which report longitudinal data, have provided evidence that leaders can be trained to use leadership behaviours that subsequently lead to safer performance among employees; leadership interventions have tended to focus on either training managers to use transformational leader behaviours (e.g., Mullen & Kelloway, 2009) or enhancing supervisory communications with employees around safety issues (e.g., Kines et al., 2010; Zohar & Polachek, 2014). For example, Zohar and Polachek (2014) implemented an intervention to increase daily safety exchanges between supervisors and employees; they found that in the experimental group there were significant positive changes in safety climate, safety behaviour, subjective workload and measures of teamwork, as well as improved safety audit data. In contrast, the control group demonstrated no significant changes. In such interventions the key changes relate to improved safety communications, in which supervisors demonstrate the importance of safety as a priority and two-way communications are enhanced, so that there is greater opportunity to exchange information about safety issues.

Interventions which include a broader range of leader behaviours, including both transformational and transactional behaviours, have been reported (e.g., Clarke & Taylor, 2015). The development of transformational leader behaviours plays an important role in influencing perceptions of safety climate and also in improving safety behaviours, especially participation, by inspiring and motivating employees (Mullen & Kelloway, 2009). Transactional leader behaviours have been more strongly linked to enforcing safety compliance than to promoting safety participation in employees (Clarke, 2013), but may also be important from the perspective of the individual leader. Transactional leader behaviours are likely to help leaders improve their ability to understand safety issues, anticipate problems and prevent safety incidents. For example, von Thiele Schwarz, Hasson and Tafvelin (2016) found that leaders' safety self-efficacy improved following leadership training, where safety self-efficacy reflects taking active control (such as the level of confidence in giving safety-related feedback and in preventing individuals from doing something risky). Training leaders in mindfulness has had limited use for safety interventions but has potential to improve safety-related behaviours, for both leaders and employees. For example, mindfulness training has been used to reduce safety workarounds performed by medical staff in health care settings (Dierynck et al., in press) and may be helpful in improving the 'flexible thinking' required by senior leaders to manage high-risk situations (Fruhen & Flin, 2016).

Conclusions

Research on safety leadership has highlighted the positive influence of constructive styles, such as transformational and authentic leadership, and also the negative effects of destructive styles, such as passive leadership. Models of safety leadership have further suggested that a combination of transformational and transactional leader behaviours may be particularly effective in promoting safety performance. We have provided a theoretical frame to integrate emerging approaches to safety leadership within the wider conceptual perspectives of self-regulation and social learning. Existing research on leadership interventions has shown that leadership training can be effective in the improvement of workplace safety. In our discussion, we identify the potential of mindfulness training for safety leaders as a means of enhancing safety-related behaviours in both leaders and employees. We have addressed new concepts that have relevance for safety leadership, but have not yet received much empirical investigation, opening up further avenues of investigation for safety researchers and practitioners.

References

Aasland, M. S., Skogstad, A., Notelaers, G., Nielsen, M. B. & Einarsen, S. (2010). The prevalence of destructive leadership behaviour. *British Journal of Management*, 21(2), 438–52.

Arnold, J. A., Arad, S., Rhoades, J. A. & Drasgow, F. (2000). The Empowering Leadership Questionnaire: The construction and validation of a new scale for measuring leader behaviors. *Journal of Organizational Behavior*, 21(3), 249–69.

Avolio, B. J., Reichard, R. J., Hannah, S. T., Walumbwa, F. O. & Chan, A. (2009). A meta-analytic review of leadership impact research: Experimental and quasi-experimental studies. *Leadership Quarterly*, 20(5), 764–84.

Bandura, A. (1977). *Social Learning Theory*. Englewood Cliffs, NJ: Prentice-Hall.

Baran, B. E. & Scott, C. W. (2010). Organizing ambiguity: A grounded theory of leadership and sensemaking within dangerous contexts. *Military Psychology*, 22(S1), S42–S69.

Barling, J., Loughlin, C. & Kelloway, E. K. (2002). Development and test of a model linking safety-specific transformational leadership and occupational safety. *Journal of Applied Psychology*, 87(3), 488–96.

Bass, B. M. (1985). *Leadership and Performance Beyond Expectations*. New York: Free Press.

Bass, B. M. (1999). Two decades of research and development in transformational leadership. *European Journal of Work and Organizational Psychology*, 8(1), 9–32.

Bass, B. M. & Avolio, B. J. (1993). Transformational leadership and organizational culture. *Public Administration Quarterly*, 17(1), 112–21.

Bass, B. M. & Riggio, R. E. (2006). *Transformational Leadership*. Mahwah, NJ: Erlbaum.

Bass, B. M. & Steidlmeier, P. (1999). Ethics, character, and authentic transformational leadership behavior. *Leadership Quarterly*, 10(2), 181–217.

Beus, J. M., Payne, S. C., Bergman, M. E. & Arthur, W. (2010). Safety climate and injuries: An examination of theoretical and empirical relationships. *Journal of Applied Psychology*, 95(4), 713–27.

Blau, P. M. (1964). *Exchange and Power in Social Life*. New York: Wiley.

Blumer, H. (1969). *Symbolic Interactionism*. Englewood Cliffs, NJ: Prentice-Hall.

Borgersen, H. C., Hystad, S. W., Larsson, G. & Eid, J. (2014). Authentic leadership and safety climate among seafarers. *Journal of Leadership & Organizational Studies*, 21(4), 394–402.
Brockner, J. & Higgins, E. T. (2001). Regulatory focus theory: Implications for the study of emotions at work. *Organizational Behavior and Human Decision Processes*, 86(1), 35–66.
Brown, K. W. & Ryan, R. M. (2003). The benefits of being present: Mindfulness and its role in psychological well-being. *Journal of Personality and Social Psychology*, 84(4), 822–48.
Brown, K. W., Ryan, R. M. & Creswell, J. D. (2007). Mindfulness: Theoretical foundations and evidence for its salutary effects. *Psychological Inquiry*, 18(4), 211–37.
Carson, J. B., Tesluk, P. E. & Marrone, J. A. (2007). Shared leadership in teams: An investigation of antecedent conditions and performance. *Academy of Management Journal*, 50(5), 1217–34.
Carver, C. S. & Scheier, M. F. (1981). The self-attention-induced feedback loop and social facilitation. *Journal of Experimental Social Psychology*, 17(6), 545–68.
Christian, M. S., Bradley, J. C., Wallace, J. C. & Burke, M. J. (2009). Workplace safety: A meta-analysis of the roles of person and situation factors. *Journal of Applied Psychology*, 94(5), 1103–27.
Christie, A., Barling, J. & Turner, N. (2011) Pseudo-transformational leadership: Model specification and outcomes. *Journal of Applied Social Psychology*, 41(12), 2943–84.
Chughtai, A., Byrne, M. & Flood, B. (2015). Linking ethical leadership to employee well-being: The role of trust in supervisor. *Journal of Business Ethics*, 128(3), 653–63.
Clark, O. L., Zickar, M. J. & Jex, S. M. (2014). Role definition as a moderator of the relationship between safety climate and organizational citizenship behavior among hospital nurses. *Journal of Business & Psychology*, 29(1), 101–10.
Clarke, S. (2006). The relationship between safety climate and safety performance: A meta-analytic review. *Journal of Occupational Health Psychology*, 11(4), 315–27.
Clarke, S. (2010). An integrative model of safety climate: Linking psychological climate and work attitudes to individual safety outcomes using meta-analysis. *Journal of Occupational and Organizational Psychology*, 83(3), 553–78.
Clarke, S. (2013). Safety leadership: A meta-analytic review of transformational and transactional leadership styles as antecedents of safety behaviours. *Journal of Occupational and Organizational Psychology*, 86(1), 22–49.
Clarke, S. & Taylor, I. (2015). Developing an intervention to improve safety leadership and safety outcomes. Paper presented at the 30th Annual Conference of the Society for Industrial and Organizational Psychology (SIOP), Philadelphia, PA, April 2015.
Clarke, S. & Ward, K. (2006). The role of leader influence tactics and safety climate in engaging employee safety participation. *Risk Analysis*, 26(5), 1175–86.
Cohen, A. (1977). Factors in successful occupational safety programs. *Journal of Safety Research*, 9(4), 168–78.

Conchie, S. M. (2013). Transformational leadership, intrinsic motivation, and trust: A moderated-mediated model of workplace safety. *Journal of Occupational Health Psychology*, 18(2), 198–210.
Conchie, S. M. & Donald, I. J. (2009). The moderating role of safety-specific trust on the relation between safety-specific leadership and safety citizenship behaviors. *Journal of Occupational Health Psychology*, 14(2), 137–47.
Conchie, S. M., Taylor, P. J. & Donald, I. J. (2012). Promoting safety voice with safety-specific transformational leadership: The mediating role of two dimensions of trust. *Journal of Occupational Health Psychology*, 17(1), 105–15.
Conchie, S. M., Taylor, P. J. & Charlton, A. (2011). Trust and distrust in safety leadership: Mirror reflections? *Safety Science*, 49(8–9), 1208–14.
Conchie, S. M., Woodcock, H. E. & Taylor, P. J. (2015). Trust-based approaches to safety and production. In S. Clarke, T. M. Probst, F. W. Guldenmund & J. Passmore (eds), *The Wiley Blackwell Handbook of the Psychology of Occupational Safety and Workplace Health*. Chichester: Wiley Blackwell, pp. 111–32.
Cullen, W. D. (1990). *The Public Inquiry into the Piper Alpha Disaster*. 2 vols. London: HMSO.
Dahl, O. & Olsen, E. (2013). Safety compliance on offshore platforms: A multi-sample survey on the role of perceived leadership involvement and work climate. *Safety Science*, 54, 17–26.
Dane, E. & Brummel, B. J. (2014). Examining workplace mindfulness and its relations to job performance and turnover intention. *Human Relations*, 67(1), 105–28.
Dierynck, B., Leroy, H., Savage, G. T. & Choi, E. (in press). The role of individual and collective mindfulness in promoting occupational safety in health care. *Medical Care Research and Review*.
Dóci, E. & Hofmans, J. (2015). Task complexity and transformational leadership: The mediating role of leaders' state core self-evaluations. *Leadership Quarterly*, 26(3), 436–47.
Dragoni, L. (2005). Understanding the emergence of state goal orientation in organizational work groups: The role of leadership and multilevel climate perceptions. *Journal of Applied Psychology*, 90(6), 1084–95.
Dulebohn, J. H., Bommer, W. H., Liden, R. C., Brouer, R. L. & Ferris, G. R. (2012). A meta-analysis of antecedents and consequences of leader–member exchange: Integrating the past with an eye toward the future. *Journal of Management*, 38(6), 1715–59.
Dunbar, R. L. M. (1975). Manager's influence on subordinates' thinking about safety. *The Academy of Management Journal*, 18(2), 364–69.
Eid, J., Mearns, K., Larsson, G., Laberg, J. C. & Johnsen, B. H. (2012). Leadership, psychological capital and safety research: Conceptual issues and future research questions. *Safety Science*, 50(1), 55–61.
Einarsen, S., Aasland, M. S. & Skogstad, A. (2007). Destructive leadership behaviour: A definition and conceptual model. *Leadership Quarterly*, 18(3), 207–16.
Eisenbeiss, S. A. & van Knippenberg, D. (2015). On ethical leadership impact: The role of follower mindfulness and moral emotions. *Journal of Organizational Behavior*, 36(2), 182–95.

Ensley, M. D., Hmieleski, K. M. & Pearce, C. L. (2006). The importance of vertical and shared leadership within new venture top management teams: Implications for the performance of startups. *Leadership Quarterly*, 17(3), 217–31.

Flin, R., Mearns, K., O'Connor, P. & Bryden, R. (2000). Measuring safety climate: Identifying the common features. *Safety Science*, 34(1–3), 177–92.

Fruhen, L. S. & Flin, R. (2016). 'Chronic unease' for safety in senior managers: An interview study of its components, behaviours and consequences. *Journal of Risk Research*, 19(5), 645–63.

Gardner, W. L., Avolio, B. J., Luthans, F., May, D. R. & Walumbwa, F. (2005). 'Can you see the real me?' A self-based model of authentic leader and follower development. *Leadership Quarterly*, 16(3), 343–72.

Griffin, M. A. & Hu, X. (2013). How leaders differentially motivate safety compliance and safety participation: The role of monitoring, inspiring, and learning. *Safety Science*, 60, 196–202.

Guediri, S. & Fruhen, L. (2015). Improving workplace safety through shared leadership. Paper presented at the Society for Industrial and Organizational Psychology 30th Annual Conference, Philadelphia, USA, April 2015.

Halbesleben, J. R. B., Leroy, H., Dierynck, B., Simons, T., Savage, G. T., McCaughey, D. & Leon, M. R. (2013). Living up to safety values in health care: The effect of leader behavioral integrity on occupational safety. *Journal of Occupational Health Psychology*, 18(4), 395–405.

Herndon, F. (2008). Testing mindfulness with perceptual and cognitive factors: External vs. internal encoding, and the cognitive failures questionnaire. *Personality and Individual Differences*, 44(1), 32–41.

Higgins, E. T. (1997). Beyond pleasure and pain. *American Psychologist*, 52(12), 1280–1300.

Higgins, E. T. (1998). Promotion and prevention: Regulatory focus as a motivational principle. In M. P. Zanna (ed.), *Advances In Experimental Social Psychology*, vol. 30. San Diego, CA: Academic Press, pp. 1–46.

Hoffmeister, K., Gibbons, A. M., Johnson, S. K., Cigularov, K. P., Chen, P. Y. & Rosecrance, J. C. (2014). The differential effects of transformational leadership facets on employee safety. *Safety Science*, 62, 68–78.

Hofmann, D. A., Jacobs, R. & Landy, F. (1995). High reliability process industries: Individual, micro, and macro organizational influences on safety performance. *Journal of Safety Research*, 26(3), 131–49.

Hofmann, D. A. & Morgeson, F. P. (1999). Safety-related behavior as a social exchange: The role of perceived organizational support and leader–member exchange. *Journal of Applied Psychology*, 84(2), 286–96.

Hofmann, D. A., Morgeson, F. P. & Gerras, S. J. (2003). Climate as a moderator of the relationship between leader–member exchange and content specific citizenship: Safety climate as an exemplar. *Journal of Applied Psychology*, 88(1), 170–8.

Hopkins, A. (2008). *Failure to learn: The BP Texas City refinery disaster*. Sydney: CCH Australia.

Hülsheger, U. R., Alberts, H. J. E. M., Feinholdt, A. & Lang, J. W. B. (2013). Benefits of mindfulness at work: The role of mindfulness in emotion regulation, emotional exhaustion, and job satisfaction. *Journal of Applied Psychology*, 98(2), 310–25.

Inness, M., Turner, N., Barling, J. & Stride, C. B. (2010). Transformational leadership and employee safety performance: A within-person, between-jobs design. *Journal of Occupational Health Psychology*, 15(3), 279–90.

Jiang, L. & Probst, T. M. (2016). Transformational and passive leadership as cross-level moderators of the relationships between safety knowledge, safety motivation, and safety participation. *Journal of Safety Research*, 57, 27–32.

Johnson, S. E. (2007). The predictive validity of safety climate. *Journal of Safety Research*, 38(5), 511–21.

Kark, R., Katz-Navon, T. & Delegach, M. (2015). The dual effects of leading for safety: The mediating role of employee regulatory focus. *Journal of Applied Psychology*, 100(5), 1332–48.

Kark, R. & Van Dijk, D. (2007). Motivation to lead, motivation to follow: The role of the self-regulatory focus in leadership processes. *Academy of Management Review*, 32, 500–28.

Kath, L. M., Marks, K. M. & Ranney, J. (2010). Safety climate dimensions, leader–member exchange, and organizational support as predictors of upward safety communication in a sample of rail industry workers. *Safety Science*, 48(5), 643–50.

Kelloway, E. K. & Barling, J. (2010). Leadership development as an intervention in occupational health psychology. *Work & Stress*, 24(3), 260–79.

Kelloway, E. K., Mullen, J. & Francis, L. (2006). Divergent effects of transformational and passive leadership on employee safety. *Journal of Occupational Health Psychology*, 11(1), 76–86.

Kines, P., Andersen, L. P. S., Spangenberg, S., Mikkelsen, K. L., Dyreborg, J. & Zohar, D. (2010). Improving construction site safety through leader-based verbal safety communication. *Journal of Safety Research*, 41(5), 399–406.

Krasikova, D. V., Green, S. G. & LeBreton, J. M. (2013). Destructive leadership: A theoretical review, integration, and future research agenda. *Journal of Management*, 39(5), 1308–38.

Lanaj, K., Chang, C. H. & Johnson, R. E. (2012). Regulatory focus and work-related outcomes: A review and meta-analysis. *Psychological Bulletin*, 138(5), 998–1034.

Latané, B. (1981). The psychology of social impact. *American Psychologist*, 36(4), 343–56.

Leroy, H., Dierynck, B., Anseel, F., Simons, T., Halbesleben, J. R. B., McCaughey, D., Savage, G. & Sels, L. (2012). Behavioral integrity for safety, priority of safety, psychological safety, and patient safety: A team-level study. *Journal of Applied Psychology*, 97(6), 1273–81.

Lord, R. G., Diefendorff, J. M., Schmidt, A. M. & Hall, R. J. (2010). Self-regulation at work. *Annual Review of Psychology*, 61, 543–68.

Luria, G. (2008). Climate strength: How leaders form consensus. *Leadership Quarterly*, 19(1), 42–53.

Luthans, F. & Avolio, B. J. (2003). Authentic leadership development. In K. S. Cameron, J. E. Dutton & R. E. Quinn (eds.), *Positive Organizational Scholarship: Foundations of a New Discipline*. San Francisco, CA: Berrett-Koehler, pp. 241–61.

Martínez-Córcoles, M., Gracia, F. J., Tomás, I. & Peiró, J. M. (2011). Leadership and employees' perceived safety behaviors in a nuclear power plant: A structural equation model. *Safety Science*, 49(8–9), 1118–29.

Martínez-Corcóles, M., Gracia, F. J., Tomás, I. & Peiró, J. M. (2014). Strengthening safety compliance in nuclear power operations: A role-based approach. *Risk Analysis*, 34(7), 1257–69.

Martínez-Córcoles, M., Gracia, F. J., Tomás, I., Peiró, J. M. & Schöbel, M. (2013). Empowering team leadership and safety performance in nuclear power plants: A multilevel approach. *Safety Science*, 51(1), 293–301.

Martínez-Córcoles, M., Schöbel, M., Gracia, F. J., Tomás, I. & Peiró, J. M. (2012). Linking empowering leadership to safety participation in nuclear power plants: A structural equation model. *Journal of Safety Research*, 43(3), 215–21.

Mullen, J. (2005). Testing a model of employee willingness to raise safety issues. *Canadian Journal of Behavioural Sciences*, 37(4), 273–82.

Mullen, J. E. & Kelloway, E. K. (2009). Safety leadership: A longitudinal study of the effects of transformational leadership on safety outcomes. *Journal of Occupational and Organizational Psychology*, 82(2), 253–72.

Mullen, J., Kelloway, E. K. & Teed, M. (2011). Inconsistent style of leadership as a predictor of safety behaviour. *Work & Stress*, 25(1), 41–54.

Mumford, M. D., Friedrich, T. L., Caughron, J. J. & Byrne, C. L. (2007). Leader cognition in real-world settings: How do leaders think about crises? *Leadership Quarterly*, 18(6), 515–43.

Nahrgang, J. D., Morgeson, F. P. & Hofmann, D. A. (2011). Safety at work: A meta-analytic investigation of the link between job demands, job resources, burnout, engagement, and safety outcomes. *Journal of Applied Psychology*, 96(1), 71–94.

National Commission on the BP Deepwater Horizon Oil Spill and Offshore Drilling (2011). *Deep Water: The Gulf Oil disaster and the future of offshore drilling: Report to the President*. Washington, DC: US Government Printing Office.

Neal, A. & Griffin, M. A. (2006). A study of the lagged relationships among safety climate, safety motivation, safety behaviour, and accidents at the individual and group levels. *Journal of Applied Psychology*, 91(4), 946–53.

Neubert, M. J., Kacmar, K. M., Carlson, D. S., Chonko, L. B. & Roberts, J. A. (2008). Regulatory focus as a mediator of the influence of initiating structure and servant leadership on employee behavior. *Journal of Applied Psychology*, 93(6), 1220–33.

Nicolaides, V. C., LaPort, K. A., Chen, T. R., Tomassetti, A. J., Weis, E. J., Zaccaro S. J. & Cortina, J. M. (2014). The shared leadership of teams: A meta-analysis of proximal, distal, and moderating relationships. *Leadership Quarterly*, 25(5), 923–42.

Nielsen, M. B., Eid, J., Mearns, K. & Larsson, G. (2013). Authentic leadership and its relationship with risk perception and safety climate. *Leadership & Organization Development Journal*, 34(4), 308–25.

Nielsen, M. B., Skogstad, A., Matthiesen, S. B. & Einarsen, S. (2016). The importance of a multidimensional and temporal design in research on leadership and workplace safety. *Leadership Quarterly*, 27(1), 142–55.

Parker, S. K., Axtell, C. M. & Turner, N. (2001). Designing a safer workplace: Importance of job autonomy, communication quality and supportive supervisors. *Journal of Occupational Health Psychology*, 6(3), 211–18.

Pearce, C. L. & Sims, H. P. (2002). Vertical versus shared leadership as predictors of the effectiveness of change management teams: An examination of aversive, directive, transactional, transformational, and empowering leader behaviors. *Group Dynamics: Theory, Research, and Practice*, 6(2), 172–97.

Probst, T. M. (2015). Organizational safety climate and supervisor safety enforcement: Multilevel explorations of the causes of accident underreporting. *Journal of Applied Psychology*, 100(6), 1899–1907.

Probst, T. M. & Brubaker, T. L. (2001). The effects of job insecurity on employee safety outcomes: Cross-sectional and longitudinal explorations. *Journal of Occupational Health Psychology*, 6(2), 139–59.

Reason, J. T. (1993). Managing the management risk: New approaches to organizational safety. In B. Wilpert & T. Qvale (eds), *Reliability and Safety in Hazardous Work Systems*. Hove, UK: Erlbaum, pp. 7–22.

Reason, J. T. (1997). *Managing the Risks of Organizational Accidents*. Aldershot, UK: Ashgate.

Reason, J. T., Manstead, A. S. R., Stradling, S. G., Baxter, J. S. & Campbell, K. (1990). Errors and violations on the road: A real distinction? *Ergonomics*, 33(10–11), 1315–32.

Reb, J., Narayanan, J. & Chaturvedi, S. (2014). Leading mindfully: Two studies on the influence of supervisor trait mindfulness on employee well-being and performance. *Mindfulness*, 5(1), 36–45.

Rodriguez, M. A. & Griffin, M. A. (2009). From error prevention to error learning: The role of error management in global leadership. *Advances in Global Leadership*, 5, 93–112.

Salancik, G. R. & Pfeffer, J. (1978). A social information processing approach to job attitudes and task design. *Administrative Science Quarterly*, 23(2), 224–53.

Schyns, B. & Schilling, J. (2013). How bad are the effects of bad leaders? A meta-analysis of destructive leadership and its outcomes. *Leadership Quarterly*, 24(1), 138–58.

Shannon, H. S. & Norman, G. R. (2009). Deriving the factor structure of safety climate scales. *Safety Science*, 47(3), 327–9.

Simons, T. (2002). Behavioral integrity: The perceived alignment between managers' words and deeds as a research focus. *Organization Science*, 13(1), 18–35.

Simons, T. (2008). *The Integrity Dividend: Leading by the Power of Your Word*. San Francisco, CA: Jossey-Bass.

Smith, T. D., Eldridge, F. & DeJoy, D. M. (2016). Safety-specific transformational and passive leadership influences on firefighter safety climate perceptions and safety behavior outcomes. *Safety Science*, 86, 92–7.

Tepper, B.J. (2000). Consequences of abusive supervision. *Academy of Management Journal*, 43(2), 178–90.

Törner, M. (2011). The 'social-physiology' of safety: An integrative approach to understanding organisational psychological mechanisms behind safety performance. *Safety Science*, 49(8–9), 1262–9.

Turner, N., Chmiel, N., Hershcovis, M. S. & Walls, M. (2010). Life on the line: Job demands, perceived co-worker support for safety, and hazardous work events. *Journal of Occupational Health Psychology*, 15(4), 482–93.

von Thiele Schwarz, U., Hasson, H. & Tafvelin, S. (2016). Leadership training as an occupational health intervention: Improved safety and sustained productivity. *Safety Science*, 81, 35–45.

Wang, D., Waldman, D. A. & Zhang, Z. (2014). A meta-analysis of shared leadership and team effectiveness. *Journal of Applied Psychology*, 99(2), 181–98.

Weick, K. E. (1995). *Sensemaking in Organisations*. London: Sage.

Weick, K. E. & Sutcliffe, K. M. (2007). *Managing the Unexpected: Resilient Performance in an Age of Uncertainty*. San Francisco, CA: Jossey-Bass.

Yule, S. (2002). Do transformational leaders lead safer businesses? Paper presented at the 25th International Congress of Applied Psychology, Singapore, July.

Zhang, J., Ding, W., Li, Y. & Wu, C. (2013). Task complexity matters: The influence of trait mindfulness on task and safety performance of nuclear power plant operators. *Personality and Individual Differences*, 55(4), 433–9.

Zhang, J. & Wu, C. (2014). The influence of dispositional mindfulness on safety behaviors: A dual process perspective. *Accident Analysis & Prevention*, 70, 24–32.

Zohar, D. (1980). Safety climate in industrial organizations: Theoretical and applied implications. *Journal of Applied Psychology*, 65(1), 96–102.

Zohar, D. (2000). A group-level model of safety climate: Testing the effect of group climate on microaccidents in manufacturing jobs. *Journal of Applied Psychology*, 85(4), 587–96.

Zohar, D. (2002a). The effects of leadership dimensions, safety climate, and assigned priorities on minor injuries in work groups. *Journal of Organizational Behavior*, 23(1), 75–92.

Zohar, D. (2002b). Modifying supervisory practices to improve sub-unit safety: A leadership-based intervention model. *Journal of Applied Psychology*, 87(1), 156–63.

Zohar, D. (2003). The influence of leadership and climate on occupational health and safety. In D. A. Hofmann & L. E. Tetrick (eds), *Health and Safety in Organizations*. San Francisco, CA: Jossey-Bass, pp. 201–30.

Zohar, D. (2008). Safety climate and beyond: A multi-level multi-climate framework. *Safety Science*, 46(3), 376–87.

Zohar, D. (2010). Thirty years of safety climate research: Reflections and future directions. *Accident Analysis and Prevention*, 42(5), 1517–22.

Zohar, D. & Luria, G. (2004). Climate as a social-cognitive construction of supervisory practices: Scripts as proxy of behavior patterns. *Journal of Applied Psychology*, 89(2), 322–33.

Zohar, D. & Polachek, T. (2014). Discourse-based intervention for modifying supervisory communication as leverage for safety climate and performance improvement: A randomized field study. *Journal of Applied Psychology*, 99(1), 113–24.

Zohar, D. & Tenne-Gazit, O. (2008). Transformational leadership and group interaction as climate antecedents: A social network analysis. *Journal of Applied Psychology*, 93(4), 744–57.

2

Senior Management Safety Leadership Behaviour

Kate C. Bowers, Mark Fleming and Andrea Bishop

The importance of senior management in shaping organizational safety culture has grown in response to the Deepwater Horizon accident in 2010. A report produced in response to the accident concluded that an organization's Chief Executive Officer (CEO) and board of directors must create a safe culture in which all employees feel responsible and motivated to prevent accidents (National Commission on the BP Deepwater Horizon Oil Spill and Offshore Drilling, 2011). Senior management maintain a strong influence on organizational culture because of their scope of influence (Day, 2014; Schein, 2004) and have been recognized in practice as a critical factor in shaping organizational safety outcomes (e.g., Health and Safety Executive, 1999; National Commission on the BP Deepwater Horizon Oil Spill and Offshore Drilling, 2011).

It is well supported that perceptions of manager commitment are critical in influencing employee safety behaviours (Beus, Payne, Bergman & Arthur, 2010; Christian, Bradley, Wallace & Burke, 2009; Clarke, 2013), and researchers have attempted to determine the characteristics of effective safety management that inform these perceptions (e.g., on safety-specific transformational leadership style Barling, Loughlin & Kelloway, 2002; Kelloway, Mullen & Francis, 2006; on authentic leadership style Eid, Mearns, Larsson, Laberg & Johnsen, 2012). Interestingly, however, there is a lack of evidence regarding how senior managers impact employee safety perceptions and behaviours (Flin, 2003; Flin & Yule, 2004; Fruhen, Mearns, Flin & Kirwan, 2013, 2014a, 2014b). Understanding how employees perceive senior manager safety commitment is a critical aspect of safety leadership that is often overlooked.

Growing evidence supports the differential impact of management influence on employee safety behaviour for various levels of management. In their investigation of organizational safety climate, Zohar and Luria (2005) established that variation in climate exists among different departments of an organization, suggesting that intervention models should assume a multilevel perspective. Adding to this, Zohar (2014) suggested that the ability to improve safety outcomes is contingent on perceptions of sincere management commitment and that these

Leading to Occupational Health and Safety: How Leadership Behaviours Impact Organizational Safety and Well-Being, First Edition.
Edited by E. Kevin Kelloway, Karina Nielsen and Jennifer K. Dimoff.

perceptions may differ for each level of management. Furthermore, literature investigating the role of senior management in organizations has highlighted that this level has a unique impact on employee safety behaviour (Clarke, 1999). Flin's (2003) summary recognized the distinctive effects of different levels of management, speculating that senior manager safety commitment is a reflection of the executive's resource management, including time, money and people. Similarly, Zohar (2014) surmised that leaders' commitment is largely perceived as investment in hazard control or risk management. Thus, it is thought that the greater the investment of time and resources to reduce potential hazards and threats to safety, the greater the reflection of commitment, and, consequently, the stronger the climate.

Research has begun to address the lack of evidence regarding senior manager safety commitment by investigating senior managers' perspectives of organizational safety practices. This includes analyses of senior managers' descriptions of safety culture (Fruhen et al., 2013) and methods assessing how senior managers perceive their influence on employee perceptions of safety commitment (Fruhen et al., 2014a, 2014b). The purpose of this chapter is to illustrate the importance of senior managers and how they can influence employees' safety-related perceptions and behaviours. To demonstrate this role, and the ways by which managers can have influence, we draw on signalling theory and empirical evidence related to senior management safety leadership.

A Framework for Leadership Influence: Signalling Theory

Signalling theory (Spence, 2002), initially developed in economics literature, has been recently adapted to explain the influence of managers in organizations (Connelly, Certo, Ireland & Reutzel, 2011). Signalling theory contends that signals are used by messengers when information asymmetry exists, that is, when different people know different things (Spence, 2002). In essence, signalling theory suggests that information communicated between two parties is relayed via a signal that must be interpreted by the receiving party (Spence, 2002). In the context of senior manager safety commitment, a high-quality signal is one that results in the perceiver believing in senior management's authentic commitment to safety. Although signalling theory may seem simplistic, the variety of characteristics that can impact signal transmission and interpretation illustrate the complexity of this process. Connelly et al. (2011) describe the characteristics that can impact interpretation of the message as:

- *sender characteristics* – perceived characteristics of the sender of the signal (e.g., credibility, trust, expertise),
- *signal characteristics* – characteristics of the descriptive quality of the signal (e.g., medium, clarity, frequency, consistency with previous messages),
- *receiver characteristics* – characteristics of the receiver that influence how a signal is perceived (e.g., an individual's ability or motivation to receive a signal), and

- *external characteristics* – characteristics that can impact signal interpretation (e.g., verifying a signal's meaning by way of countersignalling, environmental factors that can result in distortion of the message).

It is critical that leaders and practitioners consider the variety of influences that can impact the interpretation of a signal. For example, perceptions of source attributes (e.g., credibility), descriptive aspects of the message (e.g., the medium through which the message is relayed) and characteristics of the receiver (e.g., motivation or ability) can inform perception formation. The following section provides examples of signalling to illustrate more clearly the process and power of signalling.

Examples of Signalling

Signalling is a powerful method that can be commonly identified in society. The utility in signalling is that it facilitates the communication of an underlying quality that is otherwise unknown to a receiver. Luxury goods such as cars, fur coats, watches and handbags are popularly used to signal wealth. A used-car salesman may offer a five-year warranty on a previously owned vehicle to signal his assurance of the car's quality. Spence (1973) described signalling theory in the context of the job market, where employers can rely on an applicant's level of education as a credible signal of that person's underlying competence.

Kirmani and Rao (2000) provided a useful description of signalling theory in terms of high- and low-quality marketing firms. Similar to their example, the following analogy describes signalling theory in terms of buyers and sellers. In this example, two types of produce sellers exist: high- and low-quality. Sellers are aware of the quality of their produce; however, buyers are unaware of which seller is high-quality, and thus information asymmetry exists. Sellers must therefore determine if it is worthwhile to emit a signal to the buyer to demonstrate their quality. In the present example we describe how a high-quality sellers sells organic produce whereas a low-quality seller sells genetically modified produce. It is assumed that the produce are sold at similar cost.

The decision to signal information is often described in a mathematical formula whereby, when a high-quality seller (e.g. of organic produce) signals, they receive payoff 'A', and when no signal is emitted they receive payoff 'B'. When a low-quality seller (e.g. a seller of non-organic produce) signals they receive payoff 'C', and no signal results in payoff 'D'. Thus, high-quality sellers *gain* when, for high-quality setters, A (payoff from signalling) > B (payoff from not signalling) and, for low-quality sellers, D (payoff from not signalling) > C (payoff from signalling). This result occurs when emitting a signal is too costly for low-quality sellers; thus, payoff D exceeds payoff C for low-quality sellers. For example, when selling produce, the high-quality seller (organic) may advertise that their produce are certified 100% organic. However, because the low-quality seller is selling genetically modified produce, they are unable to send such a signal. In this case, the signal for the low-quality seller is too costly, as advertising their produce as organic would breach legal regulations and result in a costly fine (payoff C).

In this case, for a high-quality seller signalling organic produce (e.g., putting a 'certified organic' sticker on all produce) informs the buyer of this otherwise unobservable quality. More importantly, the buyer can be confident in choosing the high-quality seller through its advertised organic produce because the buyer is inherently aware that false advertising (sending the signal of organic when it is not) is too great a risk for a low-quality seller.

The ability of a high-quality seller to use a signal that a low-quality seller cannot fosters a separating equilibrium. The success of a signal is contingent on its credibility, and sellers will often use a 'bonding' mechanism to relay the credibility of their signal. Bonding demonstrates that a false signal would result in cost to the seller (e.g., the seller's reputation would suffer). Conversely, when companies are unable to use signals that differentiate quality (A > B and C > D), a 'pooling equilibrium' exists. In a pooling equilibrium signalling will not be effective, as no signal exists that differentiates between high- and low-quality sellers.

Much like high- and low-quality sellers in market interactions, the principle of signalling theory can be applied to managers and how their behaviour is interpreted by employees. It should be noted that the concept of signal quality (e.g., high- versus low-quality) may be differentially interpreted depending on the context in which it is used (Connelly et al., 2011). In the aforementioned example, 'quality' refers to the 'underlying, unobservable ability of the signaler to fulfill the needs or demands of an outsider observing the signal' (Connelly et al., 2011, p. 43). In the context of senior manager safety commitment, 'high-quality' describes senior managers who are able to signal to employees the true value they put on safety. Identifying signals of senior manager commitment is of great utility for organizational leadership, as sending high-quality signals will help inform perceptions of authentic safety commitment.

Signals of Senior Management Commitment to Safety

Several studies have attempted to identify how senior management demonstrate safety commitment behaviour. Broadly speaking, theorists suggest that senior management influence perceptions of safety commitment by the way in which they allocate time, money and manpower to hazard control and risk management (Flin, 2003; Zohar, 2014). More specifically, Flin and Yule's (2004) summary of senior management leadership concluded that behaviours reflecting safety commitment could be categorized under two styles of leadership: transactional and transformational. Behaviours included ensuring compliance with regulatory requirements and providing resources for a comprehensive safety programme (transactional) combined with demonstrating visible and consistent commitment to safety, demonstrating concern for people, encouraging participatory styles in middle managers and supervisors, and giving time for safety (transformational).

Similar findings were supported by Fruhen and colleagues' (2014a, 2014b) empirical investigations. In one study, the authors investigated how senior management demonstrate safety commitment (Fruhen et al., 2014a). The authors interviewed 60 senior managers (CEOs, direct reports to CEOs, and board members) from European and North American air traffic management organizations. Results showed that aspects of problem solving, specifically the number of issues considered, the information sources used, the generation of ideas, and the social competence involved, reflected senior leader commitment to safety. Senior managers also reported that personal involvement in safety matters, influence on organizational attributes and communication about safety demonstrated safety commitment. Additionally, perceiving and understanding employees' intentions and emotions were deemed a reflection of commitment.

In another two-part study, Fruhen et al. (2014b) investigated which personal attributes of senior managers most influence safety outcomes. In part one, 76 senior managers (direct reports to CEOs) completed a questionnaire about the characteristics ideal for a CEO's influence on safety. In part two nine senior managers were interviewed in order to better define the characteristics already defined in part one. Combined results indicated six attributes demonstrating commitment to safety: (1) social competence (understanding others' emotions and ability to persuade others), (2) safety knowledge (theoretical and practical understanding of safety issues, knowledge of facts and information), (3) motivation (goal motivation via context-appropriate promotion or prevention focus; see Crowe & Higgins, 1997), (4) problem solving (understanding the problem, generating ideas and planning the implementation of those ideas), (5) personality factors (e.g., approachability, empathy, reliability), and (6) interpersonal leadership skills (e.g., transactional, transformational and authentic leadership characteristics). These attributes were identified as senior managers' safety intelligence, defined as their understanding of safety issues and of relevant policies regarding safety.

Additionally, authentic leadership has recently been established as an independent style of leadership that is similar to, but separate from, transformational leadership (Tonkin, 2013) and has been shown to impact safety outcomes (Birkeland Nielsen, Eid, Mearns & Larsson, 2013; Eid et al., 2012). Transformational leadership is largely defined by behavioural characteristics, whereas authentic leadership is characterized by the personal characteristics of the leader (Avolio & Gardner, 2005). For example, a recent investigation of authentic leadership suggests that the construct is comprised of four components: (1) self-awareness (awareness of one's strengths and weaknesses and how one is viewed as a leader), (2) balanced processing (considering multiple perspectives), (3) relational transparency (presenting one's real self), and (4) internalized moral perspective (behaviour is guided by one's morals and values; Walumbwa, Avolio, Gardner, Wernsing & Peterson, 2008). It is suggested that authentic leaders have a strong sense of self that guides them in actions and decision-making (Avolio & Gardner, 2005). Moreover, employees identify with authentic leaders and their values, subsequently adopting these values as their own (Avolio & Gardner, 2005). Preliminary investigation of authentic leadership and safety outcomes has found a relationship between perceived authentic leadership and safety climate as well as lowered perceptions of risk (Birkeland Nielsen et al., 2013). Combining this knowledge with theory that signal characteristics impact message interpretation, it is reasonable to assume that perceptions of senior management's behaviour (e.g., participation in safety) and personal attributes (e.g., honesty) will impact perception formation.

Perhaps the most challenging and understudied factor in exploring how employees form perceptions of senior management's safety commitment is the variety of signals that inform perceptions. Senior manager safety commitment may be observed through senior manager behaviours and outcomes from decision-making. Thus, signals of senior manager safety commitment may be observed through direct means (e.g., observing senior management visit the worksite and speak about safety) or indirect means (e.g., inferences made from observable outcomes in the work environment or information relayed by other employees, family, friends, or the media).

Interestingly, how senior manager leadership behaviours and personal attributes are transmitted to employees depends largely on the structure of the organization. Understandably, the scale of an organization can impact how senior management engage in some forms of leadership (for example, visiting the worksite and actively participating in safety may be easier in smaller organizations with local operations). Often, the size of their organization and the multiple responsibilities they carry make it challenging for senior management to maintain consistent and frequent appearances at the worksite in order to build interpersonal relationships. Zaccaro (2001) contends that senior managers operate at a system-wide level and often do not have much opportunity to establish interpersonal relations with members of their organization. Therefore this level of management must work hard to understand and engage in indirect acts that inform employees of their safety commitment. In many organizations, senior management distribute responsibility through lower levels of management, including directors, mid-level managers and frontline supervisors. Thus senior management commitment to safety may be signalled through the behaviour and actions of lower levels of management (Flin, 2003). As well, observable outcomes in the worksite (e.g., new equipment or insufficient equipment) may lead to inferences about the value senior management place on safety.

This cascade of responsibility and interdependence among hierarchical structures enhances the complexity of signals. Signalling theory suggests that the effectiveness of signal interpretation may be impacted by the directness of the source. For example, observations of senior management engaging in safety at the worksite enhance the accuracy of signal interpretation, as employees are able to observe senior management directly and have the opportunity to clarify their understanding of senior management's statements and actions. In comparison to these direct experiences, employees may infer senior management safety commitment from published documents on organizational safety statistics, creating greater opportunity to question the credibility of the signal (e.g., how accurate are the statistics?) and the accuracy of the message source (e.g., is the message from senior management or from a marketing team?). Additionally, if signals are being transmitted indirectly through a lower-level manager, characteristics of this source can impact interpretation positively (e.g., trust in the supervisor yields message acceptance) or negatively (lack of trust in the supervisor yields message scrutiny and rejection).

The abovementioned findings support the conclusion that senior management behaviours and personal attributes impact employee perceptions and, subsequently, safety outcomes. These results highlight the criticality of understanding how senior management convincingly signal authentic safety commitment, particularly when interpersonal interaction is limited. The following sections identify four signal categories and include examples to illustrate the complexity of signals and distorting factors that can impact successful interpretation.

1) Active participation in safety
2) Allocation of resources to safety
3) Including safety in the structure of the organization
4) Consistency of actions and decision-making

Active Participation in Safety

The best-supported signal of senior management's commitment to safety is active engagement in safety. There is substantial evidence that transformational leadership and contingent reward have a positive impact on employee perceptions of manager commitment, and subsequently on safety outcomes (e.g., Barling et al., 2002; Clarke, 2013; Kelloway et al., 2006), and emerging support that authentic leadership fosters positive perceptions and safety outcomes (Birkeland Nielsen et al., 2013; Eid et al., 2012). Direct signalling of senior management's active participation in safety includes visiting worksites and engaging employees about safety, a behaviour that allows senior management to build interpersonal connections and simultaneously to engage in transformational, transactional and authentic leadership. Visiting the worksite and engaging in safety includes demonstrating an appreciation of worksite risks and compassion for individual safety, demonstrating knowledge and understanding of safety policies and procedures, promoting and rewarding safety compliance, asking questions and demonstrating an eagerness to learn as well as an ability to problem-solve, and demonstrating an understanding of employee intentions and emotions in communicated responses. Moreover, allocating time to safety by visiting the worksite and engaging employees in safety signals a priority for employee welfare. Flin (2003) surmised that senior management's time is extremely valuable; thus, expending this resource to participate in and better understand employee experiences of safety signals that this aspect of organizational functioning is more important than others (e.g., production). Senior management's personal appearances and participation at the front line allow employees to observe and experience their behaviour directly, and to ask them questions and clarify their statements. In short, senior management's active participation at the worksite gives a clear signal that senior management are allocating time to ensuring the welfare of employees over other organizational factors, so signalling their commitment to safety.

The importance of active participation in safety is further evidenced by the detrimental effects of absent leadership. Kelloway, Sivanathan, Francis and Barling (2005) identified poor leadership as being characterized by passive and abusive leadership behaviours. Passive leadership involves a lack of voluntary intervention, or intervention only when absolutely necessary, and avoidance of decision-making and role responsibilities, whereas abusive leadership includes engaging in aggressive or punitive behaviours towards employees. Empirical investigations have established a connection between passive leadership and negative safety outcomes. Zohar (2002) found that passive leadership negatively impacted safety climate, contributing to greater rates of injury. Similarly, Kelloway et al.'s (2006) investigation found that safety-specific passive leadership behaviour contributed to poorer safety climate and, in turn, to higher incidence of injury. Kelloway and colleagues (2005) describe abusive leadership as '[engagement] in aggressive or punitive behaviors toward ... employees' (p. 91).

Although active participation in safety sends a direct and therefore strong signal of safety commitment, it does not guarantee that this signal will be interpreted as intended. As described in the discussion of signalling theory, a variety of sender, signal and receiver characteristics can interact to inform perception formation (Connelly et al., 2011). Trust in management has been investigated in numerous empirical studies, and found to have an impact on perceptions of safety climate and safety outcomes (e.g., Burns, Mearns & McGeorge, 2006; Conchie, Donald & Taylor, 2006; Luria, 2010). Similarly, other personal attributes of management (e.g., reliability, openness, tolerance, empathy, responsibility; Fruhen et al., 2014b) have been suggested as impacting perceptions of senior manager safety commitment. It is therefore important that senior management consider perceptions of senior management personal attributes, as these may interfere in the interpretation of signals of safety commitment. In this case, senior management should first work to establish trust with employees as a lack of trust will negate efforts to signal genuine safety commitment.

As mentioned, it can be challenging for senior management to adequately visit the worksite and participate in safety with frontline staff (Zaccaro, 2001). In organizations of a small scale, senior management have greater ability to visit worksites and interact one to one with employees in transformational and authentic leadership styles. This task may be more challenging in organizations of larger scale (e.g., where there are thousands of employees, and worksites in multiple countries). In organizations of larger scale, senior management must use alternative (indirect) methods to demonstrate transformational, transactional and authentic leadership and inform perceptions of safety commitment. Perceptions of senior management's active participation in worksite safety through indirect sources is best inferred through lower-level management's safety behaviours. Lower-level management's engagement in safety leadership (characterized by transformational, transactional and authentic leadership behaviours) demonstrates how senior management's policies are operationalized (Zohar, 2010), subsequently informing employees of senior management decision-making. Similarly, a lack of supervisory involvement in safety may lead to inferences that senior management are unengaged in safety matters. The inference of senior manager safety commitment through a secondary (indirect) source raises the complexity of signals. The employee receiving the signal must now consider the characteristics of both senders (senior management and the supervisor). Thus, if a lack of trust exists with either management body, signal interpretation will be impacted. As well, the medium used to relay information (e.g., behavioural, verbal, in writing), combined with the clarity of the signal, can impact the success of interpretation.

Additional indirect means that senior management can use to signal active participation in safety include published documents. Senior management can produce safety-related magazines, newsletters, and personal statements or memos that are disseminated to employees. These materials can include descriptions of senior management's personal views on safety and their personal involvement in safety matters, inspirational stories, safety statistics, and recognition of safety compliance. In short, the content of published material can detail aspects of safety participation and leadership practice. The strength of these signals, however, is less than that of signals that involve interpersonal experiences. Signals translated through published mediums (indirect signals) can be impacted by a great number of source characteristics (e.g., the view of senior management or the organization's PR team), signal characteristics (for example, the published document is emailed but employees do not check their email accounts), and receiver characteristics (e.g., their ability or motivation to read the document). Thus, extra steps must be taken to ensure this type of indirect signal reaches the intended recipient and is received in the intended manner.

Allocating Resources to Safety

Senior management can also signal their commitment to safety through their resource allocation within the organization. Senior management are largely responsible for organizational strategy and formal structure, factors that have a significant impact on multiple organizational outcomes including financial performance (Day, 2014). Financial performance is an important aspect of senior management functioning (Flin, 2003); thus, contributing resources to ensure safety demonstrates a clear value for safety. Flin and Yule (2004) stated that senior management demonstrate commitment by developing and providing resources for a comprehensive safety programme. In addition to ensuring safety programmes in the workplace, allocation of finances can be inferred from new infrastructure or equipment at the worksite, the timely completion of infrastructure or equipment repairs and inspections, the development and implementation of safety training, publications that include financial reports related to safety, and information from lower-level management, co-workers or media sources. Signals of resource allocation are often strong because these outcomes can directly impact employee experience at the worksite. For example, it is unlikely that the use of new equipment would go unnoticed by an employee. As with signals of active participation in safety, however, it is not guaranteed that signals will be received appropriately. For example, employees may not interpret the appearance of new equipment at the worksite as an outcome of senior management decision-making. It is therefore useful to focus on these signals and understand how they may be improved to ensure better interpretation (e.g., by having lower-level management explain that new equipment was mandated by senior management to ensure safety). Similarly, safety publications that include statements of resource allocation can incur the same distorting characteristics as other safety publications and should therefore be used with care.

In short, allocating finances to safety demonstrates senior management's prioritization of safety above the organization's financial gain, thereby signalling a strong value for safety. It should also be noted that, similarly to allocating finances to safety, allocating sufficient manpower to safety is another form of resource allocation found to signal safety commitment (Flin, 2003). Ensuring sufficient manpower for the safe completion of tasks signals a prioritization of safety over profit, and consequently senior management's safety commitment. It is also important that senior management consider how employees may negatively perceive the balancing of resource allocation. Fruhen et al. (2014b) found that senior management described balancing safety appropriately with costs as a responsibility of senior management that demonstrated safety commitment. Senior management should be careful to ensure that the act of balancing does not signal a lack of commitment. For example, if finances are not available to address a safety concern immediately, steps should be taken to communicate why the issue is not addressed straight away, and to provide regular updates on the steps being taken to mitigate the issue until it can be appropriately dealt with. Transparency of decision-making, a quality of authentic leadership (Avolio & Gardner, 2005), allows senior management to demonstrate their concern and priority for issues when they are unable to take immediate action. A lack of response to a raised concern can signal passive leadership (Kelloway et al., 2005) and so give rise to perceptions of a lack of commitment.

Safety in the Structure of the Organization

A third way in which senior management can signal their commitment to safety is to build it into the formal structure of the organization. Senior management is primarily responsible for strategic planning and organizational structure (Day, 2014), providing ample opportunity to ensure safety is ingrained in many aspects of functioning. This includes building safety into policies and procedures, organizational values and mission statements, and other aspects of organizational structure. Importantly, organizational safety-related policies and programmes have been found to contribute significantly to safety climate and safety outcomes (DeJoy, Schaffer, Wilson, Vandenberg & Butts, 2004) and, as described by Zohar (2008), 'formal policy is explicit, relating to overt statements and formal procedures, while enforced policy or enacted practices are tacit, derived from observing senior, middle, and lower management patterns of action concerning key policy issues' (p. 376). Thus, to optimize safety within the organization, formal policies developed by senior management should underscore safety. However, the impact of these policies on perceptions of manager safety commitment depends on how policies are enforced by all other levels of management. As previously discussed, the enforcement of policy by all levels of management is part of senior management's active participation in safety, and constitutes a signal of commitment.

In order to incorporate safety in the structure of the organization, senior management can implement policies related to compliance with safety standards, safety training and safety performance feedback (DeJoy et al., 2004). Incorporating safety in numerous aspects of organizational structure works to ensure all management levels prioritize safety in all activities. Ingraining these principles in the organization promotes a focus on safety over other organizational factors (e.g., production or profit), thereby signalling safety commitment.

Consistency of Actions and Decision-making

Consistency is a critical aspect in demonstrating senior manager safety commitment. Zohar (2010) emphasized the importance of consistency between leaders' enacted and espoused values in employee perceptions of leader safety commitment. Enacted policies are messages indicating a value for safety that are visible to employees; espoused values are the underlying, authentic values for safety that leaders hold. Thus, employees must determine if a signal of safety commitment (enacted value) is representative of (consistent with) that leader's espoused value. As Zohar (2010) describes, determining the consistency of these values is a challenging task that occurs over time and across varying situations. Employees must analyse the words and actions of managers and compare their priorities across contexts to determine alignment. When alignment is experienced, employees perceive managers as authentically committed to safety. Similarly, the consistency between formal policy and management practice provides a clear example of senior management's values. Neglecting to comply with formal policies related to safety (e.g., turning a blind eye to safety to increase production speed) demonstrates a lack of value for safety (Zohar, 2008).

The signal of consistency is perhaps best exemplified through findings that demonstrate the impact of inconsistent leadership behaviour. Mullen, Kelloway and Teed (2011) defined inconsistent leadership as the interaction of passive and safety-specific transformational leadership, whereby leaders engage in these leadership behaviours at different frequencies. The authors found that passive leadership behaviour attenuated positive outcomes (greater safety compliance and safety participation) from transformational leadership behaviour. These findings highlight the importance of consistency in management's safety leadership. Thus, inconsistent acts of active safety leadership, allocating resources to safety, or implementing safety in the structure of the organization can signal a lack of safety commitment. Moreover, inconsistent behaviours directly contrast descriptions of senior management personality characteristics thought to impact safety commitment (reliability, persistence; Fruhen et al., 2014b) and qualities of authentic leadership (consistency between words and deeds; Avolio & Gardner, 2005), further supporting its importance. Moreover, Flin and Yule (2004) support the idea that clear and consistent behaviour is an important factor demonstrating senior management safety commitment.

Summary and Implications

In summary, senior management signal safety commitment through direct and indirect processes that demonstrate a genuine priority for individual welfare above competing organizational factors (i.e., production speed and profit). More specifically, combined evidence from safety leadership and signalling theory literatures supports the belief that senior management's consistent participation in safety, allocation of resources to safety and implementation of safety in organizational structure act as signals that inform perceptions of senior manager safety commitment. Although the effectiveness of these managing acts is largely supported by empirical and theoretical evidence, the complexity of the signalling process confirms that perceptions of management's intended actions or decision-making cannot be assured. Moreover, the process of signalling highlights that unintended acts by senior management can also impact perceptions positively or negatively. This finding reinforces the importance of senior management displaying consistent signals of their safety commitment and actively addressing potential distorting characteristics (e.g., perceived distrust in management, signal delivery confounded by the medium used to relay the signal, employees' lack of ability or motivation to receive a signal).

Most importantly, the evidence provided in this chapter highlights the criticality of senior management making an effort to understand the nature of signals within their own organization. This may be achieved through a combination of focus groups, interviews and surveys to ask employees about their perception of senior manager safety commitment. Understanding how employees perceive senior management's safety leadership within the organization will provide important information that can be used to better management processes. In particular, understanding the existing safety commitment signals that employees perceive, employees' motivation and ability to interpret signals, and employees' existing perceptions of varying levels of management (e.g., trustworthy versus untrustworthy) provides invaluable information that can be used to improve management practice. Consistency is an overriding principle that largely determines the effectiveness of any signal. Engaging in signals of commitment that are inconsistent will be in vain and can have a lasting negative impact on employee perceptions (e.g., unreliable, irresponsible). All management acts and decision-making should be performed in a consistent manner, with transparent and fair feedback given if a small inconsistency occurs.

Senior management should be encouraged to participate actively in safety leadership throughout the organization in order to build interpersonal relationships, to demonstrate knowledge of policies, procedures and risks, to celebrate safety compliance, to ask questions and demonstrate an openness to learn, and to demonstrate that an understanding of employee emotions and concern for individual welfare are supported as behaviours that promote perceptions of safety commitment. Moreover, senior management who are unable to personally visit worksites because of the size and scale of the organization should allocate extra effort to ensuring that signals via indirect means (e.g., the leadership of lower-level management, publications focused on management's involvement in safety) appropriately convey these qualities and are properly perceived. Similarly, senior management should ensure that sufficient resources are allocated to safety and promote the transparency of this decision-making.

Last, senior management's position fosters the ability to incorporate safety into organizational structure, including policies and procedures. Senior management should work to ensure safety is ingrained in organizational structure, as this practice will contribute to organization-wide management practices and activities.

Conclusion

It is well known that understanding and improving safety within organizations are a critical venture. This chapter provides a framework for understanding how senior management influence employee perceptions of safety commitment. Evidence from leadership and organizational safety literatures suggests that senior management's safety commitment can be signalled by direct and indirect channels through four broad categories: (1) active participation in safety, (2) allocation of resources to safety, (3) inclusion of safety in the structure of the organization, and (4) consistency in actions and decision-making. In closing, we argue that an appreciation of the employee experience, particularly as it relates to senior manager safety leadership, is essential for effective safety management. The present chapter is a further step in understanding the process of perception formation of senior manager safety commitment and provides a platform for future research.

References

Avolio, B. J. & Gardner, W. L. (2005). Authentic leadership development: Getting to the root of positive forms of leadership. *Leadership Quarterly*, 16(3), 315–38. doi: 10.1016/j.leaqua.2005.03.001.

Barling, J., Loughlin, C. & Kelloway, E. K. (2002). Development and test of a model linking safety-specific transformational leadership and occupational safety. *Journal of Applied Psychology*, 87, 488–96. doi: 10.1037/0021-9010.87.3.488.

Beus, J. M., Payne, S. C., Bergman, M. E. & Arthur, W., Jr (2010). Safety climate and injuries: An examination of theoretical and empirical relationships. *Journal of Applied Psychology*, 95(4), 713–27. doi: 10.1037/a0019164.

Birkeland Nielsen, M., Eid, J., Mearns, K. & Larsson, G. (2013). Authentic leadership and its relationship with risk perception and safety climate. *Leadership & Organization Development Journal*, 34(4), 308–25. doi: 10.1108/LODJ-07-2011-0065.

Burns, C., Mearns, K. & McGeorge, P. (2006). Explicit and implicit trust within safety culture. *Risk Analysis*, 26(5), 1139–50. doi: 10.1111/j.1539-6924.2006.00821.x.

Christian, M. S., Bradley, J. C., Wallace, J. C. & Burke, M. J. (2009). Workplace safety: A meta-analysis of the roles of person and situation factors. *Journal of Applied Psychology*, 94(5), 1103–27. doi: 10.1037/a0016172.

Clarke, S. (1999). Perceptions of organizational safety: Implications for the development of safety culture. *Journal of Organizational Behavior*, 20(2), 185–98.

Clarke, S. (2013). Safety leadership: A meta-analytic review of transformational and transactional leadership styles as antecedents of safety behaviours. *Journal of Occupational and Organizational Psychology*, 86(1), 22–49. doi: 10.1111/j.2044-8325.2012.02064.x.

Conchie, S. M., Donald, I. J. & Taylor, P. J. (2006). Trust: Missing piece(s) in the safety puzzle. *Risk Analysis*, 26(5), 1097–1104. doi: 10.1111/j.1539-6924.2006.00818.x.

Connelly, B. L., Certo, S. T., Ireland, R. D. & Reutzel, C. R. (2011). Signaling theory: A review and assessment. *Journal of Management*, 37(1), 39–67. doi: 10.1177/0149206310388419.

Crowe, E. & Higgins, E. T. (1997). Regulatory focus and strategic inclinations: Promotion and prevention in decision-making. *Organizational Behavior and Human Decision Processes*, 69(2), 117–32. doi: 10.1006/obhd.1996.2675.

Day, D. (ed.) (2014). *The Oxford Handbook of Leadership and Organizations*. New York: Oxford University Press.

DeJoy, D. M., Schaffer, B. S., Wilson, M. G., Vandenberg, R. J. & Butts, M. M. (2004). Creating safer workplaces: Assessing the determinants and role of safety climate. *Journal of Safety Research*, 35(1), 81–90.

Eid, J., Mearns, K., Larsson, G., Laberg, J. C. & Johnsen, B. H. (2012). Leadership, psychological capital and safety research: Conceptual issues and future research questions. *Safety Science*, 50(1), 55–61. doi: 10.1016/j.ssci.2011.07.001.

Flin, R. (2003). 'Danger – men at work': Management influence on safety. *Human Factors and Ergonomics in Manufacturing & Service Industries*, 13(4), 261–8. doi: 10.1002/hfm.10042.

Flin, R. & Yule, S. (2004). Leadership for safety: Industrial experience. *Quality and Safety in Health Care*, 13(suppl 2), ii45–ii51. doi: 10.1136/qshc.2003.009555.

Fruhen, L. S., Mearns, K. J., Flin, R. H. & Kirwan, B. (2013). From the surface to the underlying meaning: An analysis of senior managers' safety culture perceptions. *Safety Science*, 57, 326–34. doi: 10.1016/j.ssci.2013.03.006.

Fruhen, L. S., Mearns, K. J., Flin, R. & Kirwan, B. (2014a). Skills, knowledge and senior managers' demonstrations of safety commitment. *Safety Science*, 69, 29–36. doi: 10.1016/j.ssci.2013.08.024.

Fruhen, L. S., Mearns, K. J., Flin, R. & Kirwan, B. (2014b). Safety intelligence: An exploration of senior managers' characteristics. *Applied Ergonomics*, 45(4), 967–75. doi: 10.1016/j.apergo.2013.11.012.

Health and Safety Executive (1999). *Reducing Error and Influencing Behaviour*. Sudbury, UK: HSE Books.

Kirmani, A. & Rao, A. R. (2000). No pain, no gain: A critical review of the literature on signaling unobservable product quality. *Journal of Marketing*, 64(2), 66–79.

Kelloway, E. K., Mullen, J. & Francis, L. (2006). Divergent effects of transformational and passive leadership on employee safety. *Journal of Occupational Health Psychology*, 11(1), 76–86. doi: 10.1037/1076-8998.11.1.76.

Kelloway, E. K., Sivanathan, N., Francis, L. & Barling, J. (2005). Poor leadership. In J. Barling, E. K. Kelloway & M. R. Frone (eds.), *Handbook of Workplace Stress*. Thousand Oaks, CA: Sage, pp. 89–112.

Luria, G. (2010). The social aspects of safety management: Trust and safety climate. *Accident Analysis & Prevention*, 42(4), 1288–95. doi: 10.1016/j.aap.2010.02.006.

Mullen, J., Kelloway, E. K. & Teed, M. (2011). Inconsistent style of leadership as a predictor of safety behaviour. *Work & Stress*, 25(1), 41–54. doi: 10.1080/02678373.2011.569200.

National Commission on the BP Deepwater Horizon Oil Spill and Offshore Drilling (2011). *Deep Water: The Gulf Oil Disaster and the Future of Offshore Drilling: Report to the President*. Washington, DC: US Government Printing Office. http://www.gpo.gov/fdsys/pkg/GPO-OILCOMMISSION/pdf/GPO-OILCOMMISSION.pdf. Accessed 27 July 2016.

Schein, E. H. (2004). *Organizational Culture and Leadership*. 3rd edn. San Francisco, CA: Jossey-Bass.

Spence, M. (1973). Job market signaling. *Quarterly Journal of Economics*, 87(3) 355–74.

Spence, M. (2002). Signaling in retrospect and the informational structure of markets. *American Economic Review*, 434–59.

Tonkin, T. H. (2013). Authentic versus transformational leadership: Assessing their effectiveness on organizational citizenship behavior of followers. *International Journal of Business and Public Administration*, 10(1), 40–61.

Walumbwa, F. O., Avolio, B. J., Gardner, W. L., Wernsing, T. S. & Peterson, S. J. (2008). Authentic leadership: Development and validation of a theory-based measure. *Journal of Management*, 34(1), 89–126. doi: 10.1177/0149206307308913.

Zaccaro, S. J. (2001). *The nature of executive leadership: A conceptual and empirical analysis of success*. Washington, DC: American Psychological Association.

Zohar, D. (2002). The effects of leadership dimensions, safety climate, and assigned priorities on minor injuries in work groups. *Journal of Organizational Behavior*, 23(1), 75–92. doi: 10.1002/job.130.

Zohar, D. (2008). Safety climate and beyond: A multi-level multi-climate framework. *Safety Science*, 46(3), 376–87. doi: 10.1016/j.ssci.2007.03.006.

Zohar, D. (2010). Thirty years of safety climate research: Reflections and future directions. *Accident Analysis & Prevention*, 42(5), 1517–22. doi: 10.1016/j.aap.2009.12.019.

Zohar, D. (2014). Safety climate: Conceptualization, measurement, and improvement. In B. Schneider & K. M. Barbera (eds.), *The Oxford Handbook of Organizational Climate and Culture*. New York: Oxford University Press, pp. 317–34.

Zohar, D. & Luria, G. (2005). A multilevel model of safety climate: Cross-level relationships between organization and group-level climates. *Journal of Applied Psychology*, 90(4), 616–28. doi: 10.1037/0021-9010.90.4.616.

3

Developing Safety Leadership

Jennifer Wong, Timur Ozbilir and Jane Mullen

Organizations invest in preventive measures targeted at the work environment (e.g., work redesign, protective equipment) and at the individuals in the workplace (e.g., safety knowledge training) to lower the likelihood of accidents and injuries at work. However, having the knowledge and tools to work safely does not necessarily prevent accidents and injuries or ensure that employees work safely. Recognizing this, safety practitioners and researchers have made considerable efforts to understand other mechanisms involved with enhancing safety performance. Through these efforts, leadership has been established as a salient predictor of safety outcomes in organizations (Barling, Loughlin & Kelloway, 2002; Clarke, 2013; Mullen & Kelloway, 2011; Zohar, 2002a). In this chapter we suggest that training managers to be safety leaders is important for creating and maintaining a safe workplace because of their extensive and unique influence on their subordinates' attitudes and behaviours. The chapter is organized as follows. First, we review the literature on leadership and its effect on safety perceptions and performance. Second, we discuss how leaders exert their influence on subordinates' attitudes and behaviours, thus providing a rationale for why changes in subordinate outcomes begin with their leaders. Finally, we present the current state of knowledge on developing safety leadership behaviours, and conclude with a discussion of issues for consideration in future research.

To understand the importance of the leader's role in workplace safety, we first explore the scope of their influences. Leaders can influence the way their subordinates think, feel and act. They change the way subordinates think and feel about themselves, their leader and their job (Barling, Christie & Hoption, 2011). They can also change the way subordinates perform at work, whether in task-related performance or citizen-like behaviours. Citizen-like behaviours are pro-social behaviours beyond the expectations of typical work tasks that contribute positively to organizational effectiveness (Borman & Motowidlo, 1993; Rotundo & Sackett, 2002).

In general, effective forms of leadership (i.e., transformational leadership style, contingent reward, high-quality leader–member exchange, charismatic

Leading to Occupational Health and Safety: How Leadership Behaviours Impact Organizational Safety and Well-Being, First Edition.
Edited by E. Kevin Kelloway, Karina Nielsen and Jennifer K. Dimoff.

leadership style, participative leadership style) are associated with positive attitudes in subordinates towards their leaders (e.g., satisfaction with leaders: Judge & Piccolo, 2004; extent of identity with leader: Kark, Shamir & Chen, 2003), towards themselves (e.g., motivation: Judge & Piccolo, 2004; psychological safety: Detert & Burris, 2007; lowered stress, better well-being: see Skakon, Nielsen, Borg & Guzman, 2010 for a review), and towards their jobs (e.g., organizational commitment: Barling, Weber & Kelloway, 1996; job satisfaction: Judge & Piccolo, 2004; extent of identity with organization: Kark et al., 2003). Effective leadership is also associated with better task performance (e.g., unit-level performance: Howell & Avolio, 1993; branch-level sales performance: Barling et al., 1996; creativity, innovation: Chiaburu, Smith, Wang & Zimmerman, 2014), citizenship performance (organizational voice: Chiaburu et al., 2014) and fewer counterproductive workplace behaviours (see Kessler Bruursema, Rodopman & Spector, 2013 for a review).

Neglectful leadership (laissez-faire leadership style, management by exception) and destructive leadership (abusive supervision, petty tyranny, social undermining) have a different effect on subordinates. Both types of ineffective leadership are linked to poor attitudes in subordinates towards their leaders (e.g., diminished trust and liking of leader, increased resistance to leader: Schyns & Schilling, 2013; poor perception of leader ethicality: Ogunfowora, 2013; lowered satisfaction in leader: Judge & Piccolo, 2004), towards themselves (e.g., stress and well-being: Schyns & Schilling, 2013), and towards their jobs (e.g., more role ambiguity and role conflict: Skogstad, Einarsen, Torsheim, Aasland & Hetland, 2007; poor perception of organizational ethicality, less affective commitment: Ogunfowora, 2012). Ineffective leadership is positively associated with counterproductive workplace behaviours (e.g., towards the organization: Herschcovis & Barling, 2010) and negatively associated with general work performance (Schyns & Schilling, 2013).

Leadership and Safety Outcomes

We have established that effective leadership qualities are associated with more positive subordinate perceptions of leaders, themselves, and their jobs, better task and citizenship performance, and fewer counterproductive workplace behaviours. Ineffective leadership qualities on the other hand have the opposite effect on subordinate outcomes. We now turn to the leadership research conducted within a safety context to see if the patterns of findings are generalizable, in order to support the need for developing safety leaders at workplaces to target employee safety behaviours and attitudes.

Direct Influences on Safety Attitudes

One of the most extensively studied safety outcomes is safety climate, which is defined as the shared perception among employees regarding safety policies, procedures and practices in their organization (Neal & Griffin, 2006; Zohar, 1980). Safety climate strength has been positively associated with transformational leadership and negatively associated with passive leadership (Luria, 2008). On the other hand, laissez-faire, active management-by-exception and passive management-by-exception leadership have been negatively associated with the 'perceived leaders' prioritization of safety' dimension of safety climate (Zohar, 2002a). Overall, similarly to the trend in the general leadership literature, positive leadership is associated with stronger safety climate at work, and negative leadership is associated with weaker safety climate.

Perhaps the most important evidence on the generalizability of leadership findings to a safety context is the series of studies on safety-specific transformational leadership. Barling et al. (2002) empirically tested the effects of safety-specific transformational leadership and showed that the concept of transformational leadership can be generalized to the safety context. For example, focusing on the long-term benefits of safety goals rather than on short-term productivity pressures is a characteristic of idealized influence. Leaders who challenge their subordinates to work towards a collective goal of safety have the quality of inspirational motivation. Leaders who encourage their subordinates to think of novel ways to adhere to safety are exhibiting intellectual stimulation. Safety leaders are exhibiting individualized consideration when they are actively interested in subordinates' physical well-being.

Traditionally, most of the research (e.g., Clarke, 2013; Kelloway, Mullen & Francis, 2006) on leadership and safety has focused on the impact of different leadership styles on subordinates' safety-related behaviours. Although this approach has proved useful in developing a theoretical model to improve our understanding of the relationship between leadership and employee safety performance, measures from these studies are not always appropriate for use in training and development as they do not always focus on leaders' behaviours. With a specific focus on training, several researchers have turned their attention to observable and trainable leader behaviours that may lead to better employee safety outcomes. For example, the S.A.F.E.R. Leadership Model (Wong, Kelloway & Makhan, 2015) includes 15 leader behaviours (Wong, Ozbilir, Dimoff, MacLellan, Collins & Kelloway, 2015) that fall under the dimensions of Speak (behaviours relating to one-way dissemination of information), Act (observable behaviours that demonstrate leaders' own adherence to safety at work), Focus (behaviours that demonstrate commitment and motivation), Engage (behaviours that encourage employee involvement in safety decisions) and Recognize (behaviours that demonstrate appreciation of safety accomplishments). The measure has been shown to predict safety communication, safety climate and safety-specific trust above and beyond the effects of safety-specific transformational leadership and safety-passive leadership.

Direct Influences on Safety Performance

Safety compliance and participation are commonly studied safety performance outcomes that are task-related and citizenship-related, respectively. Safety compliance is the act of following safety rules and regulations, whereas safety participation is the willingness to participate in extra-role safety behaviours (Neal,

Griffin & Hart, 2000). We expect that the relationships in the general leadership literature should stand true in the safety context; therefore, effective safety leadership behaviours should increase safety compliance and participation. This is supported for the most part, except that active management-by-exception appears to be valuable within a safety context. This may be because active monitoring leads to higher adherence to rule-based safety compliance, and by correcting errors before they occur it may prevent future mistakes. In Clarke's (2013) meta-analysis on the full-range leadership model (Bass, 1985) and safety outcomes, transformational leadership had a stronger relationship with safety citizenship performance (e.g., engagement in safety activities) than did transactional leadership. Active transactional leadership, consisting of contingent reward and active management-by-exception, had a stronger relationship with safety task performance (e.g., responsibilities concerning rules and regulations) than did transformational leadership. Using the argument that individual leaders may alternate leadership styles or display more than one style of leadership to employees (Kelloway et al., 2006), Mullen, Kelloway and Teed (2011) investigated inconsistency in leadership styles in two samples of long-term health care workers, one comprising young workers and the other older workers. The authors reported a significant interaction between transformational leadership and passive leadership in both samples when predicting safety participation and safety compliance, such that the impact of transformational leadership on the two outcomes was attenuated when leaders also engaged in passive leadership. Therefore, it appears that in addition to the presence of effective safety leadership, the absence of ineffective leadership behaviour is also needed for maintaining safety performance outcomes.

Aside from the full-range leadership model, researchers have demonstrated that supportive leader behaviours, such as involving subordinates in decision making and encouraging open communication, have positive effects on safety compliance and safety participation (Hofmann & Morgeson, 1999). Subordinates who are involved in higher-quality leader–member exchanges, characterized by collaborative problem solving, have been shown to be more likely to reciprocate by engaging in safety citizenship behaviours (Hofmann, Morgeson & Gerras, 2003). Parker, Axtell and Turner (2001) explored the longitudinal impact of supportive supervision and reported a lagged positive effect of supportive supervision on safe working among frontline manufacturing workers 18 months later. Finally, Mullen (2005) demonstrated that employees are more willing to raise safety issues in their organizations when they perceive their leaders as more supportive.

Furthermore, empowering leadership, in which leaders generate self-management in their subordinates (Arnold, Arad, Rhoades & Drasgow, 2000), is associated with less risky behaviours (Martínez-Córcoles, Gracia, Tomás, Peiró & Schöbel, 2013); risky actions are a prime example of safety-related counterproductive workplace behaviour. The proxy for safety-related counterproductive workplace behaviours can also be injuries and accident rates. Transformational leadership, particularly the idealized influence component, and contingent reward behaviours are associated with lower injury rates (Hoffmeister et al., 2014; Zohar, 2002a). Once again, active management-by-exception appears to be beneficial in curbing counterproductive workplace behaviours in a safety context. This form of active transactional leadership is related to fewer reported injuries at work (Hoffmeister et al., 2014). Overall, it appears that in the context of safety, corrective leadership such as active management-by-exception has a positive impact on subordinates' performance, despite its negative effect on attitudes (e.g., Zohar, 2002a).

Indirect Effect on Performance through Attitudes

Leadership may also influence safety performance indirectly through subordinates' attitudes towards the leader, themselves and their job (see Wong, Kelloway & Makhan, 2015 for a review). The main mechanism by which leadership may have an impact on safety performance is through subordinates' perceptions of safety climate. The mediation role of safety climate in the relationship between leadership and safety performance has been examined in several studies. For example, focusing on the indirect effect of safety climate in the relationship between leadership styles and safety performance, Zohar (2002a) reported that both transformational leadership and the constructive leadership dimension of transactional leadership were mediated by safety climate. In a meta-analysis, Clarke (2013) found that transformational leadership was positively associated with safety participation, which was partially mediated by perceived safety climate. Furthermore, active transactional leadership was positively associated with both safety participation and safety compliance. The effect on safety participation was fully mediated by perceived safety climate, whereas the effect on safety compliance was partially mediated by perceived safety climate. In terms of the counterproductive workplace outcome of injuries, Barling et al. (2002) found that safety consciousness mediated the relationship between safety-specific transformational leadership and safety climate, which in turn predicted lower injury rates. Conversely, passive styles of leadership, including laissez-faire leadership, have been associated with increased levels of workplace injuries through their negative impact on perceptions of safety climate (Zohar, 2002b).

Other researchers have provided evidence for the mediational effect of safety climate by focusing on aspects of leadership beyond the full-range leadership model. For example, empowering leadership is associated with safety compliance behaviours through the indirect effect of safety climate (Martínez-Córcoles, Gracia, Tomás & Peiró, 2011). Examining the ways leaders gain support for policies and decisions, Clarke and Ward (2006) reported a link between leader influence tactics and employees' safety participation where perceived safety climate fully mediated the effect of inspirational appeals and partially mediated the effect of rational persuasion and consultation. Finally, several researchers have focused on the role of safety climate perceptions in how the quality of leader–member exchanges, characterized by respect, trust and obligation (Graen & Uhl-Bien, 1995), predict better subordinate safety performance. For example, in a study involving professional truck drivers, Zohar, Huang, Lee and Robertson (2014) found that higher-quality leader–member exchange between dispatchers and drivers was linked to higher levels of driver safety climate perceptions, which in turn predicted more driving safety behaviours and fewer hard braking behaviours. Similarly, in a study among soldiers, Luria (2010) focused on the relational aspect of leadership and reported that leaders who elicited trust in subordinates were influential in creating a positive climate of safety, which predicted lower injury rates.

Aside from safety climate perceptions, there are other safety-related perceptions concerning the leader, the subordinates and the workplace that mediate leadership and safety outcomes (see Wong, Kelloway & Makhan, 2015 for a review). For instance, subordinates' perceptions of management concern for safety positively predicted safety involvement through the indirect effect of perceived organizational support (Credo, Armenakis, Feild & Young, 2010). In terms of subordinates' perceptions of leaders, safety-specific transformational leadership is positively associated with safety voice behaviours through the indirect influence of disclosure trust intentions and affect-based trust in leader (Conchie, Taylor & Donald, 2012). In terms of subordinates' perceptions of themselves, intrinsic motivation mediates the relationship between safety-specific transformational leadership and safety citizenship behaviours (e.g., whistle-blowing and safety voice behaviours), and extrinsic motivation mediates the relationship between safety-specific transformational leadership and safety compliance (Conchie, 2013). Empowering leadership is positively related to subordinates' safety participation, and this relationship is mediated by collaborative team learning, which can be interpreted as a change in subordinates' perceptions of themselves because their leader fostered a stronger sense of independence (Martínez-Córcoles, Schöbel, Gracia, Tomás & Peiró, 2012). Safety leadership is negatively linked to counterproductive safety behaviours through the indirect effect of motivation. For example, supervisory influence predicts lower reports of workplace injuries through the indirect effect of motivation to avoid risk-taking behaviours (Westaby & Lowe, 2005).

Rationale for Developing Safety Leaders

Although leadership directly influences subordinates' safety attitudes and performance, research also demonstrates that leadership has an indirect effect on safety performance through changes in subordinates' safety attitudes. For example, safety-specific transformational leadership and climate have indirect effects on injury rates through safety consciousness (Barling et al., 2002). Thus, leaders' influence on subordinates' behaviour may be due to changes in subordinates' perception of the leader, of themselves or of the organization. Furthermore, if researchers can demonstrate that leaders have a unique influence on these changes in perception, we will then have empirical support for developing safety leaders at workplaces to target employee safety behaviours.

If subordinates' performance is shaped by their perceptions, it is important to investigate how this effect transpires. The theoretical foundation of this proposition can be found in Ashour's (1982) work, in which he suggests that leaders influence subordinates through two psychological processes: changing the way subordinates think about things, and exposing subordinates to various work experiences and environments. Both cognitive and experiential pathways affect subordinates' motivation and learning of behaviours.

Leaders Altering Subordinates' Attitudes

Ashour (1982) posits that the cognitive pathway to subordinates' motivation and learning is established by the subordinates observing and listening to the leader because that allows subordinates to understand what types of work behaviours can result in desirable incentives. Likewise, according to path–goal theory (House & Mitchell, 1974) and transactional leadership style (Bass, 1985), a leader is responsible for clarifying expectations, conditions, constraints and incentives around work-related matters. Leaders also serve as a chain of communication between upper management and subordinates in that they explain the intentions of workplace policy and practices to subordinates. Rationality, the act of explaining the reason behind what leaders ask of subordinates, is one of the most commonly used leader influence tactics and it is also positively related to subordinates' perceptions of power in leaders (Hinkin & Schriesheim, 1990). The effectiveness of clearly communicating safety expectations in changing subordinates' safety-related attitudes is evident in the work done on the S.A.F.E.R. Leadership Model, specifically through the 'Speak' dimension (Wong et al., 2015; Wong, Ozbilir, Dimoff et al., 2015).

In addition to the transactional establishment of effort and incentives, leaders set high standards for performance and provide the inspiration to reach these standards (Bass, 1985). For example, transformational leaders motivate by building confidence in their subordinates (Bass, 1985). Leaders can facilitate motivation and learning by enhancing other internal subordinate states, such as empowerment and efficacy (Avolio, Zhu, Koh & Bhatia, 2004). A leader can also affect subordinates' motivation by enhancing the value of the incentive to them. According to self-determination theory (Ryan & Deci, 2000), behaviours stemming from intrinsic motivation are more likely to be displayed than behaviours motivated by external rewards. Yet integration of extrinsically motivated activities can be facilitated by leaders, because leaders tend to be individuals of significance to their subordinates, meaning they are people whom subordinates want to relate to and connect with (Ryan & Deci, 2000). Thus, if leaders value certain behaviours and opinions, it is likely that subordinates will take on those values themselves and view the leaders' mission as interesting. There are leaders who use their idealized influence to encourage their subordinates to internalize the leaders' mission, to align both their values, and to find meaning in work that the subordinates do for their leaders (Jung & Avolio, 2000; Piccolo & Colquitt, 2006). Self-determination theory (Ryan & Deci, 2000) posits that these types of leaders are more effective in changing subordinates' behaviours because subordinates are more intrinsically motivated by the process (Charbonneau, Barling & Kelloway, 2001). In fact, transformational leaders are especially effective at embedding the values exemplified by their behaviours and accomplishments, so that they appear desirable to subordinates and eventually become self-rewarding, creating self-reinforcement and independence of the leaders (Bass, 1985).

Safety-specific transformational leadership training utilizes the same inspirational and value-embedding mechanisms to impact subordinates' safety behaviours (Barling et al., 2002).

Leaders also influence subordinates cognitively by creating situations where vicarious learning and motivation can take place (Ashour, 1982). Social learning of behaviours can result from observing leaders modelling those behaviours (Bandura, 1969). Watching other subordinates rewarded with incentives from the leader for acting safely is a form of vicarious learning of the appropriate types of safety behaviours (Bandura, 1977). As well, watching other subordinates and the leaders set high standards and work towards them can motivate individuals by setting off a cue for them to emulate the same behaviours (Bandura, 1977; Locke, 1970). This is comparable to how a safety leader contributes to building a strong safety culture to encourage group-based dynamics that will facilitate more safety attitudes and behaviours.

Leaders Guiding Subordinates' Performance

According to Ashour (1982), the influence of leaders does not rely solely on the cognitive pathway. After the leaders set conditions, environmental constraints and incentives for behaviours, subordinates go through the process of experiencing the reinforcement to strengthen their behaviours. In addition, leaders have control over the schedule of reinforcements and the learning environment. The experience of incentives for behaviours is essentially operant conditioning, a process of learning that is controlled by the resulting consequences and incentives (Skinner, 1953). Providing reinforcement and feedback for subordinates is a quality of transactional leaders (Bass, 1985). Experiencing leaders' feedback and goal-setting allows subordinates to achieve higher performance through an increase in their self-efficacy (Bandura, 1997). Increase in self-efficacy and competency helps with the internalization of extrinsically motivated behaviours into behaviours that are intrinsically motivating, which further facilitates the learning of behaviours (Bandura, 1997; Ryan & Deci, 2000). The effectiveness of recognition on changing subordinates' safety behaviours is evident in the work done on the S.A.F.E.R. Leadership Model, specifically through the 'Recognize' dimension (Wong, Kelloway & Makhan, 2015; Wong, Ozbilir, Dimoff et al., 2015).

According to social exchange theory (Wang, Law, Hackett, Wang & Chen, 2005), subordinates who experience certain types of behaviours from their leaders are more likely to reciprocate those same behaviours. When these behaviours are positive, the reciprocity generates a fair and trusting leader–subordinate relationship (Blau, 1964). Social exchange theory proposes that the role-modelling phenomenon occurs because the exposure to leaders' positive behaviours creates an inherent obligation in subordinates to respond in a similar manner (Blau, 1964; Podsakoff, MacKenzie, Paine & Bachrach, 2000). The theory has been used to explain the initiation of citizenship performance, including proactive contextual behaviours (Blau, 1964; Podsakoff et al., 2000). The effect of modelling the leader's safety behaviours on subordinates' own safety behaviours is evident in the work done on the S.A.F.E.R. Leadership Model, specifically through the 'Act' dimension (Wong, Kelloway & Makhan, 2015; Wong, Ozbilir, Dimoff et al., 2015).

Ashour (1982) suggested that the experiential pathway may be more impactful than the cognitive one, but influencing subordinates through one pathway is not as effective as using both. A positive match between the cognitive and the experiential pathways will increase leader credibility and power, which will feed into more positive subordinates' behaviours (Ashour, 1982). Leaders who motivate their subordinates by creating idealized goals and visions are more effective if they demonstrate commitment to providing feedback along the way to accomplishing those goals. In summary, leaders have a unique role in motivating and encouraging subordinates' learning of behaviours through cognitive and experiential processes by communicating and controlling the work–incentives associations, and by being a role model of ideals and behaviours to which subordinates want to relate.

Developing Leadership to Improve Safety Outcomes

Given the considerable body of empirical research demonstrating that leadership is a reliable predictor of subordinates' safety attitudes and performance, the issue of whether enhanced leadership behaviour results in improved employee safety outcomes has become increasingly important (Kelloway & Barling, 2010). Although the effectiveness of leadership development interventions aimed at changing leader behaviours has been well established in the literature (Avolio, Reichard, Hannah, Walumbwa & Chan, 2009; Barling, 2014), considerably fewer studies examine how changes in leader behaviour impact employee safety outcomes. To explore the issue of how leadership behaviour is developed within the context of workplace safety, we provide a summary of leadership development intervention studies aimed at changing subordinate safety performance. We identify the leadership model and behaviours that serve as the basis for the leadership training intervention and the training methodology for developing safety leadership behaviour.

Drawing on the behavioural safety approach, Zohar (2002b) designed and evaluated an eight-week leadership training intervention aimed at modifying supervisory safety practices. The intervention focused on changing supervisor safety-oriented leadership behaviour and communication of safety priority by upper management in order to improve safety outcomes at the employee level. Employees from 36 workgroups were assigned to either an experimental ($n = 18$) or control ($n = 18$) condition and asked by the researchers to describe any role-related interactions they had with their supervisor. Supervisors in the experimental condition were then provided with weekly feedback regarding the frequency of safety-oriented interactions with employees. Communication of a high safety priority was enhanced during the intervention by a half-day workshop for managers and the general manager in which they were instructed how to conduct role-episode interviews with employees and collect safety-oriented feedback for supervisors. To assess the effectiveness of the leadership intervention, safety-oriented supervisory interactions, minor injuries and safety climate were measured before the intervention, three months after the intervention and five months after the intervention. Results showed that the frequency of reported supervisory safety-oriented interactions increased in the experimental condition from a base rate of nine to 58 per cent, whereas no increase was observed in the control group. A significant decrease in minor injuries for the experimental condition was reported following the intervention, along with increased post-intervention ratings of safety climate. Safety climate scores did not increase in the control group, and the reporting of minor injuries increased during the post-intervention period.

Zohar and Luria (2003) further explored the effectiveness of supervisory-level leadership training interventions aimed at increasing safety-oriented communication between supervisors and employees. The three-month intervention was implemented across three separate organizations, and each targeted three levels of management: floor supervisors, immediate superiors and upper management. During the intervention floor supervisors were provided with feedback every two weeks regarding the frequency of safety-oriented interactions with employees. To communicate a high safety priority, immediate superiors were provided with comparative information about supervisors, which was used to review supervisor safety-oriented performance. Upper management also received summarized information regarding the shop floor supervisors' safety practices. Experience sampling methodology was used to gather information about safety-related supervisory interactions and behaviour-sampling observation was used to measure unsafe employee behaviours. Pre-intervention and post-intervention perceptions of safety climate were also collected. Similarly to Zohar's (2002b) findings, an increase of supervisory safety-oriented interactions with employees was reported across the three companies. Furthermore, unsafe behaviours declined to a near-zero frequency in two of the companies, and perceptions of safety climate improved in the one company where it was assessed.

In their intervention study spanning over nine months, Kines, Andersen, Spangenberg et al. (2010) examined daily supervisory safety-oriented verbal exchanges with workers within the construction industry. They adapted a similar leadership-based training intervention developed by Zohar and colleagues (Zohar, 2002b; Zohar & Luria, 2003), and assigned foremen to either the leadership-based intervention or the control group. Foremen in the intervention group received eight bi-weekly feedback reports regarding the percentage of safety-oriented verbal interaction with subordinates, and participated in coaching sessions aimed at increasing their safety-oriented daily verbal exchanges with workers. Researchers measured supervisory safety-oriented verbal interactions between foreman and workers using experience sampling method, and worker safety performance using safety behaviour-sampling observation measured at baseline, during the intervention and after the intervention. Perceptions of safety climate were assessed with a self-report questionnaire before and after the intervention. Baseline measurement showed that safety was perceived to be raised by foremen in 6–16% of verbal exchanges, whereas production was perceived as the priority (i.e., it featured in 85–97% of verbal exchanges). Foreman safety-oriented verbal exchanges and the attention to safety dimension of safety climate significantly increased from baseline to post-intervention follow-up in only one of the intervention groups. However, safety performance increased significantly from baseline to post-intervention follow-up in both intervention groups. No significant changes in foreman safety-oriented verbal exchanges, safety performance and safety climate were reported in the control groups. In summary, the intervention studies (Zohar, 2002b; Zohar & Luria, 2003; Kines et al., 2010) demonstrated that safety communication, monitoring and feedback facilitate better safety outcomes, and that these leadership behaviours can be enhanced through training.

Given the empirical evidence highlighting the differential effects of positive and negative leadership on safety outcomes (Griffin & Hu, 2013; Hoffmeister et al., 2014), researchers have expanded the supervisory-level leadership intervention by incorporating transformational leadership behaviour. Von Thiele Schwarz, Hasson and Tafvelin (2016) conducted a leadership development intervention study to empirically evaluate the impact of transformational leadership and applied behaviour analysis training on employee perceptions of safety climate and productivity. The leadership training was aimed at improving general leadership behaviours, safety climate, organizational learning climate, and productivity. Specifically, the study assessed whether leadership training had differential effects on employee perceptions of safety climate, which were dependent on the managers' specific focus areas for improvement (i.e., safety, leadership and productivity). A total of 76 managers completed both the baseline and the post-intervention surveys; nine managers chose to focus on safety improvement, 33 on leadership improvement, and 31 on productivity improvement. The intervention began with providing managers with 360-degree evaluation and feedback based on all the leadership behaviours in the full-range leadership model. Managers then completed the two-week lecture-based component of the intervention that focused on how contextual factors affect employee behaviour. Transformational leadership, positive transactional leader behaviours (i.e., monitoring behaviour, goal setting, feedback, rewards), and applied behaviour analysis were the focus of the lecture-based component. Each manager completed a practical block based on their chosen area for improvement in their workplace and applied the antecedents- and consequences-based intervention (i.e., goal setting, feedback). The practical block incorporated six days of feedback, coaching and internal follow-up to support managers with their improvement projects. The leadership training intervention was evaluated using a pre-test and a post-test survey. Managers provided self-ratings for transformational leadership, positive and negative transactional leadership behaviours (i.e., contingent reward and management-by-exception active) and self-efficacy. Each manager identified employees who were asked to rate their manager's leadership behaviours and provide self-ratings for expectations and actions of safety climate and productivity. Von Thiele Schwarz et al. (2016) demonstrated that employee perceptions of safety climate (i.e., actions and expectations) improved following the leadership intervention without negatively affecting self-ratings of productivity. Managers' self-reported ratings of transformational leadership behaviours, positive transactional leadership behaviours and self-efficacy increased following the leadership training intervention, and negative transactional leadership behaviours decreased. Seventy-nine per cent of managers and 32% of employees perceived that the leadership training intervention had a positive impact on safety. These findings were independent of the specific focus of the training chosen by managers (i.e., safety, productivity or general leadership).

Mullen and Kelloway (2009) evaluated a three-month safety-specific transformational leadership training intervention adapted from a training programme developed by Barling and colleagues (Barling et al., 1996; Kelloway, Barling & Helleur, 2000). Managers ($n = 54$) were randomly assigned to general transformational leadership training, safety-specific transformational leadership training or a waiting-list control group without training. Managers in each training group worked with coaches to develop specific behavioural goals (Locke & Latham, 1984), with participants in the safety-specific condition developing goals focusing on safety leadership behaviours. Using a pre-test post-test design, they found that safety-specific training enhanced leaders' safety attitudes, intentions to promote safety and self-efficacy. Data collected from leaders' direct reports showed that perceptions of safety climate in both the safety-specific and the general training were significantly higher than in the control group.

Components of Effective Leadership Interventions

The combined results of the leadership training studies suggest that the positive effects of leadership on safety outcomes (Clarke, 2013; see review by Mullen & Kelloway, 2011) can be achieved in organizations through leader-focused safety interventions. The studies begin to provide insight into what leaders can do to positively influence subordinate safety outcomes and how safety leadership behaviours can be enhanced.

The intervention studies demonstrate that developing behaviours that are characteristic of both transformational and transactional leadership styles results in improved safety outcomes. Some studies provided a clear description of the leadership behaviours that were enhanced during the intervention (e.g., safety communication), whereas others describe a general leadership style that was the focus of training. Thus, in some cases it is difficult to establish what the safety leaders did following training that resulted in positive safety outcomes. For example, it remains unclear if leaders engaged in a combination of behaviours that are characteristic of the full-range model of leadership or behaviours only characteristic of transformational leadership, or whether they focused only on specific components of transformational leadership (e.g., inspirational motivation).

Frequent supervisory safety communication was consistently shown to improve subordinate safety performance and perceptions of safety climate. In several studies, managers communicated the importance of safety and its priority within the organization by monitoring data concerning the frequency of supervisory-subordinate safety-related communication and providing supervisors with feedback. Through feedback and coaching, frontline supervisors increased safety communication by incorporating safety topics into their daily verbal communication with subordinates. The data suggest that interventions aimed at enhancing leader safety communication at the supervisory/managerial levels lead to improved safety outcomes at the employee level.

Several training programmes contained a lecture component to transfer knowledge about behaviours that are characteristic of transformational and transactional leadership, a feedback component to provide trainees with an assessment of their safety behaviours other than their own judgement of it (i.e., subordinates' ratings), and a coaching component to support the trainees in transferring what they learn to the work environment. Some researchers included 360-degree feedback before the training as a starting point to discuss areas of improvement (e.g., von Thiele Schwarz et al., 2016). Others used feedback during the coaching to keep trainees informed of their progress (Zohar & Luria, 2003). Interestingly, in von Thiele Schwarz et al.'s (2016) intervention, trainees were able to choose areas of leadership they wanted to focus on, which provided them with autonomy over the training process. This autonomy appears to be important for training outcomes, since significant improvement was observed regardless of the focal areas chosen.

Another component of an effective safety leadership intervention is a methodologically sound design for collecting data on behavioural changes. The training interventions incorporated a minimum of two time points of assessment: data on trainees' behaviours and safety outcomes were collected before and after the intervention mark. Researchers can achieve higher-quality conclusions by adding more data collection points to examine changes in behaviour, or by adding a 'yoked' training group (e.g., a general transformational leadership training group: Mullen & Kelloway, 2009). As well, collecting data from sources other than the trainees themselves (e.g., subordinates' ratings, management ratings and objective performance data) not only provides better feedback for the training, it also prevents the issues of common method variance. The experience sampling method of collecting data employed by Zohar and Luria (2003) and Kines et al. (2010) appears to be a fruitful method of assessment based on the frequency of the experience rather than pre-set time points.

Future Research

Several important issues should be considered in future studies on leadership development interventions in occupational safety. Given the evidence highlighting the differential effects of leadership facets on safety outcomes (Griffin & Hu, 2013; Hoffmeister et al., 2014) researchers suggest that leadership development intervention studies should incorporate a broader range of leadership behaviours (Clarke, 2013; Wong, Kelloway & Makhan, 2015) and the unique contribution of each behaviour should be evaluated. Models such as the S.A.F.E.R. Leadership Model (Wong, Ozbilir, Dimoff et al., 2015) hold promise for future research because they are not confined to leadership traits and styles. Furthermore, some leadership behaviours may be more effective at different levels within organizations (e.g., more effective for frontline supervisors than for CEOs and upper management; Avolio et al., 2009). Thus, the organizational level of the intervention should be considered in future leadership development studies.

In addition to examining what leaders can do, researchers suggest that there is a need to focus on the processes that lead to the intervention outcomes

(Nielsen, Taris & Cox, 2010). For example, organizational support is an important component for the success of organizational safety interventions (Hale, Guldenmund, van Loenhout & Oh, 2010) and has been shown to influence supervisors' engagement in safety leadership (Conchie, Moon & Duncan, 2013). Thus, further research is needed to identify and evaluate variables that facilitate the transfer of leadership behaviours developed through training to the work environment and processes that contribute to the effectiveness of the intervention. Accordingly, in addition to quantitative methods, researchers should consider qualitative data collection techniques (i.e., Conchie et al., 2013) to gather rich information that will provide insight into why interventions are successful.

Leadership training methodology (i.e., supervisory feedback and coaching, classroom lecture-based leadership training and 360-degree feedback) is also an important issue that warrants future research. For example, Kelloway et al. (2000) found that transformational leadership training and feedback or coaching components enhanced employee perceptions of transformational leadership, but the interaction of leadership training and feedback did not increase ratings beyond the main effects. Thus, future studies should empirically examine different combinations of training methodologies to determine how the effectiveness of leadership interventions may be enhanced and yet remain cost- and time-effective for organizations.

Given that change is expected to occur across organizational levels (i.e., training conducted at the managerial or supervisory level has safety outcomes assessed at the employee level), additional longitudinal studies with multiple data collection points are needed to investigate change over time and to ensure that lagged effects are not underestimated (Parker et al., 2001). These considerations should be taken into account when designing intervention studies, as the existing data do not provide a clear message about when or how change occurs throughout the intervention or whether improved safety performance is sustained.

With respect to outcomes that result from leader-focused safety development, researchers should consider three different types of performance outcomes, namely task, citizenship and counterproductive workplace behaviours (Rotundo & Sackett, 2002). Furthermore, given the evidence that changes in attitudes precede changes in behaviours, training research needs to incorporate both attitudinal and behavioural outcomes as indicators of training success. The proportion of research on safety climate implies that other safety attitudes are not as important. Yet, it might be valuable for research to examine other types of indirect effects of leadership (subordinates' perceptions of leaders, subordinates' perceptions of themselves). A more comprehensive understanding of how the mechanism of influence works can aid training content for developing safety leaders.

Finally, data on safety performance from various sources should be gathered to minimize the risk of common method bias. Objective evaluations of safety-related work performance, such as hard braking information collected through work equipment (Zohar et al., 2014), earplug use (Zohar, 2002b) and safety index (Kines et al., 2010), will reduce the likelihood that the results will be confounded by common method bias.

Conclusion

Our review of the literature highlights a growing body of research evidence supporting the propositions that (1) safety attitudes influence safety performance, (2) leaders have a unique role in shaping subordinates' safety attitudes and performance, (3) safety leadership can be enhanced by leadership training, and (4) changes in safety leadership behaviour are perceived by employees and associated with improved perceptions of safety climate and employee safety performance. Although a small number of studies suggest that leadership development is a viable organizational strategy for improving workplace safety, there remains a need for more intervention studies to examine what leaders can do and how these behaviours can be developed. Lastly, the processes that enhance the effectiveness of the leadership development intervention remain to be explored.

References

Arnold, J. A., Arad, S., Rhoades, J. A. & Drasgow, F. (2000). The empowering leadership questionnaire: The construction and validation of a new scale for measuring leader behaviors. *Journal of Organizational Behavior*, 21(3), 249–69. doi: 10.2307/3100332.

Ashour, A. S. (1982). A framework of a cognitive–behavioral theory of leader influence and effectiveness. *Organizational Behavior and Human Performance*, 30(3), 407–30. doi: 10.1016/0030-5073(82)90228-8.

Avolio, B. J., Reichard, R. J., Hannah, S. T., Walumbwa, F. O. & Chan, A. (2009). A meta-analytic review of leadership impact research: Experimental and quasi-experimental studies. *Leadership Quarterly*, 20, 764–84. doi: 10.1016/j.leaqua.2009.06.006.

Avolio, B. J., Zhu, W., Koh, W. & Bhatia, P. (2004). Transformational leadership and organizational commitment: Mediating role of psychological empowerment and moderating role of structural distance. *Journal of Organizational Behavior*, 25(8), 951–68. doi: 10.1002/job.283.

Bandura, A. (1969). *Principles of Behavior Modification*. New York: Holt, Rinehart & Winston.

Bandura, A. (1977). *Social Learning Theory*. Englewood Cliffs, NJ: Prentice-Hall.

Bandura, A. (1997). *Self-Efficacy: The Exercise of Control*. New York: Macmillan.

Barling, J. (2014). *The Science of Leadership: Lessons from Research and Organizational Leaders*. New York: Oxford University Press.

Barling, J., Christie, A. & Hoption, C. (2011). Leadership. In S. Zedeck (ed.), *APA Handbook of Industrial and Organizational Psychology. Volume 1: Building and Developing the Organization*. Washington, DC: American Psychological Association, pp. 183–240.

Barling, J., Loughlin, C. & Kelloway, E. K. (2002). Development and test of a model linking safety-specific transformational leadership and occupational safety. *Journal of Applied Psychology*, 87(3), 488–96. doi: 10.1037//0021-9010.87.3.488.

Barling, J., Weber, T. & Kelloway, E. K. (1996). Effects of transformational leadership training on attitudinal and financial outcomes: A field experiment. *Journal of Applied Psychology*, 81(6), 827–32. doi: 10.1037/0021-9010.81.6.827.

Bass, B. M. (1985). *Leadership and Performance Beyond Expectations*. New York: Free Press, and London: Collier Macmillan.

Blau, P. M. (1964). *Exchange and Power in Social Life*. New Brunswick, NJ: Transaction Publishers.

Borman, W. C. & Motowidlo, S. M. (1993). Expanding the criterion domain to include elements of contextual performance. In N. Schmitt, W.C. Borman & Associates, *Personnel Selection in Organizations*. San Francisco, CA: Jossey-Bass, pp. 71–98.

Charbonneau, D., Barling, J. & Kelloway, E. K. (2001). Transformational leadership and sports performance: The mediating role of intrinsic motivation. *Journal of Applied Social Psychology*, 31(7), 1521–34. doi: 10.1111/j.1559-1816.2001.tb02686.x.

Chiaburu, D. S., Smith, T. A., Wang, J. & Zimmerman, R. D. (2014). Relative importance of leader influences for subordinates' proactive behaviors, prosocial behaviors, and task performance. *Journal of Personnel Psychology*, 13(2), 70–86. doi: 10.1027/1866-5888/a000105.

Clarke, S. (2013). Safety leadership: A meta-analytic review of transformational and transactional leadership styles as antecedents of safety behaviors. *Journal of Occupational and Organizational Psychology*, 86(1), 22–49. doi: 10.1111/j.2044-8325.2012.02064.x.

Clarke, S. & Ward, K. (2006). The role of leader influence tactics and safety climate in engaging employees' safety participation. *Risk Analysis*, 26(5), 1175–85. doi: 10.1111/j.1539-6924.2006.00824.x.

Conchie, S. M. (2013). Transformational leadership, intrinsic motivation, and trust: A moderated-mediated model of workplace safety. *Journal of Occupational Health Psychology*, 18(2), 198–210. doi: 10.1037/a0031805.

Conchie, S., Moon, S. & Duncan, M. (2013). Supervisors' engagement in safety leadership: Factors that help and hinder. *Safety Science*, 51, 109–17. doi: 10.1016/2012.05.020.

Conchie, S. M., Taylor, P. J. & Donald, I. J. (2012). Promoting safety voice with safety-specific transformational leadership: The mediating role of two dimensions of trust. *Journal of Occupational Health Psychology*, 17(1), 105–15. doi: 10.1037/a0025101.

Credo, K. R., Armenakis, A. A., Feild, H. S. & Young, R. L. (2010). Organizational ethics, leader–member exchange, and organizational support: Relationships with workplace safety. *Journal of Leadership & Organizational Studies*, 17(4), 325–34. doi: 10.1177/1548051810366712.

Detert, J. R. & Burris, E. R. (2007). Leadership behavior and employee voice: Is the door really open? *Academy of Management Journal*, 50(4), 869–84. doi: 10.5465/AMJ.2007.26279183.

Graen, G. B. & Uhl-Bien, M. (1995). Relationship-based approach to leadership: Development of leader–member exchange (LMX) theory of leadership over 25 years: Applying a multi-level multi-domain perspective. *Leadership Quarterly*, 6(2), 219–47. doi: 10.1016/1048-9843(95)90036-5.

Griffin, M. A. & Hu, X. (2013). How leaders differentially motivate safety compliance and safety participation: The role of monitoring, inspiring, and learning. *Safety Science*, 60, 196–202. doi: 10.1016/j.ssci.2013.07.019.

Hale, A. R., Guldenmund, F. W., Van Loenhout, P. L. C. H. & Oh, J. I. H. (2010). Evaluating safety management and culture interventions to improve safety: Effective intervention strategies. *Safety Science*, 48(8), 1026–35. doi: 10.1016/j.ssci.2009.05.006.

Hershcovis, M. S. & Barling, J. (2010). Towards a multi-foci approach to workplace aggression: A meta-analytic review of outcomes from different perpetrators. *Journal of Organizational Behavior*, 31(1), 24–44. doi: 10.1002/job.621.

Hinkin, T. R. & Schriesheim, C. A. (1990). Relationships between subordinate perceptions of supervisor influence tactics and attributed bases of supervisory power. *Human Relations*, 43(3), 221–37. doi: 10.1177/001872679004300302.

Hoffmeister, K., Gibbons, A. M., Johnson, S. K., Cigularov, K. P., Chen, P. Y. & Rosecrance, J. C. (2014). The differential effects of transformational leadership facets on employee safety. *Safety Science*, 62, 68–78. doi: 10.1016/j.ssci.2013.07.004.

Hofmann, D. A. & Morgeson, F. P. (1999). Safety-related behavior as a social exchange: The role of perceived organizational support and leader–member exchange. *Journal of Applied Psychology*, 84(2), 286–96. doi: 10.1037/0021-9010.84.2.286.

Hofmann, D. A., Morgeson, F. P. & Gerras, S. J. (2003). Climate as a moderator of the relationship between leader–member exchange and content specific citizenship: Safety climate as an exemplar. *Journal of Applied Psychology*, 88(1), 170–8. doi: 10.1037/0021-9010.88.1.170.

House, R. J. & Mitchell, T. R. (1974). Path-goal theory of leadership. *Journal of Contemporary Business*, 3(4), 81–97.doi: 10.1177/014920639301900407.

Howell, J. M. & Avolio, B. J. (1993). Transformational leadership, transactional leadership, locus of control, and support for innovation: Key predictors of consolidated-business-unit performance. *Journal of Applied Psychology*, 78(6), 891–902. doi: 10.1037/0021-9010.78.6.891.

Judge, T. A. & Piccolo, R. F. (2004). Transformational and transactional leadership: A meta-analytic test of their relative validity. *Journal of Applied Psychology*, 89(5), 755–68. doi: 10.1037/0021-9010.89.5.755.

Jung, D. I. & Avolio, B. J. (2000). Opening the black box: An experimental investigation of the mediating effects of trust and value congruence on transformational and transactional leadership. *Journal of Organizational Behavior*, 21(8), 949–64. doi: 10.1002/1099-1379(200012)21:8<949::AID-JOB64>3.0.CO;2-F.

Kark, R., Shamir, B. & Chen, G. (2003). The two faces of transformational leadership: empowerment and dependency. *Journal of Applied Psychology*, 88(2), 246–55. doi: 10.1037/0021-9010.88.2.246.

Kelloway, E. K. & Barling, J. (2010). Leadership development as an intervention in occupational health psychology. *Work & Stress*, 24(3), 260–79.

Kelloway, E. K., Barling., J. & Helleur, J. (2000). Enhancing transformational leadership: The roles of training and feedback. *Leadership and Organizational Development Journal*, 21, 145–9.

Kelloway, E. K., Mullen, J. & Francis, L. (2006). Divergent effects of transformational and passive leadership on employee safety. *Journal of Occupational Health Psychology*, 11(1), 76–86. doi: 10.1037/1076-8998.11.1.76.

Kessler, S. R., Bruursema, K., Rodopman, B. & Spector, P. E. (2013). Leadership, interpersonal conflict, and counterproductive work behavior: An examination of the stressor–strain process. *Negotiation and Conflict Management Research*, 6(3), 180–90. doi: 10.1111/ncmr.12009.

Kines, P., Andersen, L. P., Spangenberg, S., Mikkelsen, K. L., Dyreborg, J. & Zohar, D. (2010). Improving construction site safety through leader-based verbal safety communication. *Journal of Safety Research*, 41, 399–406. doi: 10.1016/j.jsr.2010.06.005.

Locke, E. A. (1970). The supervisor as 'motivator': His influence on employee performance and satisfaction. In B. M. Bass, R. Cooper & J. A. Haas (eds.), *Managing for Accomplishment*. Lexington, MA: Lexington Books.

Locke, E. A. & Latham, G. P. (1984). *Goal Setting: A Motivational Technique that Works!* Englewood Cliffs, NJ: Prentice-Hall.

Luria, G. (2008). Climate strength: How leaders form consensus. *Leadership Quarterly*, 19(1), 42–53. doi: 10.1016/j.leaqua.2007.12.004.

Luria, G. (2010). The social aspects of safety management: Trust and safety climate. *Accident Analysis & Prevention*, 42(4), 1288–95. doi: 10.1016/j.aap.2010.02.006.

Martínez-Córcoles, M., Gracia, F., Tomás, I. & Peiró, J. M. (2011). Leadership and employees' perceived safety behaviors in a nuclear power plant: A structural equation model. *Safety Science*, 49(8–9), 1118–29. doi: 10.1016/j.ssci.2011.03.002.

Martínez-Córcoles, M., Gracia, F. J., Tomás, I., Peiró, J. M. & Schöbel, M. (2013). Empowering team leadership and safety performance in nuclear power plants: A multilevel approach. *Safety Science*, 51(1), 293–301. doi: 10.1016/j.ssci.2012.08.001.

Martínez-Córcoles, M., Schöbel, M., Gracia, F. J., Tomás, I. & Peiró, J. M. (2012). Linking empowering leadership to safety participation in nuclear power plants: A structural equation model. *Journal of Safety Research*, 43(3), 215–21. doi: 10.1016/j.jsr.2012.07.002.

Mullen, J. (2005). Testing a model of employee willingness to raise safety issues. *Canadian Journal of Behavioral Science*, 37, 273–82. doi: 10.1037/h0087262.

Mullen, J. E. & Kelloway, E. K. (2009). Safety leadership: A longitudinal study of the effects of transformational leadership on safety outcomes. *Journal of Occupational and Organizational Psychology*, 82(2), 253–72. doi: 10.1348/096317908X325313.

Mullen, J. E. & Kelloway, E. K. (2011). Occupational health and safety leadership. In J. C. Quick & L. E. Tetrick (eds), *Handbook of Occupational Health Psychology*, 2nd edn. Washington, DC: American Psychological Association, pp. 357–72.

Mullen, J., Kelloway, E. K. & Teed, M. (2011). Inconsistent style of leadership as a predictor of safety behavior. *Work & Stress*, 25(1), 41–54. doi: 10.1080/02678373.2011.569200.

Neal, A. & Griffin, M. A. (2006). A study of the lagged relationships among safety climate, safety motivation, safety behavior, and accidents at the individual and group levels. *Journal of Applied Psychology*, 91(4), 946–53. doi: 10.1037/0021-9010.91.4.946.

Neal, A., Griffin, M. & Hart, P. (2000). The impact of organizational climate on safety climate and individual behavior. *Safety Science*, 34(1), 99–109. doi: 10.1016/S0925-7535(00)00008-4.

Nielsen, K., Taris, T. & Cox, T. (2010). The future of organizational interventions: Addressing the challenges of today's organizations. *Work & Stress*, 24(3), 219–33. doi: 10.1080.02678373.2010.519176.

Ogunfowora, B. (2013). When the abuse is unevenly distributed: The effects of abusive supervision variability on work attitudes and behaviors. *Journal of Organizational Behavior*, 34(8), 1105–23. doi: 10.1002/job.1841.

Parker, S. K., Axtell, C. M. & Turner, N. (2001). Designing a safer workplace: Importance of job autonomy, communication quality, and supportive supervisors. *Journal of Occupational Health Psychology*, 6(3), 211–28. doi: 10.1037/1076-8998.6.3.211.

Piccolo, R. F. & Colquitt, J. A. (2006). Transformational leadership and job behaviors: The mediating role of core job characteristics. *Academy of Management Journal*, 49(2), 327–40. doi: 10.5465/AMJ.2006.20786079.

Podsakoff, P. M., MacKenzie, S. B., Paine, J. B. & Bachrach, D. G. (2000). Organizational citizenship behaviors: A critical review of the theoretical and empirical literature and suggestions for future research. *Journal of Management*, 26(3), 513–63. doi: 10.1177/014920630002600307.

Rotundo, M. & Sackett, P. R. (2002). The relative importance of task, citizenship, and counterproductive performance to global ratings of job performance: A policy-capturing approach. *Journal of Applied Psychology*, 87(1), 66–80. doi: 10.1037/0021-9010.87.1.66.

Ryan, R. M. & Deci, E. L. (2000). Self-determination theory and the facilitation of intrinsic motivation, social development, and well-being. *American Psychologist*, 55(1), 68–78. doi: 10.1037/0003-066X.55.1.68.

Schyns, B. & Schilling, J. (2013). How bad are the effects of bad leaders? A meta-analysis of destructive leadership and its outcomes. *Leadership Quarterly*, 24(1), 138–58. doi: 10.1016/j.leaqua.2012.09.001.

Skakon, J., Nielsen, K., Borg, V. & Guzman, J. (2010). Are leaders' well-being, behaviours and style associated with the affective well-being of their employees? A systematic review of three decades of research. *Work & Stress*, 24(2), 107–39. doi: 10.1080/02678373.2010.495262.

Skinner, B. F. (1953). *Science and Human Behavior*. New York: Macmillan.

Skogstad, A., Einarsen, S., Torsheim, T., Aasland, M. S. & Hetland, H. (2007). The destructiveness of laissez-faire leadership behavior. *Journal of Occupational Health Psychology*, 12(1), 80–92. doi: 10.1037/1076-8998.12.1.80.

von Thiele Schwarz, U., Hasson, H. & Tafvelin, S. (2016). Leadership training as an occupational health intervention: Improved safety and sustained productivity. *Safety Science*, 81, 35–45. doi: 10.1016/j.ssci.2015.07.020.

Wang, H., Law, K. S., Hackett, R. D., Wang, D. & Chen, Z. X. (2005). Leader–member exchange as a mediator of the relationship between transformational leadership and followers' performance and organizational citizenship behavior. *Academy of Management Journal*, 48(3), 420–32. doi: 10.5465/AMJ.2005.17407908.

Westaby, J. D. & Lowe, J. K. (2005). Risk-taking orientation and injury among youth workers: Examining the social influence of supervisors, coworkers, and parents. *Journal of Applied Psychology*, 90(5), 1027–35. doi: 10.1037/0021-9010.90.5.1027.

Wong, J. H. K., Kelloway, E. K. & Makhan, D. W (2015). Safety leadership. In S. Clarke, T. M. Probst, F. Guldenmund & J. Passmore (eds), *The Wiley Blackwell Handbook of the Psychology of Occupational Safety and Workplace Health*. Oxford: Wiley-Blackwell, pp. 83–110.

Wong, J. H. K., Ozbilir, T., Dimoff, J. K., MacLellan, A. M., Collins, L. & Kelloway, E. K. (2015). Leading the way to safety: The development of the S.A.F.E.R leadership model. Unpublished manuscript, Department of Psychology, Saint Mary's University, Halifax, Canada.

Zohar, D. (1980). Safety climate in industrial organizations: Theoretical and applied implications. *Journal of Applied Psychology*, 65(1), 96–102. doi: 10.1037/0021-9010.65.1.96.

Zohar, D. (2002a). The effects of leadership dimensions, safety climate, and assigned priorities on minor injuries in work groups. *Journal of Organizational Behavior*, 23(1), 75–92. doi: 10.1002/job.130.

Zohar, D. (2002b). Modifying supervisory practices to improve subunit safety: A leadership-based intervention model. *Journal of Applied Psychology*, 87(1), 156–63. doi: 10.1037/0021-9010.87.1.156.

Zohar, D., Huang, Y., Lee, J. & Robertson, M. (2014). A mediation model linking dispatcher leadership and work ownership with safety climate as predictors of truck driver safety performance. *Accident Analysis & Prevention*, 62, 17–25. doi: 10.1016/j.aap.2013.09.005.

Zohar, D. & Luria, G. (2003). The use of supervisory practices as a leverage to improve safety behavior: A cross-level intervention model. *Journal of Safety Research*, 34, 567–77.

4

The Antecedents of Transformational Leadership and Its Consequences for Occupational Health and Safety

Susanne Tafvelin

Leaders play a central part in the success of organizations, and, consequently, a large amount of research has been devoted to the study of how different leadership styles are related to important organizational outcomes. In particular, transformational leadership has attracted a vast amount of empirical research attention; since 1990, more studies have been devoted to this leadership style than to all other major theories of leadership combined (Judge & Piccolo, 2004). The findings of these efforts have been summarized in six meta-analyses, which have suggested that transformational leadership is associated with employee satisfaction, commitment, motivation, effort and performance (DeGroot, Kiker & Cross, 2000; Dumdum, Lowe & Avolio, 2002; Fuller, Patterson, Hester & Stringer, 1996; Judge & Piccolo, 2004; Lowe, Kroeck & Sivasubramaniam, 1996). In the most recent meta-analysis, Wang, Oh, Courtright and Colberg (2011) found that transformational leadership predicted performance at the individual, group and organizational levels.

Leaders are, however, responsible not only for developing and implementing strategies to ensure employee performance, but also for the health and safety of their employees. Studies have suggested that leaders have the potential to influence employee well-being above and beyond the influence of colleagues, family and friends (Gilbreath & Benson, 2004), and the role of leaders in creating a healthy and safe workplace has received increased research attention over the past decade (Clarke, Arnold & Connelly, 2015). Given the domination of transformational leadership in leadership research, and that it is a leadership style advocated by both academics and practitioners (Bass & Riggio, 2006; Desvaux, Devillard-Hoellinger & Baumgarten, 2007), it is of particular interest to understand how this leadership style is related to the health and safety of employees. Emerging empirical evidence has suggested that leadership is one of the most important workplace factors influencing well-being (Kelloway & Barling, 2010) and that, among different leadership styles, transformational leadership has the strongest relationship with employee well-being (e.g., De Hoogh & Den Hartog, 2009; Kanste, Kyngäs & Nikkilä, 2007). Although this evidence is promising,

Leading to Occupational Health and Safety: How Leadership Behaviours Impact Organizational Safety and Well-Being, First Edition.
Edited by E. Kevin Kelloway, Karina Nielsen and Jennifer K. Dimoff.

there are still important shortcomings in the literature that need to be addressed; among other things, there is still a need to explain when and why transformational leadership affects employee health and safety, and to explain the antecedents of this style of leadership.

The objective of this chapter is therefore to critically review the literature on transformational leadership in relation to occupational health and safety. I begin by describing research on the direct relationships between transformational leadership and occupational health and safety. Next, I present mechanisms explaining when and why transformational leadership affects occupational health and safety, including a proposed theoretical model that integrates the findings of mediators linking transformational leadership to employee well-being. In addition, I discuss influences on transformational leadership in terms of its antecedents. Finally, directions for future research are proposed. Because transformational leadership has been found to add to the positive effects of other leadership behaviours in the full-range model of leadership (Bass & Riggio, 2006), for the purpose of this review I will focus on transformational leadership only, excluding, for example, transactional leadership behaviours.

Consequences of Transformational Leadership: Relationships with Employee Well-Being and Safety

Occupational health is a broad concept involving all aspects of health and safety in the workplace. In this chapter, the focus is on employee psychological health and well-being; studies of employee physical health are excluded. Well-being can be defined from both a hedonic and a eudaimonic perspective, where the former is referred to as subjective well-being and includes high levels of positive affect, low levels of negative affect and high levels of life satisfaction (Ryan & Deci, 2001). Eudaimonic well-being comprises personal growth, authenticity and the pursuit of meaning in life (Ryff, 1995). Given that organizational research covers both hedonic and eudaimonic conceptualizations of well-being (Sonnentag, 2015), for the purposes of this chapter both conceptualizations are included. As a consequence, a large range of employee well-being outcomes are covered, ranging from negative to positive aspects of well-being, as well as work- and non-work-related aspects of well-being.

Employee Well-Being

In 2004, Sivanathan and colleagues pointed out that there had been surprisingly little research on transformational leadership and employee well-being (Sivanathan, Arnold, Turner & Barling, 2004). Since then, there has been a dramatic increase in the number of studies with a focus on if and how transformational leadership may be beneficial not only for employee attitudes and performance but also for employee well-being. In a review of this literature Skakon, Nielsen, Borg & Guzman (2010) found that, of the 13 studies identified, 12 reported a significant relationship between transformational leadership and increased affective well-being, job satisfaction, and reduced stress and burnout among employees. Only one study found no relationship between transformational leadership and burnout (Stordeur, D'hoore & Vandenberghe, 2001), and so Skakon et al. (2010) concluded that transformational leadership seems to be beneficial for reducing stress and enhancing employee well-being.

Studies on the relationship between transformational leadership and negative aspects of employee well-being have demonstrated that transformational leadership may reduce job-related stress (e.g., Sosik & Godshalk, 2000), burnout and depression (e.g., Perko, Kinnunen & Feldt, 2014; Seltzer, Numerof & Bass, 1989). Interestingly, a few studies have suggested that not all dimensions of transformational leadership may be equally effective at reducing employee burnout. In a study of MBA students, Seltzer et al. (1989) found that intellectual stimulation – in contrast to the other dimensions of transformational leadership – was, in fact, positively correlated with stress and burnout. These findings were later corroborated by Corrigan, Diwan, Campion and Rashid (2002), who found in a sample of mental-health teams that intellectual stimulation was unrelated to exhaustion and positively related to personal accomplishment, an aspect of burnout.

Transformational leadership has also been linked to various positive aspects of employee well-being. Early studies started with the assumption of *emotional contagion*, wherein positive emotions expressed by a transformational leader are mimicked and, thereby, experienced by employees (Cherulnik, Donley, Wiewel & Miller, 2001). Studies have supported this assumption, showing that transformational leaders tend to use positive affect words in their communication with employees (Bono & Ilies, 2006) and that employees of transformational leaders experience more optimism, happiness and enthusiasm throughout the day than employees who do not have a transformational leader (Bono, Foldes, Vinson & Muros, 2007). In addition, transformational leadership has been linked to employee affective well-being (Arnold, Turner, Barling, Kelloway & McKee, 2007; Nielsen, Randall, Yarker, & Brenner, 2008; Tafvelin, Armelius &Westerberg, 2011), vigour (Perko, Kinnunen, Tolvanen & Feldt., 2015), engagement (Tims, Bakker & Xanthopoulou, 2011), and spiritual well-being in terms of feeling that life is a positive experience and having a meaningful relationship with a higher power (McKee, Driscoll, Kelloway & Kelley, 2011).

Although studies appear to converge on the benefits of transformational leadership for employee well-being, it should be noted that most prior research used cross-sectional designs. The few longitudinal studies that explicitly tested the effect of transformational leadership on employee well-being over time showed no support for a direct effect (Nielsen & Munir, 2009; Tafvelin et al., 2011), suggesting that mediating mechanisms might be present. Furthermore, in a longitudinal study by Nielsen and Daniels (2016), transformational leadership was, in fact, positively associated with employee sickness absenteeism one year later. These results suggested that, although the short-term effects of transformational leadership on employee health and well-being are beneficial, the long-term effects may be harmful, highlighting the importance of continuing the study of transformational leadership and employee well-being.

Safety

Leaders play an important role in maintaining and improving workplace safety (e.g., Butler & Jones, 1979; Parker, Axtell & Turner, 2001). In particular, transformational leadership has been associated with increased safety behaviour in employees (e.g., Inness, Turner, Barling & Stride, 2010) and a reduced number of occupational injuries (Zohar, 2002).

In a meta-analysis, Clarke (2013) examined the relationship between transformational leadership and employee safety behaviours, differentiating between safety participation (willingness to engage in safety activities) and safety compliance (following safety rules and regulations). She found that transformational leadership predicted safety participation but not safety compliance, suggesting that transformational leadership may be beneficial to some, but not all, aspects of employee safety. Furthermore, in an effort to explore how the subdimensions of transformational leadership are related to employee safety, Hoffmeister et al. (2014) found that idealized influence and inspirational motivation were positively associated with safety participation, while intellectual stimulation and individualized consideration were unrelated to safety participation. It has been suggested that intellectual stimulation may in fact be associated with increased risk taking and therefore detrimental to employee safety, given the encouragement of creative thinking and questioning of assumptions (Clarke, 2013).

Lately, researchers have begun to distinguish between general transformational leadership and safety-specific transformational leadership, and studies have shown that safety-specific transformational leadership explains additional variance over and above that of general transformational leadership on safety outcomes (Mullen & Kelloway, 2009; Mullen, Kelloway & Teed, 2011). This has opened up a debate on whether safety-specific or general measures of transformational leadership should be used in safety research. Interested readers are referred to Barling, Loughlin and Kelloway (2002), Inness et al. (2010) and Mullen et al. (2011) for further information on this debate. Also, the meta-analysis by Clarke (2013) found that transactional leadership, not transformational leadership, predicted safety compliance, opening up a window of possibilities for leadership styles other than transformational leadership for understanding the role of leaders in workplace safety.

The Influence Process: Mediation

Despite the growing interest in transformational leadership and employee health and safety, the underlying influence process is still not well understood (Clarke et al., 2015; Skakon et al., 2010). Knowledge of the influence process, in terms of identifying how transformational leadership behaviour affects different types of mediating variables, is important for explaining why transformational leaders have a positive effect on employee well-being and safety, as well as for strengthening transformational leadership theory (van Knippenberg & Sitkin, 2013).

Mediators of the Relationship Between Transformational Leadership and Employee Well-Being

Studies examining the mechanisms by which transformational leaders may influence employee health and well-being have established support for the idea that mediators reflect followers' perceptions of themselves, their team, their leader and their work environment.

Studies of *followers' self-perceptions* have centred on the mediating effect of self-efficacy. Transformational leaders influence followers' self-efficacy through the Pygmalion effect, whereby the leaders communicate and hold high performance expectations (Sivanathan et al., 2004). They also serve as role models, showing followers how difficulties can be handled and overcome (Bass & Riggio, 2006). So far, empirical support has been found for the mediating effect of self-efficacy on well-being (Liu, Siu & Shi, 2010; Nielsen & Munir, 2009; Nielsen, Yarker, Randall & Munir, 2009) and depressive symptoms (Perko et al., 2014), but not on sleep quality (Munir & Nielsen, 2009) or job satisfaction (Nielsen et al., 2009). Other constructs related to followers' self-perceptions that have been found to mediate the effect of transformational leadership on employee well-being include empowerment (Krishnan, 2012), fulfilment of basic psychological needs (Kovjanic, Schuh, Jonas, Quaquebeke & van Dick, 2012; Stenling & Tafvelin, 2014), identification with the leader (Hobman, Jackson, Jimmieson & Martin, 2011), and self-concordant goals (Bono & Judge, 2003).

In line with studies demonstrating the mediating role of self-efficacy, a few studies have focused on *team-related mediators* in terms of collective efficacy and found mediating effects of transformational leadership on well-being (Nielsen et al., 2009; Walumbwa, Wang, Lawler & Shi, 2004). For example, in a study of Danish elderly care workers, Nielsen et al. (2009) found that team efficacy partially mediated the relationship between transformational leadership and job satisfaction and fully mediated the relationship between transformational leadership and well-being.

The studies of *followers' attitudes towards their leader* as a mediator of transformational leadership have focused on the influence of trust. Transformational leaders build trust by providing employees with support and paying close attention to their individual needs. By developing a shared vision, instilling employees with a sense of direction and role-modelling the values and norms of the organization, transformational leaders gain the trust of their followers (Bass & Riggio, 2006). In line with this, Kelloway, Turner, Barling and Loughlin (2012) found that trust in the leader mediated the relationship between transformational leadership and employee mental health in a sample of Canadian telecommunication workers as well as in a sample representative of the US workforce. In a study of Chinese employees, Liu et al. (2010) corroborated and extended these findings with job satisfaction, work stress and stress symptoms as indicators of well-being.

Finally, *followers' perceptions of their working environment* have been established as a mediator of the relationship between transformational leadership and employee health and well-being, including perceptions of meaningfulness (Arnold et al., 2007). Transformational leaders create a sense of meaning by formulating a shared vision and helping employees to see how their daily activities contribute to the goals of the organization (Arnold et al., 2007). They mentor their employees and encourage them to question assumptions regarding their working procedures, in an effort to help them to find meaning in their activities and to understand the role they play in attaining the organization's goals (Nielsen, Randall et al., 2008). In line with this, the experience of having a meaningful job has been found to mediate the effect of transformational leadership on psychological well-being (Arnold et al., 2007; Nielsen, Randall et al., 2008), work engagement (Aryee, Walumbwa, Zhou & Hartnell, 2012) and depressive symptoms (Perko et al., 2014).

The influence of transformational leadership on employee health and well-being is also mediated by other job perceptions such as involvement, opportunities for development and role clarity (Nielsen, Randall et al., 2008; Nielsen, Yarker et al., 2008). Transformational leaders encourage employees to find and to take responsibility for new ways of working and solving problems faced by the work group, thus providing opportunities for growth and participation (Nielsen, Randall et al., 2008). They also help employees to clarify their role in the organization by assisting employees to see the link between their own efforts and the goals of the organization (Nielsen, Randall et al., 2008). Finally, transformational leaders have been found to positively influence employee well-being by increasing perceptions of social support (Nielsen & Daniels, 2012), a sense of community (McKee et al., 2011) and a positive climate for innovation (Tafvelin et al., 2011), as well as by reducing work–life conflict (Munir, Nielsen, Garde, Albertsen & Carneiro, 2012) and work-related rumination away from work (Perko et al., 2014). These findings suggest that mediators related not only to the job but also to colleagues and life outside of work are important.

Although empirical studies have examined a number of different mediators to explain the influence transformational leaders have on employee well-being, theoretical work integrating these findings is still lacking (Clarke et al., 2015). Recently, the conservation of resources theory (Hobfoll, 1989) has been suggested as an overarching framework for categorizing current mediators in terms of social and personal resources (Clarke et al., 2015). Building on this, and in an effort to further the theoretical basis in this literature, I propose that self-determination theory (Deci & Ryan, 2000) can be applied as a theoretical framework to explain the psychological and motivational processes by which transformational leaders influence employee well-being. Self-determination theory may also help to explain why personal and social resources, according to conservation of resources theory, influence well-being.

Self-Determination Theory

Self-determination theory is a theoretical framework used to understand human motivation. According to self-determination theory, nurturance and growth of the human psyche are dependent on the satisfaction of three universal psychological needs: autonomy, competence and relatedness (Deci & Ryan, 2000). In the same way that the satisfaction of physical needs (e.g., hunger, thirst) is critical for physical survival, the satisfaction of psychological needs is assumed to be critical for psychological functioning, including growth, integrity and well-being

(Van den Broeck, Vansteenkiste, De Witte & Lens, 2008). *Autonomy* includes the perception of being the origin of one's own choices and decisions, the absence of pressure, and a sense that one is engaging in an action voluntarily (de Charms, 1968). The need for *competence* involves feelings of mastery and effectiveness, achieved through an effective interaction with one's environment (White, 1959). Finally, the need for *relatedness* represents a desire to be respected, understood and securely attached to others (Baumeister & Leary, 1995). Satisfaction of the three psychological needs has been postulated to enhance psychological well-being, a proposition that has been validated in empirical research (Gagné, 2014).

Within transformational leadership theory, Burns (1978) defined a transformational leader as a person who "seeks to satisfy higher needs and engages the full potential of the follower" (p. 4), while Bass (1990) described the fulfilment of followers' emotional needs as a key characteristic of transformational leadership; both emphasize the centrality of followers' needs. Transformational leaders may fulfil followers' psychological needs in several ways. By communicating a sense of meaning together with an attractive vision of the future, they inspire employees to identify with the vision and make it their own (Bass & Riggio, 2006), fulfilling the employees' need for autonomy. Furthermore, transformational leaders encourage employees to take their own initiatives while listening carefully to their suggestions and concerns, giving employees a sense of autonomy. Regarding the need for competence, transformational leaders stimulate employees' efforts to be creative and innovative by encouraging them to question old ways of doing things and to try new ways of solving problems, expanding employees' use of their capabilities (Bass & Riggio, 2006) and fulfilling their need for competence. Transformational leaders also communicate high performance expectations, along with a strong belief that these expectations will be met, giving employees confidence in their capacity. Transformational leaders provide support, feedback and coaching to ensure that employees have the ideal conditions in which to grow and develop (Bass & Riggio, 2006), fulfilling their need for competence. The need for relatedness is satisfied when a transformational leader listens attentively to the personal needs of an employee, which develops feelings of being understood and builds a close relationship between the leader and the employee (Bass & Riggio, 2006). The relationship is further deepened by role-modelling behaviours wherein the leader displays high moral and ethical standards and a strong conviction about the goals and purpose of the team. Trust in leaders is created when they earn the respect and admiration of their employees. Also, the need for relatedness is fulfilled by replacing feelings of isolation with a sense of belonging and emphasizing the importance of collective action (Sosik & Godshalk, 2000). The application of self-determination theory in the work setting has been growing (Gagné, 2014), and a number of recent studies have demonstrated that transformational leaders do influence employee need satisfaction (Hetland et al., 2015; Kovjanic et al., 2012).

Building on self-determination theory, I suggest that transformational leaders satisfy employees' basic needs and thereby increase their health and well-being, and that need satisfaction is a central psychological mechanism linking transformational leadership to employee health and well-being. This is in line with a study by Stenling and Tafvelin (2014), who found that transformational coaches influenced athlete well-being through need satisfaction among young athletes. In work settings, Kovjanic et al. (2012) demonstrated that employee need satisfaction mediated the influence of transformational leadership on job satisfaction. These findings were corroborated by Hetland et al. (2015), using both cross-sectional and diary data.

Furthermore, self-determination theory may help to explain the findings of mediators in previous research. For example, the perception of having meaningful work can fulfil the need for autonomy. Self-efficacy, the judgement of one's ability to accomplish a certain level of performance (Bandura, 1977), is closely related to the need for competence. Trust in one's leader can satisfy the need for relatedness. Following the line of thought presented by Clarke et al. (2015), many of the previously established mediators between transformational leadership and employee health and well-being may be conceptualized as resources under the conservation of resources theory. The basic tenet of conservation of resources theory is that humans are motivated to protect their current resources and to acquire new ones (Hobfoll, 1989). Resources are defined as 'objects, personal characteristics, conditions, or energies that are valued in their own right' (Hobfoll, 2001, p. 339). In addition, resources are things perceived by the individual to help them attain their goals (Halbesleben, Neveu, Paustian-Underdahl & Westman, 2014). The definition of resources, however, does not include whether a resource facilitated goal attainment. Self-determination theory is useful for understanding why individuals conserve and acquire resources (Halbesleben et al., 2014), and it may help to explain why resources increase employee health and well-being (Van den Broeck, 2010) through the process of need satisfaction. If resources are conserved and accumulated, the needs for autonomy, competence and relatedness are fulfilled (Halbesleben et al., 2014), which in turn increases well-being. This chain of proposed relationships was supported in a study by Fernet, Trépanier, Austin, Gagné & Forest (2015), who demonstrated that transformational leaders influenced employee perception of job resources, which in turn was related to feelings of being autonomous and employee psychological health. Further, Van den Broeck et al. (2008) successfully demonstrated that need fulfilment mediates the relationship between job resources and vigour.

In sum, self-determination theory may be used not only to explain the mechanisms by which transformational leaders influence employee health and well-being but also to explain why previous mediators, conceptualized as either personal or social resources, contribute to enhanced health and well-being. The proposed model is presented in Figure 4.1; echoing the line of thought of Clarke et al. (2015), I suggest that using this extended framework to guide future research is better than viewing mediators in isolation.

Mediators of the Relationship Between Transformational Leadership and Employee Safety

Although the mediating mechanisms responsible for the relationship between transformational leadership and employee safety have not yet received the same increased research attention as the mediators of well-being, the few studies

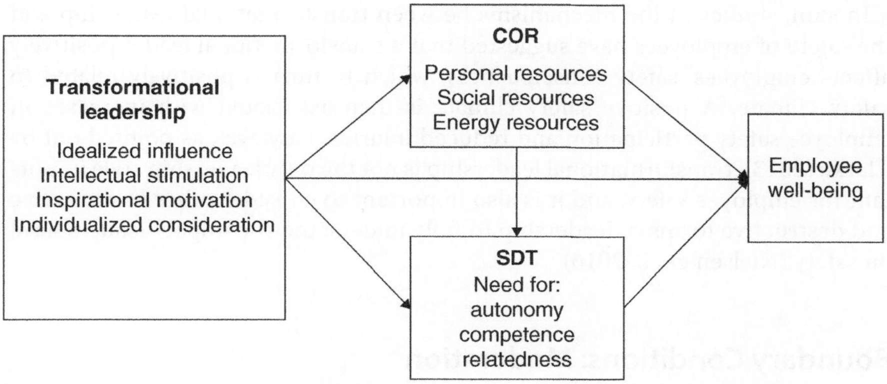

Figure 4.1 Proposed model for the mechanisms linking transformational leadership to employee health and well-being.

conducted have identified mediators reflecting followers' perceptions of themselves, their leader and their work environment.

Studies of *followers' self-perceptions* have examined the mediating potential of safety consciousness, reflecting employees' general awareness of safety issues as well as their specific knowledge and enactment of the behaviours needed to ensure safety (Barling et al., 2002). Transformational leaders foster safety consciousness by serving as role models, emphasizing the importance of safety, and stimulating employees to think about safety. In a study of Canadian restaurant workers, Barling et al. (2002) found that employees' safety consciousness partially mediated the link between safety-specific transformational leadership and safety climate, which in turn predicted safety-related events and occupational injuries. These findings were later corroborated by Kelloway et al. (2006) in a sample of undergraduate students.

To the best of my knowledge, only one study has investigated the mediating effect of *followers' attitudes towards their leader*: Conchie et al. (2012) examined the role of trust in leaders among employees at a large oil refinery in the United Kingdom. The authors found that affective trust, but not cognitive trust, mediated the relationship between transformational safety leadership and employee safety voice, suggesting that leaders who want to encourage safety voice behaviours should go beyond using good arguments and develop affective bonds with their employees.

The majority of mediational studies on transformational leadership and safety have focused on *followers' perceptions of their working environment* and the mediating effect of safety climate. Transformational leaders build a positive safety climate by calling attention to the importance of safety, encouraging employees to get involved and participate in safety-related issues. Empirically, safety climate has been found to mediate the effect of a transformational leader on safety events and occupational injuries (Barling et al., 2002; Kelloway et al., 2006), injury rates (Zohar, 2002), and safety participation (Clarke & Ward, 2006). In a recent meta-analysis, Clarke (2013) found that safety climate partially mediated the link between transformational leadership and safety participation.

In sum, studies of the mechanisms between transformational leadership and the safety of employees have suggested that a transformational leader positively affects employees' safety consciousness, which in turn is positively related to safety climate. A positive safety climate is then associated with increases in employee safety participation and reduced injuries. However, as pointed out by Clarke (2013), transformational leadership is not the only leadership style important for employee safety, and it is also important to consider other constructive and destructive forms of leadership to fully understand the impact leaders have on safety (Nielsen et al., 2016).

Boundary Conditions: Moderation

Even though transformational leadership theory is our most heavily researched leadership model at present, relatively little effort has been invested in identifying the boundary conditions under which transformational leaders are more or less effective (Avolio, Walumbwa & Weber, 2009). Some of the early work on transformational leadership did stress the importance of moderation effects (e.g., Lowe et al., 1996), but only recently have researchers devoted more attention to this aspect of the transformational leadership process. Identifying the boundary conditions of transformational leadership is important, as theoretical models are supposed to include not only the expected relationships among constructs but also the boundaries of the domains within which the theory is expected to unfold (Dubin, 1976). Also, examining whether the effects of transformational leadership are bounded facilitates efforts to identify those situations in which transformational leadership works best (Chuang, Judge & Liaw, 2012).

Empirical studies investigating moderators of transformational leadership have centred on outcomes such as effectiveness, performance, motivation, satisfaction and commitment (Judge, Woolf, Hurst & Livingston, 2006). They have identified boundary conditions related to (1) *the follower*, such as the need for autonomy (Wofford, Whittington & Goodwin, 2001) and efficacy (Zhu, Avolio & Walumbwa, 2009), (2) *the leader*, including trust (Jung, Yammarino & Lee, 2009), the level of the leader (Judge & Piccolo, 2004), and leader continuity (Tafvelin, Hyvönen & Westerberg, 2014), and finally, (3) *the context*, in terms of, for example, the organizational sector (Judge & Piccolo, 2004; Lowe et al., 1996) and climate (Felfe & Schyns, 2002). Conditions under which the effects of transformational leadership on occupational health and safety are bounded have received less research attention.

Moderators of the Relationship Between Transformational Leadership and Employee Well-Being

Studies investigating moderators of the transformational leadership and employee well-being relationship have focused on factors related to the follower. In particular, different aspects of follower personality have been examined, and the findings suggest that positive follower traits (Zhu et al., 2009), professional ambition (Holstad, Korek, Rigotti & Mohr 2014), locus of control, and neuroticism

(De Hoogh & Den Hartog, 2009), but not self-efficacy (Abate, Sewasew & Woldemeskel, 2014; Gregersen, Vincent-Höper & Nienhaus, 2014), moderate the influence transformational leaders have on employee health and well-being. For example, De Hoogh and Den Hartog (2009) found that the negative relationship between charisma and employee burnout was stronger for individuals low on internal locus of control and neuroticism. Holstad et al. (2014) demonstrated that high professional ambition among employees strengthened the relationship between transformational leadership and emotional irritation. Studies have also examined other moderators related to the follower. For example, Franke and Felfe (2011) found that the influence of individual consideration and idealized influence on employee strain was stronger when affective commitment was low, suggesting that aspects of transformational leadership play a bigger part in employee strain for employees low on commitment than employees already highly committed. Nielsen and Daniels (2016) demonstrated that *presenteeism*, showing up at work while ill, strengthened the relationship between transformational leadership and sick leave. Furthermore, Kanste et al. (2007) found that the relationship between transformational leadership and burnout was stronger among nurses with temporary positions than among their colleagues with permanent positions. Taken together, these studies suggest that followers may not benefit equally from being exposed to a transformational leader, and that factors related to follower personality, work attitudes and work status set a limit on the influence of transformational leadership on employee health and well-being.

A few studies have examined the role of context on the strength of the relationship between transformational leadership and employee well-being. De Cremer (2006) conducted an experiment with Dutch undergraduate students that showed that procedural justice was more strongly related to negative affect in the highly transformational condition. The moderating effect of procedural justice was then corroborated in a field study with self-esteem as the outcome (De Cremer, 2006). Zwingmann et al. (2014) found that when employees had a preference for high power distance, the effect of transformational leadership on employee health was stronger. They suggested that employees in cultures with a preference for high power distance may be more willing to accept influence and support from their leaders. These results suggest that it is important to consider both the organizational and the cultural contexts when examining the influence of transformational leadership on employee health and well-being. However, more studies are needed, and it is noteworthy that no studies were found that have examined how factors related to the leader may moderate the relationship between transformational leadership and employee health and well-being.

Moderators of the Relationship Between Transformational Leadership and Employee Safety

In contrast to studies of moderators on outcomes such as employee health and well-being, studies of the impact transformational leaders have on safety have primarily focused on factors related to the leader, as well as the organizational context. Leader-related moderators include supervisor-assigned safety priority (Zohar, 2002), trust (Conchie & Donald, 2009), and passive leadership style

(Mullen et al., 2011). In a study of Israeli production workers, Zohar (2002) found that assigned safety priority by a leader's immediate supervisor strengthened the relationship between the leader's transformational leadership and employee safety climate, especially under low levels of assigned safety priority. Conchie and Donald (2009) demonstrated that trust in the leader enhanced the effect of transformational leadership on employee safety: when safety-specific trust was high, safety-specific transformational leadership led to higher safety citizenship behaviours among employees. Also reflecting the importance of the leader, Mullen et al. (2011) examined how other leadership styles influenced the impact that transformational leadership has on employee safety and found that passive safety-specific leadership weakened the positive influence of safety-specific transformational leadership on employee safety participation and safety compliance. These findings highlight the downside of inconsistent safety leadership and suggest that leaders must engage in transformational safety leadership consistently.

In a study focusing on the moderating effects of factors related to the organizational context, Kapp (2012) found that safety climate moderated the relationship between transformational leadership and safety compliance, but not safety participation. Under conditions of a positive group safety climate, employee safety compliance improved as transformational leadership increased, but under conditions of a negative group safety climate, transformational leadership was unrelated to safety compliance. The results of this study suggest that organizational factors set a limit on what leadership alone can achieve when it comes to safety.

To conclude, only a few studies have examined moderators of the relationship between transformational leadership and employee safety. So far, the focus has been on the leader and, to some extent, the context, but there is no knowledge of how moderators related to the follower may bound the influence that transformational leaders have on safety.

Antecedents of Transformational Leadership

Given the positive impact of transformational leadership on important organizational outcomes, including employee well-being and safety, it is important to understand its antecedents. Why do some leaders engage in transformational leadership behaviours while others do not? And what are the conditions that make it easier for leaders to exhibit transformational leadership? Although this topic would appear to be of central interest to both practitioners and academics, it has been overlooked in the large body of transformational leadership research. One reason could be the assumption that transformational leadership is a stable personal characteristic that does not change over time or across situations (Dóci & Hofmans, 2015). However, a growing number of studies have suggested that the emergence of transformational leadership is a complex interplay of trait, state, contextual and relational influences.

Research on predictors of transformational leadership started with, and still centres on, the study of how personal characteristics may help or hinder leaders to exhibit transformational leadership behaviours. Findings have suggested that dispositional factors such as personality (Judge & Bono, 2000), intelligence (Cavazotte, Moreno & Hickmann, 2012), genetic factors (Johnson, Vernon, Harris & Jang, 2004) and gender (Eagly, Johannesen-Schmidt & van Engen, 2003) influence the extent to which leaders display transformational leadership behaviours. Among personality traits, a meta-analysis suggested that extraversion is the strongest predictor of transformational leadership, although all of the Big Five traits, except for conscientiousness, were significantly related to transformational leadership (Bono & Judge, 2004). Recent studies further indicate that the subdimensions of transformational leadership differ in how they are related to personality. For example, inspirational motivation is related to all personality traits, but only openness to experience and agreeableness affect individualized consideration (Dienert, Homan, Boer, Voelpel & Gutermann, 2015).

In their meta-analysis, Bono and Judge (2004) found that leader traits only accounted for 12 per cent or less of the variance in transformational leadership ratings and concluded that other, less stable, factors may be more important. Their findings marked a shift towards studies investigating how individually varying state-like factors such as leaders' attitudes, emotions and well-being influence the display of transformational leadership behaviours. Joseph, Dhanani, Shen, McHugh and McCord (2015) showed in a meta-analysis that leaders' positive affect explained the variance in transformational leadership ratings over and above that of extraversion and neuroticism. Similarly, Byrne et al. (2014) demonstrated that leader depression and anxiety negatively affected leaders' exhibition of transformational leadership. Also, Jin, Seo and Shapiro (2016) found that leaders' experience of pleasant emotions and commitment at work facilitated the display of transformational leadership behaviours. These findings suggest that state-like factors in terms of leader affective experiences influence transformational leadership.

Contextual factors, reflecting organizational and working conditions, have also been examined for their influence on transformational leadership. Wright and Pandey (2010) found that hierarchical decision making and communication adversely affected transformational leadership ratings. Further, centralization and size negatively predict transformational leadership, while formalization is positively related to transformational leadership (Walter & Bruch, 2010). Leaders' own working environment also plays a part. Nielsen and Cleal (2011) demonstrated that feelings of meaningfulness and high cognitive demands were positively related to self-ratings of transformational leadership, as were situations in which leaders felt they were in control, as well as those that were cognitively challenging. Also, in a laboratory experiment, leaders engaged less in transformational leadership behaviours when faced with complex tasks (Doci & Hofmans, 2015).

A few studies have examined how trait, state and contextual factors interact in their influence on transformational leadership. Perreault, Cohen and Blanchard (2016) examined how job perceptions moderated the influence of personality and found that, when leaders experienced high need satisfaction, the influence of personality on transformational leadership became weaker. In line with these findings, Zhang, Wang and Pearce (2014) demonstrated that leaders' perceptions of a dynamic work environment also weakened the influence of personality on transformational leadership. These findings suggest that contextual factors are not only important predictors of transformational leadership but may also decrease the influence of leader traits.

Another line of studies has focused on how followers influence leaders' ability to exhibit transformational leadership behaviours. Bono, Hooper and Yoon (2012) found that follower personality – in terms of agreeableness, openness, extraversion and conscientiousness – positively predicted transformational leadership ratings. Followers' self-development needs (Dvir & Shamir, 2003) and intrinsic work values (Ehrhart & Klein, 2001) have also been identified as influencing the emergence of transformational leadership. Further, Nielsen, Randall et al. (2008) demonstrated that followers' level of well-being also influenced leaders' display of transformational leadership behaviours, so that followers with higher levels of well-being over time perceived their leader as more transformational than followers with lower levels of well-being. This line of research suggests that transformational leadership is contingent upon followers' personalities, motivation and well-being. The reason for this influence is debatable (Bono et al., 2012): Is it merely that follower characteristics influence how followers perceive their leaders? Or do they in fact influence how leaders behave towards their followers? Further studies are needed to answer these questions.

To conclude, the reason why some leaders engage in transformational leadership while others do not is dependent on factors related to the leaders' personality and affective experiences, their working environment and the organizational context, and the follower. Understanding the influences on leaders' display of transformational leadership may be informative for organizations that strive for transformational leadership among their leaders, as well as for designing leadership training. If leaders are expected to exhibit transformational leadership, it is important to understand how factors related to leaders, context and followers may help or hinder the emergence of these leadership behaviours.

Directions for Future Research

Although our knowledge of the relationship between transformational leadership and employee health and safety has increased, there are still areas that deserve further research attention, and with new findings new questions will continue to arise. One issue that needs to be addressed is the influence that transformational leaders have on employee well-being over time. Most of the evidence of the health benefits of transformational leadership relies on studies that use cross-sectional designs. This is worrying, given that longitudinal studies have failed to find significant relationships (Nielsen & Munir, 2009; Tafvelin et al., 2011), or have even found adverse effects of transformational leadership on employee well-being over time (Nielsen & Daniels, 2016). One reason for these conflicting findings could be that transformational leadership has positive short-term effects on employee well-being but negative long-term effects. Transformational leaders may pressure employees to continuously perform at a high level, preventing them from recovering from pressures at work, which in the long run may lead to ill health (Nielsen and Daniels, 2016). More studies, with stronger, longitudinal designs, are needed to examine possible curvilinear relationships between transformational leadership and employee well-being. It is also of interest to examine more closely how transformational leaders influence employee recovery.

Another area of interest is to further the study of how different subdimensions of transformational leadership are related to employee well-being and safety. The few studies that have examined the subdimensions separately have suggested that there may be important variation in how they affect employee health and safety. In particular, intellectual stimulation has, in some studies, proved to be unrelated to or even detrimental to employee well-being and safety (Corrigan et al., 2002; Hoffmeister et al., 2014). The reasons for this need to be further explored to understand when and why intellectual stimulation may be harmful to employee health and safety. Also, van Knippenberg and Sitkin (2013) recently voiced concern regarding the validity of transformational leadership as a higher-order construct, recommending researchers investigate its subdimensions independently. Accordingly, investigating how the subdimensions of transformational leadership influence employee well-being and safety may be a fruitful avenue for future research.

Research on transformational leadership has also been critiqued for its lack of specification as to how transformational leaders influence their followers and under which conditions transformational leadership emerges and is effective (Pawar, 2003; van Knippenberg & Sitkin, 2013). This is also true when it comes to the influence that transformational leaders have on employee well-being and safety, and further efforts are recommended to study this aspect of the transformational leadership process, including mediators, moderators and its antecedents. Regarding the mediating process by which transformational leaders influence employee well-being, it may be helpful to use the suggested framework, which rests on conservation of resources theory and self-determination theory to stimulate ideas for future studies. It is also of interest to further identify conditions affecting when transformational leadership influences employee well-being and safety. For example, a few studies have examined how factors related to the leader may moderate the influence on employee well-being. In relation to safety, more knowledge is needed of how follower characteristics may strengthen or weaken the impact transformational leadership has. The topic of antecedents of transformational leadership seems to be increasingly studied, and much has been uncovered in only the last few years. The field has moved from mainly considering leadership traits and personality as predictors of transformational leadership to studying complex models incorporating leader characteristics, states and contextual factors, and their interactions. Here, the role of the follower in the emergence of transformational leadership seems to warrant more research attention in order to disentangle whether followers influence leadership behaviours or only their own perception of their leaders (Bono et al., 2012).

Perhaps the use of other research designs such as laboratory experiments will be a way forward to uncover the causal mechanisms linking follower characteristics to a leader's display of transformational leadership. Experimental designs, although low in ecological validity, may also be helpful, to test other aspects of the transformational leadership process as well as the differential effects of the subdimensions of transformational leadership.

Given the positive impact transformational leaders have on employee well-being and safety, training leaders to exhibit transformational leadership behaviours has been recommended as a cost-efficient intervention to improve employee health (Kelloway & Barling, 2010). Intervention studies are therefore needed to demonstrate whether transformational leadership training indeed improves employee health. As suggested by Nielsen and Daniels (2016), it is possible that such training needs to emphasize the health-related aspects within each subdimension of transformational leadership to ensure positive effects not only on performance but also on occupational health. Furthermore, when we train leaders to display transformational leadership behaviours, it is important that we understand the factors influencing training transfer. Although the transfer literature is extensive (e.g., Blume, Ford, Baldwin & Huang, 2010), less is known about how transformational leadership behaviours transfer after training. What factors help or hinder leaders' application of transformational leadership behaviours after training? This type of knowledge is important for the successful implementation of transformational leadership in organizations.

Concluding Remarks

In conclusion, the vast majority of studies suggest that transformational leaders positively impact employee well-being and safety. According to the conservation of resources theory and the self-determination theory, the influence on employee well-being may be explained by the enhancement of personal and social resources and the satisfaction of psychological needs, while safety may be promoted by transformational leaders through a positive influence on the safety climate at work. Factors related to the leader, follower and context then influence the magnitude of this positive effect as well as the emergence of transformational leadership in organizations. On the basis of this literature review, I suggest that promoting transformational leadership in organizations may be one strategy among others to ensure employee occupational health and safety.

References

Abate, G. B., Sewasew, D. T. & Woldemeskel, B. M. (2014). The moderating effect of self-efficacy on the relationships between transformational leadership and subordinates' health. *Innovare Journal of Social Sciences*, 2, 81–5.

Arnold, K. A., Turner, N., Barling, J., Kelloway, E. K. & McKee, M. C. (2007). Transformational leadership and psychological well-being: The mediating role of meaningful work. *Journal of Occupational Health Psychology*, 12(3), 193–203.

Aryee, S., Walumbwa, F. O., Zhou, Q. & Hartnell, C. A. (2012). Transformational leadership, innovative behavior, and task performance: Test of mediation and moderation processes. *Human Performance*, 25(1), 1–25.

Avolio, B. J., Walumbwa, F. O. & Weber, T. J. (2009). Leadership: Current theories, research, and future directions. *Annual Review of Psychology*, 60, 421–49.

Bandura, A. (1977). Self-efficacy: Toward a unifying theory of behavioral change. *Psychological Review*, 84(2), 191–215.

Barling, J., Loughlin, C. & E. K. Kelloway. (2002). Development and test of a model linking safety-specific transformational leadership and occupational safety. *Journal of Applied Psychology*, 87(3), 488–96.

Bass, B. M. (1990). From transactional to transformational leadership: Learning to share the vision. *Organizational Dynamics*, 18, 19–31.

Bass, B. M. & Riggio, R. E. (2006). Transformational Leadership, 2nd edn. Mahwah, NJ: Erlbaum.

Baumeister, R. F. & Leary, M. R. (1995). The need to belong: Desire for interpersonal attachments as a fundamental human motivation. *Psychological Bulletin*, 117, 497–529.

Blume, B. D., Ford, J. K., Baldwin, T. T. & Huang, J. L. (2010). Transfer of training: A meta-analytic review. *Journal of Management*, 36(4), 1065–1105.

Bono, J. E., Foldes, H. J., Vinson, G. & Muros, J. P. (2007). Workplace emotions: The role of supervision and leadership. *Journal of Applied Psychology*, 92, 1357–67.

Bono, J. E., Hooper, A. C. & Yoon, D. J. (2012). Impact of rater personality on transformational and transactional leadership ratings. *Leadership Quarterly*, 23(1), 132–45.

Bono, J. E., & Ilies, R. (2006). Charisma, positive emotions and mood contagion. *Leadership Quarterly*, 17(4), 317–34.

Bono, J. E. & Judge, T. A. (2003). Self-concordance at work: Toward understanding the motivational effects of transformational leaders. *Academy of Management Journal*, 46(5), 554–71.

Bono, J. E. & Judge, T. A. (2004). Personality and transformational and transactional leadership: A meta-analysis. *Journal of Applied Psychology*, 89(5), 901–10.

Burns, J. M. (1978). Leadership. New York: Harper & Row.

Butler, M. C. & Jones, A. P. (1979). Perceived leader behavior, individual characteristics, and injury occurrence in hazardous work environments. *Journal of Applied Psychology*, 64, 299–304.

Byrne, A., Dionisi, A. M., Barling, J., Akers, A., Robertson, J., Lys, R., Wylie, J. & Dupré, K. (2014). The depleted leader: The influence of leaders' diminished psychological resources on leadership behaviors. *Leadership Quarterly*, 25(2), 344–57.

Cavazotte, F., Moreno, V. & Hickmann, M. (2012). Effects of leader intelligence, personality and emotional intelligence on transformational leadership and managerial performance. *Leadership Quarterly*, 23(3), 443–55.

Cherulnik, P. D., Donley, K. A., Wiewel, T. S. R. & Miller, S. R. (2001). Charisma is contagious: The effect of leaders' charisma on observers' affect. *Journal of Applied Social Psychology*, 31(10), 2149–59.

Chuang, A., Judge, T. A. & Liaw, Y. J. (2012). Transformational leadership and customer service: A moderated mediation model of negative affectivity and emotion regulation. *European Journal of Work and Organizational Psychology*, 21(1), 28–56.

Clarke, H. M., Arnold, K. A. & Connelly, C. E. (2015). Improving follower well-being with transformational leadership. In S. Joseph (ed.), Positive Psychology in Practice: Promoting Human Flourishing in Work, Health, Education, and Everyday Life. Hoboken, NJ: Wiley, pp. 341–56.

Clarke, S. (2013). Safety leadership: A meta-analytic review of transformational and transactional leadership styles as antecedents of safety behaviours. *Journal of Occupational and Organizational Psychology*, 86, 22–49.

Clarke, S. & Ward, K. (2006). The role of leader influence tactics and safety climate in engaging employee safety participation. *Risk Analysis*, 26, 1175–86.

Conchie, S. M., Donald, I. J. (2009). The moderating role of safety-specific trust on the relation between safety-specific leadership and safety citizenship behaviors. *Journal of Occupational Health Psychology*, 14, 137–47.

Conchie, S. M., Taylor, P. J. & Donald, I. J. (2012). Promoting safety voice with safety-specific transformational leadership: The mediating role of two dimensions of trust. *Journal of Occupational Health Psychology*, 17, 105–15.

Corrigan, P. W., Diwan, S., Campion, J. & Rashid, F. (2002). Transformational leadership and the mental health team. *Administration and Policy in Mental Health*, 30, 97–108.

De Charms, R. (1968). Personal Causation. New York: Academic Press.

Deci, E. L. & Ryan, R. M. (2000). The 'what' and 'why' of goal pursuits: Human needs and the self-determination of behavior. *Psychological Inquiry*, 11, 227–68.

De Cremer, D. (2006). When authorities influence followers' affect: The interactive effect of procedural justice and transformational leadership. *European Journal of Work and Organizational Psychology*, 15(3), 322–51.

DeGroot, T., Kiker, D. S. & Cross, T. C. (2000). A meta-analysis to review organizational outcomes related to charismatic leadership. *Canadian Journal of Administrative Sciences*, 17, 356–71.

De Hoogh, A. H. & Den Hartog, D. N. (2009). Neuroticism and locus of control as moderators of the relationships of charismatic and autocratic leadership with burnout. *Journal of Applied Psychology*, 94(4), 1058–67.

Deinert, A., Homan, A. C., Boer, D., Voelpel, S. C. & Gutermann, D. (2015). Transformational leadership sub-dimensions and their link to leaders' personality and performance. *Leadership Quarterly*, 26(6), 1095–1120.

Desvaux, G., Devillard-Hoellinger, S. & Baumgarten, P. (2007). Women Matter: Gender Diversity, a Corporate Performance Driver. Paris: McKinsey & Company.

Dóci, E. & Hofmans, J. (2015). Task complexity and transformational leadership: The mediating role of leaders' state core self-evaluations. *Leadership Quarterly*, 26(3), 436–47.

Dubin, R. (1976). Theory building in applied areas. In M. D. Dunnette (ed.), Handbook of Industrial and Organizational Psychology. Chicago, IL: Rand McNally, pp. 17–39.

Dumdum, U. R., Lowe, K. B. & Avolio, B. J. (2002). A meta-analysis of transformational and transactional leadership correlates of effectiveness and satisfaction: An update and extension. In B. J. Avolio and F. J. Yammarino (eds), Transformational and Charismatic Leadership: The Road Ahead. Amsterdam/Oxford: JAI Press, pp. 35–65.

Dvir, T. & Shamir, B. (2003). Follower developmental characteristics as predicting transformational leadership: A longitudinal field study. *Leadership Quarterly*, 14, 327–44.

Eagly, A. H., Johannesen-Schmidt, M. C. & van Engen, M. L. (2003). Transformational, transactional, and laissez-faire leadership styles: A meta-analysis comparing women and men. *Psychological Bulletin*, 129(4), 569–91.

Ehrhart, M. G. & Klein, K. J. (2001). Predicting followers' preferences for charismatic leadership: The influence of follower values and personality. *Leadership Quarterly*, 12(2), 153–79.

Felfe, J. & Schyns, B. (2002). The relationship between employees' occupational self-efficacy and perceived transformational leadership: Replication and extension of recent results. *Current Research in Social Psychology*, 7, 137–62.

Fernet, C., Trépanier, S. G., Austin, S., Gagné, M. & Forest, J. (2015). Transformational leadership and optimal functioning at work: On the mediating role of employees' perceived job characteristics and motivation. *Work & Stress*, 29(1), 11–31.

Franke, F. & Felfe, J. (2011). How does transformational leadership impact employees' psychological strain? Examining differentiated effects and the moderating role of affective organizational commitment. *Leadership*, 7(3), 295–316.

Fuller, J. B., Patterson, C. E. P., Hester, K. & Stringer, D. Y. (1996). A quantitative review of research on charismatic leadership. *Psychological Reports*, 78, 271–87.

Gagné, M. (ed.) (2014). The Oxford Handbook of Work Engagement, Motivation, and Self-Determination Theory. New York: Oxford University Press.

Gilbreath, B. & Benson, P. G. (2004). The contribution of supervisor behaviour to employee psychological well-being. *Work & Stress*, 18(3), 255–66.

Gregersen, S., Vincent-Höper, S. & Nienhaus, A. (2014). The relation between leadership and perceived well-being: What role does occupational self-efficacy play? *Journal of Leadership Studies*, 8(2), 6–18.

Halbesleben, J. R., Neveu, J. P., Paustian-Underdahl, S. C. & Westman, M. (2014). Getting to the 'COR': Understanding the role of resources in conservation of resources theory. *Journal of Management*, 40(5), 1334–64.

Hetland, J., Hetland, H., Bakker, A. B., Demerouti, E., Andreassen, C. S. & Pallesen, S. (2015). Psychological need fulfillment as a mediator of the relationship between transformational leadership and positive job attitudes. *Career Development International*, 20(5), 464–81.

Hobfoll, S. E. (1989). Conservation of resources: A new attempt at conceptualizing stress. *American Psychologist*, 44(3), 513.

Hobfoll, S. E. (2001). The influence of culture, community, and the nested-self in the stress process: Advancing conservation of resources theory. *Applied Psychology*, 50(3), 337–421.

Hobman, E. V., Jackson, C. J., Jimmieson, N. L. & Martin, R. (2011). The effects of transformational leadership behaviours on follower outcomes: An identity-based analysis. *European Journal of Work and Organizational Psychology*, 20(4), 553–80.

Hoffmeister, K., Gibbons, A. M., Johnson, S. K., Cigularov, K. P., Chen, P. Y. & Rosecrance J. C. (2014). The differential effects of transformational leadership facets on employee safety. *Safety Science*, 62, 68–78.

Holstad, T. J., Korek, S., Rigotti, T. & Mohr, G. (2014). The relation between transformational leadership and follower emotional strain: The moderating role of professional ambition. *Leadership*, 10(3), 269–88.

Inness, M., Turner, N., Barling, J. & Stride, C. B. (2010). Transformational leadership and employee safety performance: A within-person, between-jobs design. *Journal of Occupational Health Psychology*, 15, 279–90.

Jin, S., Seo, M. G. & Shapiro, D. L. (2016). Do happy leaders lead better? Affective and attitudinal antecedents of transformational leadership. *Leadership Quarterly*, 27(1), 64–84.

Johnson, A. M., Vernon, P. A., Harris, J. A. & Jang, K. L. (2004). A behavior genetic investigation of the relationship between leadership and personality. *Twin Research*, 7(1), 27–32.

Joseph, D. L., Dhanani, L. Y., Shen, W., McHugh, B. C. & McCord, M. A. (2015). Is a happy leader a good leader? A meta-analytic investigation of leader trait affect and leadership. *Leadership Quarterly*, 4, 557–76.

Judge, T. A. & Bono, J. E. (2000). Five-factor model of personality and transformational leadership. *Journal of Applied Psychology*, 85(5), 751–65.

Judge, T. & Piccolo, R. F. (2004). Transformational and transactional leadership: A meta-analytic test of their relative validity. *Journal of Applied Psychology*, 89(5), 755–68.

Judge, T., Woolf, E. F., Hurst, C. & Livingston, B. (2006). Charismatic and transformational leadership. *Zeitschrift für Arbeits- und Organisationspsychologie*, 50(4), 203–14.

Jung, D., Yammarino, F. J. & Lee, J. K. (2009). Moderating role of subordinates' attitudes on transformational leadership and effectiveness: A multi-cultural and multi-level perspective. *Leadership Quarterly*, 20(4), 586–603.

Kanste, O., Kyngäs, H. & Nikkilä, J. (2007). The relationship between multidimensional leadership and burnout among nursing staff. *Journal of Nursing Management*, 15(7), 731–9.

Kapp, E. A. (2012). The influence of supervisor leadership practices and perceived group safety climate on employee safety performance. *Safety Science*, 50(4), 1119–24.

Kelloway, E. K. & Barling, J. (2010). Leadership development as an intervention in occupational health psychology. *Work & Stress*, 24(3), 260–79.

Kelloway, E. K., Mullen, J. E. & Francis, L. (2006). Injuring your leadership: How passive leadership affects employee safety. *Journal of Occupational Health Psychology*, 11(1), 76–86.

Kelloway, E. K., Turner, N., Barling, J. & Loughlin, C. (2012). Transformational leadership and employee psychological well-being: The mediating role of employee trust in leadership. *Work & Stress*, 26(1), 39–55.

Kovjanic, S., Schuh, S. C., Jonas, K., Quaquebeke, N. V. & van Dick, R. (2012). How do transformational leaders foster positive employee outcomes? A self-determination-based analysis of employees' needs as mediating links. *Journal of Organizational Behavior*, 33(8), 1031–52.

Krishnan, V. (2012). Transformational leadership and personal outcomes: Empowerment as mediator. *Leadership & Organization Development Journal*, 33, 550–63.

Liu, J., Siu, O. L. & Shi, K. (2010). Transformational leadership and employee well-being: The mediating role of trust in the leader and self-efficacy. *Applied Psychology*, 59(3), 454–79.

Lowe, K. B., Kroeck, K. G. & Sivasubramaniam, N. (1996). Effectiveness correlates of transformational and transactional leadership: A meta-analytic review of the MLQ literature. *Leadership Quarterly*, 7(3), 385–425.

McKee, M. C., Driscoll, C., Kelloway, E. K. & Kelley, E. (2011). Exploring linkages among transformational leadership, workplace spirituality and well-being in health care workers. *Journal of Management, Spirituality & Religion*, 8(3), 233–55.

Mullen, J. & Kelloway, K. (2009). Safety leadership: A longitudinal study of the effects of transformational leadership on safety outcomes. *Journal of Occupational and Organizational Psychology*, 82(2), 253–72.

Mullen, J., Kelloway, E. K.,& Teed, M. (2011). Inconsistent style of leadership as a predictor of safety behaviour. *Work and Stress*, 25, 41–54.

Munir, F. & Nielsen, K. (2009). Does self-efficacy mediate the relationship between transformational leadership behaviours and healthcare workers' sleep quality? A longitudinal study. *Journal of Advanced Nursing*, 65(9), 1833–43.

Munir, F., Nielsen, K., Garde, A. H., Albertsen, K. & Carneiro, I. G. (2012). Mediating the effects of work–life conflict between transformational leadership and health-care workers' job satisfaction and psychological wellbeing. *Journal of Nursing Management*, 20(4), 512–21.

Nielsen, K. & Cleal, B. (2011). Under which conditions do middle managers exhibit transformational leadership behaviors? An experience sampling method study on the predictors of transformational leadership behaviors. *Leadership Quarterly*, 22(2), 344–52.

Nielsen, K. & Daniels, K. (2012). Does shared and differentiated transformational leadership predict followers' working conditions and well-being? *Leadership Quarterly*, 23(3), 383–97.

Nielsen, K. & Daniels, K. (2016). The relationship between transformational leadership and follower sickness absence: The role of presenteeism. *Work and Stress*, 30(2), 193–208.

Nielsen, K. & Munir, F. (2009). How do transformational leaders influence followers' affective well-being? Exploring the mediating role of self-efficacy. *Work & Stress*, 23(4), 313–29.

Nielsen, K., Randall, R., Yarker, J. & Brenner, S.-O. (2008). The effects of transformational leadership on followers' perceived work characteristics and psychological well-being: A longitudinal study. *Work & Stress*, 22(1), 16–32.

Nielsen, K., Yarker, J., Brenner, S.-O., Randall, R. & Borg, V. (2008). The importance of transformational leadership style for the well-being of employees working with older people. *Journal of Advanced Nursing*, 63(5), 465–75.
Nielsen, K., Yarker, J., Randall, R. & Munir, F. (2009). The mediating effects of team and self-efficacy on the relationship between transformational leadership, and job satisfaction and psychological well-being in healthcare professionals: A cross-sectional questionnaire survey. *International Journal of Nursing Studies*, 46(9), 1236–44.
Nielsen, M. B., Skogstad, A., Matthiesen, S. B. & Einarsen, S. (2016). The importance of a multidimensional and temporal design in research on leadership and workplace safety. *Leadership Quarterly*, 27(1), 142–55.
Parker, S. K., Axtell, C. M. & Turner, N. (2001). Designing a safer workplace: Importance of job autonomy, communication quality, and supportive supervisors. *Journal of Occupational Health Psychology* 6, 211–28.
Pawar, B. S. (2003). Central conceptual issues in transformational leadership research. *Leadership & Organization Development Journal*, 24(7), 397–406.
Perko, K., Kinnunen, U. & Feldt, T. (2014). Transformational leadership and depressive symptoms among employees: Mediating factors. *Leadership & Organization Development Journal*, 35(4), 286–304.
Perko, K., Kinnunen, U., Tolvanen, A. & Feldt, T. (2015). Investigating occupational well-being and leadership from a person-centred longitudinal approach: Congruence of well-being and perceived leadership. *European Journal of Work and Organizational Psychology*, 25(1), 105–19.
Perreault, D., Cohen, L. R. & Blanchard, C. M. (2016). Fostering transformational leadership among young adults: A basic psychological needs approach. *International Journal of Adolescence and Youth*, 21(3), 341–55.
Ryan, R. M. & Deci, E. L. (2001). On happiness and human potentials: A review of research on hedonic and eudaimonic well-being. *Annual Review of Psychology*, 52, 141–66.
Ryff, C. D. (1995). Psychological well-being in adult life. *Current Directions in Psychological Science*, 4(4), 99–104.
Seltzer, J., Numerof, R. E. & Bass, B. M. (1989). Transformational leadership: Is it a source of more burnout and stress? *Journal of Health and Human Resources Administration*, 12, 174–85.
Sivanathan, N., Arnold, K. A., Turner, N. & Barling, J. (2004). Leading well: Transformational leadership and well-being. In P. A. Linley & S. Joseph (eds.) Positive Psychology in Practice. Hoboken, NJ: Wiley, pp. 241–55.
Skakon, J., Nielsen, K., Borg, V. & Guzman, J. (2010). Are leaders' well-being, behaviours and style associated with the affective well-being of their employees? A systematic review of three decades of research. *Work & Stress*, 24(2), 107–39.
Sonnentag, S. (2015). Dynamics of well-being. *Annual Review of Organizational Psychology and Organizational Behavior*, 2, 261–93.
Sosik, J. J. & Godshalk, V. M. (2000). Leadership styles, mentoring functions received, and job-related stress: A conceptual model and preliminary study. *Journal of Organizational Behavior*, 21(4), 365–90.

Stenling, A. & Tafvelin, S. (2014). Transformational leadership and well-being in sports: The mediating role of need satisfaction. *Journal of Applied Sport Psychology*, 26(2), 182–96.

Stordeur, S., D'hoore, W. & Vandenberghe, C. (2001). Leadership, organizational stress, and emotional exhaustion among hospital nursing staff. *Journal of Advanced Nursing*, 35, 533–42.

Tafvelin, S., Armelius, K. & Westerberg, K. (2011). Toward understanding the direct and indirect effects of transformational leadership on well-being: A longitudinal study. *Journal of Leadership & Organizational Studies*, 18(4), 480–92.

Tafvelin, S., Hyvönen, U. & Westerberg, K. (2014). Transformational leadership in the social work context: The importance of leader continuity and co-worker support. *British Journal of Social Work*, 44(4), 886–904.

Tims, M., Bakker, A. B. & Xanthopoulou, D. (2011). Do transformational leaders enhance their followers' daily work engagement? *Leadership Quarterly*, 22, 121–31.

Van den Broeck, A. (2010). Work motivation: A perspective from the job demands-resources model and the self-determination theory. Doctoral thesis, Katholieke Universiteit Leuven, the Netherlands.

Van den Broeck, A., Vansteenkiste, M., De Witte, H. & Lens, W. (2008). Explaining the relationships between job characteristics, burnout, and engagement: The role of basic psychological need satisfaction. *Work and Stress*, 22(3), 277–94.

van Knippenberg, D. & Sitkin, S. B. (2013). A critical assessment of charismatic–transformational leadership research: Back to the drawing board? *The Academy of Management Annals*, 7(1), 1–60.

Walter, F. & Bruch, H. (2010). Structural impacts on the occurrence and effectiveness of transformational leadership: An empirical study at the organizational level of analysis. *Leadership Quarterly*, 21(5), 765–82.

Walumbwa, F. O., Wang, P., Lawler, J. J. & Shi, K. (2004). The role of collective efficacy in the relations between transformational leadership and work outcomes. *Journal of Occupational and Organizational Psychology*, 77(4), 515–30.

Wang, G., Oh, I.-S., Courtright, S. H. & Colbert, A. E. (2011). Transformational leadership and performance across criteria and levels: A meta-analytic review of 25 years of research. *Group & Organization Management*, 36(2), 223–70.

White, R. W. (1959). Motivation reconsidered: The concept of competence. *Psychological Review*, 66, 297–333.

Wofford, J. C., Whittington, J. L. & Goodwin, V. L. (2001). Follower motive patterns as situational moderators for transformational leadership effectiveness. *Journal of Managerial Issues*, 13, 196–211.

Wright, B. E. & Pandey, S. K. (2010). Transformational leadership in the public sector: Does structure matter? *Journal of Public Administration Research and Theory*, 20(1), 75–89.

Zhang, W., Wang, H. & Pearce, C. L. (2014). Consideration for future consequences as an antecedent of transformational leadership behavior: The moderating effects of perceived dynamic work environment. *Leadership Quarterly*, 25(2), 329–43.

Zhu, W., Avolio, B. J. & Walumbwa, F. O. (2009). Moderating role of follower characteristics with transformational leadership and follower work engagement. *Group & Organization Management*, 34(5), 590–619.

Zohar, D. (2002). The effects of leadership dimensions, safety climate, and assigned priorities on minor injuries in work groups. *Journal of Organizational Behavior*, 23(1), 75–92.

Zwingmann, I., Wegge, J., Wolf, S., Rudolf, M., Schmidt, M. & Richter, P. (2014). Is transformational leadership healthy for employees? A multilevel analysis in 16 nations. *Zeitschrift für Personalforschung/German Journal of Research in Human Resource Management*, 28(1–2), 24–51.

5

Leading to a Respectful Workplace

Annilee M. Game

Introduction

A defining characteristic of the healthy workplace is respectful interpersonal behaviour among co-workers. Respectful workplaces create positive individual outcomes, whereas poor, disrespectful, working relationships impose a direct strain on individuals (Leiter, Laschinger, Day & Oore, 2011). Respect is the perceived worth accorded to one person by another that is communicated through behaviour (Spears, Ellemers & Doosje, 2005; Spears, Ellemers, Doosje & Branscombe, 2006). Little organizational research has directly explored respect. Indirectly, the respect accorded by leaders to followers is integral to conceptualizations of leadership and interactional justice (Rogers & Ashforth, 2014). However, in the context of co-worker relationships, respect is most commonly researched in relation to *workplace incivility*. In particular, (in)civility constitutes an important behavioural means of conveying (lack of) interpersonal respect (Rogers & Ashforth, 2014). Further, a respectful workplace implies the presence of shared norms of interpersonal respect that implicitly prohibit workplace incivility (e.g. interpersonal rudeness) and endorse civil (i.e., courteous and professional) interactions between co-workers (Pearson, Andersson & Porath, 2000).

Unfortunately, incivility is widespread in organizations (Pearson & Porath, 2005) and research consistently links the experience of incivility to negative well-being outcomes (Hershcovis, 2011). In the light of this, the aim of the present chapter is to assess how ethical leadership can contribute towards developing and sustaining respectful workplaces, with a specific focus on managing co-worker incivility. It is acknowledged that leadership plays an important role in shaping respectful follower interactions (e.g. Porath & Pearson, 2013), yet, to date, only a handful of researchers have explored the theoretical and empirical associations between leader behaviours and workplace incivility (e.g. Harold & Holtz, 2015; Lee & Jensen, 2014). Given that incivility constitutes a violation of *moral standards* governing workplace interactions (Pearson et al., 2000), ethical leadership theory and research may be especially relevant to understanding how leaders can curb workplace incivility and encourage respectful behaviours.

Leading to Occupational Health and Safety: How Leadership Behaviours Impact Organizational Safety and Well-Being, First Edition.
Edited by E. Kevin Kelloway, Karina Nielsen and Jennifer K. Dimoff.

There is growing evidence of beneficial individual and organizational outcomes related to ethical leadership (Brown & Mitchell, 2010). However, the role of ethical leadership in supporting respectful workplace behaviours through preventing and managing workplace incivility, and proactively promoting civility, remains (with the notable exception of Taylor & Pattie, 2014) unexplored.

This chapter explores the role of ethical leadership in helping to establish more civil (i.e. respectful) workplaces. It begins with an overview of theory and research on workplace incivility, highlighting first the negative associations between experienced incivility and employee well-being, and second the role of leaders in 'setting the tone' for acceptable behaviours. Next, the literature on ethical leadership is reviewed to assess what is currently known about the nature, processes and effects of the construct, and how this can inform understanding of the management of workplace incivility. Following this, to assist practitioners and organizations in the promotion of more respectful workplaces, the practical implications of ethical leadership theory and research are presented. Finally, directions for future research are explored.

Workplace Incivility

The reasons for the prevalence of uncivil/disrespectful interactions in contemporary organizations are not well understood. It is speculated that increasing globalization, more diverse workforces, advances in communications technology, organizational downsizing, and a trend towards greater informality in wider society and the media, have combined in the twenty-first-century workplace to create a faster-paced, high-pressure work environment in which there is no longer any time for being 'nice' to co-workers (Pearson & Porath, 2005). Workplace incivility is defined as relatively subtle acts of rude, insensitive or discourteous interpersonal behaviour that show disregard for others and violate social norms of respect (Andersson & Pearson, 1999; Pearson, Andersson & Wegner, 2001). Manifestations of incivility are diverse, including but not limited to: checking email or phones during meetings, eye-rolling, omitting to say 'please' or 'thank you' to colleagues, expressing annoyance when a colleague asks a favour, using a condescending tone, unprofessional language, ignoring colleagues' requests, terse or 'flaming' email responses, overt impatience with or disinterest in others' opinions, and giving others 'the silent treatment' (Andersson & Pearson, 1999; Cortina, Magley, Williams & Langhout, 2001; Pearson et al., 2000; Pearson et al., 2001; Pearson & Porath, 2005; Porath & Pearson, 2010).

Incivility is conceptualized as a subset of wider workplace deviance behaviours (see Robinson & Bennett, 1995), overlapping with yet distinct from more severe forms of interpersonal mistreatment such as sexual harassment and interpersonal aggression (Pearson et al., 2001). In particular, in an inductive study of business managers and legal and medical professionals, Pearson et al. (2001) demonstrated that, unlike sexual harassment and aggression, incivility is distinguished by *low intensity* and *ambiguous intent*. Low intensity characterizes typically verbal, passive and indirect behaviours (Pearson & Porath, 2005) that have a lesser negative emotional 'charge' than more intense interpersonal aggression and sexual harassment (Pearson et al. 2001). Additionally, the motivations for uncivil behaviours are viewed as ambiguous since it is often unclear whether the instigator intended to harm the target or was merely acting thoughtlessly (Pearson & Porath, 2005).

As a consequence of the ambiguity and low intensity of workplace incivility, incidents are often unreported by employees, and they are difficult for organizations to detect (Pearson & Porath, 2005). However, incivility is rarely limited to a single incident between an instigator and a target: typically targets will seek to retaliate against the instigator, often covertly (Pearson & Porath, 2005). Evidence suggests that as many as 94 per cent of employees who have experienced incivility from colleagues are likely to reciprocate in some way (Porath & Pearson, 2010). Consequently, spirals of incivility may be established which can escalate and develop into more aggressive, or even violent, interpersonal behaviours (Andersson & Pearson, 1999). Further, if targets are unable to reciprocate an act of incivility directly – perhaps because of physical distance or perceived status differences between the target and the instigator – the target may respond with displaced uncivil behaviours that target a more accessible colleague (Andersson & Pearson, 1999; Pearson et al., 2001). Additionally, in line with notions of retributive justice, employees who observe incivility perpetrated against a co-worker are likely to punish instigators with uncivil behaviours (Reich & Hershcovis, 2015). Thus, workplace incivility is a dynamic and complex social phenomenon that can spread over time throughout work units and organizations, establishing norms of disrespect (Pearson et al., 2000).

A wealth of empirical evidence indicates that workplace incivility is an especially pervasive form of interpersonal misconduct (Cortina, 2008), occurring across industries (Porath & Pearson, 2013) and cultures (Lim & Lee, 2011). Based on extensive surveys in the US and Canada over 14 years, Porath and Pearson (2013) concluded that 98% of employees experienced incivility at some point in their work lives, and as many as half were treated with disrespect on a weekly basis. Other researchers, focusing on specific occupations, have found a similarly high incidence. For example, 85% of nurses (Lewis & Malecha, 2011), 75% of university employees (Cortina & Magly, 2009) and 71% of court employees (Cortina et al., 2001) reported having experienced uncivil interactions at work in previous years. While most incivility research has focused on the experiences of targets rather than instigators, Pearson and Porath (2005) found that 'almost everyone', at least occasionally, behaves disrespectfully at work.

Outcomes of Incivility

Workplace incivility is of particular concern given growing evidence that experiencing incivility is related to negative job- and health-related outcomes for individuals. For example, experienced incivility has been associated with reduced productivity, work engagement, commitment, job and co-worker satisfaction, and increased intention to leave the organization (Cortina et al., 2001; Lim & Cortina, 2005; Lim & Lee; 2011; Pearson et al., 2001; Porath & Pearson, 2013). In terms of health and well-being, incivility has been theorized as a chronic low-level stressor that is akin to daily hassles (Lazarus & Folkman, 1984; Lim & Lee, 2011). Consequences include higher levels of psychological distress, negative affect, depression, cynicism and poorer physical health (Cortina et al., 2001; Lim & Lee, 2011; Nicholson & Griffin, 2015; Pearson et al. 2001; Pearson & Porath, 2005). Additionally, 'spillover' effects have been found in that negative emotions evoked in response to uncivil interactions at work increase self-reported work-to-family conflict (Lim & Lee, 2011). Preliminary evidence also suggests that merely being a witness to incivility at work is harmful, negatively affecting observers' job satisfaction and commitment, and contributing to burnout and turnover (Miner-Rubino & Cortina, 2007).

Much of the initial research on the effects of workplace incivility investigated between-person effects using cross-sectional research designs. There are two key limitations of this approach. First, the data are retrospective and may be subject to recall biases or memory problems, and second, the measured effects may reflect only longer-term consequences of accumulated experiences (Zhou, Yan, Che & Meier, 2015). More recently, therefore, researchers have begun to explore day-level experiences of, and reactions to, incivility. Zhou et al. (2015) found that daily variation in the experience of workplace incivility positively predicted negative affect at the end of the working day. Similarly, in a 4-week study, Beattie and Griffin (2014) reported that security employees had higher stress levels on days when they experienced more incivility. Moreover, drawing on the Effort-Recovery Model (Meijman & Mulder, 1998), Nicholson and Griffin (2015) found that the experience of day-level incivility by employees in the legal industry was negatively related to situational well-being and the ability to detach psychologically after work. Failure to detach rendered employees unable to replace depleted psychological resources; thus, workplace incivility inhibited next-day recovery.

Taken together, the evidence reviewed suggests that disrespectful workplaces pose risks to employee health and well-being in both the short and longer terms. It is in the interests of organizations to implement measures that curb incivility and promote civility. However, if possible interventions are to be facilitated, a better understanding of the antecedents of incivility is required. Incivility research has so far focused almost exclusively on the nature and outcomes of disrespectful behaviours (Harold & Holtz, 2015). Nonetheless, a consensus appears to be emerging among incivility scholars that 'leaders hold the key' (Pearson et al., 2001, p. 1414) to addressing negative workplace interactions (e.g. Cortina, 2008; Porath & Pearson, 2010, 2013). As Leiter et al. (2011, p. 1259) noted, 'incivility arises not from the failings of individuals, but from patterns of social interaction implicitly sanctioned by the management environment.' The next section, therefore, considers what is known to date about the role of leadership in workplace incivility.

Leadership and Incivility

Leaders are believed to play a pivotal role in workplace incivility because their actions (or inaction) set the tone by sending cues to employees about what kinds of interpersonal behaviours are considered acceptable in the work setting

(Andersson & Pearson, 1999; Cortina, 2008). Broadly supporting this view, an extensive, multi-method study by Pearson et al. (2001) found that, in organizations where incivility was either directly experienced or witnessed, employees reported that their leaders either ignored the problem, or appeared implicitly to tolerate it through being unable or unwilling to take action. When repeat incivility offenders are frequently seen to get away with mistreating their colleagues without repercussions (Pearson & Porath, 2005), it is theorized that this establishes a climate that facilitates organization-wide incivility (Pearson et al., 2001).

Despite these general insights about the role of leadership in incivility, there is at present a dearth of empirical research investigating how specific leadership styles either contribute to, or curb, workplace incivility. In an attempt to address this gap, Harold and Holtz (2015) proposed that incivility may be especially likely to proliferate in organizations or work units in which leaders are perceived as having a passive leadership style. Passive leadership is characterized by a combination of passive management-by-exception and *laissez-faire* leadership, which together result in a reluctance to lead proactively (Harold & Holtz, 2015). In two studies, Harold and Holtz (2015) found that passive leadership was directly and positively related to the incidence of employee behavioural (i.e. enacted) incivility, as evaluated by their co-workers and supervisors. An indirect effect was also found such that employees behaved with greater incivility when they *experienced* higher levels of co-worker incivility. The indirect effect was stronger the more passive the leader. This suggests that, consistent with Andersson and Pearson's (1999) Spiral Framework, passive leaders' tendency to overlook or ignore incivility sends inappropriate signals about expected norms of behaviour; consequently when individuals experience greater incivility from their co-workers they reciprocate in kind, so contributing to the 'spread' of incivility (Harold & Holtz, 2015).

A further study by Lee and Jensen (2014) examined the incidence of observed incivility in relation to passive leadership and active constructive leadership. Active constructive leadership combines elements of transformational and transactional leadership styles and, together with passive leadership, forms part of the full-range leadership model (e.g. Bass & Avolio, 1994; Judge & Piccolo, 2004). In line with Harold and Holtz (2015), Lee and Jensen (2014) found a direct association between passive leadership and the incidence of witnessed incivility. In addition, there was an indirect relationship with observed incivility, for both passive and active constructive leadership, which operated via fairness perceptions. Specifically, active constructive leadership was associated with reduced incivility through the establishment of positive perceptions of fair treatment in the leader–employee dyad. Conversely, passive leadership was associated with negative perceptions of fair treatment by the leader and, in turn, higher levels of incivility (Lee & Jensen, 2014). The authors suggested that social exchange mechanisms (Blau, 1964) underlie these findings. In particular, because leaders are perceived as personifying or representing the wider organization, when employees are treated with dignity and respect by leaders they feel valued and respected by the organization as a whole and reciprocate by treating others at work with respect (Lee & Jensen, 2014; Rogers & Ashforth, 2014).

The evidence reviewed, though scant, supports the view that certain leader behaviours may shape employees' perceptions of behavioural norms, which in turn affect levels of enacted and/or observed incivility. While this research is useful in building our understanding of how incivility is developed and sustained in organizations, it does not fully explain how leaders can promote respectful workplaces. The absence of uncivil behaviour, while preferable to widespread incivility, does not necessarily imply a positive and respectful working environment. It is contended that a respectful workplace additionally requires the presence of employee civility – that is, proactively 'treating others with dignity, acting with regard to others' feelings and preserving the social norms for mutual respect' (Andersson & Pearson, 1999, p. 454).

A further limitation of the existing research is that it does not fully take into account the (un)ethical nature of (in)civility and the implications of this for leading to a respectful workplace. According to Andersson and Pearson (1999), all workplaces have shared moral understandings, or implicit moral codes, which serve to guide co-worker interactions and facilitate cooperative working. The norms may vary between workplaces depending on organizational culture, and practices connected to formal/informal policies and procedures (Pearson et al., 2000). Fundamentally, however, shared norms for civility typically consist of basic moral standards (e.g. 'treat others as you would wish to be treated') that are the foundation for mutual respect (Pearson et al., 2000). Incivility constitutes a violation of this mutual respect norm (Anderson & Pearson, 1999; Pearson et al., 2001).

Given the intrinsically moral underpinnings of incivility and its inverse, civility (Pearson et al., 2001), it may be especially pertinent for incivility scholars to draw upon ethical leadership theory and research (e.g. Brown, Treviño & Harrison, 2005). Other leadership theories incorporate elements of ethical leader behaviours, especially transformational leadership (e.g. Bass & Avolio, 1994), authentic leadership (e.g. Avolio & Gardner, 2005) and spiritual leadership (e.g. Fry, 2003). Empirical evidence indicates that ethical leadership overlaps with, yet is distinct from, these other leadership theories (Brown & Treviño, 2006; Brown et al., 2005). In particular, only ethical leadership focuses on proactively influencing employee conduct (Brown & Treviño, 2006). Therefore, ethical leadership may better explain not only how leaders can prevent incivility but also how they can promote a more respectful, civil workplace. Below, the ethical leadership construct, theory and research are examined and the implications for managing workplace incivility are considered.

Ethical Leadership

The widely accepted definition of ethical leadership is 'the demonstration of normatively appropriate conduct through personal actions and interpersonal relationships, and the promotion of such conduct to followers through two-way communication, reinforcement and decision-making' (Brown et al., 2005, p. 120). This definition highlights three core components of ethical leader behaviour: ethical demonstration, promotion and decision-making. First, ethical leaders are role models demonstrating to followers those behaviours that are morally appropriate to a particular organizational context (Brown et al., 2005). Second, the leader facilitates and actively manages employee ethical conduct by directly engaging employees in ethical discussions, giving a voice to employees on ethical issues, and using reward and punishment to reinforce desired ethical conduct (Brown et al., 2005). Third, ethical leaders make principled decisions and consider the consequences of their actions for others (Brown et al., 2005).

On the basis of this definition and of inductive empirical work by Treviño, Brown and Hartman (2003), the ethical leader is further described as a *moral person* and a *moral manager* (Brown & Treviño, 2006). As a moral person the leader is seen to consistently enact moral virtues, or character traits, that convey integrity, a commitment to fair, honest and trustworthy interactions, and concern and respect for others (Brown & Mitchell, 2010). As a moral manager, the leader proactively influences employee ethical conduct through visibly role-modelling desired behaviours, communicating values, and using reward systems to hold employees accountable for their conduct (Brown & Treviño, 2006).

In order to be perceived by followers as an ethical leader, an authority figure must be *both* a moral person and a moral manager. Treviño et al. (2003) asserted that leaders who act the role of a moral manager, but are not themselves strong moral persons, may be perceived as hypocrites. Skubbin and Herzog (2016) go further to argue that, without deeply held inner moral convictions – that is, an internalized moral identity – when leaders encounter critical ethical decisions or dilemmas they are likely neither to act ethically themselves nor to act as appropriate role models for others. Conversely, possessing a moral character that is not visibly enacted (e.g. keeping silent on ethical matters) may result in a leader being seen as not genuinely caring about ethics (Brown & Mitchell, 2010).

The main theoretical foundation of ethical leadership is social learning theory (Bandura, 1977, 1986). According to social learning theory, people learn appropriate behaviours by attending to, observing and imitating the behaviours of figures who are attractive and credible role models. Ethical leaders are likely to be viewed as attractive and credible role models because, in part, of their legitimate power and status within the organization or work unit (Bandura, 1986; Brown & Treviño, 2006). Additionally, the credibility of ethical leaders is enhanced by their reliability, respectful and considerate treatment of others, and 'practising what they preach' (Brown & Mitchell, 2010). Reinforcement by ethical leaders is an important component of effective role modelling because punishment and reward help to focus followers' attention on what is deemed ethically appropriate (Brown & Treviño, 2006). Finally, social learning theory suggests a great deal of learning occurs vicariously; thus employees also learn appropriate conduct through observing how their colleagues are either rewarded or punished for (un)ethical behaviours (Brown & Treviño, 2006).

Ethical leadership theory helps to elaborate the hitherto poorly understood role of leaders in shaping employee (in)civility. In particular, social learning theory suggests that ethical leaders may reduce employee incivility by directly confronting and appropriately punishing behaviours that transgress norms of interpersonal respect. Further, to the extent that leaders – through their own behaviour – proactively demonstrate (as moral persons), and promote and reinforce (as moral managers), civility and respect at work, employees should infer these as the dominant norms and expectations for their own interpersonal conduct.

Antecedents of Ethical Leadership

From the preceding discussion it is evident that in order to serve as an effective ethical role model and influence employee conduct towards greater civility, a leader must first be perceived by their followers as being ethical. However, little is yet known about what makes employees more likely to perceive their leaders as ethical (Brown & Mitchell, 2010). While Brown and Treviño (2006) theorized a range of situational (e.g. ethical role models) and individual (e.g. personality) factors that could be important, researchers are only beginning to test these propositions empirically. For example, studies have shown that the personality traits of agreeableness and conscientiousness are positively related to follower ratings of leader ethicality (e.g. Kalshoven, Den Hartog & De Hoogh, 2011; Walumbwa & Schaubroeck, 2009). Agreeableness indicates a tendency towards being trusting, altruistic and cooperative while conscientiousness is associated with being dependable and responsible, all of which are implicit in the 'moral person' aspect of ethical leadership (Brown & Treviño, 2006; Treviño et al, 2003). Other personality-based research has found a negative association between leader Machiavellianism and ethical leadership perceptions (Den Hartog & Belschak, 2012) and a positive link with leader moral identity (Mayer, Aquino, Greenbaum & Kuenzi, 2012).

Differences in ethical reasoning capacity are also relevant antecedents. Jordan, Brown and Treviño (2013) investigated leaders' cognitive moral development (CMD) (Kohlberg, 1969), that is, independence and sophistication of moral reasoning when making ethical judgements and decisions. Jordan and colleagues found that followers' perception of their leaders as ethical was positively related to higher levels of leader CMD. Moreover, perceptions of ethicality were greatest when leaders' and followers' CMD diverged (with followers' CMD being lower). It was concluded, in line with social learning theory, that leaders visible use of more advanced ethical reasoning helps them stand out as salient, credible and attractive role models.

Going beyond research on individual differences, Brown and Treviño (2014) focused on situational antecedents to investigate whether follower perceptions of leader ethicality are influenced by the presence of an ethical role model in the leaders' early life or career. They found that, compared with role models in childhood or top management role models, leaders who reported having had an ethical role model/mentor during their career were most likely to be rated as ethical by their current followers. It is posited, again consistent with social learning theory, that (future) leaders learn from ethical career mentors by observing how they demonstrate and promote ethical standards of behaviour (Brown & Treviño, 2014).

In sum, the evidence suggests that leaders' ability to influence employee civility may depend crucially on whether the leader (despite best efforts and training) is actually perceived by employees as an ethical leader and therefore as a credible role model (Brown & Treviño, 2006). Leaders possessing particular personality traits, ethical decision-making competencies, and a past history of being supported by an ethical role model, may be more likely to be perceived as credible ethical role models and, in turn, be more effective in demonstrating, reinforcing and shaping more respectful workplace behaviours.

Outcomes of Ethical Leadership

While several studies have sought to establish the consequences of ethical leadership at both the employee and the work unit or organization level, little research has directly investigated the link between ethical leadership and the incidence of workplace incivility. Ethical leadership is commonly measured by follower ratings of perceived ethical leadership behaviours, using a 10-item, single-dimension scale, the Ethical Leadership Scale (ELS) developed and validated by Brown et al. (2005), or similar multi-dimensional scales, for example Ethical Leadership at Work (ELW) (Kalshoven, Den Hartog & De Hoogh, 2011). Positive associations have been found between perceived ethical leadership and various job-related outcomes, including employee job performance (e.g. Bouckenooghe, Zafa & Raja, 2015; Liu, Kwan, Fu & Mao, 2013; Walumbwa et al., 2011), firm-level performance (Shin, Sung, Choi & Ki, 2015), affective commitment and reduced turnover intentions (Demirtas & Akdogan, 2015). Ethical leadership has also been associated with employee well-being (Kalshoven & Boon, 2012), increased work engagement and reduced emotional exhaustion (Chugtai, Byrne & Flood, 2015) and even, via work–family spillover effects, increased family satisfaction of employees' spouses (Liao, Liu, Kwan & Li, 2015).

Only one study, to date, has focused specifically on the relationship between follower perceptions of ethical leadership and workplace incivility. Taylor and Pattie (2014) found that, in a sample of US school employees (i.e., teachers and other staff), perceptions of their principal's ethical leadership were negatively related to the frequency with which employees had engaged in self-reported incivility during the previous year. Other research indirectly supports a link between ethical leadership and workplace civility. For example, studies have shown that ethical leadership is positively related to pro-social organizational citizenship behaviours (OCBs) (e.g. Kalshoven et al., 2011; Mayer, Kuenzi, Greenbaum, Bardes & Salvador, 2009; Resick, Hargis, Shao & Dust, 2013). Like workplace civility, pro-social OCBs include interpersonally focused helping such as sharing information and going out of one's way to assist colleagues (see Podsakoff, MacKenzie, Paine & Bachrach, 2000). Conversely, follower-rated ethical leadership has been negatively related to supervisor-rated employee misconduct or deviance such as employee theft, property damage and rule breaking (e.g. Avey, Palanski & Walumbwa, 2011; Mayer, Kuenzi and Greenbaum, 2010). While the latter outcomes constitute more extreme forms of workplace deviance than incivility (Andersson & Pearson, 1999), this research nonetheless serves to underscore the significance of perceiving one's leader as ethical for shaping a respectful workplace.

Ethical Leadership Processes

Knowledge is scarce concerning specific processes by which ethical leadership influences workplace (in)civility, yet some insight can be gained by examining how ethical leadership influences follower (un)ethical conduct and OCBs. As the ethical leadership field begins to mature, a few studies have sought to build upon the social learning theoretical foundation of ethical leadership by identifying and empirically testing specific psychological mechanisms, or mediators, in the relationship between ethical leadership and employee ethical conduct. Some researchers have posited unit-level constructs (e.g. culture and climate), while others have investigated the mediating role of individual-level social cognitions. At the unit level, Mayer et al. (2010, p. 8) proposed that 'by role modeling appropriate behavior, ethical leaders help to create a climate in which doing the right thing is valued.' In a study of 300 work units across multiple organizations in the US, they found support for the mediating role of ethical climate in the relationship between ethical leadership and supervisor-rated employee misconduct.

Similarly, Schaubroeck et al. (2012) argued that the role-modelling and reinforcement behaviours associated with ethical leadership serve as primary 'embedding mechanisms' through which work unit cultural values are transmitted. Additionally, leaders may tell stories of how past employees' ethical conduct was rewarded or unethical conduct punished, thereby creating a secondary cultural embedding mechanism (Schaubroeck et al., 2012). Empirically, the researchers found that, for a sample of US army personnel, ethical leaders influenced followers' ethical cognitions and behaviours directly, and also indirectly through the cascading of an ethical culture.

At the individual level, Resick et al. (2013) proposed that leaders not only facilitate employee ethical conduct through social learning processes, they also engage in proactive *sensemaking* processes involving ethical narratives that help individuals make sense of expectations regarding ethical conduct and the treatment of others. Providing employees with such sensemaking 'anchors' helps individuals form their own ethical judgements about what constitutes fair and ethically appropriate behaviour. The propositions were tested in a sample of 190 supervisor–employee dyads. Findings suggested that employees with ethical leaders were more likely to judge workplace deviance as morally inequitable and OCBs as morally equitable. These judgements mediated the relationship between ethical leadership and employee engagement in both antisocial conduct and pro-social behaviour.

It is noteworthy that while most ethical leadership research has put social learning theory at its core, some researchers contend that social exchange theory (Blau, 1964) offers a stronger explanation of how ethical leadership shapes employee conduct, particularly in relation to OCBs (e.g. Kalshoven, Den Hartog & De Hoogh, 2013). Consistent with the earlier discussion of active constructive leadership (Lee & Jensen, 2014), the social exchange perspective suggests that when followers perceive that their leaders are treating them with fairness, integrity, trustworthiness and respect they feel an obligation to reciprocate with more pro-social behaviour (Newman, Kiazad, Miao & Cooper, 2014). Drawing on this framework, Newman and colleagues found that ethical leadership led to the development of trust, which in turn promoted reciprocal employee discretionary behaviours, directed towards co-workers and the organization.

Together, this theory and research extend our understanding of the processes by which ethical leadership may help to curb employee incivility and promote civility. Through role modelling and positive reinforcement of respectful behaviours, and by facilitating follower sensemaking and perceptions of leader fairness, ethical leaders may establish a climate (or culture) of interpersonal respect (cf. Mayer et al., 2010; Resick et al., 2013; Shaubroeck et al., 2012). Social exchange mechanisms, in turn, may create a sense of obligation among followers to reciprocate their leaders' respectful behaviours (cf. Newman et al., 2014), hence influencing a reduction in incivility and employee engagement in more positive behaviours towards co-workers.

Boundary Conditions of Ethical Leadership

In the literature reviewed so far, it is assumed that the effects of ethical leadership are uniform across individuals and work units, and that the role of ethical leadership in managing incivility should therefore be standard for all employees. Little research has explored whether ethical leadership is more or less effective under certain conditions (Avey et al., 2011). Yet it seems logical to assume that not all individuals or groups are equally receptive to ethical leaders' influence attempts. Supporting this position, Ogunfowora (2014) conducted a unit-level study in which she examined the moderating role of 'leader role modeling strength', that is, the degree of group consensus that a leader is ethical. Results indicated that the positive relationship between ethical leadership and employee engagement in unit-level OCBs is strongest in work units that share a higher level of consensus that the leader is an ethical role model.

Other studies have focused on individual-level differences as moderators. Avey et al. (2011) found that follower self-esteem moderated the relationship between ethical leadership and both OCB and deviant behaviours in such a way that the relationship was strongest for low self-esteem employees. The authors attributed the findings to the behavioural plasticity hypothesis (Brockner, 1988), which suggests that employees with low self-esteem are more influenced by contextual cues (i.e., ethical leadership) as they seek to validate their sense of self-worth. Similarly, Taylor and Pattie (2014) found that follower personality variables – conscientiousness and core self-evaluation (CSE) – were moderators of the relationship between ethical leadership and workplace incivility. In particular, the relationship was strongest for followers with lower conscientiousness and CSE. Taylor and Pattie (2014) argued that these individuals had a tendency towards lower integrity and greater likelihood of engaging in incivility; hence they had greater need of, and were more receptive to, the leader's ethical guidance. In contrast, more conscientious, high-CSE employees were more independent and confident of 'doing the right thing' so, for them, the effects of ethical leadership were weaker.

Further insight into the boundary conditions of the effects of ethical leadership is provided by Stouten, van Dijke, Mayer, de Cremer and Euwema (2013). They proposed and tested the notion that, since engaging in workplace deviance and OCBs are very different types of behaviour, ethical leadership may in fact influence follower conduct in different ways. In support, it was found that while there is an expected negative, linear relationship between ethical leadership and deviance (i.e., more ethical leadership results in less employee deviance), the relationship between ethical leadership and OCBs is curvilinear and depends on followers' perception of 'moral reproach'. Specifically, lower levels of ethical leadership support OCBs, but as ethical leadership increases employees are less likely to engage in OCBs because they perceive highly ethical leaders as looking down upon their own morality and this reduces the motivation to engage in discretionary workplace behaviours.

In the light of the above, the effectiveness of ethical leadership in creating more respectful workplaces is unlikely to be a one-size-fits-all solution. Rather, successfully shaping employee (in)civility may also depend on understanding a range of contextual variables, including the degree of group consensus regarding leader ethicality, follower personality, and followers' perceptions of how their leader perceives *them*.

Theoretical and Practical Implications

From the theory and evidence reviewed it is clear that the study of ethical leadership can make important contributions towards both understanding and managing workplace incivility. The ethical leadership literature elaborates the processes by which leaders appear to 'set the tone' or climate (Andersson & Pearson, 1999; Pearson et al., 2001) for (dis)respectful workplace behaviours. Social learning theory, underpinning ethical leadership, explains how leaders first and foremost serve as role models whose conduct is observed and imitated by their employees both directly and vicariously (Brown et al., 2005). When leaders demonstrate respect for others, it is anticipated that followers learn respect norms as the basis for their own conduct. Moreover, empirical evidence supports the view that through social learning processes, and by facilitating follower sensemaking, ethical leaders establish a climate, or culture, which serves to reduce employee negative behaviours and promote positive interactions with others and their organizations (Mayer et al., 2010; Resick et al., 2013; Shaubroeck et al., 2012). Hence, ethical leadership may be a valuable tool for establishing a work environment that is characterized by mutual interpersonal respect.

The integration of ethical leadership theory and research with workplace incivility literature can also help to elucidate the role of leaders in the spiral effect (Andersson & Pearson, 1999) by which workplace incivility can spread throughout a work unit. A key source of the spread is thought to be failure by leaders to acknowledge or respond to incivility, allowing it space to fester and grow (Pearson & Porath, 2005). In contrast, ethical leaders – as moral managers – not only demonstrate but clearly communicate expected standards of employee conduct, and they use organizational reward systems to proactively reward high standards of conduct and punish transgression of the established norms (Brown & Treviño, 2006). This suggests that ethical leadership may be effective in employee behavioural management initiatives to both disrupt and reverse the so-called spiral effect.

Overall, ethical leadership may be valuable in both the short and long terms for developing and sustaining more respectful workplaces. In the short term, ethical leaders are able to proactively confront employee incivility head on, and quickly establish expectations of acceptable interpersonal behaviour through role modelling, communication and reinforcement. In the longer term, the consistency and reliability of ethical leaders' words and deeds (Brown et al., 2005) – promoting open, honest and respectful dealings with others – may contribute towards a more durable culture of interpersonal respect that cascades throughout the organization or work unit (cf. Schaubroeck et al., 2012). It should be noted, however, that promoting civility (in contrast to preventing incivility) may require more careful attention to how 'moral' the leader is perceived to be. Efforts to enhance civility and respect may be detrimental if followers view the leader as 'morally reproaching' them (cf. Stouten et al., 2013); hence leaders need to take steps to avoid this possibility (e.g. via 360-degree appraisal, informal discussions and frank self-appraisal).

If the potential benefits of ethical leadership for workplace respectfulness are to be realized, organizational investment in identifying and developing ethical leaders is needed. The preceding discussion points to additional practical implications for organizations wishing to enhance workplace respect through the selection and training of ethical leaders. With regard to selection, the review revealed an important caveat to the effectiveness of ethical leadership in influencing employee behaviour: the leader must be perceived by followers as a strong and authentic role model (e.g. Ogunfowora, 2014). Leaders who espouse values, and manage others, according to a code of behaviour that conflicts with their own internal moral identity or personality traits may be less likely to be perceived as ethical role models despite their best efforts (see Den Hartog & Belschak, 2012; Skubbin & Herzog, 2016). Moreover, the experience of personal inauthenticity, caused by dissonance between internally felt and organizationally expected identities, is a source of stress (Ashforth & Humphrey, 1993; Wharton & Erikson, 1997). Consequently, organizations could consider developing leader selection processes to enable the identification of traits such as Machiavellianism that could pose challenges to an individual's credibility and effectiveness as an ethical leader (Den Hartog & Belschak, 2012). Additionally, it may be useful, based on the research and recommendations of Brown and Treviño (2014), to establish whether leadership candidates have themselves experienced an ethical role model or mentor, since this is related to followers' perceptions of leaders' ethicality. Information about past experiences could be obtained during interviews (Brown & Treviño, 2014), which would also allow more in-depth exploration of how the mentor or role model affected the candidates' values and behaviours towards others in the workplace.

Training and developing ethical leaders to promote respectful workplaces should focus on teaching the importance of being seen as a genuine role model for, and vocal champion of, desired behaviours such as courtesy and mutual respect. The evidence reviewed indicated that a key aspect of followers' ethical leader perceptions is leaders' level of cognitive moral development (Jordan et al., 2013). Jordan et al. suggest that higher levels of CMD can be effectively taught. This involves an intensive programme lasting between 4 and 12 weeks, facilitated by a professional trainer. Participants learn through discussion with peers, and they are challenged by the facilitator to adopt increasingly principled ways of thinking about ethical problems and dilemmas. Training needs also to instruct leaders more specifically in how to detect incivility, and to assist them in successfully managing and reinforcing employee respectful behaviour using organizational reward systems. Role play could be a useful tool to achieve this. In the light of evidence suggesting that not all employees may need or benefit from ethical leadership to the same degree (e.g. Taylor & Pattie, 2014), training should assist leaders to identify those followers who perhaps by virtue of having lower self-esteem, or a greater tendency towards incivility, are more likely to benefit from ethical leadership (Avey et al., 2011). Finally, given the importance of prior role models in the development of ethical leadership (e.g. Brown & Treviño, 2014), it is important, over time, to establish a coaching or mentoring system through which existing and future leaders within the organization can continually observe and learn how to lead to a respectful workplace.

Directions for Future Research

The practical suggestions included above are necessarily tentative until further research has been conducted. Both the ethical leadership and workplace incivility literatures are relatively young and have only recently begun to move on from describing constructs and exploring basic associations. Much remains to be done if we are to usefully extend knowledge at the interface of the two domains. The discussion of ethical leadership theory and research presented here has been purposely selective, focusing on existing scholarship that is most relevant to understanding workplace incivility and civility. The review has highlighted that, although ethical leadership researchers have investigated more severe forms of workplace deviance on the one hand, and broader positive interpersonal and organizational OCBs on the other, little research has yet focused directly on the connections between ethical leadership and workplace (in)civility. Given the prevalence and significant costs for individuals and organizations of incivility, this is an important research gap to fill.

Future research should seek to confirm whether the mediating and moderating relationships found between ethical leadership and other types of employee positive and negative conduct can be replicated and extended to workplace civility and incivility. For example, does ethical leadership influence (in)civility through the establishment of an ethical climate or culture of mutual respect? What other psychological mechanisms might be important for explaining how ethical leadership shapes employee respectful behaviours? Does perceived leader role-modelling strength, or other individual differences (e.g. locus of control) among leaders, moderate such a link (see Brown & Treviño, 2006)? Which follower individual differences (e.g. moral identity, moral disengagement) and social cognitions (e.g. attributions, ethical judgements) are important in determining the boundary conditions under which leaders' civility influence attempts are more or less effective? Finally, the role of situational or contextual factors (e.g. industry characteristics, organizational HRM policies and the presence of formal codes of conduct for civility) as potential moderators should also be explored. The answers to such questions will alleviate the dearth of research in these areas of ethical leadership more generally, as was noted in the review of the literature.

Conclusion

The aim of this chapter is to bring together the literatures on workplace incivility and ethical leadership in order to enhance our understanding of how leadership can support more respectful workplaces. From the review, it is clear that the costs to employee health and well-being of unchecked workplace incivility are high. While it has long been recognized that leadership probably plays a key role in managing workplace incivility, very little previous research has investigated this connection. The theory and research presented here suggest that, in line with well-established principles of social learning, ethical leaders may be uniquely equipped to help to create a working environment of mutual respect by modelling, communicating and reinforcing appropriate workplace behaviours. It is hoped that this review will inspire researchers to continue the promising work that is beginning to emerge on this topic.

References

Andersson, L. M. & Pearson, C. M. (1999). Tit for tat? The spiraling effect of incivility in the workplace. *Academy of Management Review*, 24, 452–71.

Ashforth, B. E. & Humphrey, R. H. (1993). Emotional labor in service roles: The influence of identity. *Academy of Management Review*, 18, 88–115.

Avey, J. B., Palanski, M. E. & Walumbwa, F. O. (2011). When leadership goes unnoticed: The moderating role of follower self-esteem on the relationship between ethical leadership and follower behavior. *Journal of Business Ethics*, 98(4), 573–82.

Avolio, B. J. & Gardner, W. L. (2005). Authentic leadership development: Getting to the root of positive forms of leadership. *Leadership Quarterly*, 16, 315–38.

Bandura, A. (1977). *Social Learning Theory*. Englewood Cliffs, NJ: Prentice-Hall.

Bandura, A. (1986). *Social Foundations of Thought and Action*. Englewood Cliffs, NJ: Prentice-Hall.

Bass, B. M. & Avolio, B. J. (1994). *Improving Organizational Effectiveness Through Transformational Leadership*. Thousand Oaks, CA: SAGE.

Beattie, L. & Griffin, B. (2014). Day-level fluctuation in stress and engagement in response to workplace incivility: A diary study. *Work & Stress*, 28, 124–42.

Blau, P. (1964). *Exchange and Power in Social Life*. New York: Wiley.

Bouckenooghe, D., Zafa, A. & Raja, U. (2015). How ethical leadership shapes employee job performance: The mediating roles of goal congruence and psychological capital. *Journal of Business Ethics*, 129, 251–64.

Brockner, J. (1988). *Self-Esteem at Work: Research, Theory and Practice*. Lexington, MA: D. C. Heath.

Brown, M. E. & Mitchell, M. S. (2010). Ethical and unethical leadership: Exploring new avenues for future research. *Business Ethics Quarterly*, 20(4), 583–616.

Brown, M. E. & Treviño, L. K. (2006). Ethical leadership: A review and future directions. *Leadership Quarterly*, 17(6), 595–616.

Brown, M. E. & Treviño, L. K. (2014). Do role models matter? An investigation of role modeling as an antecedent of perceived ethical leadership. *Journal of Business Ethics*, 122, 586–98.

Brown, M. E., Treviño, L. K. & Harrison, D. A. (2005). Ethical leadership: A social learning perspective for construct development and testing. *Organizational Behavior and Human Decision Processes*, 97(2), 117–34.

Chugtai, A., Byrne, M. & Flood, B. (2015). Linking ethical leadership with employee well-being: The role of trust in supervisor. *Journal of Business Ethics*, 128, 653–63.

Cortina, L. M. (2008). Unseen injustice: Incivility as modern discrimination in organizations. *Academy of Management Review*, 33, 55–75.

Cortina, L. M. & Magley, V. J. (2009). Patterns and profiles of response to incivility in the workplace. *Journal of Occupational Health Psychology*, 14, 272–88.

Cortina, L. M., Magley, V. J., Williams, J. H. & Langhout, R. D. (2001). Incivility in the workplace: Incidence and impact. *Journal of Occupational Health Psychology*, 6, 64–80.

Demirtas, O. & Akdogan, A. A. (2015). The effect of ethical leadership behaviour on ethical climate, turnover intention, and affective commitment. *Journal of Business Ethics*, 130, 59–67.

Den Hartog, D. N. & Belschak, F. D. (2012). Work engagement and Machiavellianism in the ethical leadership process. *Journal of Business Ethics*, 107(1), 35–47.

Fry, L. W. (2003). Toward a theory of spiritual leadership. *Leadership Quarterly*, 14, 693–727.

Harold, C. M. & Holtz, B. C. (2015). The effects of passive leadership on workplace incivility. *Journal of Organizational Behavior*, 36, 16–38.

Hershcovis, M. S. (2011). Incivility, social undermining, bullying...oh my! A call to reconcile constructs within workplace aggression research. *Journal of Organizational Behavior*, 32, 499–519.

Jordan, J., Brown, M. E. & Treviño, L. K. (2013). Someone to look up to: Executive–follower ethical reasoning and perceptions of ethical leadership. *Journal of Management*, 29, 660–83.

Judge, T. A. & Piccolo, R. F. (2004). Transformational and transactional leadership: A meta-analytic test of their relative validity. *Journal of Applied Psychology*, 89, 755–68.

Kalshoven, K. & Boon, C. T. (2012). Ethical leadership, employee well-being, and helping the moderating role of human resource management. *Journal of Personnel Psychology*, 11, 60–8.

Kalshoven, K., Den Hartog, D. N. & De Hoogh, A. H. B. (2011). Ethical leadership at work questionnaire (ELW): Development and validation of a multidimensional measure. *Leadership Quarterly*, 22, 51–69.

Kalshoven, K., Den Hartog, D. N.. & De Hoogh, A. H. B. (2013). Ethical leadership and followers' helping and initiative: The role of demonstrated responsibility and job autonomy. *European Journal of Work and Organisational Psychology*, 22, 165–81.

Kohlberg, L. (1969). Stage and sequence: The cognitive-developmental approach to socialization. In D. A. Goslin (ed.), *Handbook of Socialization and Research*. Chicago, IL: Rand McNally, pp. 347–480.

Lazarus, R. S. & Folkman, S. (1984). *Stress, Appraisal, and Coping*. New York: Springer.

Lee, J. & Jensen, J. M. (2014). The effects of active constructive and passive corrective leadership on workplace incivility and the mediating role of fairness perceptions. *Group and Organization Management*, 39(4), 416–43.

Leiter, M., Laschinger, H. K. S., Day, A. & Oore, D. G. (2011). The impact of civility interventions on employee social behavior, distress, and attitudes. *Journal of Applied Psychology*, 96, 1258–74.

Lewis, P. S. & Malecha, A. (2011). The impact of workplace incivility on the work environment, manager skill, and productivity. *Journal of Nursing Administration*, 41(1), 41–7.

Liao, Y., Liu, X. Y., Kwan, H. K. & Li, J. (2015). Work–family effects of ethical leadership. *Journal of Business Ethics*, 128, 535–45.

Lim, S. & Cortina, L. M. (2005). Interpersonal mistreatment in the workplace: The interface and impact of general incivility and sexual harassment. *Journal of Applied Psychology*, 90, 483–96.

Lim, S. & Lee, A. (2011). Work and non-work outcomes of workplace incivility: Does family support help? *Journal of Occupational Health Psychology*, 16, 95–111.

Liu, J., Kwan, H. K., Fu, P. P. & Mao, Y. (2013). Ethical leadership and job performance in China: The roles of workplace friendships and traditionality. *Journal of Occupational and Organizational Psychology*, 86, 564–84.

Mayer, D. M., Aquino, K., Greenbaum, R. L. & Kuenzi, M. (2012). Who displays ethical leadership, and does it matter? An examination of antecedents and consequences of ethical leadership. *Academy of Management Journal*, 55, 151–71.

Mayer, D. M., Kuenzi, M. & Greenbaum, R. L. 2010. Examining the link between ethical leadership and employee misconduct: The mediating role of ethical climate. *Journal of Business Ethics*, 95, 7–16.

Mayer, D. M., Kuenzi, M., Greenbaum, R., Bardes, M. & Salvador, R. (2009). How low does ethical leadership flow? Test of a trickle-down model. *Organizational Behavior and Human Decision Processes*, 108, 1–13.

Meijman, T. F. & Mulder, G. (1998). Psychological aspects of workload. In P. J. D. Drenth, H. Thierry & C. J. de Wolff (eds.), *Handbook of Work and Organizational Psychology. Volume 2: Work Psychology*. 2nd edn. Hove, UK: Psychology Press, pp. 5–33.

Miner-Rubino, K. & Cortina, L. M. (2007). Beyond targets: Consequences of vicarious exposure to misogyny at work. *Journal of Applied Psychology*, 92, 1254–69.

Newman, A., Kiazad, K., Miao, Q. & Cooper, B. (2014). Examining the cognitive and affective trust-based mechanisms underlying the relationship between ethical leadership and organisational citizenship: A case of the head leading the heart? *Journal of Business Ethics*, 123, 113–23.

Nicholson, T. & Griffin, B. (2015). Here today but gone tomorrow: Incivility affects after-work and next day recovery. *Journal of Occupational Health Psychology*, 20, 21825.

Ogunfowora. B. (2014). It's all a matter of consensus: Leader role modelling strength as a moderator of the links between ethical leadership and employee outcomes. *Human Relations*, 67, 1467–90.

Pearson, C. M., Andersson, L. M. & Porath, C. L. (2000). Assessing and attacking workplace incivility. *Organizational Dynamics*, 29, 123–37.

Pearson, C. M., Andersson, L. M. & Wegner, J. W. (2001). When workers flout convention: A study of workplace incivility. *Human Relations*, 54, 1387–1419.

Pearson, C. M. & Porath, C. L. 2005. On the nature, consequences and remedies of workplace incivility: No time for 'nice'? Think again. *Academy of Management Executive*, 19, 7–18.

Podsakoff, P. M., MacKenzie, S. B., Paine, J. B. & Bachrach, D. G. (2000). Organizational citizenship behavior: A critical review of the theoretical and empirical literature and suggestions for future research. *Journal of Management* 26, 513–63.

Porath, C. L. & Pearson, C. M. (2010). The cost of bad behavior. *Organizational Dynamics*, 39, 64–71.

Porath, C. L. & Pearson, C. M. (2013). The price of incivility: Lack of respect hurts morale – and the bottom line. *Harvard Business Review*, January–February, 115–21.

Reich, T. C. & Hershcovis, M. S. (2015). Observing workplace incivility. *Journal of Applied Psychology*, 100, 203–15.

Resick, C. J., Hargis, M. B., Shao, P. & Dust, S. B. (2013). Ethical leadership, moral equity judgments, and discretionary workplace behaviour. *Human Relations*, 66, 951–72.

Robinson, S. L. & Bennett, R. J. (1995). A typology of deviant workplace behaviors: A multidimensional scaling study. *Academy of Management Journal*, 38, 555–72.

Rogers, K. M. & Ashforth, B. E. (2014). Respect in organizations: Feeling valued as 'We' and 'Me'. *Journal of Management*. doi: 10.1177/0149206314557159.

Schaubroeck, J. M., Hannah, S. T., Avolio, B. J., Kozlowski, S. W. J., Lord, R. G., Treviño, L. K., Dimotakis, N. & Peng, A. C. (2012). Embedding ethical leadership within and across organization levels. *Academy of Management Journal*, 55, 1053–78.

Shin, Y., Sung, S. Y., Choi, J. N. & Ki, M. S. (2015). Top management ethical leadership and firm performance: Mediating role of ethical and procedural justice climate. *Journal of Business Ethics*, 129, 43–57.

Skubbin, S. & Herzog, L. (2016). Internalized moral identity in ethical leadership. *Journal of Business Ethics*, 133, 249–60.

Spears, R., Ellemers, N. & Doosje, B. (2005). Let me count the ways in which I respect thee: Does competence compensate or compromise lack of liking from the group? *European Journal of Social Psychology*, 35, 263–79.

Spears, R., Ellemers, N., Doosje, B. & Branscombe, N. R. (2006). The individual within the group: Respect! In T. Postmes and J. Jetten (eds), *Individuality and the Group: Advances in Social Identity*. London: Sage, pp. 175–95.

Stouten, J., van Dijke, M., Mayer, D. M., de Cremer, D. & Euwema, M. C. (2013). Can a leader be too ethical? The curvilinear effects of ethical leadership. *Leadership Quarterly*, 24, 680–95.

Taylor, S. G. & Pattie, M. W. (2014). When does ethical leadership affect workplace civility? The moderating role of follower personality. *Business Ethics Quarterly*, 24, 595–616.

Treviño, L. K., Brown, M. & Hartman, L. P. (2003). A qualitative investigation of perceived executive ethical leadership: Perceptions from inside and outside the executive suite. *Human Relations*, 56, 5–37.
Walumbwa, F. O., Mayer, D. M" Wang, P., Wang, H" Workman, K. & Christensen, A. L. (2011). Linking ethical leadership to employee performance: The roles of leader–member exchange, self-efficacy, and organizational identification. *Organizational Behavior and Human Decision Processes*, 115, 204–13.
Walumbwa, F. O. & Schaubroeck, J. (2009). Leader personality traits and employee voice behavior: Mediating roles of ethical leadership and work group psychological safety. *Journal of Applied Psychology*, 94, 1275–86.
Wharton, A. S. & Erikson, R.J. (1993). Managing emotions on the job and at home: Understanding the consequences of multiple emotional roles. *Academy of Management Review*, 18, 457–86.
Zhou, Z. E., Yan, Y., Che, X. X. & Meier, L. L. (2015). Effect of workplace incivility on end of work negative affect: Examining individual and organizational moderators in a daily diary study. *Journal of Occupational Health Psychology*, 20, 117–30.

6

Leading the Psychologically Healthy Workplace

The RIGHT Way

E. Kevin Kelloway, Samantha A. Penney and Jennifer K. Dimoff

Employers and researchers alike have increasingly come to recognize the enormous costs associated with poor employee health and safety in the workplace. Many organizations have implemented healthy workplace programmes and policies (Goetzel & Ozminkowski, 2008; Goetzel, Roemer, Liss-Levinson & Samoly, 2008) to address these concerns. For example, organizations can improve the physical and mental health of their employees by offering access to employee assistance programmes (EAPs), by introducing health promotion activities, and by providing programmes that support the physical, social, personal and professional lives of employees (American Psychological Association, 1999; Health Canada, 2004). More broadly, a healthy workplace has been defined as one in which organizational goals of profitability and productivity are integrated with employees' desire for well-being (Sauter, Lim & Murphy, 1996).

Perhaps more specifically, healthy workplace programmes are 'employer-sponsored initiatives directed at improving the health and well-being of workers' (Goetzel et al., 2008, p. 4). Much of the extant research supports the idea that the implementation of such programmes serves to drive down health care costs and improve organizational outcomes concerning such matters as absenteeism and productivity (e.g., Aldana, 2001; Grawitch, Gottschalk & Munz, 2006; Kelloway & Day, 2005; Schmidt, Welch & Wilson, 2000), which suggests that organizations that introduce and cultivate healthy workplace programmes are more likely to reap the financial benefits associated with having healthy employees. Although it has been difficult to isolate and quantify the financial impact of such programmes (for a review see Dimoff, Kelloway & MacLellan, 2014), it is clear that healthy workplace programmes have been the focus of a tremendous amount of qualitative and quantitative research examining their effectiveness. Healthy workplace programmes have been associated with reductions in risk factors, such as high blood pressure, excess body fat and elevated levels of cholesterol (Goetzel et al., 2002; Goetzel, Shechter, Ozminkowski, Marmet, Tabrizi & Roemer, 2007), as well as improvements in organizational outcomes, such as reduced turnover, better accident rates, and even competitive marketplace advantage (Greening & Turban, 2000; Harter, Schmidt & Killham, 2003; Schmidt et al., 2000).

Leading to Occupational Health and Safety: How Leadership Behaviours Impact Organizational Safety and Well-Being, First Edition.
Edited by E. Kevin Kelloway, Karina Nielsen and Jennifer K. Dimoff.

Emerging from the healthy workplace movement has been the definition of a 'psychologically healthy workplace' that goes beyond physical well-being to include a focus on the psychosocial aspects of health. As Kelloway and Day (2005) suggest, a psychologically healthy workplace encompasses a focus on both reducing or mitigating the effects of job stressors and providing resources to employees. At least two models of psychologically healthy workplaces have emerged that emphasize this point. First, the American Psychological Association has created a psychologically healthy workplace programme based on five major features of the organization: recognition, involvement, growth and development, health and safety, and work–family balance (see, for example, Grawitch, Gottshalk & Muntz, 2006). Second, the Mental Health Commission of Canada worked with the Canadian Standards Association to produce Standard Z1003, a standard for psychological health and safety in the workplace that specifies 13 areas that should be included in an assessment of the psychosocial environment.

A Focus on Leaders

In attempting to identify the elements of a psychologically healthy and safe workplace, researchers and practitioners have focused on the notion of the 'workplace'. We adopt a different strategy in suggesting that the creation of psychological healthy workplaces is directly tied to the actions of organizational leaders. This suggestion is consistent with a burgeoning body of research literature documenting the extensive effects that leadership has on employee well-being (Mullen & Kelloway, 2011).

Thus, the quality of organizational leadership has been linked to an array of outcomes within occupational health psychology: positive outcomes such as psychological well-being (e.g., Arnold, Turner, Barling, Kelloway & McKee, 2007; McKee, Driscoll, Kelloway & Kelley, 2011) and organizational safety climate (e.g., Zohar, 2002), and negative outcomes, including employee stress (e.g., Offermann & Hellmann, 1996), cardiovascular disease (e.g., Kivimaki, Ferrie, Brunner et al., 2005; Wager, Fieldman & Hussey, 2003), workplace incidents and injuries (e.g., Barling, Loughlin & Kelloway, 2002; Kelloway, Mullen & Francis, 2006; Mullen & Kelloway, 2009) and health-related behaviours, such as alcohol use (e.g., Bamberger & Bacharach, 2006). In short, virtually every outcome variable in the field of occupational health psychology is empirically related to organizational leadership (Mullen & Kelloway, 2011).

The RIGHT Way

Taking the American Psychological Association definition of a psychologically healthy workplace as our starting point, we suggest that leaders create a psychologically healthy workplace through their actions with respect to (1) recognition, (2) involvement, (3) growth and development, and (4) health and safety. We depart from the largely individually focused American Psychological Association model to add a fifth element – teamwork – which we suggest is critical to the creation of a psychologically healthy workplace.

Recognition

Employee recognition has appeared sporadically in the research literature for over three decades, receiving attention from experts aiming to identify new factors in employee performance and motivation (Godkin, Parayitam & Natarajan, 2010; Magnus, 1981), as well as those interested in effective leader–follower relationships (Luthans, 2000). However, despite the obvious importance of the topic there has been surprisingly little research on employee recognition (Tetrick & Haimann, 2014). In an influential review, Grawitch et al. (2006) identified recognition as one of the five categories of healthy workplace practices that define a psychologically healthy workplace.

Most researchers and managers would recognize that employees' level of motivation is influenced by the sense that they are valued by others (Amabile & Kramer, 2007). Empirically, employee recognition is associated with higher levels of employee engagement, motivation and satisfaction (Krueger et al., 2002; Shiraz, Rashid & Riaz, 2011). A lack of recognition even places employees at greater risk of experiencing psychological distress (Brun, Biron, Martel & Hivers, 2003). Not surprisingly, research also indicates that employees consider personalized recognition for the work they do to be an integral part of the rewards they receive at work (Luthans, 2000).

Brun and Dugas (2008) identified four sub-dimensions, each representing a different *object* of recognition (what is being recognized): the *personal* dimension (recognizing the employee as an individual), the *achievement* dimension (recognizing the results of the employee's performance), the *work performance* dimension (focusing on *how* someone does their job) and, finally, the *job dedication* dimension (recognizing the commitment and loyalty of an employee to their job or organization) (Brun & Dugas, 2008).

Recognition can come from a number of sources, including co-workers, subordinates, supervisors, the organization's leadership, and even society as a whole (Brun & Dugas, 2008). Although the source of recognition has been taken into consideration in some studies (e.g., Godkin et al., 2010), relatively little research has focused on the specific impact which different sources have on individual perceptions of employee recognition.

Given the importance of social proximity to the source of recognition, it seems reasonable to focus on recognition from employees' immediate supervisors, since they are often in the best position to observe employees and provide recognition for meaningful contributions (Godkin et al., 2010). Employees tend to perceive their supervisors as representatives of the organization (Eisenberger et al., 2010). This being so, recognition from the supervisor likely guides employee perceptions of organization-level recognition.

Recognition can also vary along a dimension of formality. Many organizations establish formal programmes for 'reward and recognition' that administer monetary and other forms of rewards, typically based on employee performance. Although some data suggest that these programmes can be effective in increasing performance (e.g., Stajkovic & Luthans, 2003), formal programmes are often based on the one 'winner' receiving the reward (e.g., employee of the month programmes). Such programmes may have unintended, and negative, consequences (for a review see Tetrick & Haimann, 2014).

However, recognition can also come more informally as supervisors thank individuals for a particular job or commend them on a specific aspect of their job performance. Informal recognition of this sort can convey the same sense of value that is intended by more formal systems but is not limited by constraints on the availability of the reward. Indeed, in describing their approach to transformational leadership training, Kelloway and Barling (2000) noted the importance of setting micro-goals – small behaviours that can be performed on a daily basis. 'Tell five employees a day that they are doing a good job' is one such goal that is frequently used; it has the effect of increasing employees' sense that they are recognized and that their contributions are valued at work.

At the organizational level, senior leaders striving to cultivate psychologically healthy organizations can help to facilitate employee recognition by encouraging mid-level managers to recognize employees' day-to-day performance. While favourable performance is often praised during annual performance reviews, this formal recognition may have limited capacity to improve employee attitudes and behaviours (Tetrick & Haimann, 2014). Instead, seemingly smaller and more frequent acts of recognition may be more motivating for employees; timely, specific and sincere 'pat-on-the-back' recognition for a well-executed task may have a greater effect than a more formalized reward that is received months, or even years, later.

Mid-level managers, rather than senior executives, are often in a good position to notice and recognize employees who have performed well, engaged in organizational citizenship behaviours (OCBs), or engaged in other activities or behaviours that benefit the organization and its employees (Eisenberger et al., 2010; Godkin et al., 2010). Thus, while the presence of formal recognition programmes and procedures may be appreciated by employees, it may be the less formal, day-to-day recognition that encourages and engages employees in the short and long term.

According to a recent study (Dimoff, Kelloway & Pitfield, 2014), this less formal recognition has been linked to increased engagement or 'love of job', whereby an employee feels passion for the work itself and affective commitment towards the organization, and has close relationships with others at work. Findings suggest that employees who receive more recognition from their manager are more engaged at work and tend to 'love' their job more than their peers who do not receive praise at work (Dimoff et al., 2014). These findings highlight the power of seemingly small acts of recognition that can easily be facilitated by managers at any level of an organization.

Involvement

Employee involvement means empowering employees through increasing their autonomy and involvement in decision-making (Grawitch, Trares & Kohler, 2007). Employee involvement initiatives can encompass minor practices such as open-door policies, employee surveys and communication of organizational information, and major practices such as high-involvement systems, self-managed work teams, and joint employee–management committees (Grawitch, Ledford, Ballard & Barber, 2009). In terms of employee outcomes in healthy workplaces, employee involvement initiatives are related to employee well-being (Grawitch et al., 2007; Grawitch et al., 2009), emotional exhaustion (Grawitch et al., 2007), employee morale (Vandenberg, Richardson & Eastman, 1999) and job satisfaction (Zatzick & Iverson, 2011). In addition to employee outcomes, employee involvement initiatives are related to organizational outcomes, such as absenteeism (Lawler, 1991), turnover, return on equity (Vandenberg et al., 1999) and firm performance (Gibson, Porath, Benson & Lawler, 2007). Furthermore, employee involvement initiatives are related to organizational commitment (Grawitch et al., 2007) and attitudes towards management, fairness and blame during organizational downsizing (Martin, Parsons & Bennett, 1995). Therefore, employee involvement initiatives are related to both employee and organizational effectiveness outcomes, and are an important part of healthy workplaces.

Leaders are in a unique position to increase employee involvement given that they are typically involved in organizational decision making and work closely with employees. For example, transformational leadership has been shown to be significantly related to a climate of involvement (Richardson & Vandenberg, 2005). In terms of specific components of transformational leadership, individualized consideration may be particularly valuable in promoting employee involvement. Leaders that exhibit individualized consideration mentor employees and focus their attention on employees' individual needs (Barling, Christie & Hoption, 2011). Therefore, through their leadership role, leaders who exhibit individualized consideration may be able to empower, support and encourage employees to get involved in employee involvement programmes that meet their individual needs (e.g., joining a joint management–employee committee; completing an employee survey). Therefore, when making organizational decisions or deciding on practices or programmes for employees, leaders should try to involve employees in decision making through various means (e.g., surveys, joint management–employee committees). Moreover, by involving employees in decisions, organizations and leaders will be in a better position to make decisions and offer programmes based on employee needs (Grawitch et al., 2009).

Leaders who involve employees in decisions that affect their daily lives or jobs may also foster environments categorized by trust and mutual respect. Through employee involvement, leaders and employees have the opportunity to exchange information and communicate openly about issues that affect the organization (Grawitch et al., 2009). When they do so, this communication helps to facilitate openness, trust, and a desire to become more involved in future organizational decisions or pursuits (Grawitch et al., 2009). Thus, employee involvement helps to initiate a social exchange process, whereby (1) leaders provide employees with information and autonomy, and (2) employees, in turn, perceive their leaders as more trustworthy, prompting them to become more involved in the pursuit of organizational goals or decisions.

As a consequence, both employees and leaders reap the benefits of this leader-facilitated process. For instance, employees who have the opportunity to be involved in key decisions are likely to also experience positive personal and professional outcomes, such as improved well-being and morale (Grawitch et al., 2007; Grawitch et al., 2009; Vandenberg et al., 1999). Managers who facilitate employee involvement also benefit from employee feedback and greater insight into unique employee experiences (Grawitch et al., 2009). As a result of employee and leader benefits, organizations also benefit from employee involvement. For instance, organizations that support and encourage employee involvement may observe increased employee productivity and lower levels of unproductive turnover. However, mid-level managers often dictate the extent to which organizations will observe these positive outcomes (Fenton-O'Creevy, 1998). If managers do not support employee involvement and fail to encourage employees, the organization may not gain significant improvements in employee attitudes and productivity (Fenton-O'Creevy, 1998). Psychologically healthy workplace environments should help foster managers' support for employee involvement, and lower the risk that managers will resist employee involvement practices because of negative attitudes or perceived threats to self-interest – potential unintended consequences of employee involvement practices (Fenton-O'Creevy, 1998). To be effective and to gain adequate support from mid-level leaders, employee involvement programmes should have clear goals and receive visible support from senior management (Fenton-O'Creevy, 1998).

Growth and Development

'Growth and development' refers to providing employees with opportunities and programmes to gain and expand their skills, knowledge and abilities (Grawitch et al., 2006). Employee growth and development initiative examples include tuition reimbursements, on-the-job training, leadership development programmes, and career advancement opportunities (Grawitch et al., 2006; Grawitch et al., 2007). Satisfaction with growth and development programmes has been shown to be related to employee well-being and organizational commitment (Grawitch et al., 2007). Similarly, on-the-job training is related to both organizational commitment and reduced turnover intentions (Benson, 2006). Furthermore, training and internal career opportunities have been shown to predict organizational effectiveness and job satisfaction (Browne, 2000). Accordingly, providing employees with growth and development opportunities can demonstrate to employees that their organization is willing to invest in them and that it values employee contributions and employability (Lee & Bruvold, 2003).

Mayo (2000) suggested that leadership is an important contributor to a climate for growth and development. He further highlighted how growth and development opportunities can increase human capital and value among employees, so leaders should put effort into promoting growth and development opportunities and programmes for employees (Mayo, 2000). In terms of transformational leadership, intellectual stimulation behaviour is likely to be related to the promotion of growth and development opportunities among employees, given that intellectual stimulation is associated with promoting personal growth and development among employees (Barling et al., 2011). Therefore, leaders who intellectually stimulate employees may be able to instil confidence in them and encourage them to seek out, or provide them with, opportunities to expand their skills, knowledge and abilities.

Through intellectual stimulation and supportive management behaviours, leaders can help employees become more creative with their work. Although not desirable in all occupations, creativity can help employees expand and utilize existing skills, knowledge and abilities in novel ways (Oldham & Cummings, 1996). Arguably, managers who are able to foster creativity within their employees are helping employees grow and develop. The benefits of such growth and development are not only observed by employees – through an expanded skill set – but are also observed by the leader and the organization. For instance, much research suggests that organizations that foster creativity and risk-taking behaviours among employees can achieve competitive advantage within the marketplace (Shalley & Gilson, 2004; Woodman, Sawyer & Griffin, 1993).

Leaders and managers who are supportive and manage in a non-controlling fashion are likely to be able to help employees grow, develop and flourish (Oldham & Cummings, 1996). Specifically, leaders can encourage employee growth and development by providing employees with the time and security to attend workshops, receive additional education, or even engage in other activities, such as volunteer or fundraising work. To do so, leaders must provide practical support for such activities and engender a culture in which employees feel that such growth and development opportunities are valued by the organization.

Van de Ven and Poole's (1995) process theory posits that the strategies, procedures and management practices of an organization can determine how organizational inputs (e.g., growth and development opportunities) become outputs (e.g., competitive advantage for the employee and the organization). Managers' behaviours not only reflect the organization's cultures and values, but also impact whether or not, and the extent to which, employee growth will be achieved (Damanpour, 1991; Van de Ven & Poole, 1995). For instance, managers that support employee growth and development are likely to communicate openly about opportunities, and provide ample time and resources for employees seeking out such opportunities.

Health and Safety

As this volume attests, leaders play numerous roles in enhancing the health and safety of employees. Recognizing that the role of leadership in traditional occupational health and safety is reviewed extensively elsewhere in this volume, here we limit our consideration to the role that leaders play in increasing, or mitigating, workplace stress.

In their review of how poor leadership leads to stress, Kelloway, Sivanathan, Francis & Barling (2005) suggested that an often overlooked possibility is that leaders are a root cause of many of the stressors experienced by employees in organizations (see also chapter 9 for a review of the nature and effects of destructive leadership in organizations). For example, leaders who fail to give clear directions or to effectively communicate expectations may create a sense of role ambiguity for employees. Supervisors who do not effectively manage workloads may increase employees' experience of work overload and, potentially, work–family conflict, thereby decreasing their overall well-being. Close and controlling supervision can result in employees experiencing increased anxiety and stress. Dimoff and Kelloway (in press) also point to the potential role of organizational leaders as resource facilitators, helping individual employees obtain the resources they need to be able to accomplish their jobs and maintain their well-being. They argue that managers see their employees frequently and may be ideally positioned to observe the changes in behaviour that are associated with increased strain (Dimoff, Kelloway & Burnstein, 2016). Training managers in supportive behaviours (e.g., Dimoff et al., 2016; Hammer, Kossek, Anger, Bodner & Zimmerman, 2011) has been shown to be effective in reducing indices of employee strain.

Moreover, through a contagion process, leaders' stress levels and poor well-being can affect employee stress and well-being (Skakon, Nielsen, Borg & Guzman, 2010). For example, Theorell, Emdad, Arnetz and Weingarten (2001) demonstrated that leaders' stress levels were associated with employee stress levels. Therefore, given that leaders act as role models for employees, it is important for leaders to promote not only the health and well-being of their employees, but their own health and well-being.

These findings are consistent with transformational leadership theory (Bass, 1985), which emphasizes leaders' concern for the individual as a component of effective leadership. By acting as role models who consistently do what is moral and right, and not necessarily personally beneficial, transformational leaders gain the respect and trust of their followers and positively affect their well-being.

Teamwork

The importance of teams is rarely mentioned in the literature dealing with psychologically healthy workplaces. For example, a recent book surveying the literature on healthy workplaces does not have a chapter dealing with the importance of teams (Day, Kelloway & Hurrell, 2014). This silence is in stark contrast to the growing importance of teams in organizations. Teams of all sorts are endemic in organizations. Of particular importance is the growth in the number of project teams and the projectification (Bredin & Söderlund, 2011) of the workplace that relies increasingly on the work of these teams (see Chiocchio, Kelloway & Hobbs, 2015 for a review).

Hackman (1991) proposed a widely cited set of criteria for team effectiveness when he suggested that teams could be judged to be effective to the extent that they (1) produce an acceptable good or service (as judged by the employers or consumers of the good or service), (2) grow as a team in their ability to continue to produce competent work, and (3) enhance the well-being of the individuals comprising the teams. By incorporating team members' well-being as an explicit criterion for team effectiveness, Hackman highlighted the role of teams and teamwork in creating a psychologically healthy workplace.

The actions of a leader can substantially contribute to the sense of group cohesion. Inspirational motivation, one of the core components of transformational leadership (Bass, 1985), emphasizes collaborative group work to further the groups' goals and mission, and raises groups' expectations about their performance. In a longitudinal study, Keller (1992) showed that employee perceptions of transformational leadership predicted group-level project quality and appropriate budgeting and scheduling. Moreover, his zero-order correlations showed that charismatic leadership (a combination of idealized influence and inspirational motivation) was consistently associated with employee and management ratings of group-level project quality and appropriate budgeting and scheduling, while intellectual stimulation was not. In a laboratory study, Sosik, Avolio and Kahai (1997) showed that transformational leadership was more strongly associated with group potency than transactional leadership was. Jung and Sosik (2002) showed that transformational leadership was associated with team cohesion, group potency and group effectiveness. Similarly, Pillai and Williams (2004) found that transformational leadership was associated with group cohesion and self-efficacy in teams.

Moreover, leaders are in a unique position to foster team coherence, orientation (Kozlowski, Gully, McHugh, Salas & Cannon-Bowers, 1996) and team building, particularly among the development of new teams or onboarding of new team members. For example, Major, Kozlowski, Chao and Gardner (1995) suggested that a positive relationship between a leader and a team was important in facilitating effective socialization among team members. Furthermore, it has been suggested that leaders play an important role in shaping a safe team climate among employees working in teams (Nembhard & Edmondson, 2006). Thus, it is clear that the characteristics of transformational leaders that contribute to positive individual-level employee outcomes can also result in positive group-level outcomes in a team context (Kozlowski & Bell, 2003).

Conclusions

We have suggested that organizational leaders play an important role in creating employees' perceptions that they (1) are valued and recognized in the workplace, (2) are involved in the decisions that affect them, (3) have the opportunities to grow and develop through their work, (4) work in an environment that cares about their health and safety and (5) belong to effective and cohesive teams in the workplace. Although these features have been ascribed to the workplace, we argue that managers are the visible manifestation of the workplace for most employees and it is the actions of organizational leaders as individuals that have the most direct impact on employees. The promotion of a psychologically healthy workplace, therefore, is tied directly to the behaviour of leaders.

So how can leaders promote a psychologically healthy workplace? As previously mentioned, we believe that the key lies in leaders performing small but critical tasks as part of a daily routine. Thus, when leaders compliment employees on a job well done they foster the sense of recognition. When leaders ask employees for their opinion on an organizational issue they contribute to their sense of involvement. Coaching employees and assessing how the organization can provide the resources employees need to acquire new skills and develop existing skills contribute to growth and development. Talking about health and safety on a daily basis is a key component (Wong, Kelloway & Makhan, 2016), and an effective means (Mullen & Kelloway, 2009), of safety leadership. Finally, focusing on team building and team cohesion through setting group goals, coaching, knowledge sharing, and focusing on group dynamics is a leadership function that leads to both more effective teams and a psychologically healthy workplace.

References

Aldana, S. G. (2001). Financial impact of health promotion programs: A comprehensive review of the literature. *American Journal of Health Promotion*, 15, 296–320.

Amabile, T. M. & Kramer, S. J. (2007). Inner work life: Understanding the subtext of business performance. *Harvard Business Review*, 85(5), 72–83.

American Psychological Association (1999). Creating a psychologically healthy workplace. https://www.apaexcellence.org/resources/creatingahealthyworkplace/. Accessed 30 July 2016.

Arnold, K., Turner, N., Barling, J., Kelloway, E. K. & McKee, M. (2007). Transformational leadership and psychological well-being: The mediating role of meaningful work. *Journal of Occupational Health Psychology*, 12, 193–203.

Bamberger, P. A. & Bacharach, S. B. (2006). Abusive supervision and subordinate problem drinking: Taking resistance, stress and subordinate personality into account. *Human Relations*, 59(6), 723–52.

Barling, J., Christie, A. & Hoption, A. (2011). Leadership. In S. Zedeck (ed.) *APA Handbook of Industrial and Organizational Psychology. Volume 1: Building and Developing the Organization*. Washington, DC: American Psychological Association, pp. 183–240.

Barling, J., Loughlin, C. & Kelloway, E. K. (2002). Development and test of a model linking safety-specific transformational leadership and occupational safety. *Journal of Applied Psychology*, 87, 488–96.

Bass, B. M. (1985). *Leadership and performance beyond expectations*. New York: Basic Books.

Benson, G. S. (2006). Employee development, commitment and intention to turnover: a test of 'employability' policies in action. *Human Resource Management Journal*, 16(2), 173–92.

Bredin, K. & Söderlund, J. (2011). The HR quadriad: A framework for the analysis of HRM in project-based organizations. *International Journal of Human Resource Management*, 22(10), 2202–21.

Browne, J. H. (2000). Benchmarking HRM practices in healthy work organizations. *American Business Review*, 18(2), 54–61.

Brun, J.-P., Biron, C., Martel, J. & Hivers, H. (2003), *L'Évaluation de la santé mentale au travail: une analyse des pratiques de gestion des ressources humaines*, Montréal: Institut de Recherche Robert-Sauvé en santé et en sécurité du travail.

Brun, J. & Dugas, N. (2008). An analysis of employee recognition: Perspectives on human resources practices. *The International Journal of Human Resource Management*, 19 (4), 716–30.

Chiocchio, F., Kelloway, E. K. & Hobbs, B. (eds) (2015). *The Psychology and Management of Project Teams*. New York: Oxford University Press.

Damanpour, F. (1991). Organizational innovation: A meta-analysis of effects of determinants and moderators. *Academy of Management Journal*, 34, 555–90.

Day, A., Kelloway, E. K. & Hurrell, J. J. (eds) (2014). *Workplace Well-being: How to Build Psychologically Healthy Workplaces*. Chichester, UK: Wiley-Blackwell.

Dimoff, J. K. & Kelloway, E. K. (in press). Organizational leaders as resource facilitators. In P. Perrewé, J. Halbesleben & C. Rose (eds), *Research in Occupational Stress and Well-Being*. Bingley, UK: Emerald.

Dimoff, J. K., Kelloway, E. K. & Burnstein, M. (2016). Mental health awareness training (MHAT): The development and evaluation of an intervention for workplace leaders. *International Journal of Stress Management*, 23(2), 167–89.

Dimoff, J. K., Kelloway, E. K. & MacLellan, A. S. (2014). Health and performance: Science or advocacy? *Journal of Organizational Effectiveness: People and Performance*, 1, 316–34.

Dimoff, J. K., Kelloway, E. K. & Pitfield, L. (2014). Engaging your employees: The power of recognition. Paper presented at 'Looking at the past – planning for the future: Capitalizing on OHP multidisciplinarity', the 11th conference of the European Academy of Occupational Health Psychology, University of London, 14–16 April.

Eisenberger, R., Karagonlar, G., Stinglhamber, F., Neves, P., Becker, T. E., Gonzalez-Morales, M. G. & Steiger-Mueller, M. (2010). Leader–member exchange and affective organizational commitment: The contribution of supervisor's organizational embodiment. *Journal of Applied Psychology*, 95, 1085–1103.

Fenton-O'Creevy, M. (1998). Employee involvement and the middle manager: Evidence from a survey of organizations. *Journal of Organizational Behavior*, 19(1), 67–84.

Gibson, C. B., Porath, C. L., Benson, G. S. & Lawler, E. I. (2007). What results when firms implement practices: The differential relationship between specific practices, firm financial performance, customer service, and quality. *Journal of Applied Psychology*, 92(6), 1467–80.

Godkin, L., Parayitam, S. & Natarajan, L. (2010). An empirical study of attitudes toward recognition among civilian municipal employees in a US city. *Journal of Organizational Culture, Communication and Conflict*, 14(2), 51–61.

Goetzel, R. Z. and Ozminkowski, R. J. (2008), The health and cost benefits of worksite health promotion programs. *Annual Review of Public Health*, 29, 303–23.

Goetzel, R. Z., Ozminkowski, R. J., Bruno, J. A., Rutter, K. R., Isaac, F. and Wang, S. (2002), The long-term impact of Johnson & Johnson's health & wellness program on employee health risks. *Journal of Occupational Environmental Medicine*, 44, 417–24.

Goetzel, R. Z., Roemer, E. C., Liss-Levinson, R. C. and Samoly, D. K. (2008). Workplace health promotion: Policy recommendations that encourage employers to support health improvement programs for their workers. A Prevention Policy Paper commissioned by Partnership for Prevention, Emory University. https://www.prevent.org/data/files/initiatives/workplacehealtpromotion-policyrecommendations.pdf. Accessed 30 July 2016.

Goetzel, R. Z., Shechter, D., Ozminkowski, R. J., Marmet, P. F., Tabrizi, M. J. and Roemer, E. C. (2007). Promising practices in employer health and productivity management efforts: Findings from a benchmarking study. *Journal of Occupational and Environmental Medicine*, 49, 111–30.
Grawitch, M. J., Gottschalk, M. and Munz, D. C. (2006). The path to a healthy workplace: A critical review linking healthy workplace practices, employee well-being, and organizational improvements. *Consulting Psychology Journal: Practice and Research*, 58, 129–47.
Grawitch, M. J., Ledford, G. E., Jr, Ballard, D. W. & Barber, L. K. (2009). Leading the healthy workforce: The integral role of employee involvement. *Consulting Psychology Journal: Practice and Research*, 61(2), 122–35.
Grawitch, M. J., Trares, S. & Kohler, J. M. (2007). Healthy workplace practices and employee outcomes. *International Journal of Stress Management*, 14(3), 275–93.
Greening, D. W. and Turban, D. B. (2000). Corporate social performance as a competitive advantage in attracting a quality workforce, *Business and Society*, 39, 254–80.
Hackman, J. R. (1991). Work teams in organizations: An orienting framework. In J. R. Hackman (ed.), *Groups that Work (and Those that Don't)*. San Francisco, CA: Jossey-Bass, pp. 1–14.
Hammer, L. B., Kossek, E. E., Anger, W. K., Bodner, T. & Zimmerman, K. L. (2011). Clarifying work–family intervention processes: The roles of work–family conflict and family-supportive supervisor behaviors. *Journal of Applied Psychology*, 96, 134–50.
Harter, J. K., Schmidt, F. L. and Killham, E. A. (2003). *Employee Engagement, Satisfaction, and Business-Unit-Level Outcomes: A Meta-Analysis*. Princeton, NJ: The Gallup Organization.
Health Canada (2004). *About Healthy Workplace*. http://www.nqi.ca/HealthyWorkplace/default.aspx.
Jung, D. I. & Sosik, J. J. (2002). Transformational leadership in work groups: The role of empowerment, cohesiveness, and collective-efficacy on perceived group performance. *Small Group Research*, 33, 313–36.
Keller, R. T. (1992). Transformational leadership and the performance of research and development project groups. *Journal of Management*, 18, 489–501.
Kelloway, E. K. & Day, A. L. (2005). Building healthy workplaces: What we know so far. *Canadian Journal of Behavioural Science*, 37, 223–35.
Kelloway, E. K., Mullen, J. & Francis, L. (2006). Divergent effects of passive and transformational leadership on safety outcomes. *Journal of Occupational Health Psychology*, 11(1), 76–86.
Kelloway, E. K. & Barling, J. (2000). What we've learned about developing transformational leaders. *Leadership and Organization Development Journal*, 21, 157–61.
Kelloway, E. K. & Barling, J. (2010). Leadership development as an intervention in occupational health psychology. *Work & Stress*, 24(3), 260–79.
Kelloway, E. K., Sivanathan, N., Francis, L. & Barling, J. (2005). Poor leadership. In J. Barling, E. K. Kelloway & M. R. Frone (eds), *Handbook of Workplace Stress*. Thousand Oaks, CA: Sage, pp. 89–112.

Kelloway, E. K., Teed, M. & Prosser, M. (2008). Leading to a healthy workplace. In A. Kinder, R. Hughes & C. L. Cooper (eds), *Employee Well-being Support: A Workplace Resource*. Chichester, UK: John Wiley & Sons, pp. 25–38.

Kivimaki, M., Ferrie, J. E., Brunner, E., Head, J., Shipley, M. J., Vahtera, K. & Marmot, M. (2005). Justice at work and reduced risk of coronary heart disease among employees: The Whitehall II Study. *Archives of Internal Medicine*, 165, 2245–51.

Kozlowski, S. J. & Bell, B. S. (2003). Work groups and teams in organizations: Review and update. In W. C. Borman, D. R. Ilgen & R. J. Klimoski (ed.), *Handbook of Psychology. Volume 12: Industrial and Organizational Psychology*. Hoboken, NJ: John Wiley & Sons, pp. 333–75.

Kozlowski, S. W., Gully, S. M., McHugh, P. P., Salas, E. & Cannon-Bowers, J. A. (1996). A dynamic theory of leadership and team effectiveness: Developmental and task contingent leader roles. In G. R. Ferris (ed), *Research in Personnel and Human Resources Management*, vol. 14. Greenwich, CT: JAI Press, pp. 253–305.

Krueger, P., Brazil, K., Lohfeld, L., Edward, H. G., Lewis, D. & Tjam, E. (2002). Organization specific predictors of job satisfaction: Findings from a Canadian multi-site quality of work life cross-sectional survey. *BMC Health Services Research*, 2(6) (unpaginated).

Lawler, E. E. (1991). Participative management strategies. In J. W. Jones, B. D. Steffy & D. W. Bray (eds), *Applying Psychology in Business: The Handbook for Managers and Human Resource Professionals*. Lexington, MA: Lexington Books, pp. 578–86.

Lee, C. H. & Bruvold, N. T. (2003). Creating value for employees: Investment in employee development. *International Journal of Human Resource Management*, 14(6), 981–1000.

Luthans, K. (2000). Recognition: A powerful but often overlooked leadership tool to improve employee performance. *Journal of Leadership Studies*, 7(1), 31–9.

Magnus, M. (1981). Employee recognition: A key to motivation. *Personnel Journal*, 60, 103–6.

Major, D. A., Kozlowski, S. W., Chao, G. T. & Gardner, P. D. (1995). A longitudinal investigation of newcomer expectations, early socialization outcomes, and the moderating effects of role development factors. *Journal of Applied Psychology*, 80(3), 418–31.

Martin, C. L., Parsons, C. K. & Bennett, N. (1995). The influence of employee involvement program membership during downsizing: Attitudes toward the employer and the union. *Journal of Management*, 21(5), 879–90.

Mayo, A. (2000). The role of employee development in the growth of intellectual capital. *Personnel Review*, 29(4), 521–33.

McKee, M. C., Driscoll, C., Kelloway, E. K. & Kelley, E. (2011). Exploring linkages among transformational leadership, workplace spirituality and well-being in health care workers. *Journal of Management, Spirituality & Religion*, 8(3), 233–55.

Mullen, J. & Kelloway, E. K. (2009). Safety leadership: A longitudinal study of the effects of transformational leadership on safety outcomes. *Journal of Occupational and Organizational Psychology*, 20, 253–72.

Mullen, J. & Kelloway, E. K. (2011). Leading to occupational health and safety. In J. Campbell Quick and L. Tetrick (eds), *Handbook of Occupational Health Psychology*. Washington, DC: APA Books.

Nembhard, I. M. & Edmondson, A. C. (2006). Making it safe: The effects of leader inclusiveness and professional status on psychological safety and improvement efforts in health care teams. *Journal of Organizational Behavior*, 27(7), 941–66.

Nielsen, K. (2014). Leadership and climate in a psychologically healthy workplace. In A. Day, E. K. Kelloway & J. H. Hurrell, Jr. *Workplace Well-being: How to Build Psychologically Healthy Workplaces*. Chichester, UK: John Wiley & Sons, pp. 226–44.

Offermann, L. R. & Hellmann, P. S. (1996). Leadership behavior and subordinate stress: A 360° view. *Journal of Occupational Health Psychology*, 1, 382–90.

Oldham, G. R. & Cummings, A. (1996). Employee creativity: Personal and contextual factors at work. *Academy of Management Journal*, 29(3), 607–34.

Pillai, R. & Williams, E. A. (2004). Transformational leadership, self-efficacy, group cohesiveness, commitment, and performance. *Journal of Organizational Change Management*, 17, 144–59.

Richardson, H. A. & Vandenberg, R. J. (2005). Integrating managerial perceptions and transformational leadership into a work-unit level model of employee involvement. *Journal of Organizational Behavior*, 26(5), 561–89.

Sauter, S., Lim, S. & Murphy, L. (1996), Organizational health: A new paradigm for occupational stress research at NIOSH. *Japanese Journal of Occupational Mental Health*, 4, 248–54.

Schmidt, W. C., Welch, L. and Wilson, M. G. (2000). Individual and organizational activities to build better health. In L. R. Murphy and C. L. Cooper (eds), *Healthy and Productive Work: An International Perspective*. London: Taylor & Francis, pp. 133–47.

Shalley, C. E. & Gilson, L. L. (2004). What leaders need to know: A review of social and contextual factors that can foster or hinder creativity. *Leadership Quarterly*, 15, 33–53.

Shiraz, N., Rashid, M. & Riaz, A. (2011). The impact of reward and recognition programs on employee's motivation and satisfaction. *Interdisciplinary Journal of Contemporary Research in Business*, 3(3), 1428–34.

Skakon, J., Nielsen, K., Borg, V. & Guzman, J. (2010). Are leaders' well-being, behaviours and style associated with the affective well-being of their employees? A systematic review of three decades of research. *Work & Stress*, 24(2), 107–39.

Sosik, J. J., Avolio, B. J. & Kahai, S. S. (1997). Effects of leadership style and anonymity on group potency and effectiveness in a group decision support system environment. *Journal of Applied Psychology*, 82, 89–103.

Stajkovic, A. D. & Luthans, F. (2003). Behavioral management and task performance in organizations: Conceptual background, meta-analysis, and test of alternative models. *Personnel Psychology*, 56(1), 155–94.

Tetrick. L. E. & Haimann, C. R. (2014). Employee recognition. In A. Day, E. K. Kelloway & J. R. Hurrell, Jr. (eds), *Workplace Well-being: How to Build Psychologically Healthy Workplaces*. Chichester, UK: John Wiley & Sons, pp. 161–74.

Theorell, T., Emdad, R., Arnetz, B. & Weingarten, A. (2001) Employee effects of an educational program for managers at an insurance company. *Psychosomatic Medicine*, 63, 724–33.

Vandenberg, R. J., Richardson, H. A. & Eastman, L. J. (1999). The impact of high involvement work processes on organizational effectiveness: A second-order latent variable approach. *Group & Organization Management*, 24(3), 300–39.

Van de Ven, A. H. & Poole, M. S. (1995). Explaining development and change in organizations. *Academy of Management Review*, 20, 510–40.

Woodman, R. W., Sawyer, J. E. & Griffin, R. W. (1993). Toward a theory of organizational creativity. *Academy of Management Review*, 18, 293–321.

Wager, N., Fieldman, G. & Hussey, T. (2003). The effect on ambulatory blood pressure of working under favourably and unfavourably perceived supervisors. *Occupational and Environmental Medicine*, 60, 468–74.

Wong, J. H. K., Kelloway, E. K. & Makhan, D. W. (2016). Safety leadership. In S. Clarke, T. M. Probst, F. W. Guldenmund & J. Passmore (eds), *The Wiley Blackwell Handbook of the Psychology of Occupational Safety and Workplace Health*. Chichester, UK: Wiley, pp. 83–110.

Zatzick, C. D. & Iverson, R. D. (2011). Putting employee involvement in context: A cross-level model examining job satisfaction and absenteeism in high-involvement work systems. *International Journal of Human Resource Management*, 22(17), 3462–76.

Zohar, D. (2002). The effects of leadership dimensions, safety climate, and assigned priorities on minor injuries in work groups. *Journal of Organizational Behavior*, 23, 75–92.

7

Leadership and Work–Family Conflict

Ana Isabel Sanz-Vergel and Alfredo Rodríguez-Muñoz

Employees' Work–Family Conflict: Is it Exclusively Their Problem?

Work–Family Conflict: A Universal Phenomenon

The problem of juggling work with family life is not new but it has increased over recent years mainly because of economic and societal issues. In the 1970s, Pleck (1977) emphasized that work and family were two related spheres that influenced each other, both negatively and positively. Scholars use the term 'work–family conflict' to refer to this problem, which was defined as 'a form of interrole conflict in which the role pressures from the work and family domains are mutually incompatible in some respect' (Greenhaus & Beutell, 1985, p. 77). The experience of work–family conflict has traditionally been associated with two major changes in society.

The first one is the globalization of the economy. Companies have entered into a spiral of competitiveness which is affecting employees, who have to work long hours at the expense of their leisure and family time. Working during 'unsocial hours' has become usual among workers (Geurts, Rutte & Peeters, 1999; Roberts, 2007), who feel the pressure to do it to adjust to cultural norms (Perlow, 1995). The second main change leading to higher work–family conflict is a sociological change. Women have entered the workforce and the number of dual-earner couples has increased over the world. For example, in 2014, 47.7 per cent of families had both members of the couple working (Bureau of Labor Statistics, 2014), whereas in Europe this percentage is even higher, reaching 65 per cent (Eurofound, 2015). In Asia, female labour participation is likewise increasing (Lu & Cooper, 2015). This means that the traditional roles associated with women and men are now blurred and both members of a couple have to take responsibility for work and family tasks (Allen, Herst, Bruck & Sutton, 2000). This situation may be stressful for employees, so the role of managers is crucial as they may encourage or discourage employees from balancing work and life (Thompson, Beauvais & Lyness, 1999).

Leading to Occupational Health and Safety: How Leadership Behaviours Impact Organizational Safety and Well-Being, First Edition.
Edited by E. Kevin Kelloway, Karina Nielsen and Jennifer K. Dimoff.

The phenomenon of work–family conflict is universal and affects both women and men all over the world. Cross-cultural studies have demonstrated that employees face this problem in both eastern and western countries. For example, Aryee, Fields and Luk (1999) conducted a study among Hong Kong employees to test a model of work–family conflict developed by Frone, Russell and Cooper (1992) among US employees. They found similarities between the Hong Kong and the US samples. For example, the main reason leading to work–family conflict was a high level of job stressors or job conflict. E. J. Hill (2005) tested a cross-cultural model of the work–family interface using IBM survey responses from 48 countries. The results suggested the existence of a 'transportable rather than a culturally specific or gender-specific' work–family interface model, in which the causes and consequences of work–family conflict are similar among employees in diverse cultures.

Interestingly, in these 'classic models' of the work–family interface, the importance of leadership styles and the role of the manager are not taken into account. However, all of them emphasize how important it is that the organization provides employees with policies to help them balance work and life. Thus, what seems clear is that work–family conflict is not a problem that belongs exclusively to employees but also to the organization in general, and to senior and line managers in particular.

Work–Family Conflict and Work–Family Facilitation: Two Different Processes

To understand better the role of managers and leadership styles in the work–family process, it is important to have in mind a clear picture of the causes and consequences of work–family conflict. As we pointed out previously, work–family conflict occurs when there are difficulties in attending to both family and work responsibilities (Greenhaus & Beutell, 1985). In subsequent studies on work–family issues, Frone and colleagues (Frone, 2000; Frone et al., 1992; Frone, Yardley & Markel, 1997) distinguished between two types of conflict, arguing that the definition by Greenhaus and Beutell involved a bidirectional relationship between these two domains. Specifically, work–family conflict occurs when work-related demands interfere with home responsibilities (e.g., answering work-related emails at home) whereas family–work conflict takes place when family responsibilities interfere with work activities (e.g., receiving phone calls from family members during working time). Several studies have demonstrated that these two constructs can be distinguished both theoretically and empirically (e.g., Frone et al., 1992; Geurts, Taris, Kompier et al., 2005; Kelloway, Gottlieb & Barham, 1999; Kossek & Ozeki, 1998; Netemeyer, Boles & McMurrian, 1996).

The top part of Figure 7.1 represents the 'traditional model of work–family conflict', including the main antecedents and consequences of this phenomenon. As regards the antecedents, most studies have shown that the best predictors of work–family conflict are work-related demands such as the number of work hours or work overload, whereas the main predictors of family–work conflict are family-related demands such as the number of children (e.g., Amstad, Meier, Fasel, Elfering & Semmer, 2011; Aryee et al., 1999; Frone et al., 1992). As regards the

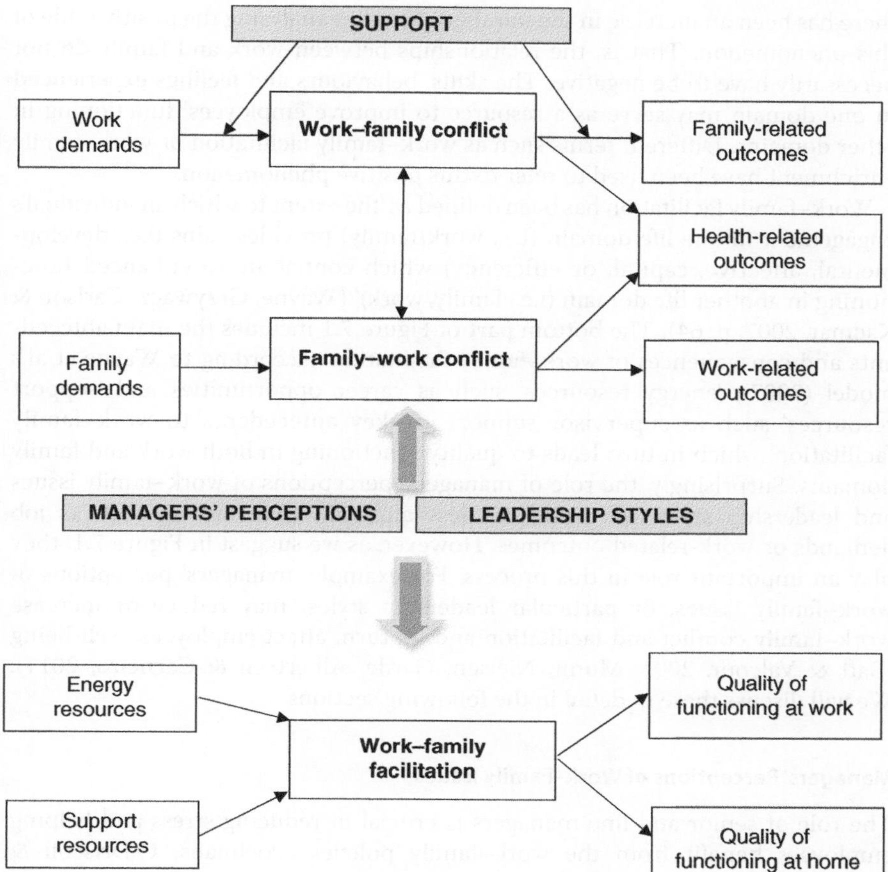

Figure 7.1 Traditional models of work–family conflict and facilitation.

potential consequences, Ford, Heinen and Langkamer (2007) found that work–family conflict was related to family-related outcomes such as reduced family satisfaction, whereas family–work conflict was related to work-related outcomes such as reduced job satisfaction. More recently, Sanz-Vergel, Rodríguez-Muñoz and Nielsen (2015) found that family–work conflict was related to conflicts with colleagues, which in turn was positively related to conflicts with the spouse. Other studies have found that both types of conflict can be related to both work- and family-related outcomes such as reduced satisfaction, health problems and absenteeism (E. J. Hill, 2005; Kinnunen, Feldt, Geurts & Pulkkinen, 2006; Kinnunen & Mauno, 1998). Finally, support from supervisors, colleagues and family members is a crucial moderator in this process, buffering the effects of stressors on work–family conflict, and the effects of work–family conflict on health and work-related outcomes (Fox & Dwyer, 1999; Goff, Mount & Jamison, 1990; Voydanoff, 2002).

The negative side of the work–family interface has been the main area of research within this field over the last 40 years. However, during the last decade there has been an increase in the number of studies analysing the positive side of this phenomenon. That is, the relationships between work and family do not necessarily have to be negative. The skills, behaviours and feelings experienced in one domain may serve as a resource to improve employees' functioning in other domains. Different terms such as work–family facilitation or work–family enrichment have been used to refer to this positive phenomenon.

Work–family facilitation has been defined as 'the extent to which an individual's engagement in one life domain (i.e., work/family) provides gains (i.e., developmental, affective, capital, or efficiency) which contribute to enhanced functioning in another life domain (i.e., family/work)' (Wayne, Grzywacz, Carlson & Kacmar, 2007, p. 64). The bottom part of Figure 7.1 includes the main antecedents and consequences of work–family facilitation. According to Wayne et al.'s model (2007), 'energy resources' such as career opportunities and 'support resources' such as supervisor support are key antecedents to work–family facilitation, which in turn leads to quality functioning in both work and family domains. Surprisingly, the role of managers' perceptions of work–family issues and leadership styles have received less attention than factors such as job demands or work-related outcomes. However, as we suggest in Figure 7.1, they play an important role in this process. For example, managers' perceptions of work–family issues, or particular leadership styles, may reduce or increase work–family conflict and facilitation and, in turn, affect employees' well-being (Batt & Valcour, 2003; Munir, Nielsen, Garde, Albertsen & Carneiro, 2011). We will discuss these in detail in the following sections.

Managers' Perceptions of Work–Family Issues

The role of senior and line managers is crucial in reducing stress and helping employees benefit from the work–family policies (Poelmans, O'Driscoll & Beham, 2005). The development of a work–family supportive culture is the first milestone for the policies to work efficiently and be appropriately used. To achieve it, it may be necessary to change how managers approach work–family issues. Managers may put obstacles in the way of employees achieving a good work–life balance if they perceive work and family issues to be exclusively the employees' problem. For example, in a study conducted among 4,000 Spanish employees working in 800 different organizations, it was found that 61.6 per cent of the senior managers considered that work–family issues should be solved by the employees privately and 42.6 per cent reported that family responsibilities limited females' level of productivity (Women's Institute, Spanish Ministry of Labour, 2005).

These underlying assumptions about the division of labour and the separation of work and home are the basis of an organizational culture that may support or hinder work–family balance. Lewis (2001) mentions four assumptions made in the 'traditional' model of work. Table 7.1 summarizes these assumptions and their potential negative consequences for the creation of a supportive work–family culture.

The first is related to the gendered assumptions about how women and men separate work and home. If managers conceive that women still have the traditional

Table 7.1 Managers' assumptions about work–family issues.

Areas	Possible managers' assumptions	Potential consequences
Gender and family responsibilities	Males are breadwinners Women will experience more family–work conflict and perform less well	Preference for employees without family commitments Difficulties for women to be hired and promoted
Long work hours	Working long hours is a sign of commitment It will increase productivity	Presenteeism Lack of work–family balance and health problems
Full-time work	It demonstrates higher commitment Full-time employees perform better	Fewer career opportunities for employees who need part-time jobs to balance work and family
Entitlements and favours	The use of work–family policies is a favour and not a right	Employees are afraid of using benefits Employees using benefits are excluded from promotion

role of taking care of the family, they will value male workers or women without family commitments. This assumption was empirically tested in a study by Hoobler, Wayne and Lemmon (2009), who demonstrated that supervisors (both male and female) perceived that women had greater family–work conflict and that this conflict affected their performance and their adjustment to the organization and to the specific job. Because of this perceived mismatch, supervisors did not see women as possible candidates for promotion. The second assumption is related to norms about time. The ideology of long hours as an indicator of commitment and productivity should be avoided. Indeed, it has been found that work hours and work overload lead to higher work–family conflict and health problems and do not increase performance (e.g., Holman, Joyeux & Kask, 2008; Ilies, Huth, Ryan & Dimotakis, 2015). The third assumption is related to the concept of a full-time job as the typical work pattern, while part-time jobs are considered as atypical and generally performed by women who have to attend to family responsibilities. This underlying assumption may result in unfair processes such as poor performance appraisals or fewer opportunities for promotion.

On the other hand, Batt and Valcour (2003) demonstrated that understanding supervisors were able to alleviate stress by showing simple behaviours such as kind words when the employee had a family problem or flexibility to accommodate their needs. Also, identifying how managers relate work–family issues to strategic issues will play a role in the organization. For example, Xiao and O'Neill (2010) proposed a theoretical model in which work–family issues were considered as a competitive advantage. In this model, manager characteristics, including factors such as personality, the existence of a mentor, and the level of experience, were proposed as a predictor of the organizational culture and the workplace flexibility, which in turn affected employees' family life. They conducted in-depth interviews with 49 hotel managers and found that management perceptions of work–family issues differed among hotels, which resulted in different human resource strategies. For example, caring about 'people-related issues' was cited as a competitive advantage in some hotels but not in others. In this study it was also found that hotel managers acted as role models and it was easier for employees to balance work and family if the managers also cared about their own work–family life. Finally, Manfredi and Doherty (2006) pointed out that leadership styles and attitudes towards work–life balance filter down through different levels of management, influencing work–family practices.

The Role of the Leader in Creating a Work–Family Culture

Leadership Styles and Followers' Work–Family Conflict and Facilitation

To date, evidence about the effects of leadership styles has primarily been focused on job-related outcomes, and little empirical research has examined the effects of leadership beyond the workplace. The existence of this gap in the field is surprising, especially considering the significant influence that leaders can exert over several aspects of employees' lives (McCarthy, Darcy & Grady, 2010). Supervisors or immediate managers are the frontline representatives for the organization and the people most involved in employee's daily work activity, including work–life balance decisions (Major & Lauzun, 2010).

Of the limited number of studies which empirically bridge the work–family and leadership literatures, one dominant approach has been based on leader supportiveness as a predictor of subordinate outcomes, such as work–family conflict or family-friendly policy use (e.g., Hammer, Kossek, Anger, Bodner & Zimmerman, 2011; Michel, Pichler & Newness, 2014; Van Daalen, Willemsen & Sanders, 2006). This support can be emotional, such as by discussing family-related issues, or instrumental, such as by approving family-related requests. The second approach is relationship-based, analysing how leaders interact with their employees, and how this evolves over time. This view is exemplified by the leader–member exchange theory (e.g., Major & Morganson, 2011). A third emerging line of research, still anecdotal, applies leadership styles, such as transformational or servant leadership, to the study of work–family interaction.

There is evidence that supervisor support can reduce work–family conflict levels. Leaders who show understanding towards followers' family issues have been found to reduce followers' work–family conflict (Van Daalen, Willemsen & Sanders, 2006). Similarly, Allen (2001) showed that supervisor support influenced employees' perceptions of the organization as family-supportive, which reduced the level of experienced work–family conflict. Carlson and Perrewé (1999) demonstrated that having a supervisor who is supportive leads to lower scores on work–family conflict. Meta-analytical studies have also confirmed the link between support from supervisor and reduced work–family conflict (Ford, Heinen & Langkamer, 2007; Kossek, Pichler, Bodner & Hammer, 2011).

In general terms, it is argued that a high-quality leader–member exchange relationship alleviates interference between work and family. In support of this view, R. T. Hill, Morganson, Matthews and Atkinson (2015) showed that work–family conflict is reduced through a process of social exchange between the supervisor and employee. In the same vein, Major, Fletcher, Davis and Germano (2008) found that leader–member exchange relationship is associated with reduced work interference with family. Similar results were obtained by Bernas and Major (2000), Lapierre, Hackett and Taggar (2006), and Tummers and Bronkhorst (2014).

With regard to leadership styles and work–family interface, in recent years some researchers have begun to explore this neglected area. Munir et al. (2012) and Hammond, Cleveland, O'Neill, Stawski and Jones Tate (2015) found transformational leadership to be negatively associated with work–family conflict. A recent study extended the research by showing that employee perceptions of servant leadership was negatively related to work–family conflict (Tang, Kwan, Zhang & Zhu, 2015).

Conservation of resources theory (COR) (Hobfoll, 1989) provides the theoretical underpinning for understanding why leadership behaviours may help to diminish interference of work with family. Leaders may boost employees' resources to deal with stress at work, thus reducing work–family conflict. For instance, transformational leaders may provide employees with autonomy and self-efficacy through empowerment (Piccolo & Colquitt, 2006). This is crucial, since work–family conflict has often been conceptualized as a response to threats to resources (e.g., time or energy). Therefore, leaders might compensate for resources lost because of job demands, and provide resources for combining employees' work and family. Hammond et al. (2015) explored the role of work-relevant resources (autonomy, positive affect and managerial support) as the explanatory mechanism by which transformational leaders influence the experience of conflict across work and family domains. They found that the abovementioned resources mediated the relationship between transformational leadership and work–family conflict.

However, COR also suggests that managing multiple roles (work and home) may offer the potential to acquire and accumulate resources, from which the other domain benefits as well. Therefore, leaders may help not only to prevent work–family conflict, but also to promote work–family facilitation (also known as work–family enrichment). Carlson, Ferguson, Kacmar, Grzywacz and Whitten (2006) showed that when employees can negotiate with their supervisors for scheduling flexibility, they tend to report a high level of work–life enrichment. Similarly, both authentic (Jiang & Men, in press) and servant leadership (Tang et al., 2015) are positively related to work–family facilitation.

In our effort to disentangle the effects of the dynamics of leadership on the relationship between work and family, it is worth mentioning that beyond the abovementioned effects the leader may have an indirect role. Based on a within-individual approach, Goh, Ilies and Wilson (2015) showed that the relationship between daily workload and daily work–family conflict was moderated by supervisor work–family support. Similarly, Harris, Harris, Carlson and Carlson (2015) also found that leader–member exchange quality acted as a buffering variable, in this case between technology overload and work–family conflict. Regarding transformational leadership, a study conducted by Wang and Walumbwa (2007) found that it moderated the relationship between work flexibility benefits and both organizational commitment and work withdrawal, and that between childcare benefits and work withdrawal.

Work–Family Policies and Positive Organizational Outcomes

The question of how work–family policies or practices are linked to optimal organizational functioning has been of great interest to both academics and practitioners. Broadly speaking, work–family policies are defined as '*any employer sponsored benefit or working condition that helps an employee to balance work and non-work demands*' (Cascio, 2000, p. 166). As pointed out by Sánchez-Vidal, Cegarra-Leiva and Cegarra-Navarro (2012), we can find more than 100 human resource practices that organizations could implement to achieve a balance between work and life, and there is no widely accepted approach to classifying them. It is possible to distinguish between three general types of family-friendly practices, namely policies (e.g., flexible work arrangements), services (e.g., resource programmes concerning dependent care options) and benefits (e.g., childcare subsidies; Hammer, Neal, Newsom, Brockwood & Colton, 2005).

Research on the consequences of work–family policies indicates the benefits for organizations. Among such consequences, a distinction can be made between outcomes that are individually oriented (they have benefits primarily for the employee, e.g., job satisfaction) and those that are organizationally oriented (they have benefits mainly for the organization, e.g., financial performance). First, at the individual level, work–family policies have been associated with a wide variety of advantages, including an increased organizational commitment, decreased turnover, decreased job burnout and increased job satisfaction (Butts, Casper & Yang, 2013). Work–family policies are also effective in reducing work–family conflict. For instance, Mandeville, Halbesleben and Whitman (in press) found that the utilization of family-friendly policies reduced the level of work–family conflict among employees. Furthermore, a recent study suggests that family-friendly work arrangements influence not only employees' work–family conflict but also their partners' level of work–family conflict (Schooreel & Verbruggen, 2016).

Literature on work–family policies has emphasized the need to distinguish between the availability of work–family policies and the actual use that employees make of these offered policies depending on contextual factors (Blair-Loy & Wharton, 2002). One noteworthy aspect of this research is that work–family policies have benefits even when employees do not use these policies. For instance, Scandura and Lankau (1997) showed that simple availability of work–family policies increased employees' job satisfaction. Meta-analytic findings suggest that availability and use of work–family support policies are related to more positive work attitudes. However, the effects associated with policy availability were generally stronger than those associated with use (Butts et al., 2013). It is quite likely that those who use work–family policies are more aware of their shortcomings, and therefore less satisfied. Indeed, when managers consider that work–family policies are a favour instead of a right, employees may feel that they will be considered to be less committed employees and will avoid using these policies.

For example, in a study of faculty members, the members mentioned fear of their use of policies being regarded as a 'red flag' (Castañeda et al., 2015).

Among organizational outcomes, several researchers have provided support for positive effects of work–family policies on performance. For instance, Konrad and Mangel (2000) found a positive association between the number of work–life programs offered and performance (measured as sales per employee). Work–family policies have been linked with both self-reported performance and supervisor ratings of performance (Butts et al., 2013). Similarly, in a study of Fortune 500 list companies, it was found that firm announcements of work–family initiatives were positively related to shareholder return (Arthur, 2003). Additionally, work–family policies are relevant for retaining and attracting highly qualified professionals (Harrington & Ladge, 2009) and reducing absenteeism (Dalton & Mesch, 1990).

Lastly, despite the present-day consensus about the positive effects of work–family policies, earlier research found that these practices may sometimes lead to negative outcomes. Research has found a positive relationship between work–family policies and decreased job satisfaction (Thomas & Ganster, 1995), increased intentions to stay (Glass & Riley, 1998) and higher work–family conflict (Goff et al., 1990). This inconsistent pattern of results can be explained mainly by two factors. First, most research examines outcomes without considering possible mediators. As discussed above, research has long stressed the critical role of supervisors in the implementation of work and family policies. These interventions are more likely to be effective when employees perceive support from supervisors for the use of family-friendly practices (e.g., Major & Lauzun, 2010). Second, a first step is to communicate the availability of these policies to employees effectively, which is not the common practice with work–family policies. Yeandle, Wigfield, Crompton and Dennett (2002) found that 50 per cent of employees were unaware of the family-friendly practices offered by their organizations.

Avenues for Future Research: Integrating the Leader Level in Work–Family Studies

Theoretical Challenges

Throughout this chapter, we have examined the main theoretical models that have been described in the work–family literature. It seems clear that most of the studies focus on possible antecedents such as job and family demands, whereas managers' perceptions of work–family issues and the role of leadership styles are still not well represented in this field. For that reason, one of the main theoretical challenges is to develop a theoretical framework that incorporates the figure of the manager and the role of leadership styles.

As can be seen in Figure 7.2, we propose a multilevel model that includes not only employees' perceptions of work–family conflict but also the roles that other people in the organization have in this process. For example, the role of the team is crucial; when colleagues are working towards a common goal instead of against

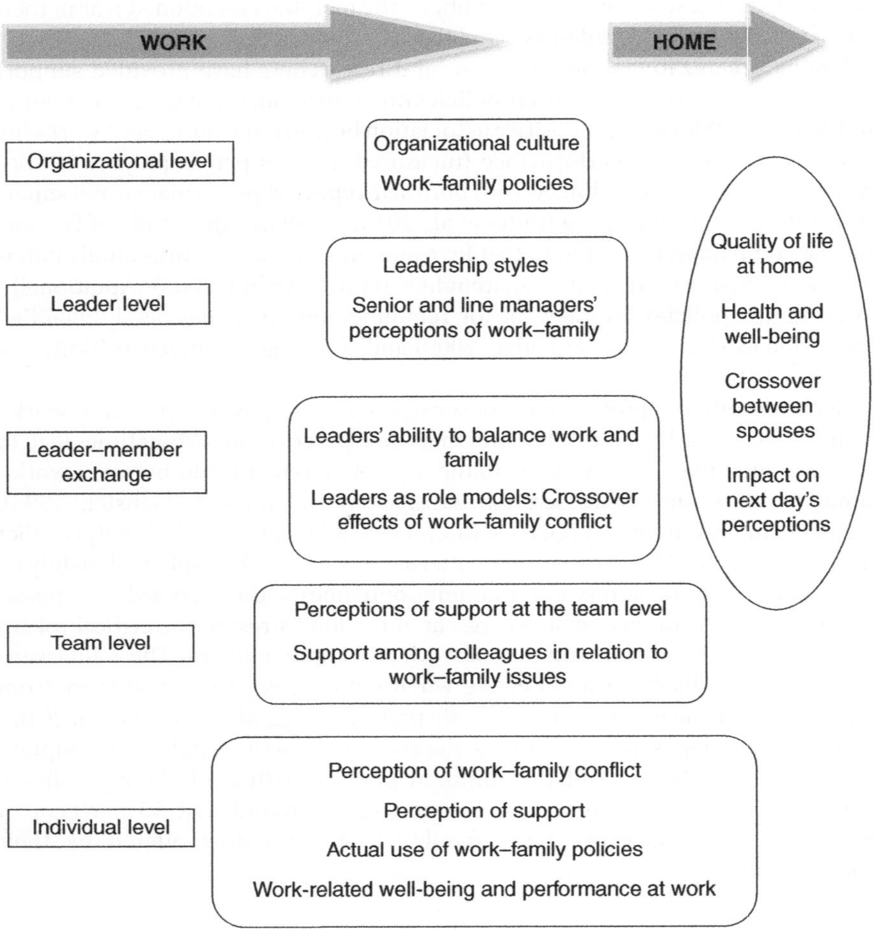

Figure 7.2 Multilevel model of the work–family interface.

each other, employees will have the necessary support if a family problem is interfering with work. In a previously mentioned study among dual-earner couples, it was found that family–work conflict led to more conflict with colleagues (Sanz-Vergel et al., 2015). Future studies should analyse why this is the case, and include variables that may explain this relationship. For example, it may be that family–work conflict prevents employees from doing their job, which results in higher work overload for colleagues.

Also, the perceptions of colleagues about work–family issues may be affecting this relationship. As may happen with managers, colleagues may have a negative view of people bringing family problems into the work domain. In order to have a team where all employees collaborate, leaders should make clear to the team that work–family balance is valued. Therefore, both the team level and the leader level should be included in studies on work–family. Also, more studies are needed on how leaders' own levels of work–family conflict cross over to the followers.

The role of leaders as role models has not been sufficiently analysed so far. The few existing studies show that leaders' work–family facilitation crosses over to followers, which increases their job performance (Carlson, Ferguson, Kacmar, Grzywacz & Whitten, 2011), whereas leaders' family–work conflict leads to feelings of burnout, which in turn leads to followers' higher feelings of burnout. These studies open a door to future studies on the crossover effects from leaders to team members and the importance of leaders' own ability to balance work and family (Ten Brummelhuis, Haar & Roche, 2014).

In addition, more studies on leadership styles would help us identify the main characteristics of the leader supportive of work–family issues. For example, Kossek and Hammer (2008) identified the main behaviours shown by this type of leader: they offer emotional and social support for family, they are a good role model for work and non-work balance, they offer tangible support with scheduling conflicts, and they work effectively with associates to creatively solve conflicts between work and non-work. Kossek and Hammer demonstrated the success of a training intervention during which supervisors learned family-supportive behaviours and how to transfer those behaviours onto the actual job.

Taken together, what these findings suggest is that (1) a combination of specific behaviours ensures the appropriate environment that will help the organization deal with work–family issues, and (2) these supportive behaviours can be trained. The leader level is the core part of the model, as it is only through the work of the senior and line managers that the appropriate work–family policies can be designed and implemented, creating an organizational culture which actually supports the employee. The multilevel model allows us to examine the dynamic interactions between the different levels of analysis, and scholars have emphasized the need to adopt a multilevel approach in the study of work-related stress and well-being (Bakker & Daniels, 2013).

Finally, both domains, work and home, should be analysed, given that what happens at work spills over to the home domain and has an impact on employees' privates lives, affecting not only employees' own health and well-being, but also their families' (Bakker & Demerouti, 2013). In our multilevel model, spillover and crossover processes should be analysed in order to achieve a complete understanding of the existing dynamics within each domain, and between domains.

Methodological Challenges

Regarding methodological challenges, a clear gap in the literature is to know how work–family policies relate to employee work attitudes, and why several practices are not effective. Although the field has advanced in terms of cross-level analysis within boundaries (work and non-work), most intervention studies fail to include cross-level examinations. For instance, it would be interesting to test more frequently a three-level mediational design, whereby a predictor variable at organizational level (e.g., family-friendly organizational culture) affects another variable designated as mediator (e.g., leader support), which, in turn, affects the employee's outcome (e.g., performance). A design with a similar approach was carried out by Las Heras, Bosch and Raes (2015), in which it was found that perceived organizational support and family-supportive supervisor behaviours were underlying mechanisms that explained the relationship between family-friendly organizational culture and employees' turnover intentions and satisfaction with work–family balance. This type of design is relevant, since it allows the researcher to control for specific variance changes at each level of analysis.

In this area, despite the accumulation of findings, many central questions have not received clear answers, and we need a more thorough understanding of how work–family policies impact on employee and workplace business outcomes. In addition, most work–life balance policies and programmes are not evidence-based, and the scarce research evidence is based on weak experimental designs or correlational studies (Hammer et al., 2016). Therefore, a further issue worthy of consideration is the need for more methodologically rigorous and evidence-based research on the effectiveness of work–family workplace interventions. Randomized control trials designs can be helpful for this aim.

Future research also might benefit from evaluating work–family policies more broadly by considering their impact on the multiple stakeholders (e.g., society, families). There has been a call for more multisource data and multilevel relationships in work–family studies (Kossek, Baltes & Matthews, 2011). In their recent review of methods in work and occupational health psychology, Spector and Pindek (2016) found that the use of a single source of information in work–family literature was around 40 per cent, and the use of multiple data sources was still somewhat limited (e.g., Ilies, Huth, Ryan & Dimotakis, 2015; Ilies, Wilson & Wagner, 2009). In this area, how organization policies affect one's life outside of work has yet to be explored more deeply. Recent methodological advances provide the opportunity to examine the impact of work domain on non-work life. For instance, the Actor–Partner Interdependence Model (APIM) (Cook & Kenny, 2005) is a proper way to analyse data from research design with dyads. APIM was designed to deal with violations of statistical independence, as well as for investigating dyadic effects in close relationships. Specifically, the APIM allows examination of how an individual's predictor variable simultaneously and independently relates to his or her own criterion variable (actor effect) and to his or her partner's criterion variable (partner effect). In APIM, the partner effect allows testing of the mutual (i.e. reciprocal) influence between the members of the dyad.

Another issue that is of interest for future research concerns the adoption of a within-individual approach. One of the most salient criticisms within the field has been the reliance on cross-sectional designs, despite the recognition that work processes and relationships between the work and family domains are inherently dynamic (e.g., Ohly, Sonnentag, Niessen & Zapf, 2010). Several meta-analyses on the effects of work–life policies base their conclusions primarily on correlational designs (Allen, Johnson, Kiburz & Shockley, 2013; Butts, Casper & Yang, 2013; Gajendran & Harrison, 2007; Mesmer-Magnus & Viswesvaran, 2006; Michel, Kotrba, Mitchelson, Clark & Baltes, 2011). In such between-individual designs, it is very difficult to explore the day-to-day processes through which work influences employees' family lives. Diary studies have been recommended to collect work and non-work experiences in individuals' natural life contexts (Butler, Song & Ilies, 2013). These experiences may take place during the course of a working week, or during longer time frames such as weeks or months.

This methodology reduces the likelihood of retrospective recall bias, because the amount of time between the experience and the report of these experiences is reduced (Ohly et al., 2010).

Empirical research using diary designs has clearly shown daily fluctuations within the same person in work–family conflict. Butler et al. (2013) have indicated that the amount of total variance in work–family conflict that may be attributed to within-person fluctuations ranges from 48 to 72 per cent. Other recent diary studies showed that estimates of within-person variability range from 49 to 52 per cent, which means that this work experience varies significantly from one day to another (Derks, Bakker, Peters & van Wingerden, 2016; Goh et al., 2015; Ilies et al., 2015). An emerging line of research which fits perfectly with this type of design is the study of state leadership behaviours, or, in other words, leadership as a dynamic phenomenon. Recent studies have begun to use a within-person perspective for studying daily fluctuations of leader behaviours (Dóci, Stouten & Hofmans, 2015). For instance, Tims, Bakker and Xanthopoulou (2011) found daily fluctuations in transformational leadership. Specifically, it was shown that 75 per cent of the variation on transformational leadership was attributable to within-person variations. It is plausible to argue that leader behaviour will not be the same every day, and it may change on a daily basis in terms of intensity according to environmental factors. As previous research indicates that supervisor behaviour has a great impact on employees' work–family conflict, future studies can examine how individual's daily work–family conflict is influenced by daily leadership support. Overall, these findings stress the importance of adopting a within-person approach, as complementary to between-person, in the study of the work–family interface.

References

Allen, T. D. (2001). Family-supportive work environments: The role of organizational perceptions. *Journal of Vocational Behavior*, 58, 414–35.

Allen, T. D., Herst, D., Bruck, C. & Sutton, M. (2000). Consequences associated with work-to-family conflict: A review and agenda for future research. *Journal of Occupational Health Psychology*, 5, 278–308.

Allen, T. D., Johnson, R. C., Kiburz, K. M. & Shockley, K. M. (2013). Work–family conflict and flexible work arrangements: Deconstructing flexibility. *Personnel Psychology*, 66(2), 345–76.

Amstad, F. T., Meier, L. L., Fasel, U., Elfering, A. & Semmer, N. K. (2011). A meta-analysis of work–family conflict and various outcomes. *Journal of Occupational Health Psychology*, 16, 151–69.

Arthur, M. M. (2003). Share price reactions to work–family initiatives: An institutional perspective. *Academy of Management Journal*, 46(4), 497–505.

Aryee, S., Fields, D. & Luk, V. (1999). A cross-cultural test of a model of the work–family interface. *Journal of Management*, 25, 491–511.

Bakker, A. B. & Daniels, K. (2013). *A Day in the Life of a Happy Worker*. Hove, UK: Psychology Press.

Bakker, A. B. & Demerouti, E. (2013). The Spillover–Crossover model. In J. Grzywacz & E. Demerouti (eds), *New Frontiers in Work and Family Research*. Hove, UK: Psychology Press, pp. 53–69.

Batt, R. & Valcour, P. M. (2003). Human resources practices as predictors of work–family outcomes and employee turnover. *Industrial Relations*, 42, 189–220.

Bernas, K. H. & Major, D. A. (2000). Contributors to stress resistance: Testing a model of women's work–family conflict. *Psychology of Women Quarterly*, 24, 170–8.

Blair-Loy, M. & Wharton, A. S. (2002). Employees use of work–family policies and the workplace context. *Social Forces*, 80, 813–45.

Bureau of Labor Statistics (2014). Employment characteristics of families summary. http://www.bls.gov/news.release/famee.nr0.htm. Accessed 11 January 2016.

Butler, A. B., Song, Z. & Ilies, R. (2013). Experience sampling methods for work–family research: A review and research agenda. In J. Grzywacz & E. Demerouti (eds), *New Frontiers in Work and Family Research*. New York: Psychology Press, pp. 133–49.

Butts, M. M., Casper, W. J. & Yang, T. S. (2013). How important are work–family support policies? A meta-analytic investigation of their effects on employee outcomes. *Journal of Applied Psychology*, 98(1), 1–25.

Carlson, D. S., Ferguson, M., Kacmar, K. M., Grzywacz, J. G. & Whitten, D. (2011). Pay it forward: The positive crossover effects of supervisor work–family enrichment. *Journal of Management*, 37, 770–89.

Carlson, D. S. & Perrewé, P. L. (1999). The role of social support in the stressor-strain relationship: An examination of work–family conflict. *Journal of Management*, 25(4), 513–40.

Cascio, W. F. (2000). *Costing Human Resources: The Financial Impact of Behaviour in Organizations*. Boston, MA: Thompson Learning.

Castañeda, M., Zambrana, R., Marsh, K., Vega, W., Becerra, R. & Pérez, D. J. (2015). Role of institutional climate on underrepresented faculty perceptions and decision making in use of work–family policies. *Family Relations*, 64, 711–25.

Cook, W. & Kenny, D. A. (2005). The Actor–Partner Interdependence Model: A model of bidirectional effects in developmental studies. *International Journal of Behavioral Development*, 29, 101–9.

Dalton, D. R. & Mesch, D. J. (1990). The impact of flexible scheduling on employee attendance and turnover. *Administrative Science Quarterly*, 370–87.

Derks, D., Bakker, A. B., Peters, P. & van Wingerden, P. (2016). Work-related smartphone use, work–family conflict and family role performance: The role of segmentation preference. *Human Relations*, 69(5), 1045–68.

Dóci, E., Stouten, J. & Hofmans, J. (2015). The cognitive-behavioral system of leadership: Cognitive antecedents of active and passive leadership behaviors. *Frontiers in Psychology*, 6, 1344, doi: 10.3389/fpsyg.2015.01344.

Eurofound (2015). *Sixth European Working Conditions Survey*. doi: 10.2806/59106.

Ford, M. T., Heinen, B. A. & Langkamer, K. L. (2007). Work and family satisfaction and conflict: A meta-analysis of cross-domain relations. *Journal of Applied Psychology*, 92, 57–80.

Fox, M. L. & Dwyer, D. J. (1999). An investigation of the effects of time and involvement in the relationship between stressors and work–family conflict. *Journal of Occupational Health Psychology*, 4, 164–74.

Frone, M. R. (2000). Work–family conflict and employee psychiatric disorders: The national comorbidity survey. *Journal of Applied Psychology*, 85, 888–95.

Frone, M. R., Russell, M. & Cooper, M. L. (1992). Antecedents and outcomes of work–family conflict: Testing a model of the work–family interface. *Journal of Applied Psychology*, 77, 65–78.

Frone, M. R., Yardley, J. K. & Markel, K. (1997). Developing and testing an integrative model of the work–family interface. *Journal of Vocational Behavior*, 50, 145–67.

Gajendran, R. S. & Harrison, D. A. (2007). The good, the bad, and the unknown about telecommuting: Meta-analysis of psychological mediators and individual consequences. *Journal of Applied Psychology*, 92(6), 1524–41.

Geurts, S., Rutte, C. & Peeters, M. (1999). Antecedents and consequences of work–home interference among medical residents. *Social Science & Medicine*, 48, 1135–48.

Geurts, S., Taris, T. W., Kompier, M. A. J., Dikkers, J. S. E., Van Hooff, M. L. M. & Kinnunen, U. M. (2005). Work–home interaction from a work psychological perspective: Development and validation of a new questionnaire, the SWING. *Work & Stress*, 19, 319–39.

Glass, J. L. & Riley, L. (1998). Family responsive policies and employee retention following childbirth. *Social Forces*, 76(4), 1401–35.

Goff, S. J., Mount, M. K. & Jamison, R. L. (1990). Employer supported child care, work–family conflict and absenteeism: A field study. *Personnel Psychology*, 43, 793–809.

Goh, Z., Ilies, R. & Wilson, K. S. (2015). Supportive supervisors improve employees' daily lives: The role supervisors play in the impact of daily workload on life satisfaction via work–family conflict. *Journal of Vocational Behavior*, 89, 65–73.

Greenhaus, J. & Beutell, N. (1985). Sources of conflict between work and family roles. *Academy of Management Review*, 10, 76–88.

Hammer, L. B., Johnson, R. C., Crain, T. L., Bodner, T., Kossek, E. E., Davis, K. D., Kelly, E. L., Buxton, O. M., Karuntzos, G., Chosewood, L.C. & Berkman, L. (2016). Intervention effects on safety compliance and citizenship behaviors: Evidence from the work, family, and health study. *Journal of Applied Psychology*, 101(2), 190–208.

Hammer, L. B., Kossek, E. E., Anger, W. K., Bodner, T. & Zimmerman, K. L. (2011). Clarifying work–family intervention processes: The roles of work–family conflict and family-supportive supervisor behaviors. *Journal of Applied Psychology*, 96(1), 134–50.

Hammer, L. B., Neal, M. B., Newsom, J., Brockwood, K. J. & Colton, C. (2005). A longitudinal study of the effects of dual-earner couples' utilization of family-friendly workplace supports on work and family outcomes. *Journal of Applied Psychology*, 90, 799–810.

Hammond, M., Cleveland, J. N., O'Neill, J. W., Stawski, R. S. & Jones Tate, A. (2015). Mediators of transformational leadership and the work–family relationship. *Journal of Managerial Psychology*, 30(4), 454–69.

Harrington, B. & Ladge, J. J. (2009). Work–life integration: Present dynamics and future directions for organizations. *Organizational Dynamics*, 38(2), 148–57.
Harris, K. J., Harris, R. B., Carlson, J. R. & Carlson, D. S. (2015). Resource loss from technology overload and its impact on work–family conflict: Can leaders help? *Computers in Human Behavior*, 50, 411–17.
Hill, E. J. (2005). Work–family facilitation and conflict, working fathers and mothers, work–family stressors and support. *Journal of Family Issues*, 26, 793–819.
Hill, R. T., Morganson, V. J., Matthews, R. A. & Atkinson, T. P. (2016). LMX, breach perceptions, work–family conflict, and well-being: A mediational model. *Journal of Psychology*, 150(1), 132–49.
Hobfoll, S. E. (1989). Conservation of resources: A new attempt at conceptualizing stress. *American Psychologist*, 44(3), 513–24.
Holman, C., Joyeux, B. & Kask, C. (2008). Labor productivity trends since 2000, by sector and industry. *Monthly Labor Review*, 131, 64–82.
Hoobler, J. M., Wayne, S. J. & Lemmon, G. (2009). Bosses' perceptions of family–work conflict and women's promotability: Glass ceiling effects. *Academy of Management Journal*, 52, 939–57.
Ilies, R., Huth, M., Ryan, A. M. & Dimotakis, N. (2015). Explaining the links between workload, distress, and work–family conflict among school employees: Physical, cognitive, and emotional fatigue. *Journal of Educational Psychology*, 107, 1136–49.
Ilies, R., Wilson, K. S. & Wagner, D. T. (2009). The spillover of daily job satisfaction onto employees' family lives: The facilitating role of work–family integration. *Academy of Management Journal*, 52(1), 87–102.
Jiang, H. & Men, R. L. (in press). Creating an engaged workforce: The impact of authentic leadership, transparent organizational communication, and work–life enrichment. *Communication Research*. doi: 10.1177/0093650215613137.
Kelloway, E. K., Gottlieb, B. H. & Barham, L. (1999). The source, nature, and direction of work and family conflict: A longitudinal investigation. *Journal of Occupational Health Psychology*, 4, 337–46.
Kinnunen, U., Feldt, T., Geurts, S. & Pulkkinen, L. (2006). Types of work–family interface: Well-being correlates of negative and positive spillover between work and family. *Scandinavian Journal of Psychology*, 47, 149–62.
Kinnunen, U. & Mauno, S. (1998). Antecedents and outcomes of work–family conflict among employed women and men in Finland. *Human Relations*, 51, 157–77.
Konrad, A. M. & Mangel, R. (2000). The impact of work–life programs on firm productivity. *Strategic Management Journal*, 21(12), 1225–37.
Kossek, E. E., Baltes, B. B. & Matthews, R. A. (2011). How work–family research can finally have an impact in organizations. *Industrial and Organizational Psychology*, 4(3), 352–69.
Kossek, E. E. & Hammer, L. B. (2008). Family Supportive Supervisory Behaviors (FSSB) Intervention Study: Effects on Employee's Work, Family, Safety & Health Outcomes. Summary of Findings from the National Institute for Occupational Safety and Health Grant # U010H008788. Portland State University and Michigan State University.

Kossek, E. E. & Ozeki, C. (1998). Work–family conflict, policies, and the job–life satisfaction relationship: A review and directions for organizational behavior–human resources research. *Journal of Applied Psychology*, 83, 139–49.
Kossek, E. E., Pichler, S., Bodner, T. & Hammer, L. B. (2011). Workplace social support and work–family conflict: A meta-analysis clarifying the influence of general and work–family-specific supervisor and organizational support. *Personnel Psychology*, 64(2), 289–313.
Lapierre, L. M., Hackett, R. D. & Taggar, S. (2006). A test of the links between family interference with work, job enrichment and leader–member exchange. *Applied Psychology*, 55(4), 489–511.
Las Heras, M., Bosch, M. J. & Raes, A. M. (2015). Sequential mediation among family friendly culture and outcomes. *Journal of Business Research*, 68(11), 2366–73.
Lewis, S. (2001). Restructuring workplace cultures: The ultimate work–family challenge? *Women in Management Review*, 16, 21–9.
Lu, L. & Cooper, C. L. (eds) (2015). *Handbook of Research on Work–Life Balance in Asia*. Cheltenham, UK: Edward Elgar.
Major, D. A., Fletcher, T. D., Davis, D. D. & Germano, L. M. (2008). The influence of work–family culture and workplace relationships on work interference with family: A multilevel model. *Journal of Organizational Behavior*, 29(7), 881–97.
Major, D. A. & Lauzun, H. M. (2010). Equipping managers to assist employees in addressing work–family conflict: Applying the research literature toward innovative practice. *Psychologist-Manager Journal*, 13(2), 69–85.
Major, D. A. & Morganson, V. J. (2011). Coping with work–family conflict: A leader–member exchange perspective. *Journal of Occupational Health Psychology*, 16(1), 126–38.
Mandeville, A., Halbesleben, J. & Whitman, M. (in press). Misalignment and misperception in preferences to utilize family-friendly benefits: Implications for benefit utilization and work–family conflict. *Personnel Psychology*. doi: 10.1111/peps.12124.
Manfredi, S. & Doherty, L. (2006). Leadership styles for work–life balance. Centre for Diversity Policy Research, Oxford Brookes University. https://www.brookes.ac.uk/services/hr/cdprp/resources/leadership_styles_wlb.pdf. Accessed 14 January, 2016.
McCarthy, A., Darcy, C. & Grady, G. (2010). Work–life balance policy and practice: Understanding line manager attitudes and behaviors. *Human Resource Management Review*, 20(2), 158–67.
Mesmer-Magnus, J. R. & Viswesvaran, C. (2006). How family-friendly work environments affect work/family conflict: A meta-analytic examination. *Journal of Labor Research*, 27(4), 555–74.
Michel, J. S., Kotrba, L. M., Mitchelson, J. K., Clark, M. A. & Baltes, B. B. (2011). Antecedents of work–family conflict: A meta-analytic review. *Journal of Organizational Behavior*, 32(5), 689–725.
Michel, J., Pichler, S. & Newness, K. (2014). Integrating leader affect, leader work–family spillover, and leadership. *Leadership & Organization Development Journal*, 35(5), 410–28.

Munir, F., Nielsen, K., Garde, A. H., Albertsen, K. & Carneiro, I. G. (2012). Mediating the effects of work–life conflict between transformational leadership and health-care workers' job satisfaction and psychological wellbeing. *Journal of Nursing Management*, 20(4), 512–21.

Netemeyer, R. G., Boles, J. S. & McMurrian, R. (1996). Development and validation of work–family conflict and family–work conflict scales. *Journal of Applied Psychology*, 81(4), 400–10.

Ohly, S., Sonnentag, S., Niessen, C. & Zapf, D. (2010). Diary studies in organizational research: An introduction and some practical recommendations. *Journal of Personnel Psychology*, 9, 79–93.

Perlow, L. A. (1995). Putting the work back into work/family. *Group and Organization Management*, 20, 227–39.

Piccolo, R. F. & Colquitt, J. A. (2006). Transformational leadership and job behaviors: The mediating role of core job characteristics. *Academy of Management Journal*, 49(2), 327–40.

Pleck, J. H. (1977). The work–family role system. *Social Problems*, 24, 417–27.

Poelmans, S., O'Driscoll, M. & Beham, B. (2005). An overview of international research on the work–family interface. In S. Poelmans (ed.), *Work and Family: An International Research Perspective*. Mahwah, NJ: Erlbaum, pp. 3–46.

Roberts, K. (2007). Work–life balance: The sources of the contemporary problem and the portable outcomes. *Employee Relations*, 29, 334–51.

Sánchez-Vidal, M. E., Cegarra-Leiva, D. & Cegarra-Navarro, J. G. (2012). Gaps between managers' and employees' perceptions of work–life balance. *International Journal of Human Resource Management*, 23(4), 645–61.

Sanz-Vergel, A. I., Rodríguez-Muñoz, A. & Nielsen, K. (2015). The thin line between work and home: The spillover and crossover of daily conflicts. *Journal of Occupational and Organizational Psychology*, 88, 1–18.

Scandura, T. A. & Lankau, M. J. (1997). Relationships of gender, family responsibility and flexible work hours to organizational commitment and job satisfaction. *Journal of Organizational Behavior*, 18(4), 377–91.

Schooreel, T. & Verbruggen, M. (2016). Use of family-friendly work arrangements and work–family conflict: Crossover effects in dual-earner couples. *Journal of Occupational Health Psychology*, 21(1), 119–32.

Spector, P. E. & Pindek, S. (2016). The future of research methods in work and occupational health psychology. *Applied Psychology*, 65(2), 412–31.

Tang, G., Kwan, H. K., Zhang, D. & Zhu, Z. (2015). Work–family effects of servant leadership: The roles of emotional exhaustion and personal learning. *Journal of Business Ethics*. doi: 10.1007/s10551-015-2559-7.

Ten Brummelhuis, L. L., Haar, J. M. & Roche, M. (2014). Does family life help to be a better leader? A closer look at crossover processes from leaders to followers. *Personnel Psychology*, 67, 917–49.

Thomas, L. T. & Ganster, D. C. (1995). Impact of family-supportive work variables on work–family conflict and strain: A control perspective. *Journal of Applied Psychology*, 80(1), 6–15.

Thompson, C., Beauvais, L. & Lyness, K. (1999). When work–family benefits are not enough: The influences of work–family culture on benefit utilization, organizational attachment, and work–family conflict. *Journal of Vocational Behavior*, 54, 329–415.

Tims, M., Bakker, A. B. & Xanthopoulou, D. (2011). Do transformational leaders enhance their followers' daily work engagement? *Leadership Quarterly*, 22(1), 121–31.

Tummers, L. & Bronkhorst, B. (2014). The impact of leader–member exchange (LMX) on work–family interference and work–family facilitation. *Personnel Review*, 43(4), 573–91.

Van Daalen, G., Willemsen, T. M. & Sanders, K. (2006). Reducing work–family conflict through different sources of social support. *Journal of Vocational Behavior*, 69(3), 462–76.

Voydanoff, P. (2002). Linkages between the work–family interface and work, family and individual outcomes: An integrative model. *Journal of Family Issues*, 23, 138–64.

Wang, P. & Walumbwa, F. O. (2007). Family-friendly programs, organizational commitment, and work withdrawal: The moderating role of transformational leadership. *Personnel Psychology*, 60, 397–427.

Wayne, J. H., Grzywacz, J. G., Carlson, D. S. & Kacmar, K. M. (2007). Work–family facilitation: A theoretical explanation of primary antecedents and consequences. *Human Resource Management Review*, 17, 63–76.

Women's Institute, Spanish Ministry of Labour (2005). *Estudio sobre la conciliación de la vida familiar y la vida laboral: Situación actual, necesidades y demandas.* [Study on the reconciliation between work and family: Current situation, needs and demands]. https://www.um.es/estructura/unidades/u-igualdad/recursos/2013/007-conciliacion.pdf. Accessed 31 July 2016.

Xiao, Q. & O'Neill, J. W. (2010). Work–family balance as a potential strategic advantage: A hotel general manager perspective. *Journal of Hospitality & Tourism Research*, 34, 415–39.

Yeandle, S., Wigfield, A., Crompton, R. & Dennett, J. (2002). *Employed Carers and Family-Friendly Employment Policies*. Bristol: Policy Press for the Joseph Rowntree Foundation.

8

Leaders as Resources

How Managers and Supervisors Can Socially Support Employees Towards Better Mental Health and Well-Being

Jennifer K. Dimoff and E. Kevin Kelloway

Mental health problems and illnesses are among the leading causes of disability and premature death in the developed world (Watson Wyatt Worldwide, 2007). In Canada, the United States, and many European countries, mental health problems are prevalent and financially costly. According to the Mental Health Commission of Canada (2012) and the Center for Disease Control (CDC) (2014) in the United States, mental health problems affect 20 per cent of adults each year and cost the global economy hundreds of billions of dollars each year. The prevalence rates are similar throughout Europe, where mental health-related costs are also burdensome (McDaid, 2011; McDaid & Park, 2011). Compared to other costly and prevalent illnesses, such as cancer, heart disease and diabetes, mental health problems are prevalent among a younger demographic – working-age adults (Canadian Mental Health Association, 2013; Mental Health Commission of Canada (MHCC), 2012). Consequently, many organizations have begun to adopt health-promotion and illness-prevention programmes aimed at reducing costs and improving employee health.

Although there has been much debate surrounding how best to achieve these goals, there is consensus that organizations can play an important role in improving employee mental health, and that the workplace is an appropriate setting for developing and sustaining positive health practices (Conti & Burton, 1995; Cooper & Cartwright, 1994; Goetzel, Ozminkowski, Sederer & Mark, 2002; Kelloway & Barling, 2010). In this chapter, we focus on the roles that frontline managers can play in helping to improve the mental health and well-being of employees. Thus, we describe (1) how organizational leaders and frontline managers can support employee mental health, and (2) how managers can be trained to help facilitate resource-use and help-seeking behaviour among struggling employees.

Employee Mental Health: The Role of the Workplace

Mental health has been described as the foundation for overall health and well-being, and as long ago as 1954 the World Health Organization went as far as to claim that there is no health without mental health (for review, see Kolappa,

Leading to Occupational Health and Safety: How Leadership Behaviours Impact Organizational Safety and Well-Being, First Edition.
Edited by E. Kevin Kelloway, Karina Nielsen and Jennifer K. Dimoff.

Henderson & Kishore, 2013). Mental health is considered a state of positive well-being, whereby individuals are able to cope with everyday challenges, live and work productively, and respond adaptively to stressors (World Health Organization, 2004). When mental health is compromised, mental health problems and illnesses can become debilitating, reducing or eliminating the ability to think properly or regulate thoughts, emotions and behaviours (Baicker, Cutler & Song, 2010; Caveen, Dewa & Goering, 2006; Goetzel et al., 2002; Karasek & Theorell, 1990; Shain, Arnold & GermAnn, 2012). Fortunately, most mental health problems are treatable, and most people with mental health problems can recover and return to a normal level of functioning if they are able to receive timely and effective treatment (Canadian Mental Health Association, 2013). This is where organizations and leaders can play a substantial role. First, workplaces can strive to develop and uphold psychologically healthy workplace principles. Second, and as a by-product of their psychologically healthy workplace, organizations can strive to provide social support networks for employees, both informally and formally.

Psychologically healthy workplaces are places that have a strong people-centred culture that is characterized by open communication, employee involvement, support for employee development, and support for employee work–life balance (American Psychological Association, 2011; Grawitch, Gottschalk & Munz, 2006; Kelloway & Day, 2005). The more an organization develops and cultivates these characteristics, the better the workplace will serve as a buffer against poor employee mental health (Grawitch et al., 2006; Kelloway & Day, 2005). For instance, typical work-related stressors and pressures, such as work–life imbalance, can be reduced, if not eliminated, through healthy workplace initiatives (Grawitch et al., 2006; Grawitch, Ledford, Ballard & Barber, 2009). Moreover, there is evidence that greater results can be achieved when healthy workplace programmes target both psychological and physical health, rather than physical health alone (Cooper, 1985; Cooper & Cartwright, 1994; Grawitch et al., 2009). Some organizations that have added psychologically healthy programmes have observed increases in employee job satisfaction, self-esteem and organizational commitment. For instance, the UK Post Office's adoption of an employee counselling programme led to a reduction in absenteeism of over 60 per cent, and a significant increase in employee life-satisfaction (Allinson, Cooper & Reynolds, 1989; Cooper & Sadri, 1991).

Supportive leadership is a key component of the success of any psychologically healthy workplace programme or initiative (Kelloway & Day, 2005). Leaders, managers and supervisors who espouse the values of psychologically healthy workplaces are likely to behave in ways that support employees and boost the psychological health of employees. Leaders' behaviours also help to establish normative behaviours within the workplace (Eisenberger, Stinglhamber, Vandenberghe, Sucharski & Rhoades, 2002; Wayne, Shore & Liden, 1997). Given the high level of stigma and uncertainty surrounding mental health and mental health problems (Canadian Medical Association, 2013; Cooper, Corrigan & Watson, 2003), leaders' attitudes, values and behaviours surrounding employee mental health are likely to be influential. Resultantly, if an organization seeks to improve employee mental health and well-being, it may be best to first turn to its leaders (Dimoff, Kelloway & Burnstein, 2016; Nielsen & Randall, 2009; Nielsen, Randall, Holten & González, 2010). This is especially relevant given that managers are often viewed as organizational agents (Nielsen & Randall, 2009; Nielsen, Randall, Holten & González, 2010) – individuals capable of spearheading change and who reflect the organization, its values, its mission, and its policies and programmes.

According to much research by Eisenberger and colleagues (Eisenberger, Huntington, Hutchinson & Sowa, 1986; Eisenberger & Stinglhamber, 2011; Kurtessis, Eisenberger, Ford, Buffardi, Stewart & Adis, 2015; Rhoades & Eisenberger, 2002), the extent to which employees feel supported by their organization is largely dependent on their relationships with their supervisors. Perceptions of supervisor support (PSS) can be described as the extent to which managers are seen to be supportive of employee contributions and employee well-being (Eisenberger et al., 2002; Rhoades & Eisenberger, 2002). To a large extent, these perceptions initiate a social exchange process, whereby employees who feel supported by their supervisors exert greater effort, commitment, and desire to help the organization succeed (Kurtessis et al., 2015; Liden, Sparrowe & Wayne, 1997; Shore & Shore, 1995). Unsurprisingly, employees who feel supported by their managers and their organizations tend to experience positive outcomes – higher levels of job satisfaction, less job stress and burnout – and report lower levels of turnover intentions (Kurtessis et al., 2015; Riggle, Edmondson & Hansen, 2009). Ultimately, employee mental health, well-being and performance can be significantly impacted by leaders who are willing and able to provide social support at work.

Employee Mental Health: Support from Leaders

Described as 'the social resources that persons perceive to be available or that are actually provided by non-professionals in the context of both formal support groups and informal helping relationships' (Cohen, Gottlieb & Underwood, 2000, p. 4), social support can be critical to health and productivity. According to decades of research, social support is a strong protectant, or buffer, against various somatic health complaints and psychological disorders, and can even help make individuals more resilient against strain (Beehr, 1995; Östberg & Lennartsson, 2007; Viswesvaran, Sanchez & Fisher, 1999).

Social support from supervisors has been indirectly and directly linked to employee health and well-being (Ganster, Fusilier & Mayes, 1986). For instance, social support is thought to enhance mental health by helping to improve employee coping behaviour, by increasing self-esteem, by bolstering morale (Heller, Swindle & Dusenbury, 1986; Lazarus & Folkman, 1984), and by providing instrumental tools to help employees perform well (Van der Doef & Maes, 1999). Consequently, social support from leaders can take many forms, best categorized by House (1981) into four primary 'social support types': emotional, instrumental, informational and appraisal support.

Emotional support largely involves the portrayal of feelings of trust, caring and personal consideration (House, 1981). Emotional support can help to reassure employees, provide them with psychological need fulfilment, and protect self-esteem (House, 1981). Instrumental support often involves more tangible resources or assistance, such as time, materials or skills (House, 1981). To be instrumentally supportive, managers can provide employees with a wide range of support, from specific tools and training and career development opportunities, to greater levels of autonomy and work–life balance. Informational support involves information, advice or guidance, and can be facilitated through clear and honest communication (House, 1981). Managers who communicate with employees about deadlines or new protocols are engaging in informationally supportive behaviours. Appraisal support can come in the form of feedback or evaluation, making it somewhat distinct from informational support (House, 1981). To demonstrate appraisal support, supervisors can help with goal setting and can provide timely feedback and fair performance evaluations for employees.

Despite the distinct categorizations of the four 'types' of social support, employees rarely distinguish between the types of support they experience or receive (Tardy, 1994). Unsurprisingly, the four types of social support are often highly correlated, suggesting that employees feel a sense of global support regardless of the type of support they receive (Barling, MacEwen & Pratt, 1988). For instance, instrumental support is often perceived as being helpful because of its emotional meaning (Barling et al., 1988; Tardy, 1994); when managers provide their time, expertise or resources, they are signalling that they care about their employees. Thus, the actual behaviours or types of social support may be of lesser consequence than the presence of any or all types of social support.

Within the context of mental health, it is likely that managers will employ all four types of social support in unison, albeit relying on emotional, instrumental and informational support more often. For instance, managers must (1) be compassionate (i.e., emotionally supportive) when addressing warning signs, (2) take time out of their day to meet with a struggling employee and possibly make accommodations (i.e., instrumental support), and (3) be ready to provide information about available resources, such as employee assistance programs (EAPs) (i.e., informational support).

Regardless of the type of support received, employees who feel supported by their leaders are likely to be in a better position to respond to challenges than those who lack support (Dimoff & Kelloway, in press; Gottlieb & Bergen, 2010). Social support from leaders may empower employees to have the confidence to respond to stressors on their own, without drawing upon resources within their networks, such as human resources, accommodation plans or employee assistance programmes (Gottlieb & Bergen, 2010). Conversely, social support from leaders may empower employees to do just the opposite – to draw upon workplace resources in order to cope efficiently with challenges or stressors (Dimoff & Kelloway, in press). Thus, social support may enable employees to make adaptive decisions and to marshal their own resources, as well as the organization's resources, in order to remain healthy and productive (Dimoff & Kelloway, in press).

Still, it may not be about the type of support delivered so much as the way by which it is delivered. For instance, well-intentioned but unsuitable, clumsy or overbearing support can be unhelpful and even psychologically damaging

(Steinberg & Gottlieb, 1994). This consequence could be especially problematic if experienced by an employee with a mental health problem. For instance, a leader who provides information about mental health, but does so reluctantly or begrudgingly, is unlikely to be perceived as providing support (Fisher, Nadler & Whitcher-Alagna, 1982; Gottlieb, 1992; Pasch & Bradbury, 1998). This is dysfunctional, maladaptive social support and can have negative consequences that hinder well-being (Ingram, Betz, Mindes, Schmitt & Smith, 2001; Semmer, Amstrad, Elfering & Kalin, 2006). Thus, it is important that managers know what to do, but also *how* to do it.

Social Support in Action: Workplace Mental Health Training for Leaders

The hierarchical manager–employee relationship puts managers in a good position to influence employee behaviours. Given that supervisors and managers play a central role in providing organizational rewards, facilitating resources and administering discipline, leaders can be perceived as organizational agents of support (Wayne et al., 1997) – gatekeepers to resources that can help employees, both professionally and personally. Typically, leaders are in a position where they have the opportunity to work with and interact with employees on a regular or semi-regular basis. As a result, leaders have the opportunity to get to know their employees and learn about their regular or typical behaviours. In doing so, leaders have the opportunity to demonstrate various forms of social support, such as emotional support, when making an effort to get to know individual employees as people, not just as workers. Indeed, many employees report that they would welcome support from their managers, especially during times of difficulty (Irvine, 2011). Unfortunately, many managers lack the knowledge, skills and confidence to recognize and provide assistance to struggling employees (Ipsos Reid, 2012; Thorpe & Chénier, 2011).

Yet, workplace mental health training, tailored specifically to managers and supervisors, may have the potential to provide leaders with the skills and the confidence to actively support employees who are struggling (Dimoff et al., 2016). Developed in Canada in 2012, the Mental Health Awareness Training (MHAT) for workplace leaders was designed specifically to provide leaders with the knowledge and confidence to take supportive action when employees are struggling. Leader-related data suggested that the three-hour training programme was capable of improving leaders' knowledge about mental health and their confidence with regard to managing employee mental health issues at work. More importantly, a pattern of effects also suggests that by targeting knowledge and self-efficacy, the training was capable of improving leaders' attitudes towards mental health problems, as well as their intentions to use their skills and promote mental health in the workplace. Thus, improvements in knowledge helped to facilitate reductions in stigmatizing attitudes, and improvements in self-efficacy (along with improvements in knowledge and attitudes) helped to facilitate improvements in leaders' promotion intentions. This training also resulted in a significant return on investment nine months after the training was delivered.

The saving was largely attributable to a 19-day reduction in disability claim duration. The authors reasoned that the reduction was probably attributable to early recognition and action on the part of leaders.

According to this work, leaders must engage in an almost cyclical process, whereby they (1) recognize warning signs that an employee is struggling, (2) identify sources of support or ways that they can help, and (3) provide support by helping the employee engage resources (Dimoff & Kelloway, in press; Dimoff et al., 2016). This work, along with the work of others (e.g., Kitchener & Jorm, 2002; Pinfold, Stuart, Thornicroft & Arboleda-Florez, 2005), suggests that support for mental health is a skill, or a set of skills, that can be taught or trained. While only 33% of managers report having had training designed to help them recognize and intervene with employees showing signs of distress, most managers want to help (Ipsos Reid, 2012). In a report released by Ipsos Reid in 2012, 80% of managers reported that they felt it was part of their job to provide support. Even more encouragingly, 63% reported that they would be able to do their jobs more effectively if they had more information about how to support and assist employees.

Recognition of Warning Signs

According to Goetzel et al. (2002) and Hepburn, Kelloway and Franche (2010), early recognition can improve the prognosis for mental health problems and can even prevent illness-escalation. It is important to note that recognition, or detection, is not diagnosis. Managers are not, and should not be, diagnosing or providing treatment for employee mental health problems – they are not counsellors, psychologists or doctors – but they should be capable of recognizing when employees need extra support (Gates, 1993; Nieuwenhuijsen, Verbeek, de Boer, Blonk & van Dijk, 2004). Unlike their untrained peers, mangers who have received workplace mental health training will be better informed about mental health and will probably be more attuned to the signs of developing mental health issues (Dimoff, Kelloway & Burnstein, 2016). Many of these signs, such as reduced work quality, missed deadlines, increased absenteeism, and interpersonal conflicts at work, are issues that managers are likely addressing within the context of performance management anyway (Attridge & Wallace, 2010; Conti & Burton, 1995; Dimoff & Kelloway, 2013; Goetzel et al., 2002; Shain et al., 2012; Sparks, Faragher & Cooper, 2001).

According to Corrigan and Watson (2005), a certain level of factual information about mental health and mental health problems is required in order to facilitate early recognition. Leaders should be educated not only on the signs of a developing mental health problem, but also on the prevalence rates of different mental health problems, and how mental health problems can be treated. Along similar lines, the content of the training should focus on issues most prevalent in the organization or industry (Dimoff & Kelloway, 2013; Dimoff et al., 2016). In many cases, depression and anxiety are the most prevalent mental illnesses among individuals in the working population (Mental Health Commission of Canada, 2012). Thus, training content might focus on improving understanding of anxiety and depression, as well as the warning signs and treatment options associated with each. Generally, less prevalent issues or very specific disorders, such as schizophrenia, warrant less attention than more common illnesses. To disseminate information effectively in a short period of time, lecture-style training methods can help provide managers with the basic information and knowledge that they will need in order to recognize warning signs and support employees (Dimoff, Kelloway & Burnstein, 2016; Noe & Peacock, 2006).

Identifying Sources of Support

Beyond recognizing signs of employee mental health problems, managers with mental health training are also in a good position to address these issues by providing employees with appropriate support and referral to available workplace resources and programmes (Dimoff & Kelloway, 2013; Kitchener & Jorm, 2002, 2008; Shain et al., 2012). Many employees are unaware of organizational resources and treatment options for mental health problems (Goetzel et al., 2002). If leaders are trained to communicate about these resources it is more likely that employees will use them (Nieuwenhuijsen et al., 2004). Leaders can communicate informally about mental health by bringing attention to specific workplace programmes and policies that may help employees who are struggling. Leaders can also do this more formally by incorporating 'psychological health and safety' discussions into weekly staff meetings or 'toolkit' discussions that might otherwise be reserved for discussions of engagement, satisfaction or physical health and safety. Ultimately, managers are in a position to 'help employees help themselves', a task that is much more manageable in environments where stigma is low and employees feel safe to seek support from their manager (Edmondson, 1999).

Mental health awareness training for managers can also help break down workplace barriers and improve the overall psychological health of the workplace (Corrigan & Matthews, 2003). For instance, stigma, *or negative, disrespectful and untrue judgements based on what people think they know about someone and their situation*, is one of the primary barriers to help-seeking behaviours among employees (Attridge & Wallace, 2010; Andrews, Henderson & Hall, 2001). In fact, two out of three people with mental health problems report that they do not seek treatment or support, solely because they are afraid of being stigmatized or discriminated against (Canadian Medical Association, 2013). This is especially true in working populations, where employees are concerned that a mental health issue may label them as 'weak', 'crazy' or 'not promotion material'. As a result, many employees fear that disclosure of a mental health problem could negatively impact their career (Corrigan & Matthews, 2003; Irvine, 2011). If managers are aware of this fear and are provided with the skills to openly discuss mental health in the workplace, employees may become less fearful of being stigmatized and more likely to seek support. Leaders can help to reduce this fear by normalizing mental health issues and bringing awareness of mental health and mental health problems. For instance, leaders can mention the ways they work to promote and protect their own mental health, through sleep or healthy eating habits, and can establish ground-rules for the workplace that help employees create balance between their work and personal lives.

Providing Support

In addition to training leaders how to identify sources of support and communicate about them, the training should also help managers feel comfortable about assisting someone who is showing warning signs (Corrigan & Watson, 2005; Dimoff et al., 2016). To do so, the training should be designed to improve participants' existing interpersonal and management skills (or help participants develop new skills). The training must also help participants feel comfortable about using these new skills within their workplaces. To help increase this comfort level, the relevance of the material must be clear. Customized training content has been linked to improvements in leaders' intentions to promote mental health, and is thought to be important to long-term use (Dimoff & Kelloway, 2013; Gottlieb & McLeroy, 1994; Wallerstein & Weinger, 1992). The more relevant training content is to the organization and its unique needs and resources, the more likely it is that managers will be able to apply the content to their day-to-day work lives (Dimoff & Kelloway, 2013; Nielsen & Randall, 2009; Nielsen et al., 2010). For example, if mental health literacy in a particular area is poor (e.g., there is a lack of understanding of stress and workplace stressors), additional time or information can be allocated to improving specific literacies or background knowledge about this very specific area.

The training must also aim to improve participants' comfort level with regard to interacting with people with known mental health problem (Corrigan & Watson, 2005). Exposure to individuals, or stories of individuals, with mental health problems can help decrease stigma and discrimination (Corrigan & Watson, 2005). Active learning methods, or 'learning by doing' methods, such as case studies, simulations or role-play scenarios, can help improve confidence and skill-use (Noe & Peacock, 2006). The more realistic the case study or method is within the work setting and the organization, the more comfortable leaders will feel (Levenstein, 1996; Noe & Peacock, 2006). Customized case studies seem to be effective in improving skill use among leaders who have attended mental health training designed for the workplace (Dimoff et al., 2016). Regardless of the specific content or the methods used, it is absolutely essential that the training be delivered in a socially supportive environment that facilitates effective learning (Vuori, Toppinen-Tanner & Mutanen, 2012).

Conclusions

Twenty per cent of adults in the developed world will experience a mental health problem this year (Mental Health Commission of Canada, 2012). This high prevalence is associated with seemingly insurmountable financial and human costs (Goetzel et al., 2002; Mental Health Commission of Canada, 2012; World Health Organization, 2004). Low levels of mental health literacy, combined with a lack of understanding of resources and treatment, prevent people from seeking or receiving help for mental health issues (Goetzel et al., 2002; Irvine, 2011; Kitchener & Jorm, 2002; Prince et al., 2007). To improve resource use and prevent long-term costs, many organizations are turning to frontline managers and supervisors as the first line of defence against poor employee mental health.

Mental health management programmes and mental health training for managers have been associated with positive returns on investment (ROI), increased mental health literacy and improvements in employee health and well-being (Conti & Burton, 1995; Dimoff & Kelloway, 2014; Israel, Baker, Goldenhar, Heaney & Schurman, 1996; Kitchener & Jorm, 2002, 2008). Supervisors who show concern for their employees and display earnest efforts to help their employees tend to engender commitment on behalf of employees (Hepburn et al., 2010). Similarly, support from supervisors is associated with improvements in employee mental health, as well as speedier returns to work for individuals on disability leave (i.e., a leave from work due to a physical or mental health condition, injury or impairment) (DeLange, Taris, Kompier, Houtman & Bongers, 2004; Nieuwenhuijsen et al., 2004).

By training managers to be more aware of employees' health and well-being, organizations may help their management teams become more supportive – a consequence that can lead to improved employee relations, lower stress levels among both managers and employees, and improved cooperation within the overall workforce. Organizations, management teams and individual employees are likely to benefit from workplaces that cultivate a strong perception of social support. To improve the overall health and well-being of employees, organizations must play an active role in promoting social support at work, providing managers with the tools and the training to effectively support their employees, and encouraging employees to use resources and engage in help-seeking behaviours.

References

Attridge, M. & Wallace, S. (2010). *Able-Minded: Return to work and accommodations for workers on disability leave for mental disorders.* Vancouver, BC, Canada: Human Solutions.

Allinson, T., Cooper, C. L. & Reynolds, P. (1989). Stress counselling in the workplace: The Post Office experience. *The Psychologist,* 2(9), 384–88. doi: 10.1177/001872679404700405.

American Psychological Association (2011). *Psychologically Healthy Workplace Program: Awards and Best Practice Honors.* Washington, DC: American Psychological Association.

Andrews, G., Henderson, S. & Hall, W. (2001). Prevalence, comorbidity, disability and service utilisation: Overview of the Australian National Mental Health Survey. *British Journal of Psychiatry,* 178, 145–53.

Baicker, K., Cutler, D. & Song, Z.(2010). Workplace wellness programs can generate savings. *Health Affairs,* 29(2), 1–8. doi: 10.1377/hlthaff.2009.0626.

Barling, J., MacEwen, K. E. & Pratt, L. I. (1988). Manipulating the type and the source of social support: An experimental investigation. *Canadian Journal of Behavioral Science,* 20, 140–53.

Beehr, T. A. (1995). *Psychological Stress in the Workplace.* London: Routledge.

Canadian Medical Association (2013). Mental health. https://www.cma.ca/En/Pages/mental-health.aspx. Accessed 3 August 2015.

Canadian Mental Health Association. (2013). Fast Facts about Mental Illness. www.cmha.ca/media/fast-facts-about-mental-illness/. Accessed 17 August 2016.
Caveen, M., Dewa, C. S. & Goering, P. (2006). The influence of organizational factors on return-to-work outcomes. *Canadian Journal of Community Mental Health*, 25(2), 121–42. 10.7870/cjcmh-2006-0017. Accessed 1 August 2016.
Centers for Disease Control (2014). *Workplace Health Promotion: Depression*. http://www.cdc.gov/workplacehealthpromotion/health-strategies/depression/index.html. Accessed 17 August 2016.
Cohen, S., Gottlieb, B. & Underwood, L. (2000). *Social Relationships and Health: Challenges for Measurement and Intervention*. New York: Oxford University Press.
Thorpe, K. & Chénier, L. (2011). *Building Mentally Healthy Workplaces: Perspectives of Canadian Workers and Front-Line Managers*. Toronto, ON: Conference Board of Canada.
Conti D. J. & Burton, W. N. (1995). The cost of depression in the workplace. *Behavioral Healthcare Tomorrow*, 4, 25–7.
Cooper, A. E., Corrigan, P. W. & Watson, A. C. (2003). Mental illness stigma and care seeking. *Journal of Nervous and Mental Disease*, 191(5), 339–41.
Cooper, C. L. (1985). The road to health in American firms. *New Society*, 73, 335–6.
Cooper, C. L. & Cartwright, S. (1994). Healthy mind, healthy organization: A proactive approach to occupational stress. *Human Relations*, 47(4), 455–71. doi: 10.1177/001872679404700405.
Cooper, C. L. & Sadri, G. (1991). The impact of stress counseling at work. *Journal of Social Behavior and Personality*, 6(7), 411–23.
Corrigan, P. W. & Matthews, A. K. (2003). Stigma and disclosure: Implications for coming out of the closet. *Journal of Mental Health*, 12, 235–48.
Corrigan, P. W. & Watson, A. C. (2005). Findings from the National Comorbidity Survey on the frequency of dangerous behavior in individuals with psychiatric disorders. *Psychiatry Research*, 136(2–3) 153–62.
DeLange, A. H., Taris, T. W., Kompier, M. A. J., Houtman, I. L. D. & Bongers, P. M. (2004). The relationships between work characteristics and mental health: Examining normal, reversed, and reciprocal relationships in a 4-wave study. *Work and Stress*, 18(2), 149–66.
Dimoff, J. K. & Kelloway, E. K. (2013). Bridging the gap: Workplace mental health research in Canada. *Canadian Psychology/Psychologie Canadienne*, 54, 203.
Dimoff, J. K. & Kelloway, E. K. (in press). Resource utilization model: Organizational leaders as resource facilitators. In P. L. Perrewé & D. C. Ganster (eds), Research in Occupational Stress and Wellbeing, 14. Bingley, UK: Emerald.
Dimoff, J. K., Kelloway, E. K. & Burnstein, M. D. (2016). Mental health awareness training (MHAT): The development and evaluation of an intervention for workplace leaders. *International Journal of Stress Management*, 23(2), 167–89.
Edmondson, A. (1999). Psychological safety and learning behavior in work teams. *Administrative Science Quarterly*, 44, 350–83.
Eisenberger, R., Huntington, R., Hutchison, S. & Sowa, D. (1986). Does pay for performance increase or decrease perceived self-determination and intrinsic motivation? *Journal of Personality and Social Psychology*, 77, 1026–40.

Eisenberger, R. & Stinglhamber, F. (2011). *Perceived Organizational Support: Fostering Enthusiastic and Productive Employees*. Washington, DC: American Psychological Association.
Eisenberger, R., Stinglhamber, F., Vandenberghe, C., Sucharski, I. L. & Rhoades, L. (2002). Perceived supervisor support: Contributions to perceived organizational support and employee retention. *Journal of Applied Psychology*, 87, 565–73.
Fisher, J. D., Nadler, A. & Whitcher-Alagna, S. (1982). Recipient reactions to aid. *Psychological Bulletin*, 91, 27–54.
Ganster, D.C., Fusilier, M. R. & Mayes, B. T. (1986). Role of social support in the experience of stress at work. *Journal of Applied Psychology*, 71(1), 102–10.
Gates, L. (1993). The role of the supervisor in successful adjustment to work with a disabling condition: Issues for disability policy and practice. *Journal of Occupational Rehabilitation*, 3, 179–90. doi: 10.1007/BF01097428.
Goetzel, R., Ozminkowski, R., Sederer, L. & Mark, T. (2002). The business case for quality mental health services: Why employers should care about the mental health and well- being of their employees. *Journal of Occupational and Environmental Medicine*, 44, 320–30.
Gottlieb, B. H. (1992). Quandaries in translating support concepts to intervention. In H. O. F. Veiel & U. Baumann (eds). *The Meaning and Measurement of Social Support*. Washington, DC: Hemisphere, pp. 293–309.
Gottlieb, B. H. & Bergen, A. E. (2010). Social support concepts and measures. *Journal of Psychosomatic Research*, 69, 511–20.
Gottlieb, N. H. & McLeroy, K. R. (1994). Social health. In M. P. O'Donnell & J. S. Harris (eds), *Health Promotion in the Workplace*. 2nd edn. Albany, NY: Delmar.
Grawitch, M. J., Gottschalk, M. & Munz, D. C. (2006). The path to a healthy workplace: A critical review linking healthy workplace practices, employee well-being, and organizational improvement. *Consulting Psychology Journal: Practice and Research*, 58(3), 129–47. doi: 10.1037/1065-9293.58.3.129.
Grawitch, M. J., Ledford, G. E., Ballard, D. W. & Barber, L. K. (2009). Leading the healthy workforce: The integral role of employee involvement. *Consulting Psychology Journal: Practice and Research*, 61(2), 122–35. doi: 10.1037/a0015288.
Heller, K., Swindle, R. W. & Dusenbury, L. (1986). Component social support processes: Comments and integration. *Journal of Consulting and Clinical Psychology*, 54(4), 466–70.
Hepburn, C. G., Kelloway, E. K. & Franche, R. (2010). Early employer response to workplace injury: What injured workers perceive as fair and why these perceptions matter. *Journal of Occupational Health Psychology*, 15, 409–20.
House, J. S. (1981). *Work Stress and Social Support*. Reading, MA: Addison-Wesley.
Ingram, K. M., Betz, N. E., Mindes, E. J., Schmitt, M. M. & Smith, N. G. (2001). Unsupportive responses from others concerning a stressful life event: Development of the Unsupportive Social Interactions Inventory. *Journal of Social and Clinical Psychology*, 20, 173–207.
Ipsos Reid (2012). Four in five (84%) managers and supervisors believe it's part of their job to intervene with employees who are showing signs of depression. Press release, 9 October. http://www.workplacestrategiesformentalhealth.com/pdf/GWLFactum1DepressionintheWorkplace_clean.pdf. Accessed 1 August 2016.

Irvine, A. (2011). Something to declare? The disclosure of common mental health problems at work. *Disability & Society*, 26, 179–92.

Israel, B., Baker, E., Goldenhar, L., Heaney, C. & Schurman, S. (1996). Occupational stress, safety, and health: Conceptual framework and principles for effective prevention interventions. *Journal of Occupational Health Psychology*, 1, 261–86.

Karasek, R. & Theorell, T. (1990). *Healthy Work: Stress Productivity and the Reconstruction of Working Life*. New York: John Wiley & Sons.

Kelloway, E. K. & Barling, J. (2010). Leadership development as an intervention in occupational health psychology. *Work & Stress*, 24, 260–79.

Kelloway, E. K. & Day, A. L. (2005). Building healthy workplaces: What we know so far. *Canadian Journal of Behavioural Science*, 37(4), 223–35.

Kitchener, B. A. & Jorm, A. F. (2002). Mental health first aid training for the public: Evaluation of effects on knowledge, attitudes and helping behavior. *BMC Psychiatry*, 2, 1–6.

Kitchener, B. A. & Jorm, A. F. (2008). Mental health first aid: An international programme for early intervention. *Early Intervention in Psychiatry*, 2, 55–61.

Kolappa, K., Henderson, D. C. & Kishore, S. P. (2013). No physical health without mental health: Lessons unlearned? *Bulletin of the World Health Organization*. http://www.who.int/bulletin/volumes/91/1/12-115063/en/.

Kurtessis, J. N., Eisenberger, R., Ford, M. T., Buffardi, L. C., Stewart, K. A. & Adis, C. S. (2015). Perceived organizational support: A meta-analytic evaluation of organizational support theory. *Journal of Management*, 22(10), 1–31.

Lazarus, R. S. & Folkman, S. (1984). *Stress, Appraisal, and Coping*. New York: Springer.

Levenstein, C. (1996) Policy implications of intervention research: Research on the social context for intervention. *American Journal of Independent Medicine*, 29, 358–61.

Liden, R. C., Sparrowe, R. & Wayne, S. J. (1997). Leader–member exchange theory: The past and potential for the future. *Research in Personnel and Human Resources Management*, 15, 47–119.

McDaid, D. (2011). Making the Long-Term Economic Case for Investing in Mental Health to Contribute to Sustainability. European Union. http://ec.europa.eu/health/mental_health/docs/long_term_sustainability_en.pdf.

McDaid, D. & Park, A. (2011). Investing in mental health and well-being: Findings from the DataPrev project. *Health Promotion International*, 26(suppl. 1): i108–39.

Mental Health Commission of Canada (2012). *Changing Directions, Changing Lives: The Mental Health Strategy for Canada*. Calgary, AB: Mental Health Commission of Canada.

Nielsen, K. & Randall, R. (2009). Managers' active support when implementing teams: The impact on employee well-being. *Applied Psychology: Health and Well-being*, 1, 374–90.

Nielsen, K., Randall, R., Holten, A. & Gonzalez, E. (2010). Conducting organizational-level occupational health interventions: What works? *Work & Stress*, 24, 234–59.

Nieuwenhuijsen, K., Verbeek, J., de Boer, A. G. E. M., Blonk, R. & van Dijk, F. J. H. (2004). Supervisory behaviour as a predictor of return to work in employees absent from work due to mental health problems. *Journal of Occupational and Environmental Medicine*, 61, 817–23.

Noe, R. & Peacock, M. (2006). *Employee Training and Development*. 1st Canadian Edition. McGraw-Hill Ryerson.

Östberg, V. & Lennartsson, C. (2007). Getting by with a little help: The importance of various types of social support for health problems. *Scandinavian Journal of Public Health*, 35, 197–204.

Pasch, L. A. & Bradbury, T. N. (1998). Social support, conflict, and the development of marital dysfunction. *Journal of Consulting and Clinical Psychology*, 66, 219–30.

Pinfold, V., Stuart, H., Thornicroft, G. & Arboleda-Florez, J. (2005). Working with young people: The impact of mental health awareness programmes in schools in the UK and Canada. *World Psychiatry*, 4, 48–52.

Prince, M., Patel, V., Saxena, S., Maj, M., Maselko, J., Phillips, M. R. & Rahman, A. (2007). No health without mental health. *Lancet*, 370, 859–77.

Rhoades, L. & Eisenberger, R. (2002). Perceived organizational support: A review of the literature. *Journal of Applied Psychology*, 87, 698–714.

Riggle, R. J., Edmondson, D. R. & Hansen, J. D. (2009). A meta-analysis of the relationship between perceived organizational support and job outcomes: 20 years of research. *Journal of Business Research*, 62, 1027–30.

Semmer, N. K., Amstad, F., Elfering, A. & Kälin, W. (2006). Dysfunctional social support. Paper presented at the APA/NIOSH Conference on 'Work, Stress, and Health', March, Miami, FL.

Shain, M., Arnold, I. & GermAnn, K. (2012). The road to psychological safety: Legal, scientific, and social foundations for a Canadian National Standard on Psychological Safety in the Workplace. *Bulletin of Science, Technology & Society*, 32(2), 142–62.

Shore, L. M. & Shore, T. H. (1995). Perceived organizational support and organizational justice. In R. S. Cropanzano & K. M. Kacmar (eds), *Organizational Politics, Justice, and Support: Managing the Social Climate of the Workplace*. Westport, CT: Quorum, pp. 149–64.

Sparks, K., Faragher, B. & Cooper, C. L. (2001). Well-being and occupational health in the 21st century workplace. *Journal of Occupational and Organizational Psychology*, 74, 489–509.

Steinberg, M. & Gottlieb, B. H. (1994). The appraisal of spousal support by women facing conflicts between work and family. In B. R. Burleson, T. L. Albrecht, & I. G. Sarason (eds), *Communication of Social Support: Messages, Interactions, Relationships, and Community*. Thousand Oaks, CA: Sage, pp. 152–74.

Tardy, C. H. (1994). Counteracting task-induced stress: Studies of instrumental and emotional support in problem-solving contexts. In B. R. Burleson, T. L. Albrecht & I. G. Sarason (eds), *Communication of Social Support: Messages, Interactions, Relationships, and Community*. Thousand Oaks, CA: Sage, pp. 71–87.

Van der Doef, M. & Maes, S. (1999). The job demand-control (-support) model and psychological well-being: A review of 20 years of empirical research. *Work & Stress*, 13, 87–114.

Viswesvaran, C., Sanchez, J. & Fisher, J. (1999). The role of social support in the process of work stress: A meta-analysis. *Journal of Vocational Behavior*, 54, 314–34.

Vuori, J., Toppinen-Tanner, S. & Mutanen, P. (2012). Effects of resource-building group intervention on career management and mental health in work organizations: Randomized controlled field trial. *Journal of Applied Psychology*, 97, 273–86.

Wallerstein, N. & Weinger, M. (1992). Health and safety education for worker empowerment. *American Journal of Industrial Medicine*, 22, 619–35.

Watson Wyatt Worldwide (2007). Staying@work: Effective presence at work. 2007 Survey Report: Canada. https://www.easna.org/wp-content/uploads/2010/08/WatsonWyattStayingatWorkSurvey.pdf. Accessed 1 August 2016.

Wayne, S. J., Shore, L. M. & Liden, R. C. (1997). Perceived organizational support and leader–member exchange: A social exchange perspective. *Academy of Management Journal*, 40, 82–111.

World Health Organization (2004). *Promoting Mental Health: Concepts, Emerging Evidence, Practice: Summary Report.* Geneva: World Health Organization.

9

Destructive Forms of Leadership and Their Relationships with Employee Well-Being

Anders Skogstad, Morten Birkeland Nielsen and Ståle Einarsen

Introduction

Numerous studies have documented the bright side of leadership, such as transactional, transformational, task-oriented and considerate leadership (see, e.g., Judge & Piccolo, 2004; Judge, Piccolo & Ilies, 2004). At the turn of the century a corresponding documentation for the dark side of leadership was sorely missing. In hindsight, it may be a surprise that academic efforts to study the 'dark side' of leadership have been relatively sparse. One explanation for this imbalance may be found in the conception of leadership itself, where leadership traditionally has been equated with supportive and efficient leadership (Kellerman, 2004; Yukl & Van Fleet, 1992). Yet all human beings are in principle capable of enacting 'good' as well as 'bad' deeds, as proved by the history of mankind (Zimbardo, 2004). A basic premise of human life is therefore that human interactions include the enactment and experience of both positive and negative social exchanges (Rook, 1998), and that both types of exchanges also exist in superior–subordinate relationships. Leaders will at times enact behaviour which the other party in the relationship will perceive as negative or even destructive, especially if consistently repeated over time and related to a power imbalance between the two parties (see also Einarsen, Hoel, Zapf & Cooper, 2011).

In response to the lack of knowledge about the potential negative impact of leadership on the well-being and health of subordinates, there has recently been a striking growing interest in the dark side of leadership among both academics and practitioners. As an illustration, a Google search (11 March 2016) with the search term 'dealing with a mean boss' provided some 2430 results. Similarly, a Google Scholar search for academic papers on 'abusive supervision' yielded 4810 hits, while a search on 'destructive leadership' resulted in 1550 hits. Considering that exposure to destructive leadership has been described as one of the most emotionally salient and disturbing affective events experienced in the work arena (Matta, Erol-Korkmaz, Johnson & Biçaksiz, 2014; Simon, Hurst, Kelley & Judge, 2015), a better grasp of the dark side of leadership is important

Leading to Occupational Health and Safety: How Leadership Behaviours Impact Organizational Safety and Well-Being, First Edition.
Edited by E. Kevin Kelloway, Karina Nielsen and Jennifer K. Dimoff.

with regard to both theoretical models of leadership and our understanding of the well-being of organizations and their employees.

In this chapter we first discuss the behaviours that characterize destructive leaders and define the very concept of 'destructive leadership'. We will thereafter provide an overview of what is known about the relationships between active and passive forms of destructive leadership and indicators of well-being among subordinates, such as job dissatisfaction, affective organizational commitment, emotional exhaustion and psychological distress. As the research field of destructive leadership is still quite young, there are still many unanswered questions with regard to the mediating and moderating factors that can explain the relationships between destructive forms of leadership and their outcomes. In this chapter we therefore take a closer look at *how* and *when* destructive leadership is related to negative well-being outcomes. We particularly look at subordinates' strong negative emotions when confronted with destructive leadership, and present strategies that subordinates may use to cope with such superiors' hostile behaviours in order to prevent their potentially harmful outcomes, i.e. in terms of subordinate emotional exhaustion. Finally, we will present an overview of measures against destructive leadership on both a societal and an organizational level.

Conceptualizing Destructive Leadership

An Overarching Definition

The increasing interest in destructive forms of leadership is reflected by a steadily growing number of terms and concepts describing the dark side of leadership. Over the last decades studies have been conducted that have employed concepts such as 'abusive supervision' (Tepper, 2000), 'despotic leadership' (De Hoogh & Den Hartog, 2008), 'petty tyranny' (Ashforth, 1994), 'poor leadership' (Kelloway, Sivanathan, Francis & Barling, 2005), 'toxic leaders' (Lipman-Blumen, 2005), 'social undermining' by leaders (Duffy, Ganster & Pagon, 2002) and 'destructive leadership' (Aasland, Skogstad, Notelaers, Nielsen & Einarsen, 2010) (see Table 9.1 for an overview). Nonetheless, there is still no overall consensus as regards the definition of what destructive leadership is, and what it is *not* (Craig & Kaiser, 2013). While many scholars in the last century focused on destructiveness from a personality perspective, for example in the form of narcissism and Machiavellianism (see, e.g., O'Connor, Mumford, Clifton, Gessner & Connelly, 1996), contemporary researchers mainly focus on subordinates' perceptions of leaders' destructive behaviours and styles, and their consequences for individuals as well as for the organization (Schyns & Schilling, 2013).

A question much debated within the literature is which behaviours should be included in definitions of destructive leadership. Following Blake and Mouton (1985), and their Managerial Grid, leadership can be described as directed either towards subordinates or towards work tasks (goal attainment) (Einarsen, Aasland & Skogstad, 2007). Accordingly, destructive leadership has been characterized by behaviours such as theft and embezzlement directed towards the organization, as well as humiliating subordinates with harsh comments, blaming them for things they are not responsible for, ignoring employees who are in need

Table 9.1 An overview of terms and concepts used to describe destructive forms of leadership.

Terms and concepts	References
Laissez-faire method of leadership	Lewin, Lippitt & White (1939)
Authoritarian leaders	Adorno, Frenkel-Brunswik, Levinson & Sandford (1950)
Machiavellian leaders	Christie & Geis (1970)
Intolerable bosses	Lombardo & McCall (1984)
Personalized charismatic leadership	House & Howell (1992)
The dark side of charisma	Hogan, Raskin & Fazzini (1990)
The dark side of leadership	Conger (1990)
Crazy bosses	Bing (1992)
Petty tyranny	Ashforth (1994)
Flawed leadership	Hogan (1994)
Derailed leadership	Shackleton (1995)
Brutal bosses	Hornstein (1996)
Passive leadership	Den Hartog, Muijen & Koopman (1997)
Passive-avoidant leadership	Avolio, Bass & Jung (1999)
Abusive supervision	Tepper (2000)
Despotic leaders	Aronson (2001)
Leaders' social undermining	Duffy et al. (2002)
Impaired managers	Lubit (2004)
Bad leadership	Kellerman (2004)
Poor leadership	Kelloway et al. (2005)
Toxic leaders	Lipman-Blumen (2005)
Destructive leadership	Einarsen et al. (2007)
Negative leadership	Schilling (2009)

of help, and in extreme cases even threatening or physically assaulting subordinates. In studies of counterproductive behaviour by organization members in general, a similar division has been proposed in which the said behaviour is directed either at the resources, goal attainment and effectiveness of the organization, or at hurting other organization members (see, e.g., Gruys & Sackett, 2003; Sackett & DeVore, 2001). The latter category of behaviour would in our case be leadership practices that are destructive mainly in terms of subordinates' motivation and well-being. Using the notion that a given manager or supervisor may behave constructively towards the organization while being destructive towards subordinates, or vice versa, Einarsen, Aasland and Skogstad (2007) conceptualize three main forms of destructive leadership, namely:

Tyrannical leadership; leaders are constructive in terms of organizational factors, and destructive towards subordinates' motivation, well-being or effectiveness.

Supportive but disloyal leadership; leaders are destructive as seen from the organization's perspective, but may still be highly supportive and motivating as seen by the subordinates.

Derailed leadership; leaders act in a destructive manner towards both subordinates and the organization.

On the basis of such a broader and more inclusive perspective, we may define destructive leadership as '*The systematic and repeated behaviour by a leader, supervisor or manager that violates the legitimate interest of the organisation by undermining and/or sabotaging the organisation's goals, tasks, resources, and effectiveness and/or the motivation, well-being or job satisfaction of subordinates*' (Einarsen et al., 2007, p. 208). Following this definition, destructive leadership may be directed both towards subordinates and towards the organization, the latter by sabotaging or stealing from the organization, for example. Many scholars support such a broad view of destructive leadership or leadership behaviours (Craig & Kaiser, 2013; Thoroughgood, Tate, Sawyer & Jacobs, 2012), which makes it possible to map all those destructive leadership behaviours that may influence employees' well-being, be it directly or indirectly. Yet, in this literature overview, we will concentrate on behaviours directed at subordinates, irrespective of the effect on the organization, as this is where the greatest extent of research has been conducted so far, and because this chapter focuses on employee well-being.

Destructive Leadership Directed Towards Subordinates

As described above, researchers have proposed a number of concepts that arguably fall within this domain of destructive leadership. For instance, Bennett J. Tepper, a prominent scholar within the field, used the term 'abusive supervision' to describe subordinates' perceptions of 'the extent to which supervisors engage in *the sustained display of hostile verbal and nonverbal behaviors, excluding physical contact*' (Tepper, 2000, p. 178; italics in original). An argument in support of this relatively narrow definition of destructive leadership is that a core element in the leadership process has been described as that of influencing other people, as compared to influencing the organizations as such (see also Schyns & Schilling, 2013).

Setting up a complete and all-inclusive list of the specific behaviours within this domain of destructive leadership will probably be very difficult or even impossible. However, looking at Arnold H. Buss's (1961) seminal work and the categorization of aggressive types of behaviours is an excellent foundation for an even more nuanced understanding of what destructive leadership towards subordinates is, and is not. Buss describes aggressive behaviours on three dimensions, namely active-passive, physical-verbal and direct-indirect. Verbal forms of aggression involve harm to others through words rather than deeds, whereas physical forms of aggression involve overt actions. Direct forms of aggression are reflected through behaviours delivered directly to the victim, while indirect forms involve the actions of other agents or assaults on persons or objects valued by the victim. Finally, active aggression produces harm through the performance of behaviour while passive aggression delivers harm through the withholding of behaviour.

Accordingly, all destructive behaviours can adequately be described by those three dimensions. In the field of destructive leadership, yelling at a subordinate is an example of a verbal-active-direct behaviour, talking badly about a subordinate behind his or her back is an example of a verbal-active-indirect behaviour, theft from the organization is an example of physical-active-indirect behaviour, while giving the subordinate the 'silent treatment' is an example of (non-)verbal-passive-direct behaviour. Accordingly, we may see that destructive leadership directed towards subordinates may come in many shapes and forms, yet with a basic distinction between active and passive forms.

A basic question in psychology, as well as in philosophy and law, has been the following: which is worse, the enactment of destructive deeds or the avoidance of action when there is a need for action? The answer to this question will to a high degree depend on the type and criticality of the need addressed. Laissez-faire leadership, defined as the avoidance or absence of leadership (Bass & Avolio, 1994), is a type of non-responsive leadership in situations where followers probably are in need of a leader's help and support (Hinkin & Schriesheim, 2008; Schriesheim, Wu & Scandura, 2009; Skogstad, Hetland, Glasø & Einarsen, 2014). Accordingly, and in line with Buss (1961), who defines such passivity as a form of aggressiveness, we take the position that laissez-faire leadership is a type of destructive leadership. This constitutes a contingency perspective on destructive leadership by focusing on situations where there is a concrete need for leadership, and where subordinates have legitimate expectations of leadership action (see also Einarsen et al., 2007). In line with other scholars (see, e.g., Yang, 2015), we agree that leader passivity is not destructive per se. There has to be a situation where the subordinate is in need of help or some sort of assistance, and has legitimate expectations of receiving this help from his or her superior. In contrast, there are various situations where leaders should refrain from action, for instance in situations where the subordinate should be empowered, or where the subordinates perceive the leader's actions to be unnecessary or even intrusive, as in the case of over-helping (Gilbert & Silvera, 1996). From such a balanced approach to leadership, destructive leadership is about not knowing when to act and when not to act, be it by non-responsiveness when leader assistance is critical or by enacting hostile and offensive behaviour in general.

What About Intent?

Many definitions of workplace aggression include intentionality as a central element (see, e.g., Neuman & Baron, 1998). Accordingly, whether intentionality should be a criterion in definitions of destructive leadership has been discussed at length (Craig & Kaiser, 2013). However, only two of twelve definitions of destructive forms of leadership (social undermining and despotic leadership) explicitly include intentionality (Schyns & Schilling, 2013), and many scholars choose 'a no call for intent' position where destructive leadership may include both leader behaviour which intended to harm the target and non-intentional behaviours that result from thoughtlessness, insensitivity, lack of competence, and so on. Consequently, the core question may concern not whether the behaviour was intended or not, but the degree to which subordinates experience the behaviour as hostile, unfair or humiliating. Another argument for not including intentionality in definitions of destructive leadership is that it is difficult for the target to decide if an action was intentional or not (Buss, 1961). However, in line with Mikula (2003) and his attribution-of-blame model, one may expect that the effects of destructive leadership may be strengthened when followers perceive that the leader may be blamed, rather than blaming the organization or the subordinate him- or herself. We may conclude that a variety of active as well as passive forms of destructive leadership have been identified, characterized as being hostile, unjust, harmful and illegitimate for the individual or the organization. In what follows we will document the consistent negative associations between destructive leadership and a broad range of well-being outcomes.

Relationships Between Destructive Forms of Leadership and Employee Well-Being

There are reasons to believe that destructive forms of leadership will be differently associated with different subordinate behavioural, attitudinal and health outcomes. A simple illustration of this is that most would expect a physical attack by a superior on a subordinate to have different immediate health effects on the subordinate from those that would occur in a situation in which a leader avoids helping a subordinate who has signalled that they are in need of help. Below we present findings on the relationships between active and passive forms of destructive leadership with regard to employee well-being.

The concept of occupational well-being is very broad, and has been defined to include affective, cognitive, professional and social aspects, as well as psychosomatic complaints and other strain indicators (Danna & Griffin, 1999; Horn, Taris, Schaufeli & Schreurs, 2004; Sivanathan, Arnold, Turner & Barling, 2004; Skakon, Nielsen, Borg & Guzman, 2010; Warr, 1987, 1994). According to research on the relationship between destructive leadership and employee well-being the majority of studies have been conducted on the affective dimension, which includes job satisfaction, affective organizational commitment and emotional exhaustion (Horn et al., 2004). This research has been synthesized in four meta-analyses. Zhang and Liao (2015) documented 20 studies on job satisfaction and emotional exhaustion, 10 studies on affective organizational commitment, and seven studies on depression. Mackey, Frieder, Brees and Martinko (2015) reported from 17 studies on job satisfaction, 15 studies on emotional exhaustion, nine studies on organizational commitment, and six studies on depression. Schyns and Schilling (2013) reported 21 studies on job satisfaction and 24 studies on emotional exhaustion and depression, while Hershcovis & Barling (2010) reported 12 studies on job satisfaction, 11 studies on psychological well-being, six studies on physical well-being, and six studies on affective organizational commitment. In the following we will present a summary of these meta-analyses. It should be noted that the studies by Zhang and Liao (2015) and Mackey et al. (2015) only report findings on abusive supervision, whereas Schyns and Schilling (2013) employs the broader concept of destructive leadership. As none of the existing meta-analyses have reported associations between passive destructive leadership and well-being, we will present relevant primary studies that include findings on passive-avoidant leadership. This will substantiate our understanding of the degree to which passive-avoidant leadership styles may have negative effects, just as active destructive styles may have.

Relationships Between Destructive Leadership and Job Satisfaction

Job satisfaction is the most frequently examined outcome of destructive leadership. Theoretically, job satisfaction has been related to both emotional and cognitive evaluative components. Many scholars emphasize the affective dimension of job satisfaction (see, e.g., Horn et al., 2004; Warr, 1987, 1994), where job satisfaction is perceived to represent affective well-being on a pleasure–displeasure axis. Brief and Weiss (2002) state that job satisfaction may be approached productively in at least two ways. First, if job satisfaction is defined as an evaluative judgement, then affect at work can be defined as an antecedent to it. Second, if job satisfaction is primarily defined by an affective component, then affect at work can be seen to be an indicator of job satisfaction. To our knowledge, all conducted studies show a consistent link between destructive forms of leadership and job satisfaction. Most of these studies have been conducted on abusive supervision, for example Bowling and Michel (2011), all documenting negative relationships between subordinates' reports of abusive supervision and job satisfaction. Likewise, a study by Skogstad et al. (2014) showed a negative relationship between tyrannical leadership and job satisfaction. The abovementioned meta-analyses (Hershcovis & Barling, 2010; Mackey et al., 2015; Schyns & Schilling, 2013; Zhang & Liao, 2015) reported correlations between abusive supervision and job satisfaction of –.39, –31, –34, and –.35, respectively (weighted mean correlations, which are reported in all the referred meta-analyses). For other forms of active destructive leadership Schyns and Schilling (2013) found a highly comparable correlation (–.35).

While the relationships between active forms of destructive leadership and job satisfaction have been abundantly studied, there are fewer studies which have reported findings on passive-avoidant forms, such as laissez-faire leadership. However, laissez-faire leadership has been included in some meta-analyses on the full-range leadership model employing the Multifactor Leadership Questionnaire (Bass & Avolio, 1990). For instance, DeRue, Nahrgang, Wellman and Humphrey (2011) found an association (estimated true $r = -.28$) between laissez-faire leadership and job satisfaction. Accordingly, two cross-sectional findings by Skogstad, Aasland et al. (2014) showed comparable correlations ($r = -.26$, $r = -.25$). Barling and Frone (2016) show a significant relationship between passive leadership and overall work attitude, including job satisfaction and organizational affective commitment ($r = -.42$). Interestingly, their study shows that passive leadership is linked to overall work attitude via the two sequential paths of role stressors and psychological work fatigue. The negative associations between laissez-faire leadership and job satisfaction support the notion that passive-avoidant forms of leadership should be considered as destructive. However, as cross-sectional findings can only be used to establish associations, but not causal relationships, these relationships should be studied further, and especially within a longitudinal design, which is rare in leadership research (Martinko, Harvey, Brees & Mackey, 2013). In one of the few existing longitudinal studies on destructive leadership and well-being, Skogstad, Aasland et al. (2014) found that tyrannical leadership was significantly related to job satisfaction over a six-month lag, while laissez-faire leadership was not. In a representative sample of the Norwegian workforce they found opposite relationships between the two destructive leadership styles and job satisfaction over a two-year lag in that tyrannical leadership was not related to subsequent changes in job satisfaction two years later, while increases in laissez-faire leadership were related to subsequent reduced job satisfaction. This may indicate that the influence of tyrannical and laissez-faire leadership on job satisfaction differs over time and that active destructive leaderships may have more profound and short-term effects, whereas the impact of passive-avoidant forms develops more slowly.

Relationships Between Destructive Leadership and Organizational Commitment

Like job satisfaction, affective organizational commitment, reflecting an employee's degree of identification with the goals of the organization and their desire to remain a part of it (Meyer & Allen, 1991), can be placed on a pleasure–displeasure axis (Horn et al., 2004). Not surprisingly, abusive supervision has been shown to be associated with a lowered level of subordinate affective commitment (Aryee, Chen, Sun & Debrah, 2007; Tepper, 2000), and Tepper's study showed that abusive supervision was equally related to followers' normative commitment, reflecting the degree to which employees feel an obligation to stay in the organization. The meta-analyses by Hershcovis & Barling (2010), Mackey et al. (2015) and Zhang and Liao (2015) showed that the magnitude of the association between abusive supervision and affective organizational commitment ($r = -.26$, $r = -.23$ and $r = -.30$, respectively) is somewhat lower than the association found between abusive supervision and job satisfaction. The meta-analysis by Schyns and Schilling (2013) found negative relationships between both abusive supervision ($r = -.19$) and other forms of active destructive leadership ($r = -.28$) with organizational commitment in general.

As shown in a meta-analysis by Jackson, Meyer, and Wang (2013), the relationship between passive destructive leadership and affective organizational commitment has only been examined in a limited number of studies ($k = 8$). Their study showed a weighted average correlation between laissez-faire leadership and affective commitment of – .29, which is on an equal level with that of abusive supervision, while the associations between laissez-faire leadership and normative and continuance commitment respectively were lower ($\rho = -.16$ and $\rho = -.08$) In their time-lagged study Chênevert, Vandenberghe, Doucet and Ayed (2013) found a comparable correlation ($r = -.25$) between passive leadership (T1) and affective commitment (T2), where role ambiguity fully mediated a negative relationship between passive leadership and affective organizational commitment. As noted earlier, Barling and Frone (2016) found a significant relationship between passive leadership and overall work attitude, including job satisfaction and organizational affective commitment (r = −.42). These studies indicate that the relationship between passive destructive leadership and affective organizational commitment may be on equal levels with those for abusive supervision.

Relationships Between Destructive Leadership and Emotional Exhaustion

Emotional exhaustion, considered as the core component in burnout (see e.g., Shirom, 1989), has been defined as a chronic state of physical and emotional depletion that results from excessive job or personal demands and continuous stress (Cropanzano, Rupp & Byrne, 2003). In addition to emotional exhaustion, the burnout concept also includes depersonalization (cynicism) and inefficacy (reduced personal accomplishment) (Maslach, Schaufeli & Leiter, 2001). The findings from four meta-analyses show relatively consistent associations between abusive supervision and destructive leadership, and emotional exhaustion. Zhang and Liao's (2015) meta-analysis found an association of .35, while Mackey et al. (2015) yielded an association of .32. Likewise, Schyns and Schilling's (2013) meta-analysis, using a measure of strain including exhaustion as well as depression, showed the same strength of relationship as the study by Zhang and Liao. Montano, Reeske, Franke and Hüffmeier (2016), in their online meta-analysis on relationships between leadership and mental health and job performance, report a corresponding relationship with this outcome (ρ = .31). We also note that Schyns and Schilling's study showed weaker associations with the included indicator of strain (r = .21) for other forms of active destructive leadership than for abusive supervision.

To our knowledge there is no meta-analysis on the relationship between passive destructive leadership and emotional exhaustion. However, a study by Hetland, Sandal and Johnsen (2007) showed that passive-avoidant leadership was positively related to emotional exhaustion (r = .22), and even more so to cynicism (r = .34). Accordingly, Zopiatis and Constanti (2010) found a laissez-faire leadership style to be associated with emotional exhaustion (r = .29), and even more strongly with depersonalization (r = .35). Likewise, Kanste, Kyngas and Nikkila (2007) found laissez-faire leadership to be related to emotional exhaustion (r = .18). In a comparable study Theorell et al. (2012) showed 'non-listening' to be negatively related to emotional exhaustion (r = .28). Barling and Frone's (2016) study showed a comparable correlation (r = .23) between passive leadership and psychological work fatigue. Zwingmann, Wolf and Richter (2016) show that follower perceptions of laissez-faire leadership also predicted leaders' reports of emotional exhaustion 24 months later (β = .38, p = .046). In conclusion, these findings suggest that passive-avoidant leadership is a relatively strong predictor of subordinate emotional exhaustion, as well as of leaders' own emotional exhaustion, although the relationship for subordinates is somewhat weaker than that found for abusive supervision.

Relationships Between Destructive Leadership and Psychological Well-Being

'Psychological well-being' refers to the psychological aspects of health-related behaviours. Being an indicator of general psychological well-being, psychological distress is a general term that is used to describe unpleasant feelings or emotions that impact one's level of functioning. In psychiatry, 'psychological distress' is considered an umbrella term that includes symptoms of both anxiety and depression. While emotional exhaustion overlaps with depression, they are considered as different phenomena (Glass & McKnight, 1996). In one of the first studies on abusive supervision, Tepper (2000) found it to be positively related to depression ($r = .18$). Similarly, Martinko, Harvey, Brees and Mackey (2013) and Tepper, Moss, Lockhart and Carr (2007) showed that abusive supervision was closely related to a variety of indicators of psychological well-being such as detachment, psychological distress, fatigue, insomnia, somatic health complaints and job strain. The meta-analyses by Hershcovis & Barling (2010), Mackey et al. (2015), Montano et al. (2016) and Zhang and Liao (2015) support this consistent negative relationship ($r = -.31$, $r = -.21$, $r = -.16$ and $r = -.29$ respectively). While the available evidence is somewhat limited, the findings are relatively consistent in showing that exposure to active destructive leadership is associated with an increase in depression and distress.

The evidence for a relationship between passive-avoidant leadership and psychological well-being is even scarcer. Nonetheless, the established associations between passive destructive leadership and psychological well-being seem to correspond to the associations found for active destructive leadership. In a study across 16 countries comprising 93,576 subordinates in 11,177 teams, Zwingmann et al. (2014) found laissez-faire leadership to be negatively associated with psychological well-being (the WHO-5 Index) in 16 subsamples ($r = -.19$ to $r = -.43$). Similarly, in a representative study of the Norwegian working population, Skogstad, Einarsen, Torsheim, Aasland and Hetland (2007) found that a laissez-faire leadership style was associated with psychological distress in that laissez-faire leadership was related to psychological distress through stressors in the work arena and exposure to bullying. In a longitudinal study of 2272 governmental employees exposed to the Oslo terror bombing attack in 2011, laissez-faire leadership was bivariately associated with psychological distress over a one-year period ($r = -.26$). However, this relationship became insignificant when stability in distress and fair, empowering and supportive leadership were adjusted for (Birkeland, Nielsen, Knardahl & Heir, 2015).

Relationship Between Destructive Leadership and Other Indicators of Well-Being

While the majority of existing studies have examined the influence of destructive leadership on job satisfaction, commitment, emotional exhaustion or psychological well-being, there are also some studies which have assessed other indicators of well-being. In their meta-analysis of leadership and mental health, Montano et al. (2016) showed negative associations between destructive leadership and psychological function, stress, affective symptoms and health complaints (respectively $\rho = -.33$, $\rho = .32$, $\rho = .29$ and $\rho = .11$). The meta-analysis by Schyns and Schilling (2013) showed a negative relationship between abusive supervision and an outcome including physical well-being and life satisfaction ($r = -.37$), while the meta-analysis by Mackey et al. (2015) and the review by Skakon et al. (2010) documented associations between abusive supervision and job tension

($r = .21$). Similarly, the meta-analysis by Zhang and Liao (2015) showed a consistent relationship between abusive supervision and unhealthy symptoms ($r = .24$), and Nielsen, Matthiesen and Einarsen (2005) found tyrannical leadership to be associated with three symptoms of post-traumatic stress. As regards passive destructive forms of leadership, Barling and Frone (2016) found passive leadership to be related to overall mental health, including mental and emotional health as well as depressive symptoms ($r = .17$). This study shows that passive leadership is linked to overall mental health via the two sequential paths of role stressors and psychological work fatigue. In the study by Zwingmann et al. (2014) laissez-faire leadership was associated with physical health in the form of headache, backache and fatigue ($r = -.15$ to $r = -.29$). In a study using four indicators of job-related affective well-being (high pleasure–high arousal, high pleasure–low arousal; low pleasure–high arousal, low pleasure–low arousal), Kelloway, Turner, Barling and Loughlin (2012) found that laissez-faire leadership was negatively related to all four measures of affective well-being in the range between $r = -.35$ and $r = -.37$). Likewise, Rowold and Schlotz (2009) found laissez-faire leadership to be positively associated with three measures of chronic stress, and Nielsen et al. (2005) found laissez-faire leadership to be correlated with two symptoms of post-traumatic stress.

Workplace Bullying and its Relationships with Subordinates' Mental and Somatic Health

A considerable literature on the relationships between workplace mistreatment and the health and well-being of its targets has evolved over the last three decades, employing the concept of workplace bullying and harassment (see also Einarsen et al., 2011). The concept of workplace bullying tends to look more at long-term and systematic exposure to emotional abuse by other organization members, and the victimization process that may evolve from such situations, than at the role of the specific perpetrator. Yet in practice, workplace bullying is most often about long-term exposure to abusive supervision (Einarsen, Skogstad & Glasø, 2013). According to Lutgen-Sandvik, Tracy and Alberts (2007), workplace bullying is a type of interpersonal aggression at work that goes beyond simple incivility and is marked by the characteristic features of frequency, intensity, duration and power imbalance (p. 837).

A range of studies internationally and in all kinds of industries have documented the detrimental impact such bullying may have on the health and well-being of its targets (see Hogh, Mikkelsen & Hansen, 2011 for an overview). Employing longitudinal designs and time lags of one to five years, studies have provided ample evidence for bullying as an antecedent of subsequent health-related problems in those targeted, be it symptoms of depression and anxiety (Einarsen & Nielsen, 2015), cardiovascular disease (Kivimäki et al., 2003), sleep difficulties (Hansen, Hogh, Garde & Persson, 2014), neck pain (Kääriä, Laaksonen, Rahkonen, Lahelma & Leino-Arjas, 2012), and fibromyalgia (Kivimaki et al., 2004). Meta-analyses show that these relationships are not only strong but also highly consistent across studies and samples (Nielsen & Einarsen, 2012; Nielsen, Magerøy, Gjerstad & Einarsen, 2014).

Being systematically exposed to abusive supervision over a long time period therefore seems to be highly detrimental to one's mental as well as one's physical health. A Swedish prospective study among 3122 male employees showed that working for a bad leader in the mid-1990s was related to more instances of ischaemic heart diseases (IHD) over the following 8–10 years (Nyberg et al., 2009). Records of employee hospital admissions with a diagnosis of acute myocardial infarction, unstable angina and deaths from heart disease were used to ascertain IHD. Altogether 74 IHD events occurred during the mean follow-up period of 9.7 years. Having a bad leader was associated with higher IHD risk, controlling for education, social class, income, perceived physical load at work, smoking, physical exercise, body mass index, blood pressure, lipids, fibrinogen and diabetes. Regarding passive forms of destructive leadership, Diebig, Bormann and Rowold (2016) found laissez-faire leadership to predict followers' hair cortisol levels, a biological marker of stress. Although a cause–effect relationship between destructive leadership and subsequent health-related problems is yet to be firmly established, the evidence on the prospective association is considered strong enough to warrant preventive measures by employers to protect employees against abuse and mistreatment from their superiors.

Summary of Findings on Destructive Leadership and Well-Being

The above documentation shows a consistent picture in which abusive supervision and laissez-faire leadership are negatively related to job satisfaction, affective organizational commitment, and health and well-being. Correspondingly, both forms of destructive leadership show a positive relationship with emotional exhaustion, psychological distress and other indicators of strain. The meta-analysis by Schyns and Schilling (2013) also supports the notion that abusive supervision and other measures of predominantly active forms of destructive leadership yield comparable results. However, the presented studies on active forms of destructive leadership are restricted to person-directed behaviours, as compared to those which are directed towards the organization. Hence, future studies should scrutinize the effects of organization-directed behaviours, or the combination of organization- and individual-directed behaviours (see, e.g., Aasland et al., 2010). There is reason to believe that destructive behaviours directed at the organization also have indirect consequences for individuals' well-being by reducing the quality of the leader–member relationship in general, reducing subordinates' trust in the leader, and generating insecurity in regard to receiving adequate follow-up as well as career development.

Because of the restricted number of studies that have examined relationships between laissez-faire leadership and well-being, these results have to be interpreted with caution, and more studies are needed to justify firmer conclusions. Still, the presented studies yield a consistent picture that supports the notion that laissez-faire leadership is something more than just an incompetent and ineffective form of leadership. In this regard there is reason to emphasize that with few exceptions studies of laissez-faire leadership employ the Multifactor Leadership Questionnaire (MLQ) measure (Bass & Avolio, 1990), in which this leadership form is defined not only as a type of non-leadership, but as a type of

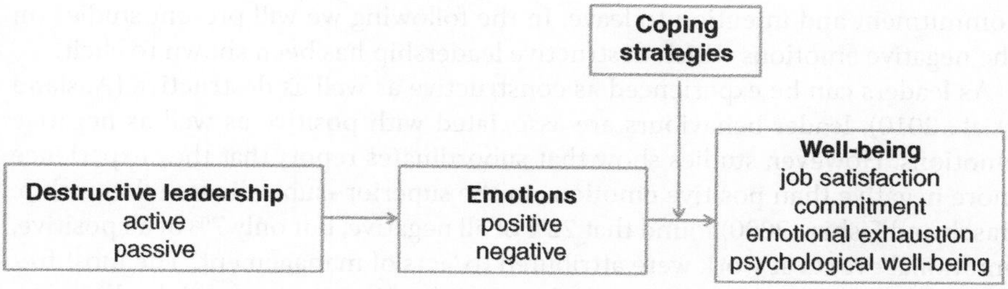

Figure 9.1 Relationships between destructive leadership and occupational well-being.

non-responsive leadership in situations where subordinates or the organization are in need of leader action.

The presented overview yields a simplified picture of relationships between destructive leadership and occupational well-being by documenting direct and mainly cross-sectional bivariate relationships. This is a first step in understanding the consequences of destructive leadership. In a second step one has to investigate why and when destructive leadership is related to various well-being outcomes. A core issue in explaining why destructive forms of leadership are consistently related to negative outcomes may be found in the strong negative emotions that have shown to be triggered by destructive leadership behaviours. With regard to when destructive leadership has an impact on the well-being of subordinates, coping strategies seems to be especially important. We will take a closer look at which strategies have shown to be successful and unsuccessful in coping with destructive leadership, and avoid the dramatic end-state of emotional exhaustion. A graphic overview of the relationships is provided in Figure 9.1.

Emotional Responses to Destructive Forms of Leadership

Destructive leadership, by being perceived as hostile, offensive, unjust and illegitimate, is probably one of the most emotionally salient and disturbing affective events employees may experience at work. According to Affective Events Theory (Weiss & Cropanzano, 1996) destructive leadership behaviours may be defined as work events which immediately trigger subordinate affective responses, where such responses are attempts to gain control over events related to survival (Robert, 1980). Weiss and Cropanzano (1996) propose, and substantiate, that these affective responses mediate the relationship between work events and outcomes such as job satisfaction. In support of this claim – that destructive leadership constitutes a negative work event – Glasø, Skogstad, Notelaers and Einarsen (2016) have found that negative emotions fully mediate the relationships between tyrannical leadership and work engagement and intention to leave. Likewise, Glasø and Notelaers (2012) found that negative emotions partly mediated the relationship between workplace bullying and job satisfaction, and partly mediated the relationship between workplace bullying, and organizational commitment and intention to leave. In the following we will present studies on the negative emotions which destructive leadership has been shown to elicit.

As leaders can be experienced as constructive as well as destructive (Aasland et al., 2010), leader behaviours are associated with positive as well as negative emotions. However, studies show that subordinates report that they experience more negative than positive emotions in the superior–subordinate relationship. Basch and Fisher (2000) found that 22% of all negative, but only 7% of all positive, emotional events at work were attributed to 'acts of management'. The most frequent negative emotions experienced as a result of interactions with leaders were anger, disgust, bitterness, unhappiness and disappointment. In line with this, Dasborough (2006) found that employees reported far more negative than positive incidents with their superiors when recalling leader emotion-evoking behaviours. While constructive leadership behaviour was associated with feelings such as pleasure, calmness and enthusiasm, destructive behaviour elicited emotions of frustration, disappointment, fear, rejection, anxiousness, loathing, annoyance and anger. Glasø and Einarsen (2006) presented subordinates with, altogether, 70 different epithets of moods, emotions and emotion-laden judgements which can be experienced in a relationship with a superior. Interestingly their study showed that three of four factors reflected negative emotions. The only factor representing positive emotions was labelled 'recognition'; it consisted of positive emotions such as feeling glad, content, excited, enthusiastic, happy and acknowledged. Among the three factors reflecting negative emotions, the frustration factor included feeling resigned, annoyed, angry, frustrated and disappointed, while the violation factor included feeling insulted, despised and humiliated. The last factor, uncertainty, included feeling uncertain, anxious and embarrassed. These studies document the fact that subordinates experience a broad range of negative emotions in their contact with superiors.

In line with our distinction between active and passive forms of destructive leadership, Dasborough (2006) distinguished between destructive leader behaviour such as yelling and being arrogant, and behaviour such as lack of awareness, respect, support and acknowledgement. Dasborough stated that a lack of leader support was followed by an increase in employees' feelings of being betrayed and disappointed. These findings support the notion that a repeated lack of leader support, when there is a need for such support, will trigger negative emotions in the same way as active destructive forms of leadership, such as yelling, do. Lack of leadership when it is needed has been shown to be associated with uncertainty in the form of role ambiguity (Skogstad, Hetland et al., 2014), and uncertainty has been shown to trigger negative affective reactions (Lind & Van den Bos, 2002). Leaders' non-responsiveness may also be a hindrance to subordinates' goal attainment, which has been shown to trigger negative emotions such as anger (Cropanzano, Stein & Nadisic, 2011). In line with this, Kessler, Bruursema, Rodopman and Spector (2013) found that laissez-faire leadership correlated positively with negative emotions in co-worker dyads. Negative emotions correlated with self-reported passive-avoidant leadership ($r = .40$) as well as co-worker-reported passive-avoidant leadership ($r = .29$). In severe cases, for example when a leader gives a subordinate the silent treatment as a part of laissez-faire leadership, the subordinate may perceive this as a type of interpersonal rejection (see e.g., Leary, 2001); here the predominant emotion appears to be 'hurt feelings'. Studies on the features of 'hurt feelings' suggest that this may be a distinct negative emotion that is associated with feelings of being devalued, unwanted and rejected (Smart Richman & Leary, 2009). There is reason to believe that laissez-faire leadership, often characterized by not responding to follower needs, triggers such emotions of 'hurt feelings'. This passive-avoidant leadership style may also trigger emotions of rage and humiliation, because the subordinate may not complete his or her work task, and in the long run it may hamper career development. However, there is also reason to believe that leaders' non-responsiveness, when the subordinate is in need of help, may trigger in the subordinate 'hot' affective responses such as anger and disgust, for example when the subordinate perceives the leader as highly incompetent. Which emotions will be triggered by a given destructive act may be difficult to predict, not least because such behaviour will be part of a pattern, manifesting itself over time, in which different constructive as well as destructive acts will be enacted (Aasland et al., 2010). In this regard, there is reason to believe that a combination of constructive and destructive acts may have the worst consequences, as indicated by Duffy et al. (2002). We may conclude that active as well as passive forms of destructive leadership elicit a variety of negative emotions which will subsequently influence employees' well-being. In the following section we will have a closer look at which subordinates' coping strategies may be used when confronted with destructive leadership to prevent emotional exhaustion, one of the most severe negative well-being outcomes.

Subordinates' Coping Strategies when Confronted with Destructive Leadership

Destructive leadership is by definition a repeated phenomenon (Einarsen et al., 2007). It will often be experienced as a series of linked episodes, and if not coped with successfully may result in emotional exhaustion and a wide range of symptoms of psychological distress. Harvey, Stoner, Hochwarter and Kacmar (2007) suggest that the relationship between abusive supervision and emotional exhaustion probably stems from the nature of the interpersonal conflict in conjunction with the continuous assault on subordinates' feelings, self-esteem and self-efficacy. In support of this view Leiter and Maslach (1988) point to interpersonal conflict as particularly salient in the burnout process, while reviews on burnout document qualitative and quantitative work loads, role conflict and role ambiguity, lack of participation and lack of social support as precursors of emotional exhaustion and burnout (Maslach et al., 2001; Seidler et al., 2014; Shirom, 2003).

Although many employees are exposed to leadership behaviours that may be perceived as destructive, it is unlikely that all will react to this exposure in the same manner. Following most perspectives on stress (Bakker, Demerouti & Sanz-Vergel, 2014; Lazarus & Folkman, 1984), it is far more probable that the effects of destructive leadership on employees are dependent upon a range of personal and organizational characteristics such as individual dispositions and resilience, coping behaviours, social support and leadership. The basic premise of most stress models is that the strength of the relation between a stressor and an outcome differs as a function of moderator variables. Hence, with regard to destructive leadership, an understanding of moderating variables will contribute to explaining when and under what conditions destructive leadership is related to well-being. The Transactional Model of Stress (Lazarus & Folkman, 1984) suggests that the nature and severity of reactions following exposure to a given stressor are functions of a dynamic interplay between event characteristics and individual appraisal and coping processes. Consequently, it is likely that individual attempts at coping could influence the outcomes of destructive leadership. In the following sections we will explain how various forms of coping may determine the impact of destructive leadership.

Confronted with destructive leaders, subordinates have been shown to employ a range of different responses. In some cases they respond with various types of retaliation towards the organization or other organizational members (Martinko et al., 2013), or they may try to solve the problem of being exposed to destructive leadership (May, Wesche, Heinitz & Kerschreiter, 2014). Destructive leadership represents a significant workplace stressor, and in line with cognitive appraisal theory (see, e.g., Cropanzano et al., 2011; Lazarus, 2006) subordinates will first make a primary appraisal of possible outcomes by evaluating whether anything is at stake, and, if there is a stake, what the outcome may be. Accordingly, subordinates will ascertain the overall favourability, or unfavourability, of the event with respect to their individual goals. Experiencing leaders' destructive acts will certainly make most subordinates feel that there is a stake which cannot be ignored, and that the outcomes may be threatening as well as harmful. During a secondary appraisal, coloured by emotions, subordinates will, on the grounds that they are exposed to systematic destructive acts, evaluate their own coping resources to respond effectively to the destructive leader.

Coping may be defined as '*constantly changing cognitive and behavioral efforts to manage specific external and/or internal demands that are appraised as taxing or exceeding the resources of the person*' (Lazarus & Folkman, 1984, p. 141; italics in original). There are many ways to group coping responses, and a classification of different coping strategies into a broader architecture has not yet been agreed upon (Carver & Connor-Smith, 2010). However, a commonly used distinction is Lazarus and Folkman's (1984) classification of coping strategies into problem-focused coping, which covers attempts to actively eliminate the problem, and emotion-focused coping, which describes attempts to attenuate discomfort by altering perception or appraisal of the problem. Another distinction is between approach and avoidance coping (Carver & Connor-Smith, 2010). Combining these two categories of coping strategies, May et al. (2014) define four basic types of coping, namely problem-focused approach coping, emotion-focused approach coping, problem-focused avoidance coping and emotion-focused avoidance coping. An illustration of different forms of coping according to this system is provided in Table 9.2.

Confronted with a destructive leader, subordinates can approach the destructive leader with the goal of reducing, eliminating or managing the stressor of destructive leadership. Alternatively, the subordinate may avoid the leader, with the goal of ignoring, avoiding or withdrawing from the destructive leader or the

Table 9.2 Examples of subordinates' coping strategies in response to destructive leadership.

	Approach coping	Avoidance coping
Problem-focused coping	*General coping strategies*	*General coping strategies*
	Problem solving (mc)	Avoiding contact with leader (lc)
	Seeking instrumental support (mc)	Work withdrawal (lc)
	Upward influence tactics	
	Ingratiating (lc)	
	Rational persuasion (mc)	
	Exchange/negotiating (mc)	
	Exerting pressure (hc)	
Emotion-focused coping	*General coping strategies*	*General coping strategies*
	Acceptance (lc)	Denial (lc)
	Cognitive restructuring (lc)	Wishful thinking (lc)
	Seeking emotional support (lc)	Substance abuse (lc)

Note: lc = low confrontativeness; mc = moderate confrontativeness; hc = high confrontativeness.
Source: adapted from May et al., 2014.

emotional consequences of this contact. Examples of problem-focused approach coping are ingratiation and exerting pressure on the destructive leader.

An important aspect of subordinate coping behaviour is its level of confrontativeness, especially in the subordinate–superior relationship. Problem-focused approach coping characterized by high confrontativeness will probably provoke the abusive leader, which may lead to even more destructive leader behaviour. In agreement with this, a study by D. Yagil (2006) showed that a forceful subordinate upward influence tactic is positively associated with abusive leadership. In comparison, ingratiation is a type of coping characterized by low confrontativeness. Examples of subordinate emotion-focused approach coping are verbally attacking the superior, which is a highly confronting coping style. Emotion-focused strategies low in confrontativeness are those that avoid contact with the leader, such as withdrawal from the organization by absenteeism or quitting the job altogether. It is highly understandable that subordinates wish to withdraw from the emotionally painful relationship. However, more studies substantiate that this is not a successful coping strategy as regards facilitating well-being and preventing emotional exhaustion. Yet a study by Kant, Skogstad, Torsheim and Einarsen (2013) showed that abusive supervision tended to increase among superiors high on trait anger when interacting with a mild, non-angry subordinate, while subordinates high on trait anger did not experience more abusive supervision from high versus low trait anger superiors. Hence, it may be that the strategy of the subordinate is also dependent on the particular leaders and her or his characteristics. If so, this line of research is still only in its infancy.

Another issue is how different coping strategies work when it comes to the outcomes of being exposed to destructive leadership. Various studies have shown that approach coping strategies, in general, tend to defuse the negative effects of stress, while avoidance strategies tend to worsen such effects (Carver & Connor-Smith, 2010). Similarly, a meta-analysis by Shin, Park, Ying et al. (2014) shows that emotion-focused strategies, in general, are positively associated, while problem-focused strategies are negatively related, to emotional exhaustion. It is interesting to note that this study shows that the positive association for emotion-focused strategies is clearly stronger ($r = .33$) than the negative association for problem-focused strategies ($r = -.05$), indicating that the consequences of using passive strategies may be severe.

The few studies we have found of the effects of subordinates' coping strategies on the destructive leadership–emotional exhaustion relationship confirm the findings by Shin et al. (2014) that approach strategies, in general, are more effective than avoidance strategies. Tepper et al. (2007 found that when subordinates used an approach coping strategy by openly discussing relationship problems with the superior, the abusive supervision–emotional exhaustion relationship was reduced, while avoiding the superior strengthened this relationship. The authors suggest that the strategy of avoiding contact may have negative consequences through creating role ambiguity, and reinforce subordinates' self-image as a target of further victimization. A study by Yagil, Ben-Zur and Tamir (2011) supports these findings by showing that while direct communication with the destructive superior was most weakly related to abusive supervision, avoiding contact was most strongly related to abusive supervision. Similarly, Frieder, Hochwarter and DeOrtentiis (2015) found that those subordinates exhibiting proactive voice behaviours in general, when confronted with abusive supervision, in combination with being able to manage their personal resources, reported lower levels of emotional exhaustion. Likewise, in their study on interpersonal influence, Harvey et al. (2007) found that the positive relationship between abusive supervision and emotional exhaustion decreased when subordinates scored higher on positive affect and used an active upward-influence tactic. However, in studying subordinates coping with destructive leadership, one should also emphasize the perceptions and actions of the destructive superior. A fruitful approach is to consider subordinates' coping behaviour as being part of an interaction process in which leaders' perceptions of subordinates' responses as either aggressive, submissive or constructive will influence leader responses. May et al. (2014) propose that subordinates who wish to be perceived as constructive by their destructive leaders should engage in moderately confrontational coping strategies, that is, problem-focused approach strategies like rational persuasion or negotiation.

There is reason to believe that the degree to which a subordinate experiences having a high or low coping potential will influence the likelihood of their displaying constructive approaching coping styles rather than unconstructive avoiding coping styles. There is also reason to believe that the coping potential will be higher in subordinates scoring high on core self-evaluations (Judge, Locke & Durham, 1997), which are high self-esteem, high self-efficacy, low neuroticism and an internal locus of control. They are all traits which will probably help employees to experience control over their environment, including their superiors, and some studies support the notion that core self-evaluations are important in preventing emotional exhaustion when confronted by destructive leaders. A study by Wu and Hu (2009) showed that core self-evaluations, measured by one indicator, were negatively related to abusive supervision. Vogel and Mitchell (2015) found a negative relationship between self-esteem and abusive supervision, while Kiazad, Restubog, Zagenczyk, Kiewitz and Tang (2010) found that organization-based self-esteem moderated the relationship between authoritarian leadership behaviour and perceptions of abusive supervision, in that this relationship was more positive for those subordinates with low levels of organization-based self-esteem. Likewise, a study by Lian et al. (2014) showed that self-control capacity was negatively associated with abusive supervision, and that self-control influenced the relationship between abusive supervision and supervisor-directed aggression. The strongest association was found for subordinates reporting to be low on self-control and perceiving their superior to be low in coercive power. Further, Wei and Si (2011) found that locus of control moderated the relationship between abusive supervision and subordinates' counterproductive work behaviour towards the organization in such a way that this relationship is stronger for subordinates who are external as compared to internal in their locus of control. We have not identified any study on core self-evaluations as moderators in the destructive leadership–emotional exhaustion relationship. However, in one study the moderating effect of subordinates' susceptibility to emotional contagion was studied (Wu & Hu, 2009). The higher the susceptibility to emotional contagion, the higher the likelihood that subordinates were 'infected' by the destructive leaders' negative emotions. Accordingly, this study showed that the negative relationship between abusive supervision and emotional exhaustion was stronger at a high level of susceptibility to emotional contagion than at a low level of susceptibility.

These findings substantiate the view that we may expect that subordinate characteristics will be important in coping with destructive superiors. However, and in line with conservation of resources theory applied to burnout (Hobfoll & Freedy, 1993), there is also reason to believe that being consistently exposed to destructive leadership behaviours over time will probably deplete subordinates completely of their personal resources, so that constructive problem-focused coping will no longer be an option (see also Shirom, 2003). And this may especially be the case because of the power imbalance in the superior–subordinate relationship which dramatically restricts the options subordinates have as regards responses and coping opportunities. When power inferiority is experienced as high by the subordinate, active approach coping strategies are probably supressed (Aquino, Tripp & Bies, 2006; Klaussner, 2014). In line with this view Zapf and Gross (2001), in a qualitative study, showed that while most victims of bullying started with constructive conflict-solving strategies, they followed up by changing their strategies several times, and finally tried to leave the organization. Hence, within a coping framework, the only alternatives left for subordinates may in most cases be avoidance coping strategies, such as withdrawing from the leader–follower relationship, and ultimately from the organization. From the perspective of the victimized subordinate and the organization this is a highly unsatisfactory solution. Accordingly, Klaussner (2014), in addition to those coping strategies described by May et al. (2014) (see Table 9.2), includes organizational measures against destructive leadership. In line with this approach Schat and Kelloway (2003) found that instrumental organizational support moderated the effects of workplace violence on emotional well-being, somatic health and job-related affect. Likewise, informational support buffered the effect of violence in the workplace on emotional well-being. However, organizational measures may be difficult to employ because of factors such as lower power positions and low work self-esteem (Harlos, 2010) and the loss of personal resources (cf. conservation of resources theory; Hobfoll & Freedy, 1993). Hence, the organization as such should implement policies against destructive leadership and offer systems and resources to effectively confront leaders' illegitimate and unacceptable behaviours.

Societal and Organizational Measures Against Destructive Leadership and its Outcomes

Faced with the relatively high prevalence of destructive leadership in contemporary organizations (see Aasland et al., 2010) and its potentially devastating outcomes, particularly regarding subordinate health and well-being, a range of measures is needed to prevent and manage the problem and to heal the wounds of those affected. Measures on both an organizational and a societal level are necessary, as are preventive measures of a primary, secondary and tertiary nature (see Vartia et al., 2011). While primary prevention is about measures taken to reduce the possibility of a certain risk or to avoid a given problem from happening in the first place, secondary prevention is about managing the problem when present. That is, secondary prevention may be about increasing the resources of those affected, but is mainly about stopping and reversing the problem at hand, in our case a process of destructive leadership. Tertiary prevention is about reducing the negative impact exposure to destructive leadership may have on the health and well-being of those affected and, if possible, healing, and repairing the health-related outcomes in, targets.

At the societal level, primary prevention is about setting up a national legal framework that protects employees against mistreatment from their superiors and employers (see Yamada, 2011) by stating the employers' duty of care and responsibility to act when problems of destructive leadership arise. An alternative primary prevention on a societal level is the use of collective agreements covering the problem of destructive leadership. Such measures may also oblige organizations to develop internal policies and codes of conduct with the aim of preventing destructive leadership from happening, and also to ensure that the organization has proper means and procedures in place to investigate and follow up on any employee complaints. An example of a collective agreement on the management of destructive leadership may be found in the Framework Agreement on Violence and Harassment at Work (European Social Dialogue, 2007) signed by the social dialogue partners in Europe. Under this agreement all employers are obliged to develop policies for the prevention of bullying and harassment at work and to install proper procedures to handle complaints. Where destructive leadership practices amount to bullying and harassment, it would be covered by such policies and this collective agreement.

Secondary prevention on a societal level is about having legal systems, labour inspectorates or industrial tribunals in place to manage complaints when resolution is not secured within the organization itself. (See also Hoel and Einarsen (2010) for a discussion of the Swedish ordinance against workplace bullying.) Tertiary prevention on a societal level may also include setting up treatment facilities for those subordinates affected and with health impairment attributed to the menace of destructive leadership. Such tertiary prevention may be accomplished by setting up a system for legal and health-related counselling or by setting up occupational health clinics for the treatment and rehabilitation of targets of destructive leadership. For examples of such interventions see Schwickerath et al. (2011) and Tehrani, Einarsen, Hoel, Zapf and Cooper (2011).

Primary, secondary and tertiary interventions are needed at the organizational level too. Primary interventions on an organizational level are mainly about trying to prevent leaders from becoming destructive in the first place. Although the antecedents and risk factors for destructive leadership are far less understood than are its outcomes, there are reasons to believe that the following may help to reduce the risk of destructive leadership:

- Selection and recruitment procedures tailored to reduce the risk of recruiting destructive leaders.
- Leadership training and leadership education programmes that both promote leadership styles that are fair and effective, and address how leaders may restore a healthy working relation with subordinates if they find themselves displaying destructive behaviour.
- The establishment of a culture that supports effective and fair leadership styles and discourages destructive leadership practices at all levels of the organization.
- Keeping the stress level of managers and supervisors manageable and teaching them stress and anger management.

Furthermore, employers should have sound policies in place that promote their duty of care to all employees and their devotion to securing a working environment free from any kind of bullying, harassment and emotional abuse, be it from peers or from managers, leaders and supervisors. A sound policy against destructive leadership must establish fair complaints procedures and the possibility of redress for those involved (see also Hoel and Einarsen, 2011). In the abovementioned Framework Agreement (European Social Dialogue, 2007, p. 3) the main underlying principles of such a complaints procedure are as follows:

- It is in the interest of all parties to proceed with the necessary discretion to protect the dignity and privacy of all.
- No information should be disclosed to parties not involved in the case.
- Complaints should be investigated and dealt with without undue delay.

- All parties involved should get an impartial hearing and fair treatment.
- Complaints should be backed up by detailed information.
- False accusations should not be tolerated and may result in disciplinary action.
- External assistance may help.

The last principle in this framework agreement also speaks to tertiary prevention on an organizational level, that is, the need for the organization to set up a structure of victim support, including the need for rehabilitation and reintegration of those employees who may have been suffering victimization during the process. Such a support and rehabilitation process may involve occupational counselling, health-related services, and possibly professional rehabilitation (see also Tehrani et al., 2011).

Looking at interventions this way builds on the very assumption that it is within the duty of care of any employer to protect its employees against the abuse, harassment and mistreatment that may stem from the misuse of power by destructive managers, even if employees may react and cope differently with instances of exposure to a destructive leader, as discussed above. Hence, even if the actual enactment of destructive leadership may hinge upon characteristics of both the superior and the subordinate in question, as indicated by the evidence presented earlier in this chapter (see also Kant et al., 2013), it is still the actual behaviour exhibited by the person in charge that must be the focal point of the organization's measures. Following this line of argument, it is worth noticing that it is a complaint procedure and not a mediation procedure that is at the heart of most legal frameworks and collective agreements in this field, as exemplified by the European Framework Agreement. Hence, setting up a support system with the possibility of counselling on how to manage and cope with a highly destructive boss must come in addition to, and not at the expense of, a well-run complaints and grievance system (see also Hoel and Einarsen, 2011).

Yet, as filing a complaint against a destructive boss is probably a highly stressful event in and of itself, subordinates may well choose to make an effort to cope with and manage the problem individually. Hence, an individual-level primary prevention strategy would be to seek training programmes on how to be bully-proof and how to avoid coming into conflict with one's superiors in the first place. A secondary individual-level strategy would be to seek legal as well as personal counselling on how to cope with a given situation, be it through counselling systems set up by the organization itself or by its occupational health services, through the union if the individual is a member, or by seeking private legal or social counselling. In this, the labour inspector may also be a source of such resources, at least in principle. As documented in the preceding paragraphs, it seems to be very difficult to cope with destructive leaders. Hence, it is important that one seeks advice and counselling from professionals. And for those employees that suffer long-term consequences a tertiary preventive strategy is to seek professional, medical and psychological treatment to recover from one's experiences, trying to avoid post-traumatic symptoms, rebuild one's coping resources and restore one's self-confidence.

Conclusion and Directions for Future Research

The research field of destructive leadership is still young. Nevertheless, the many studies on this phenomenon leave no doubt about the fact that many employees indeed experience a variety of destructive leadership practices, be they active or passive-avoidant, with severe detrimental outcomes for the health and well-being of those targeted. Yet we still have limited knowledge about those leader, follower and organizational characteristics that create these situations, the potential moderators that may buffer or enhance the potential outcomes, and the mechanisms involved in explaining the many observed negative effects. By now we have some knowledge about how subordinates may cope with abusive superiors. However, there is strong reason to believe that employees in general have limited resources to cope with such hostile leader behaviours, which again may trigger strong negative emotions and drain those exposed of their personal resources. Furthermore, from an ethical point of view it is highly questionable to reduce the problem of destructive leadership to an issue of individual coping among subordinates. We take the position that we must hold the organization responsible for identifying measures against destructive leadership, be it primary, secondary or tertiary interventions. If superiors are destructive, we need to better understand how subordinates might safely complain and blow the whistle on abusive supervisors (see e.g., Hoel & Einarsen, 2011) and how organizations can set up safe policies and procedures to protect subordinates against such detrimental experiences with their leaders, as well as building support systems to assist those targeted.

This said, there is a strong need for more advanced research on destructive leadership, yielding better answers to *why* and *when* destructive leadership has such detrimental negative effects on employees' well-being. One general problem in this regard is the lack of longitudinal research designs, which is a problem for leadership research in general (see, e.g., Shamir, 2011), yet with research on workplace bullying and health as a notable exception (Nielsen et al., 2014). The meta-analyses presented in this chapter document associations, including some longitudinal ones, between exposure to destructive leadership and employee health and well-being. Without longitudinal designs there may always be arguments for a reverse or reciprocal relationship between destructive leadership and well-being, for example that demotivated and dissatisfied subordinates may start to perceive their superiors as more destructive, reflecting the so-called 'gloomy' perception mechanism (De Lange, Taris, Kompier, Houtman & Bongers, 2005). Further, with few exceptions studies on leadership focus on either constructive or destructive forms (Schyns & Schilling, 2013). Because most leaders, over time, will enact positive as well as negative behaviours (Aasland et al., 2010) we propose future studies to include both types, in order to secure an optimal range of leader behaviours and styles that may influence employees' well-being. Another challenge in destructive leadership research is the lack of overarching theories directing empirical research. A review of the research field shows that a wide range of moderators and mediators have been examined (see, e.g., Martinko et al., 2013). However, it is difficult to relate the different studies and variables to each other. Hopefully, in a future, more mature, stage of destructive leadership research, such overarching models will guide empirical research, and that will help us to better answer the questions of *why* and *when* destructive leadership has such detrimental effects on occupational well-being.

References

Aasland, M. S., Skogstad, A., Notelaers, G., Nielsen, M. B. & Einarsen, S. (2010). The prevalence of destructive leadership behaviour. *British Journal of Management*, 21(2), 438–52.

Adorno, T. W., Frenkel-Brunswik, E., Levinson, D. J. & Sanford, R. N. (1950). *The Authoritarian Personality*. New York: Harper.

Aquino, K., Tripp, T. M. & Bies, R. J. (2006). Getting even or moving on? Power, procedural justice, and types of offense as predictors of revenge, forgiveness, reconciliation, and avoidance in organizations. *Journal of Applied Psychology*, 91(3), 653–68.

Aronson, E. (2001). Integrating leadership styles and ethical perspectives. *Canadian Journal of Administrative Sciences/Revue Canadienne des Sciences de l'Administration*, 18(4), 244–56.

Aryee, S., Chen, Z. X., Sun, L. Y. & Debrah, Y. A. (2007). Antecedents and outcomes of abusive supervision: Test of a trickle-down model. *Journey of Applied Psychology*, 92(1), 191–201. doi: 10.1037/0021-9010.92.1.191.

Ashforth, B. (1994). Petty tyranny in organizations. *Human Relations*, 47(7), 755–78.

Avolio, B. J., Bass, B. M. & Jung, D. I. (1999). Re-examining the components of transformational and transactional leadership using the Multifactor Leadership Questionnaire. *Journal of Occupational and Organizational Psychology*, 72(4), 441–62.

Bakker, A. B., Demerouti, E. & Sanz-Vergel, A. I. (2014). Burnout and work engagement: The JD–R approach. *Annual Review of Organizational Psychology and Organizational Behavior*, 1(1), 389–411.

Barling, J. & Frone, M. R. (2016). If only my leader would just do something! Passive leadership undermines employee well-being through role stressors and psychological resource depletion. *Stress and Health*. doi: 10.1002/smi.2697.

Basch, J. & Fisher, C. (2000). Affective events–emotions matrix: A classification of work events and association emotions. In N. M. Ashkanasy, C. E. J. Härtel & Zerbe (eds), *Emotions in the Workplace: Research, Theory, and Practice*. Westport, CT: Quorum Books, pp. 36–48.

Bass, B. M. & Avolio, B. J. (1990). *Transformational Leadership Development: Manual for the Multifactor Leadership Questionnaire*. Palo Alto, CA: Consulting Psychologists Press.

Bass, B. M. & Avolio, B. J. (1994). *Improving Organizational Effectiveness Through Transformational Leadership*. Thousand Oaks, CA: Sage.

Bing, S. (1992). *Crazy Bosses: Spotting Them, Serving Them, Surviving Them*. New York: William Morrow and Company.

Birkeland, M. S., Nielsen, M. B., Knardahl, S. & Heir, T. (2015). Time-lagged relationships between leadership behaviors and psychological distress after a workplace terrorist attack. *International Archives of Occupational and Environmental Health*, 89(4), 1–9.

Blake, R. R. & Mouton, J. S. (1985). *The Managerial Grid III*. Houston, TX: Gulf Publishing Company.

Bowling, N. A. & Michel, J. S. (2011). Why do you treat me badly? The role of attributions regarding the cause of abuse in subordinates' responses to abusive supervision. *Work & Stress*, 25(4), 309–20. doi: 10.1080/02678373.2011.634281.

Brief, A. P. & Weiss, H. M. (2002). Organizational behavior: Affect in the workplace. *Annual Review of Psychology*, 53(1), 279–307.

Buss, A. H. (1961). *The Psychology of Aggression*. New York: Wiley.

Carver, C. S. & Connor-Smith, J. (2010). Personality and coping. *Annual Review of Psychology*, 61, 679–704. doi: 10.1146/annurev.psych.093008.100352.

Chênevert, D., Vandenberghe, C., Doucet, O. & Ayed, A. K. B. (2013). Passive leadership, role stressors, and affective organizational commitment: A time-lagged study among health care employees. *Revue Européenne de Psychologie Appliquée/European Review of Applied Psychology*, 63(5), 277–86.

Christie, R. & Geis, F. L. (1970). *Studies in Machiavellianism*: New York: Academic Press.

Conger, J. A. (1990). The dark side of leadership. *Organizational Dynamics*, 19(2), 44–55.

Craig, S. B. & Kaiser, R. B. (2013). Destructive leadership. In M. G. Rumsey (ed.), *The Oxford Handbook of Leadership*. Oxford: Oxford University Press, pp. 439–54.

Cropanzano, R., Rupp, D. E. & Byrne, Z. S. (2003). The relationship of emotional exhaustion to work attitudes, job performance, and organizational citizenship behaviors. *Journal of Applied Psychology*, 88(1), 160–9.

Cropanzano, R., Stein, J. H. & Nadisic, T. (2011). *Social Justice and the Experience of Emotion*: New York: Routledge.

Danna, K. & Griffin, R. W. (1999). Health and well-being in the workplace: A review and synthesis of the literature. *Journal of Management*, 25(3), 357–84.

Dasborough, M. T. (2006). Cognitive asymmetry in employee emotional reactions to leadership behaviors. *Leadership Quarterly*, 17(2), 163–78. doi: 10.1016/j.leaqua.2005.12.004.

De Hoogh, A. H. & Den Hartog, D. N. (2008). Ethical and despotic leadership, relationships with leader's social responsibility, top management team effectiveness and subordinates' optimism: A multi-method study. *Leadership Quarterly*, 19(3), 297–311.

de Lange, A. H., Taris, T. W., Kompier, M. A., Houtman, I. L. & Bongers, P. M. (2005). Different mechanisms to explain the reversed effects of mental health on work characteristics. *Scandinavian Journal of Work, Environment & Health*, 31(1), 3–14.

Den Hartog, D. N., J. J. Muijen & P. L. Koopman (1997). Transactional versus transformational leadership: An analysis of the MLQ. *Journal of Occupational and Organizational Psychology*, 70(1), 19–34.

DeRue, D. S., Nahrgang, J. D., Wellman, N. & Humphrey, S. E. (2011). Trait and behavioral theories of leadership: An integration and meta-analytic test of their relative validity. *Personnel Psychology*, 64(1), 7–52.
Diebig, M., Bormann, K. C. & Rowold, J. (2016). A double-edged sword: Relationship between full-range leadership behaviors and followers' hair cortisol level. *Leadership Quarterly*, 27(4), 684–96.
Duffy, M. K., Ganster, D. & Pagon, M. (2002). Social undermining in the workplace. *Academy of Management Journal*, 45, 331–51.
Einarsen, S., Aasland, M. S. & Skogstad, A. (2007). Destructive leadership behaviour: A definition and conceptual model. *Leadership Quarterly*, 18(3), 207–16. doi: 10.1016/j.leaqua.2007.03.002.
Einarsen, S., Hoel, H., Zapf, D. & Cooper, C. L. (2011). The concept of bullying and harassment at work: The European tradition. *Bullying and Harassment in the Workplace: Developments in Theory, Research, and Practice*. 2nd edn. Boca Raton, FL: CRC Press, pp. 3–40.
Einarsen, S. & Nielsen, M. B. (2015). Workplace bullying as an antecedent of mental health problems: A five-year prospective and representative study. *International Archives of Occupational and Environmental Health*, 88(2), 131–42.
Einarsen, S., Skogstad, A. & Glasø, L. (2013). When Leaders are Bullies. The Wiley-Blackwell handbook of the psychology of leadership, change, and organizational development, 129–154.
European Social Dialogue (2007). Framework Agreement on Harassment and Violence at Work. 26 April. Brussels: European Trade Union Confereration.
Frieder, R. E., Hochwarter, W. A. & DeOrtentiis, P. S. (2015). Attenuating the negative effects of abusive supervision: The role of proactive voice behavior and resource management ability. *Leadership Quarterly*, 26(5), 821–37.
Gilbert, D. T. & Silvera, D. H. (1996). Overhelping. *Journal of Personality and Social Psychology*, 70(4), 678–90.
Glasø, L. & Einarsen, S. (2006). Experienced affects in leader–subordinate relationships. *Scandinavian Journal of Management*, 22(1), 49–73.
Glasø, L. & Notelaers, G. (2012). Workplace bullying, emotions, and outcomes. *Violence and Victims*, 27(3), 360–77.
Glasø, L., Skogstad, A., Notelaers, G. & Einarsen, S. (2016). Leadership, emotions and outcomes: Symmetrical and asymmetrical relationships. Unpublished MS.
Glass, D. & McKnight, J. (1996). Perceived control, depressive symptomatology, and professional burnout: A review of the evidence. *Psychology and Health*, 11(1), 23–48.
Gruys, M. L. & Sackett, P. R. (2003). Investigating the dimensionality of counterproductive work behavior. *International Journal of Selection and Assessment*, 11(1), 30–42.
Hansen, Å. M., Hogh, A., Garde, A. H. & Persson, R. (2014). Workplace bullying and sleep difficulties: A 2-year follow-up study. *International Archives of Occupational and Environmental Health*, 87(3), 285–94.
Harlos, K. (2010). If you build a remedial voice mechanism, will they come? Determinants of voicing interpersonal mistreatment at work. *Human Relations*, 63(3), 311–29.

Harvey, P., Stoner, J., Hochwarter, W. & Kacmar, C. (2007). Coping with abusive supervision: The neutralizing effects of ingratiation and positive affect on negative employee outcomes. *Leadership Quarterly*, 18, 264–80.

Hershcovis, M. S., & Barling, J. (2010). Towards a multi-foci approach to workplace aggression: A meta-analytic review of outcomes from different perpetrators. *Journal of Organizational Behavior*, 31(1), 24–44.

Hetland, H., Sandal, G. M. & Johnsen, T. B. (2007). Burnout in the information technology sector: Does leadership matter? *European Journal of Work and Organizational Psychology*, 16(1), 58–75. doi: 10.1080/13594320601084558.

Hinkin, T. R. & Schriesheim, C. A. (2008). An examination of 'nonleadership': From laissez-faire leadership to leader reward omission and punishment omission. *Journal of Applied Psychology*, 93(6), 1234–48. doi: 10.1037/a0012875.

Hobfoll, S. E. & Freedy, J. (1993). Conservation of resources: A general stress theory applied to burnout. In W. B. Schaufeli, C. Maslach & T. Marek (eds), *Professional Burnout: Recent Developments in Theory and Research*. Washington, DC: Taylor & Francis, pp. 115–29.

Hoel, H. & Einarsen, S. (2010). The Swedish Ordinance against Victimization at Work: A critical assessment,. *Comparative Labor Law & Policy Journal*, 32(1), 225–50.

Hoel, H. & Einarsen, S. (2011). Investigating complaints of bullying and harassment. In S. Einarsen, H. Hoel, D. Zapf & C. L. Cooper (eds), *Bullying and Harassment in the Workplace: Developments in Theory, Research, and Practice*. 2nd edn. Boca Raton, FL: Taylor & Francis Group, pp. 341–57.

Hogan, R. (1994). Trouble at the top: Causes and consequences of managerial incompetence. *Consulting Psychology Journal*, 46(1), 9–15.

Hogan, R., Raskin, R. & Fazzini, D. (1990). The dark side of charisma. In K. E. Clark & M. B. Clark (eds), *Measures of Leadership*. West Orange, NJ: Leadership Library of America, pp. 343–54.

Hogh, A., Mikkelsen, E. G. & Hansen, A. M. (2011). Individual consequences of workplace bullying/mobbing. In S. Einarsen, H. Hoel, D. Zapf & C. L. Cooper, *Bullying and Harassment in the Workplace: Developments in Theory, Research, and Practice*. 2nd edn. Boca Raton, FL: CRC Press, pp. 107–28.

Horn, J. E., Taris, T. W., Schaufeli, W. B. & Schreurs, P. J. (2004). The structure of occupational well-being: A study among Dutch teachers. *Journal of Occupational and Organizational Psychology*, 77(3), 365–75.

Hornstein, H. A. (1996). *Brutal Bosses and Their Prey: How to Identify and Overcome Abuse in the Workplace*. New York: Riverhead Books.

House, R. J. & Howell, J. M. (1992). Personality and charismatic leadership. *Leadership Quarterly*, 3(2), 81–108.

Jackson, T. A., Meyer, J. P. & Wang, X.-H. F. (2013). Leadership, commitment, and culture: A meta-analysis. *Journal of Leadership & Organizational Studies*, 20(1), 84–106.

Judge, T. A., Locke, E. A. & Durham, C. C. (1997). The dispositional causes of job satisfaction: A core evaluations approach. *Research in Organizational Behavior*, 19, 151–88.

Judge, T. A. & Piccolo, R. F. (2004). Transformational and transactional leadership: A meta-analytic test of their relative validity. *Journal of Applied Psychology*, 89(5), 755–68.

Judge, T. A., Piccolo, R. F. & Ilies, R. (2004). The forgotten ones? The validity of consideration and initiating structure in leadership research. *Journal of Applied Psychology*, 89(1), 36–51.

Kääriä, S., Laaksonen, M., Rahkonen, O., Lahelma, E. & Leino-Arjas, P. (2012). Risk factors of chronic neck pain: A prospective study among middle-aged employees. *European Journal of Pain*, 16(6), 911–20.

Kanste, O., Kyngäs, H. & Nikkilä, J. (2007). The relationship between multidimensional leadership and burnout among nursing staff. *Journal of Nursing Management*, 15(7), 731–39. doi: 10.1111/j.1365–2934.2006.00741.x.

Kant, L., Skogstad, A., Torsheim, T. & Einarsen, S. (2013). Beware the angry leader: Trait anger and trait anxiety as predictors of petty tyranny. *Leadership Quarterly*, 24(1), 106–24.

Kellerman, B. (2004). *Bad Leadership: What It Is, How It Happens, Why It Matters*. Boston, MA: Harvard Business School Press.

Kelloway, E. K., Sivanathan, N., Francis, L. & Barling, J. (2005). Poor leadership. In J. Barling, E. K. Kelloway & M. R. Frone (eds), *Handbook of Workplace Stress*. Thousand Oaks, CA: Sage Publications, pp. 89–112.

Kelloway, E. K., Turner, N., Barling, J. & Loughlin, C. (2012). Transformational leadership and employee psychological well-being: The mediating role of employee trust in leadership. *Work & Stress*, 26(1), 39–55. doi: 10.1080/02678373.2012.660774.

Kessler, S. R., Bruursema, K., Rodopman, B. & Spector, P. E. (2013). Leadership, interpersonal conflict, and counterproductive work behavior: An examination of the stressor–strain process. *Negotiation and Conflict Management Research*, 6(3), 180–90.

Kiazad, K., Restubog, S. L. D., Zagenczyk, T. J., Kiewitz, C. & Tang, R. L. (2010). In pursuit of power: The role of authoritarian leadership in the relationship between supervisors' Machiavellianism and subordinates' perceptions of abusive supervisory behavior. *Journal of Research in Personality*, 44(4), 512–19. doi: 10.1016/j.jrp.2010.06.004.

Kivimäki, M., Leino-Arjas, P., Virtanen, M., Elovainio, M., Keltikangas-Jarvinen, L., Puttonen, S., Vartia, M., Brunner, E. & Vahtera, J. (2004). Work stress and incidence of newly diagnosed fibromyalgia: Prospective cohort study. *Journal of Psychosomatic Research*, 57(5), 417–22.

Kivimäki, M., Virtanen, M., Vartia, M., Elovainio, M., Vahtera, J. & Keltikangas-Järvinen, L. (2003). Workplace bullying and the risk of cardiovascular disease and depression. *Occupational and Environmental Medicine*, 60(10), 779–83.

Klaussner, S. (2014). Engulfed in the abyss: The emergence of abusive supervision as an escalating process of supervisor–subordinate interaction. *Human Relations*, 67(3), 311–32.

Lazarus, R. S. (2006). *Stress and Emotion: A New Synthesis*. New York: Springer.

Lazarus, R. S. & Folkman, S. (1984). *Stress, Appraisal, and Coping*. New York: Springer.

Leary, M. R. (2001). *Interpersonal Rejection*. New York: Oxford University Press.

Leiter, M. P. & Maslach, C. (1988). The impact of interpersonal environment on burnout and organizational commitment. *Journal of Organizational Behavior*, 9(4), 297–308.

Lewin, K., Lippitt, R. & White, R. K. (1939). Patterns of aggressive behavior in experimentally created 'social climates'. *Journal of Social Psychology*, 10(2), 269–99.

Lian, H., Brown, D. J., Ferris, D. L., Liang, L. H., Keeping, L. M. & Morrison, R. (2014). Abusive supervision and retaliation: A self-control framework. *Academy of Management Journal*, 57(1), 116–39.

Lind, E. A. & Van den Bos, K. (2002). When fairness works: Toward a general theory of uncertainty management. *Research in Organizational Behavior*, 24, 181–223.

Lipman-Blumen, J. (2005). *The Allure of Toxic Leaders: Why We Follow Destructive Bosses and Corrupt Politicians – and How We Can Survive Them*. Oxford: Oxford University Press.

Lombardo, M. M. & McCall, M. W. (1984). *Coping with an Intolerable Boss*. Greensboro, NC: Center for Creative Leadership.

Lubit, R. (2004). The tyranny of toxic managers: Applying emotional intelligence to deal with difficult personalities. *Ivey Business Journal*, 68(4), 1–7.

Lutgen-Sandvik, P., Tracy, S. J. & Alberts, J. K. (2007). Burned by bullying in the American workplace: Prevalence, perception, degree and impact. *Journal of Management Studies*, 44(6), 837–62.

Mackey, J. D., Frieder, R. E., Brees, J. R. & Martinko, M. J. (2015). Abusive supervision: A meta-analysis and empirical review. *Journal of Management*. doi: 10.1177/0149206315573997.

Martinko, M. J., Harvey, P., Brees, J. R. & Mackey, J. (2013). A review of abusive supervision research. *Journal of Organizational Behavior*, 34(S1), S120–S137. doi: 10.1002/job.1888.

Maslach, C., Schaufeli, W. B. & Leiter, M. P. (2001). Job burnout. *Annual Review of Psychology*, 52(1), 397–422.

Matta, F. K., Erol-Korkmaz, H. T., Johnson, R. E. & Biçaksiz, P. (2014). Significant work events and counterproductive work behavior: The role of fairness, emotions, and emotion regulation. *Journal of Organizational Behavior*, 35(7), 920–44.

May, D., Wesche, J. S., Heinitz, K. & Kerschreiter, R. (2014). Coping with destructive leadership: Putting forward an integrated theoretical framework for the interaction process between leaders and followers. *Zeitschrift für Psychologie*, 222(4), 203–13.

Meyer, J. P. & Allen, N. J. (1991). A three-component conceptualization of organizational commitment. *Human Resource Management Review*, 1(1), 61–89.

Mikula, G. (2003). Testing an attribution-of-blame model of judgments of injustice. *European Journal of Social Psychology*, 33(6), 793–811. doi: 10.1002/ejsp.184.

Montano, D., Reeske, A., Franke, F. & Hüffmeier, J. (2016). Leadership, followers' mental health and job performance in organizations: A comprehensive meta-analysis from an occupational health perspective. *Journal of Organizational Behavior*. doi: 10.1002/job.2124.

Neuman, J. H. & Baron, R. A. (1998). Workplace violence and workplace aggression: Evidence concerning specific forms, potential causes, and preferred targets. *Journal of Management*, 24(3), 391–419.

Nielsen, M. B. & Einarsen, S. (2012). Outcomes of exposure to workplace bullying: A meta-analytic review. *Work & Stress*, 26(4), 309–32.
Nielsen, M. B., Magerøy, N., Gjerstad, J. & Einarsen, S. (2014). Workplace bullying and subsequent health problems. *Tidsskrift for den Norske laegeforening: tidsskrift for praktisk medicin, ny raekke*, 134(12–13), 1233–8.
Nielsen, M. B., Matthiesen, S. B. & Einarsen, S. (2005). Ledelse og personkonflikter: Symptomer på posttraumatisk stress blant ofre for mobbing fra ledere. *Nordisk Psykologi*, 57(4), 391–415.
Nyberg, A., Alfredsson, L., Theorell, T., Westerlund, H., Vahtera, J. & Kivimäki, M. (2009). Managerial leadership and ischaemic heart disease among employees: The Swedish WOLF study. *Occupational and Environmental Medicine*, 66(1), 51–5.
O'Connor, J., Mumford, M. D., Clifton, T. C., Gessner, T. L. & Connelly, M. S. (1996). Charismatic leaders and destructiveness: An historiometric study. *Leadership Quarterly*, 6(4), 529–55.
Robert, P. (1980). *Emotion: A Psychoevolutionary Synthesis*. New York: Harper and Row.
Rook, K. S. (1998). Investigating the positive and negative sides of personal relationships: Through a lens darkly? In B. H. Spitzberg & W. R. Cupach (eds), *The Dark Side of Close Relationships*. Mahwah, NJ: Lawrence Erlbaum Associates, pp. 369–93.
Rowold, J. & Schlotz, W. (2009). Transformational and transactional leadership and followers' chronic stress. *Leadership Review*, 9(2), 35–48.
Sackett, P. R. & DeVore, C. J. (2001). Counterproductive behaviors at work. In N. Anderson, D. S. Ones, H. K. Sinangil & C. Viswesvaran (eds), *Handbook of Industrial, Work and Organizational Psychology. Volume 1: Personnel Psychology*, pp. 145–64.
Schat, A. C. & Kelloway, E. K. (2003). Reducing the adverse consequences of workplace aggression and violence: The buffering effects of organizational support. *Journal of Occupational Health Psychology*, 8(2), 110–22.
Schilling, J. (2009). From ineffectiveness to destruction: A qualitative study on the meaning of negative leadership. *Leadership*, 5, 102–28.
Schriesheim, C. A., Wu, J. B. & Scandura, T. A. (2009). A meso measure? Examination of the levels of analysis of the Multifactor Leadership Questionnaire (MLQ). *Leadership Quarterly*, 20(4), 604–16. doi: 10.1016/j.leaqua.2009.04.005.
Schwickerath, J., Zapf, D., Einarsen, S., Hoel, H., Zapf, D. & Cooper, C. (2011). Inpatient treatment of bullying victims. In S. Einarsen, H. Hoel, D. Zapf & C. L. Cooper (eds), *Bullying and Harassment in the Workplace: Developments in Theory, Research, and Practice*. 2nd edn. Boca Raton, FL: Taylor & Francis Group, pp. 397–422.
Schyns, B. & Schilling, J. (2013). How bad are the effects of bad leaders? A meta-analysis of destructive leadership and its outcomes. *Leadership Quarterly*, 24(1), 138–58. doi: 10.1016/j.leaqua.2012.09.001.
Seidler, A., Thinschmidt, M., Deckert, S., Then, F., Hegewald, J., Nieuwenhuijsen, K. & Riedel-Heller, S. G. (2014). The role of psychosocial working conditions on burnout and its core component emotional exhaustion: A systematic review. *Journal of Occupational Medicine and Toxicology*. doi: 10.1186/1745-6673-9-10.

Shackleton, V. (1995). Leaders who derail. In ibid., *Business Leadership*. London: Routledge, pp. 89–100.

Shamir, B. (2011). Leadership takes time: Some implications of (not) taking time seriously in leadership research. *Leadership Quarterly*, 22(2), 307–15. doi: 10.1016/j.leaqua.2011.02.006.

Shin, H., Park, Y. M., Ying, J. Y., Kim, B., Noh, H. & Lee, S. M. (2014). Relationships between coping strategies and burnout symptoms: A meta-analytic approach. *Professional Psychology: Research and Practice*, 45(1), 44–56.

Shirom, A. (1989). Burnout in work organizations. In C. L. Cooper & I. Robertson (eds), *International Review of Industrial and Organizational Psychology*. Chichester: John Wiley and Sons, pp. 25–48.

Shirom, A. (2003). Job-related burnout: A review. In J. C. Quick & L. E. Tetrick, *Handbook of Occupational Health Psychology*. Washington, DC: American Psychological Association, pp. 245–64.

Simon, L. S., Hurst, C., Kelley, K. & Judge, T. A. (2015). Understanding cycles of abuse: A multimotive approach. *Journal of Applied Psychology*, 100(6), 1798–1810.

Sivanathan, N., Arnold, K. A., Turner, N. & Barling, J. (2004). *Leading well: Transformational leadership and well-being. Paper presented at the Second International Positive Psychology Summit*, Washington, DC.

Skakon, J., Nielsen, K., Borg, V. & Guzman, J. (2010). Are leaders' well-being, behaviours and style associated with the affective well-being of their employees? A systematic review of three decades of research. *Work & Stress*, 24(2), 107–39. doi: 10.1080/02678373.2010.495262.

Skogstad, A., Aasland, M. S., Nielsen, M. B., Hetland, J., Matthiesen, S. B. & Einarsen, S. (2014). The relative effects of constructive, laissez-faire, and tyrannical leadership on subordinate job satisfaction. *Zeitschrift für Psychologie*, 222(4), 221–32. doi: 10.1027/2151-2604/a000189.

Skogstad, A., Einarsen, S., Torsheim, T., Aasland, M. S. & Hetland, H. (2007). The destructiveness of laissez-faire leadership behavior. *Journal of Occupational Health Psychology*, 12(1), 80–92.

Skogstad, A., Hetland, J., Glasø, L. & Einarsen, S. (2014). Is avoidant leadership a root cause of subordinate stress? Longitudinal relationships between laissez-faire leadership and role ambiguity. *Work & Stress*, 28(4), 323–41. doi: 10.1080/02678373.2014.957362.

Smart Richman, L. & Leary, M. R. (2009). Reactions to discrimination, stigmatization, ostracism, and other forms of interpersonal rejection: A multimotive model. *Psychological Review*, 116(2), 365–83. doi: 10.1037/a0015250.

Tehrani, N., Einarsen, S., Hoel, H., Zapf, D. & Cooper, C. (2011). Workplace bullying: The role for counselling. In S. Einarsen, H. Hoel, D. Zapf & C. L. Cooper (eds), *Bullying and Harassment in the Workplace: Developments in Theory, Research, and Practice*. 2nd edn. Boca Raton, FL: Taylor & Francis Group, pp. 381–96.

Tepper, B. J. (2000). Consequences of abusive supervision. *Academy of Management Journal*, 43(2), 178–90.

Tepper, B. J., Moss, S. E., Lockhart, D. E. & Carr, J. C. (2007). Abusive supervision, upward maintenance communication, and subordinates' psychological distress. *Academy of Management Journal*, 50(5), 1169–80.

Theorell, T., Nyberg, A., Leineweber, C., Hanson, L. L. M., Oxenstierna, G. & Westerlund, H. (2012). Non-listening and self centered leadership: Relationships to socioeconomic conditions and employee mental health. *PloS ONE*, 7(9), e44119.

Thoroughgood, C. N., Tate, B. W., Sawyer, K. B. & Jacobs, R. (2012). Bad to the bone: Empirically defining and measuring destructive leader behavior. *Journal of Leadership & Organizational Studies*, 19(2), 230–55. doi: 10.1177/1548051811436327.

Vartia, M., Leka, S., Einarsen, S., Hoel, H., Zapf, D. & Cooper, C. (2011). Interventions for the prevention and management of bullying at work. In S. Einarsen, H. Hoel, D. Zapf & C. L. Cooper (eds), *Bullying and Harassment in the Workplace: Developments in Theory, Research, and Practice*. 2nd edn. Boca Raton, FL: Taylor & Francis Group, pp. 359–79.

Vogel, R. M. & Mitchell, M. S. (2015). The motivational effects of diminished self-esteem for employees who experience abusive supervision. *Journal of Management*. doi: 10.1177/0149206314566462.

Warr, P. (1987). *Work, Unemployment, and Mental Health*. Oxford: Clarendon Press.

Warr, P. (1994). A conceptual framework for the study of work and mental health. *Work & Stress*, 8(2), 84–97.

Wei, F. & Si, S. (2011). Tit for tat? Abusive supervision and counterproductive work behaviors: The moderating effects of locus of control and perceived mobility. *Asia Pacific Journal of Management*, 30(1), 281–96. doi: 10.1007/s10490-011-9251-y.

Weiss, H. M. & Cropanzano, R. (1996). Affective events theory: A theoretical discussion of the structure, causes and consequences of affective experiences at work. *Research in Organizational Behavior: An Annual Series of Analytical Essays and Official Reviews*, 18, 1–74.

Wu, T.-Y. & Hu, C. (2009). Abusive supervision and employee emotional exhaustion: Dispositional antecedents and boundaries. *Group & Organization Management*, 34(2), 143–69.

Yagil, D. (2006). The relationship of abusive and supportive workplace supervision to employee burnout and upward influence tactics. *Journal of Emotional Abuse*, 6(1), 49–65.

Yagil, D., Ben-Zur, H. & Tamir, I. (2011). Do employees cope effectively with abusive supervision at work? An exploratory study. *International Journal of Stress Management*, 18(1), 5–23.

Yamada, D. C. (2011). Workplace bullying and the law: Emerging global responses. In S. Einarsen, H. Hoel, D. Zapf & C. L. Cooper (eds), *Bullying and Harassment in the Workplace: Developments in Theory, Research, and Practice*. 2nd edn. Boca Raton, FL: Taylor & Francis Group, pp. 469–84.

Yang, I. (2015). Positive effects of laissez-faire leadership: Conceptual exploration. *Journal of Management Development*, 34(10), 1246–61.

Yukl, G. & Van Fleet, D. D. (1992). Theory and research on leadership in organizations. In M. D. Dunnette & L. M. Hough (eds), *Handbook of Industrial and Organizational Psychology*, vol. 3. Palo Alto, CA: Consulting Psychologists Press, pp. 147–97.

Zapf, D. & Gross, C. (2001). Conflict escalation and coping with workplace bullying: A replication and extension. *European Journal of Work and Organizational Psychology*, 10, 497–522.

Zhang, Y. & Liao, Z. (2015). Consequences of abusive supervision: A meta-analytic review. *Asia Pacific Journal of Management*, 32(4), 959–87.

Zimbardo, P. G. (2004). A situationist perspective on the psychology of evil: Understanding how good people are transformed into perpetrators. In A. Miller (ed.), *The Social Psychology of Good and Evil: Understanding Our Capacity for Kindness and Cruelty*. New York: Guilford Press, pp. 21–50.

Zopiatis, A. & Constanti, P. (2010). Leadership styles and burnout: Is there an association? *International Journal of Contemporary Hospitality Management*, 22(3), 300–20.

Zwingmann, I., Wegge, J., Wolf, S., Rudolf, M., Schmidt, M. & Richter, P. (2014). Is transformational leadership healthy for employees? A multilevel analysis in 16 nations. *Zeitschrift für Personalforschung/German Journal of Research in Human Resource Management*, 28(1–2), 24–51.

Zwingmann, I., Wolf, S. & Richter, P. (2016). Every light has its shadow: A longitudinal study of transformational leadership and leaders' emotional exhaustion. *Journal of Applied Social Psychology*, 46(1), 19–33.

10

Leaders Can Make or Break an Intervention – But Are They the Villains of the Piece?

Karina Nielsen

Organizational occupational health interventions can be defined as those interventions that aim to improve employee health and well-being through the way work is organized, designed and managed (Nielsen, 2013). Such interventions typically go through five phases: initiation, identification of sources of poor well-being and heath (screening), development of action plans, implementation of action plans, and evaluation of processes and outcomes (Nielsen, Randall, Holten & Rial Gonzalez, 2010). In some European countries systematic approaches to managing employee well-being have been developed such as the Management Standards (UK), Work Positive (Ireland), START (Germany), SOBANE (Belgium), and INAIL (Italy) (Zoni & Lucchini, 2012). A similar framework exists in Canada: the Canadian Psychological Safety and Health national standard (http://www.mentalhealthcommission.ca/English/issues/workplace/national-standard).

All these methods emphasize the importance of senior management in supporting organizational occupational health interventions. The SOBANE method states that senior management should openly express the priority it gives to safety and health and commit itself to follow up on issues identified in the screening phase. The Canadian Standard emphasizes the importance of leadership or senior management in reinforcing the development and sustainability of a psychologically healthy workplace. It also states that senior managers should support line management during the process, establish the objectives, lead and influence organizational culture in a positive way, and engage employees where necessary. The UK Management Standards state that senior management plays a key role in shaping the culture of the organization. Furthermore, the Management Standards say that line managers play a crucial role in designing jobs that ensure the quality of working life. Line managers are seen as responsible for spreading information about change, fostering both upward and downward communication. In line with this, Work Positive states that line managers play an important role in bridging the gap between employees and the wider organization, are responsible for implementing action plans, and are therefore crucial to ensuring that organizational interventions are successful.

Leading to Occupational Health and Safety: How Leadership Behaviours Impact Organizational Safety and Well-Being, First Edition.
Edited by E. Kevin Kelloway, Karina Nielsen and Jennifer K. Dimoff.

In other words, although senior management may be a necessary prerequisite for organizational interventions to succeed, it is suggested that line managers take on the day-to-day management and therefore have the power to make or break an intervention. In the present chapter I therefore focus on leaders at the level of line managers. There is ample evidence in the literature that leaders at the line management level play an important role in organizational occupational health interventions. Kompier, Geurts, Grundemann, Vink and Smulders (1998) compiled the experiences from 10 Dutch organizational interventions and found that line managers were most often responsible for intervention implementation. A few years later, Kompier, Cooper and Geurts (2000) conducted a review of 13 European organizational occupational health interventions and again found that the main strategy for implementing such interventions was to allocate overall responsibility to line managers. Leaders at the line management level are important in ensuring successful interventions for at least four reasons. (1) They function as the link between senior management and shop floor workers. They communicate the decisions made by senior management to employees on the floor and communicate the reactions of shop floor workers to senior management. (2) They are responsible for translating the decisions of senior management into a concrete strategy and, in collaboration with employees, for developing and implementing actual changes in the way work is organized, designed and managed. (3) They play a key role in prioritizing the intervention in a hectic working day with many conflicting priorities, and keep the momentum going. (4) Finally they need to manage employees' expectations about change (Guth & Macmillan, 1986; Nielsen & Randall, 2009; Parker & Williams, 2001). The role of line managers as leaders of organizational occupational health interventions is also reflected in national policies for managing psychosocial risks. For example, the British Management Standards identify the line manager as having the main responsibility for ensuring employee well-being (Donaldson-Feilder, Yarker & Lewis, 2011). In the light of this key role, there has been an increasing interest in how line managers are the leaders that may make or break an intervention. Nielsen, Randall, Holten and Rial González (2010) called for a better understanding of the role such managers play in making or breaking organizational occupational health interventions. In the present chapter I discuss the ways in which line managers may make or break an intervention, but I also go beyond this discussion and explore the reasons why such leaders may choose to make or break interventions and how, in the future, we can make it easier for leaders to make, rather than break, the interventions that they are responsible for.

The Leader as the Driver of Change

Several examples can be found in the literature of how leaders can make an intervention. They may do so either by functioning as role models or proactively by assuming responsibility for planning and implementing the intervention.

Do You See What I See? Leaders' Attitudes Shaping Employee Attitudes and Intervention Outcomes

It has been argued that organizational actors, both leaders and employees, need to have positive attitudes towards an intervention in order to accept it and that the interdependencies in attitudes are important to ensuring a successful intervention outcome (Guth & Macmillan, 1986). The social identity theory of leadership (SITOL) (Hogg, 2001) may help explain why the interdependent relationship between leaders and employees influences intervention outcomes (Nielsen, 2013). According to SITOL, when employees and leaders share norms and values (the leader is perceived to be prototypical of the values and norms favoured by the group) employees are more likely to support the activities advocated by their leader (Haslam & Platow, 2001; Hogg, 2001), and so to work together to achieve the objectives. In other words, the more employees and managers share perceptions, the more likely they are to support an intervention.

An example of such shared perceptions can be found in Hasson et al. (2016), who conducted an intervention in a paper and pulp mill in Sweden. It has been argued that a certain level of 'organizational maturity' is needed for an organizational intervention to succeed (Nielsen, Fredslund, Christensen & Albertsen, 2006). Such organizational maturity would imply that employees and managers need to feel they have an organizational learning climate before the intervention. They need a certain level of resources – that is, an existing learning climate – in order to engage in activities that further enhance the organizational learning climate, thus creating a positive gain spiral (Hobfoll, 1989). According to SITOL, if employees and leaders share a perception that the existing organizational learning climate is at a high level they will be more likely to support the intervention and work proactively to implement changes to improve the organizational learning climate, because the organizational maturity will be sufficient for them to work comfortably together. Hasson et al. (2016) found support for this proposition: when employees and leaders reported having a good organizational learning climate before the intervention, they would report improvements in the organizational learning climate after the intervention. The smallest improvements in organizational learning climate were observed in situations where the leader believed the organizational learning climate was better than reported by his or her employees.

In summary, it would appear that, before initiating an organizational occupational health intervention, we need to (1) consider the shared perceptions of leaders' and employees' existing working climate and (2) take additional initiatives to correct any misalignments between the leaders and their employees.

It has been argued that organizational actors, both leaders and their employees, need to have positive attitudes towards an intervention if they are to accept and implement any changes introduced and to maintain their engagement throughout the intervention period. A key element of the role of a leader is to shape the expectations and attitudes of employees. According to the norm of reciprocity (Gouldner, 1960) and social exchange theory (Blau, 1964), employees are likely to respond positively to favourable treatment and to reciprocate positive leader behaviours. If employees perceive that leaders advocate an organizational occupational health intervention and make it clear that they see value in the intervention, employees may be more likely themselves to adopt these attitudes and to be more ready for change (Coyle-Shapiro, 1999; Nielsen & Randall, 2011). SITOL would suggest that the more employees identify with their leader the more ready they are for change (Jetten, Postmes & McAuliffe, 2002). Readiness for change can be seen as *positive dispositions towards a change* (Herold, Fedor & Caldwell, 2007) and as including the leaders' and employees' views on whether the intervention is appropriate, whether they can use the intervention and whether they support the particular intervention (Armenakis & Bedeian, 1999). Where the leaders and employees share a perception of an intervention as useful and see where they can contribute actively towards its successful implementation, they may be more likely to jointly work towards implementing it (Nielsen & Daniels, 2012; Nielsen & Randall, 2011). In other words, participants need to be ready for change to ensure a successful outcome of the intervention (Rafferty, Jimmieson & Armenakis, 2013; Richardson & Rothstein, 2008). It can thus be expected that when leaders are ready for change they may inspire their employees to be more ready for the intervention too.

Nielsen and Randall (2011) explored the impact of leaders' and employees' readiness for change on the outcomes of an organizational occupational health intervention. The intervention consisted of the implementation of a teamwork structure in a Danish elder care home. The aim of the intervention was to ensure retention of staff, reduce absenteeism and increase job satisfaction and affective well-being. The implementation of a teamwork structure was expected to bring about these outcomes through the creation of jobs that were characterized by employees supporting each other and having greater influence over how to do the job; as each would be responsible for a smaller number of clients, it was believed their jobs would be perceived as more meaningful and they would become clear about their role within the organization (Nielsen & Randall, 2012).

Extending the perspectives on the necessity of a certain level of organizational maturity, Nielsen and Randall (2011) found that when leaders and employees were already satisfied with their jobs, both parties were more ready for change. Only employees who were satisfied with their jobs held positive expectations of what could be achieved through the intervention. Conversely, it was found that where working conditions were already good, leaders and employees were less ready for change. This finding suggests a ceiling effect: where the conditions that the intervention aimed to change were already good, leaders and employees saw little need for change.

Nielsen and Randall (2011) also found that leaders' readiness for change was positively related to employees' readiness for change and employees' readiness for change was in turn related to improved working conditions and, through improved working conditions, to better affective well-being and greater job satisfaction.

In summary, the study by Nielsen and Randall (2011) suggests that (1) we need to examine the context in which an organizational occupational health intervention is introduced (there may need to be some improvements at the same time, as leaders and employees need to be reasonably satisfied with their existing job if they are to welcome changes to their work), and (2) leaders' expectations of change are related to their employees' readiness for change, which implies that it is important to acknowledge the role of leaders in shaping their employees' perceptions of the intervention. These perceptions impact on the intervention's ability to improve working conditions and employee well-being. However, leaders' positive attitudes towards the intervention may be a necessary but not sufficient requirement for making changes in the way work is organized, designed and managed; their behaviours may also be critical to a successful intervention outcome.

Leaders' Behaviours: Job Crafting to Make or Break Interventions

Job crafting has been defined as 'the physical and cognitive changes individuals make in the task or relational boundaries of their work' (Wrzesniewski & Dutton, 2001, p. 179). By altering task and relational boundaries, leaders can change the content of their own jobs and those of others (Wrzesniewski, LoBuglio, Dutton & Berg, 2013; Nielsen, Randall & Christensen, 2015). When organizational occupational health interventions are introduced, many changes to the way work is organized, designed and managed take place: new goals are established, roles are altered, and relationships between employees and leaders are renegotiated (Seo, Putnam & Bartunek, 2004). Such changes create a window of opportunity in which leaders may actively job craft new ways of working (Kira, van Eijnatten & Balkin, 2003; Petrou, Demerouti & Schaufeli, 2015; Nielsen et al., 2015; Wrzesniewski and Dutton, 2001). Most often senior management only make the decision to introduce an organizational occupational health intervention, and it then becomes the responsibility of line managers to make concrete changes to the way work is organized, designed and managed according to the intentions of senior management to improve employee health and well-being (Nielsen et al., 2015).

It could be argued that, in the process of implementing organizational occupational health interventions, leaders may job craft in two ways. First, they may craft the process through deciding whether to engage themselves in the process of planning and implementing the intervention, and they decide how to involve employees in the process. For example, they may limit employee participation to responding to a questionnaire, and take responsibility themselves for developing action plans. Alternatively, they may choose to allocate responsibility for developing action plans to employees and establish ad hoc working groups where employees (in collaboration with leaders) make decisions on how to implement the intervention. Second, they may also job craft by making concrete changes to the way work is organized, designed and managed, addressing the sources of poor health and well-being. For example, if lack of communication is identified as a source of stress, they may choose to develop systems that ensure employees are kept informed through memos and regular meetings.

Although, to date, few studies have focused directly on leaders' job crafting during organizational occupational health interventions, there is evidence to suggest that the behaviours of leaders play a role in determining a successful intervention outcome.

In a study in the process and engineering industry, Björklund, Grahn, Jensen and Bergström (2007) examined the intervention process: they explored whether getting feedback on risk assessment was sufficient to detect improvements in working conditions and employee health and well-being, or whether it was also important to develop action plans to address the issues identified in risk assessment. Björklund et al. (2007) found that in groups where improvements could be detected, employees had received feedback on the risk assessment and action plans had been implemented. They ascribed these activities to the leaders. Most activity had taken place in groups where leaders already had an empowering leadership style and involved their employees. These results suggest that leaders took the opportunity to job craft changes to the working environment of employees by using the risk assessment feedback: empowering leaders were the drivers of change, making sure results were fed back to employees and action plans were developed.

Similar findings were reported by Sørensen and Holman (2014). In a study of Danish knowledge workers, it was reported that leaders ensured the implementation of the intervention and maintained employee awareness through the dissemination of posters and leaflets. In summary, the results of these two studies suggest that line managers drive successful interventions.

Nielsen and Randall (2009) found that leaders' job crafting to involve employees in the intervention process was related to improvements in employees' social support, their perceptions of having meaningful work, and role clarity. These positive changes in working conditions were in turn related to the employees' well-being.

In summary, these studies suggest that it is important for leaders to assume responsibility for making changes happen and to actively support the intervention process; when they do, they may be instrumental in successful intervention outcomes.

Leaders Can Break an Intervention

Just as leaders may job craft to make an intervention, they may also break the intervention. For example, Weyman and Boocock (2015) conducted an intervention focused on managing musculoskeletal disorders and found that leaders prevented modification requests from being reported upwards in the system.

In the UK the Management Standards, the national strategy to manage psychosocial risks, emphasizes the importance of the leader in implementing the Management Standards (Donaldson-Feilder et al., 2011). Following the introduction of the Management Standards, some studies have looked into the experiences of organizations that have worked to implement them. Mellor, Mackay, Packham et al. (2011) found that organizational actors who were interviewed about the process reported that the unavailability of leaders was a problem. Also, Biron, Gatrell and Cooper (2010) found that, of leaders who participated in workshops on how to use the Management Standards and the associated Stress Indicator, only a third subsequently conducted a survey using the tool. In summary, these studies indicate that leaders intentionally broke the intervention.

Why Do Leaders Break Interventions? Are They the Villains of the Piece?

Organizational occupational health interventions may challenge the adaptive resources of leaders (Monat & Lazarus, 1991). Broaden-and-build theory (Fredrickson, 2001) may explain why resourceful leaders play an important role in a successful intervention outcome. According to broaden-and-build theory, leaders high in positive states, that is, leaders who have plenty of resources, both individual and contextual, made available to them, have broader thought–action repertoires. Such broad repertoires enable creative and flexible thinking and therefore may explain how resourceful leaders are the ones who proactively implement changes (Fredrickson, 2001). Resourceful leaders may be in a position where they can identify which intervention activities may have the biggest impact, and having interpersonal resources may enable the leader to identify which key stakeholders should be involved in ensuring momentum. Resources, in the context of organizational occupational health interventions, comprise both the personal resources of the leader and the resources available in the organizational context (Nielsen & Randall, 2013).

What Am I Doing? Leaders' Lack of Personal Resources

In the case of the musculoskeletal intervention mentioned above (Weyman & Boocock, 2015), leaders struggled after the implementation of a concurrent intervention that introduced a teamworking structure: They felt overwhelmed as their role changed from one solely of responsibility for sorting out their employees' problems with technology at work to one that also incorporated dealing with interpersonal conflicts within the new teams. In other words, leaders felt they lacked the personal resources, skills and competencies to deal with interpersonal conflicts: they perceived themselves as experts in the job, not in people. Biron et al. (2010) found that although leaders had participated in workshops on how to conduct an assessment of psychosocial risks using the Management Standards' Stress Indicator Tool (Edwards, Webster, Van Laar & Easton, 2008) they did not feel equipped to deal with sensitive stress issues. Furthermore, Biron et al. (2010) found that leaders who reported having good working conditions in terms of communication and relationships at work, and who reported having good mental and physical health, were the ones that actively engaged in using the Stress Indicator Tool. Biron et al. (2010) also reported that some leaders felt that assessing psychosocial risks was irrelevant to their staff; they felt leaders themselves had much worse working conditions. As a consequence, these leaders did not use the tool. Leaders also felt that the workshops were inappropriate: talking about sensitive stress-related issues in sessions with people from other departments deterred leaders from engaging in in-depth discussions.

In summary, leaders resisted change because they did not feel they had the necessary resources to deal with the changes introduced by the organizational occupational health intervention.

Providing Leaders with the Resources to Make Interventions

It has been found that training can provide leaders with the resources necessary to make interventions work. Nielsen and Daniels (2012) explored whether training new team leaders could build leaders' individual resources. In a cluster-randomized, controlled trial, it was found that leaders who had undergone training in how to implement and manage newly created teams experienced their jobs as more challenging and reported better well-being. One caveat was noted: these positive findings only applied if employees reported being willing to work in teams. If employees were not supportive, leaders who had been on the training course had poorer well-being than those leaders who had not. In summary, it would appear that training can help build resources, but only in cases where the training is transferred to a supportive environment.

Nielsen, Randall and Christensen (2010) examined the effects of team leader training in the elder care industry in Denmark. Using a cluster-randomized, controlled design, they found that employees whose leader had received training reported being more involved in their jobs and were more satisfied with their jobs than employees whose leaders had not been trained.

When Training is Not Enough

If we analyse the two leader training studies in more detail (Nielsen & Daniels, 2012; Nielsen, Randall & Christensen, 2010), we find the picture to be more complex than anticipated: training is not without its challenges. As mentioned above, it was only when leaders who had been on a training course returned to a team whose members were willing to work in a team that leaders were able to benefit from the training. This result indicates that it is only where the surrounding environment is supportive that leaders can apply the learning they have acquired during training.

In the Nielsen, Randall & Christensen (2010) study, it was found that although leaders held positive perceptions of the training and some leaders changed their behaviours and their attitudes towards teamwork, employees' job involvement and job satisfaction only increased marginally or remained stable. In the control group, these outcomes worsened. A contextual analysis revealed that ongoing changes such as merging elder care centres and downsizing had made it difficult for line managers and their followers to focus on team implementation. Although leaders found the training had provided them with the resources to implement change, they had not been able to reap the benefits of the training course and implement team organization according to plan. Despite these limitations, employees did benefit from trained leaders compared to employees whose leaders had not received training (Nielsen, Randall & Christensen, 2010).

Nielsen, Randall and Christensen (2015) explored how leaders job crafted a teamwork structure that was introduced to improve employee health and well-being. The implementation of teamwork was supported by voluntary training of leaders and their employees. Combining qualitative and quantitative methods, Nielsen et al. (2015) found that groups with trained leaders were better at implementing teamwork than groups whose leader had received no training. However, they also found that contextual factors other than whether leaders had received training also influenced whether teams were successfully implemented. First, some leaders reported that lack of support from senior management and the organizational turbulence caused by downsizing and mergers prevented teamwork implementation. Only leaders who saw the lack of support as the go-ahead to do as they pleased benefited from the training and crafted a role as team leaders. Second, lack of buy-in from employees also presented a problem. Some leaders reported that older employees were resistant to the implementation of teams.

In summary, it can be concluded that when leaders break an intervention it may be because the organizational context is not supportive of their using their resources to make changes happen.

A Model of the Leader's Role in Organizational Occupational Health Interventions

Although research on how leaders may make or break organizational occupational health interventions is still in its infancy, using current research I have attempted to develop a preliminary model of how leaders' job crafting functions in relation to such interventions. First, I suggest that leaders play a crucial role in developing a psychologically healthy workplace. Leaders need to job craft to plan and implement the intervention process itself. Leaders need to craft a role for themselves and decide to what extent they want to involve employees, and whom in particular they may rely on as intervention champions. Leaders also need to job craft to make changes to the way work is organized, designed and managed. For example, if action plans are developed that call for a change in the meeting structure, leaders may need to make changes to how often meetings take place, who is involved in planning the agenda, who leads the meetings and how minutes are taken.

Second, a number of factors may influence leaders' job crafting behaviours. Leaders' and their employees' readiness for change may influence the leaders' job crafting in relation both to the process itself and also to how they shape the content of the intervention. For example, if employees' feedback to the leader suggests that they have little faith that the intervention will bring about a positive outcome, the leader may invest a little time in involving employees in the planning and implementation of the intervention. It is also possible that if leaders do not believe the intervention is appropriate they will make little attempt to make changes to the way work is organized, designed and managed. Likewise, if leaders do not feel they have sufficient knowledge and skills to manage the intervention process, they may ignore the intervention altogether. Finally, if they perceive that the intervention is not being prioritized by management and that organizational resources, such as supporting training, are not being made available, leaders may opt for as little engagement as possible.

Third, I suggest that the extent to which leaders and employees share an understanding of the current situation, and therefore also of the need to make changes, may moderate the relationship between the extent to which leaders job craft and their ability to promote a psychologically healthy workplace. When leaders and employees have a shared understanding of the current situation, leaders may job-craft changes to the way work is organized, designed and managed that successfully address the issues raised. For example, if leaders and employees agree that

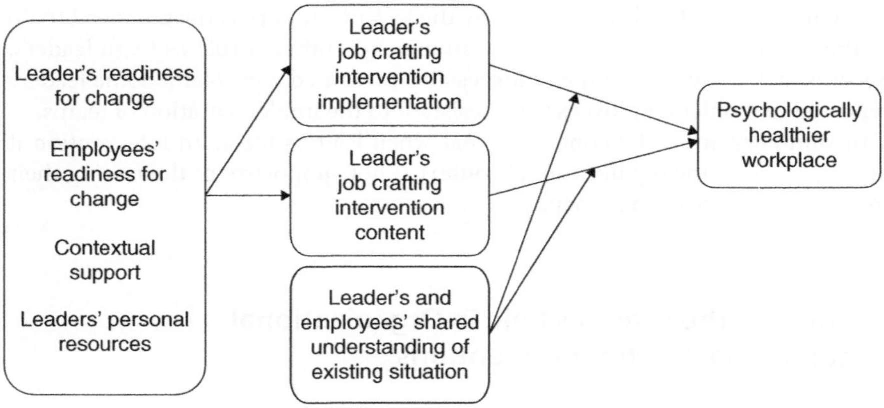

Figure 10.1 Model of the leader's role in organizational occupational health interventions.

meeting structure is a problem, and what the problem is, they may implement changes to the meeting structure that employees find useful and that bring about a psychologically more healthy workplace. (See Figure 10.1.)

So What Can We Do Differently?

What we can learn from the present studies is that leaders can make or break an intervention, but sometimes they do so with good reason. Leaders may not be able to make sense of the goals of the intervention, or perhaps the intervention is not needed.

A thorough needs analysis should be conducted before the initiation of an organizational occupational health intervention to ensure that leaders are ready for change, and if they are not, measures should be put in place to prepare them mentally and skills-wise to manage change. A needs analysis should also include whether it is the right time to introduce the intervention. During turbulent times, when downsizing, mergers and other organizational changes are going on, it may be better not to initiate such interventions, because other initiatives divert the leader's attention from the organizational occupational health intervention.

To prepare both leader and employees, supporting initiatives may need to be put in place. Training leaders in the first phase of the intervention may be important to give them the necessary skills to manage the health and well-being of subordinates and to manage change, but training subordinates may be equally important. For example, training that involves leader and their employees may facilitate the joint development of the objectives of the organizational occupational health intervention and may provide leaders and employees with knowledge of how to manage health and well-being in the workplace. Joint training may also help leaders and employees to develop a shared understanding of problems and opportunities and help them implement changes. Training may increase readiness for change, as employees and leaders then understand what can be gained from the intervention and are provided with tools for using the intervention to better their situation.

Support from senior management also plays a key role in how leaders can implement changes. If leaders are poorly supported, that is, they are not allocated the decision power to make changes, they may be restricted in how much they can do to actively support the intervention and make changes happen.

To understand why the same intervention may succeed or fail in one organization (Greasley & Edwards, 2015), there is a need to evaluate the implementation of the intervention at the local level rather than assume that the intervention will have the same effect across departments. In other words, there should be a systematic evaluation of how leaders' involvement may have influenced intervention outcomes. Randall, Nielsen and Tvedt (2009) developed a process evaluation questionnaire that among other things captured the role of the leader's involvement, including communication, involvement of employees in the process and taking responsibility for making changes. This measure can be integrated into effect evaluation and used to understand whether different intervention outcomes in different departments in the same organization can be explained by the leader's actions. This provides valuable information about the circumstances in which an organizational occupational health intervention may succeed or fail.

Concluding Remarks

In conclusion, I argue that although leaders may be able to make or break an organizational occupational health intervention, they may not be the villains of the piece. Many other contextual factors influence leaders' ability to job craft during an intervention and to ensure that changes to the way work is organized, designed and managed are introduced to ensure a successful intervention outcome.

References

Armenakis, A. A. & Bedeian, A. G. (1999). Organizational change: A review of theory and research in the 1990s. *Journal of Management*, 25, 293–315.

Biron, C., Gatrell, C. & Cooper, C. L. (2010). Autopsy of a failure: Evaluating process and contextual issues in an organizational-level work stress intervention. *International Journal of Stress Management*, 17(2), 135–58.

Björklund, C., Grahn, A., Jensen, I. & Bergström, G. (2007). Does survey feedback enhance the psychosocial work environment and decrease sick leave? *European Journal of Work and Organizational Psychology*, 16, 76–93.

Blau, P. M. 1964. *Exchange and Power in Social Life*. New York: Wiley.

Coyle-Shapiro, J. A.-M. (1999). Employee participation and assessment of an organizational change intervention: A three-way study of total quality management. *Journal of Applied Behavioral Science*, 35, 439–56.

Donaldson-Feilder, E., Yarker, J. & Lewis, R. (2011). *Preventing Stress in Organizations: How to Develop Positive Managers*. Chichester, UK: Wiley-Blackwell.

Edwards, J. A., Webster, S., Van Laar, D., & Easton, S. (2008). Psychometric analysis of the UK Health and Safety Executive's Management Standards work-related stress Indicator Tool. *Work & Stress,* 22(2), 96–107.

Fredrickson, B. L. (2001). The role of positive emotions in positive psychology. *American Psychologist,* 56, 218–26.

Gouldner, A. W. 1960. The norm of reciprocity: A preliminary statement. *American Sociological Review,* 25, 161–78.

Greasley, K. & Edwards, P. (2015). When do health and well-being interventions work? Managerial commitment and context. *Economic and Industrial Democracy,* 36, 355–77.

Guth, W. D. & Macmillan, I. C. (1986). Strategy implementation versus middle manager self-interest. *Strategic Management Journal,* 7, 313–27.

Haslam, S. A. & Platow, M. J. (2001). The link between leadership and followership: How affirming social identity translates vision into action. *Personality and Social Psychology Bulletin,* 27, 1469–79.

Hasson, H., von Thiele Schwarz, U., Nielsen, K. & Tafvelin, S. (2016). Are we all in the same boat? The role of perceptual distance in organizational health interventions. *Stress & Health.* doi: 10.1002/smi.2703

Herold, D. M., Fedor, D. B. & Caldwell, S. D. (2007). Beyond change management: A multilevel investigation of contextual and personal influences on employees' commitment to change. *Journal of Applied Psychology,* 92, 942–51.

Hobfoll, S. E. (1989). Conservation of resources: A new attempt at conceptualizing stress. *American Psychologist,* 44(3), 513–24.

Hogg, M. A. (2001). A social identity theory of leadership. *Personality and Social Psychology Review,* 5, 184–200.

Jetten, J., Postmes, T. & McAuliffe, B. J. (2002). We're all individuals: Group norms of individualism and collectivism, levels of identification, and identity threat. *European Journal of Social Psychology,* 32, 189–207.

Kira, M., van Eijnatten, F. M. & Balkin, D. B. (2010). Crafting sustainable work: Development of personal resources. *Journal of Organizational Change Management,* 23, 616–32.

Kompier. M., Cooper, C. & Geurts, S. (2000). A multiple case study approach to work stress prevention in Europe. *European Journal of Work and Organizational Psychology,* 9, 371–400.

Kompier, M., Geurts, S., Grundemann, R., Vink, P. & Smulders, P. (1998). Cases in stress prevention: The success of a participative and stepwise approach. *Stress Medicine,* 14, 155–68.

Mellor, N., Mackay, C. Packham, C., Jones, R., Palferman, D., Webster, S. & Kelly, P. (2011). 'Management standards' and work-related stress in Great Britain: Progress on their implementation. *Safety Science,* 49, 1040–6.

Monat, A. & Lazarus, R. S. (1991). Introduction: Stress and coping – some current issues and controversies. In A. Monat & R. S. Lazarus (eds), *Stress and Coping: An Anthology.* New York: Columbia University Press, pp. 1–16.

Nielsen, K. (2013). Review article: How can we make organizational interventions work? Employees and line managers as actively crafting interventions. *Human Relations,* 66, 1029–50.

Nielsen, K. & Daniels, K. (2012). Enhancing team leaders' well-being states and challenge experiences during organizational change: A randomized controlled study. *Human Relations*, 65, 1207–31.

Nielsen, K., Fredslund, H., Christensen, K. B. & Albertsen, K. (2006). Success or failure? Interpreting and understanding the impact of interventions. *Work & Stress*, 20(3), 272–87.

Nielsen, K. & Randall, R. (2009). Managers' active support when implementing teams: The impact on employee well-being. *Applied Psychology: Health and Well-being*, 1, 374–90.

Nielsen, K. & Randall, R. (2011). The importance of middle manager support for change: A case study from the financial sector in Denmark. In P.-A. Lapointe, J. Pelletier & F. Vaudreuil (eds), *Different Perspective on Work Changes: Papers from the Second International Workshop on Work and Intervention Practices, Québec, August 27, 28, 29, 2008*. Quebec: Presse de l'Université Laval, pp. 95–102.

Nielsen, K. & Randall, R. (2012). The importance of employee participation and perception of changes in procedures in a teamworking intervention. *Work and Stress*, 29, 91–111.

Nielsen, K. & Randall, R. (2013). Opening the black box: Presenting a model for evaluating organizational-level interventions. *European Journal of Work and Organizational Psychology*, 22(5), 601–17.

Nielsen, K., Randall, R. & Christensen, K. B. (2010). Does training managers enhance the effects of implementing team-working? A longitudinal, mixed methods field study. *Human Relations*, 63(11), 1719–41.

Nielsen, K., Randall, R. & Christensen, K. B. (2015). Do different training conditions facilitate team implementation? A quasi-experimental mixed methods study. *Journal of Mixed Methods Research*. doi: 10.1177/1558689815589050.

Nielsen, K., Randall, R, Holten, A. L. & Rial González, E. (2010). Conducting organizational-level occupational health interventions: What works? *Work & Stress*, 24, 234–59.

Parker, S. & Williams, H. (2001). *Effective Teamworking: Reducing the Psychosocial Risks*. Sudbury, UK: HSE Books.

Petrou, P., Demerouti, E. & Schaufeli, W. (2015). Job crafting in changing organizations: Antecedents and implications for exhaustion and performance. *Journal of Occupational Health Psychology*, 20, 470–80.

Rafferty, A. E., Jimmieson, N. L. & Armenakis, A. (2013). Change readiness: A multilevel review. *Journal of Management*, 39(1), 110–35.

Randall, R., Nielsen, K. & Tvedt, S. D. (2009). The development of five scales to measure employees' appraisals of organizational-level stress management interventions. *Work & Stress*, 23, 1–23.

Richardson, K. M. & Rothstein, H. R. (2008). Effects of occupational stress management intervention programs: A meta-analysis. *Journal of Occupational Health Psychology*, 13, 69–93.

Seo, M. G., Putnam, L. L. & Bartunek, J. M. (2004). Dualities and tensions of planned organizational change. In M. Poole and A. H. Van de Ven (eds), *Handbook of Organizational Change and Innovation*. New York: Oxford University Press, pp. 73–107.

Sørensen, O. H. & Holman, D. (2014). A participative intervention to improve employee well-being in knowledge work jobs: A mixed-methods evaluation study. *Work & Stress*, 28(1), 67–86.

Weyman, A. & Boocock, M. (2015). Managing work-related musculoskeletal disorders – Socio-technical 'solutions' and unintended psychosocial consequences. In M. Karanika-Murray & C. Biron (eds), *Derailed Organizational Interventions for Stress and Well-Being: Confessions of Failure and Solutions for Success*. Dordrecht: Springer, pp. 45–58.

Wrzesniewski A. & Dutton, J. E. (2001). Crafting a job: Revisioning employees as active crafters of their work. *Academy of Management Review* 26(2): 179–201.

Wrzesniewski, A., LoBuglio, N., Dutton, J. E. & Berg, J. M. (2013). Job crafting and cultivating positive meaning and identity in work. In A. B. Bakker (ed.), *Advances in Positive Organizational Psychology*. Bingley, UK: Emerald Group, pp. 281–302.

Zoni, S. & Lucchini, R. G. (2012). European approaches to work-related stress: A critical review on risk evaluation. *Safety and Health at Work*, 3(1), 43–9.

11

Developing Positive Leadership for Employee Well-Being and Engagement

Emma Donaldson-Feilder and Rachel Lewis

This chapter aims to present a body of research by the authors of the chapter on positive leadership, that is, leadership that is aimed at positively enhancing both employee well-being and engagement. The chapter will highlight the importance of this focus, with a review of the literature linking leadership and employee health, well-being and engagement. The authors will then present the results of a research programme aimed initially at identifying those management behaviours necessary for enhancing employee health, well-being and engagement, and then research aimed at addressing the question of whether positive leadership can be developed. The chapter will conclude with evidence from a research programme identifying the success factors associated with developing leadership for employee health, well-being and engagement.

Links Between Leadership and Employee Well-Being and Engagement

Leadership and Employee Well-Being

Since 2006, the literature exploring the link between leadership and employee well-being has grown dramatically and the consistent message is that the way employees are managed is a key determinant of their well-being (e.g. Kelloway & Barling, 2010; Skakon, Nielsen, Borg & Guzman, 2010).

The academic literature has explored links between well-being and a range of existing leadership models. These leadership models can be categorized into four clusters: transformational and transactional leadership behaviours; negative leadership behaviours; supportive behaviours; and task- and relationship-focused behaviours (Donaldson-Feilder, Munir & Lewis, 2013). There is also a group of studies using other leadership and management indices. These four clusters are explored briefly in the paragraphs below.

Leading to Occupational Health and Safety: How Leadership Behaviours Impact Organizational Safety and Well-Being, First Edition.
Edited by E. Kevin Kelloway, Karina Nielsen and Jennifer K. Dimoff.

Transformational and Transactional Leadership

Transformational leadership continues to be the dominant theory in leadership research and the most widely published leadership theory in *Leadership Quarterly* for the past two decades (Gardner, Lowe, Moss, Mahoney & Cogliser, 2010; Lowe & Gardner, 2000). According to Bass (1985, 1998, 1999) transformational leaders generate enthusiasm for a 'vision', show individualized consideration, create opportunities for employees' development, set high expectations for performance, and act as role models to gain the respect, admiration and trust of employees. Transformational leadership theory can be described as a 'full-range model', meaning that as well as displaying transformational behaviours, leaders also need (according to Bass, 1985, 1998) to display transactional behaviours, which involve a more straightforward exchange between the leader and their direct report, in which the employee is suitably rewarded for good performance; it also contrasts with laissez-faire leadership, characterized by a passive leadership style, an avoidance of action, a lack of feedback and communication, and a general indifference to employee well-being and performance (Sosik & Godshalk, 2000).

Research suggests that there are positive effects of transformational leadership and negative effects of laissez-faire leadership on a variety of employee well-being outcomes (e.g., Alimo-Metcalfe & Alban-Metcalfe, 2001; Hetland, Sandal & Johnsen, 2007; Kuoppala, Lamminpaa, Liira & Vainio, 2008; Nielsen, Randall, Yarker & Brenner, 2008; Sosik & Godshalk, 2000). There are also studies linking these forms of leadership to other employee outcomes relevant to well-being, such as retention (McDaniel & Wolf, 1992), empowerment and self-efficacy (e.g. Brossoit, 2001; Hetland et al., 2007), meaningfulness (Arnold, Turner, Barling, Kelloway & McKee, 2007), optimism and happiness (Bono, Foldes, Vinson & Muros, 2007), and conflict (e.g. Hauge, Skogstad & Einarsen, 2007; Skogstad, Einarsen, Torsheim, Aasland & Hetland, 2007). For a full review on the links between transformational leadership and employee well-being see Arnold and Connelly (2014).

Negative Leadership

While laissez-faire leadership largely seems to have a negative impact due to lack of action, there is a growing body of literature that suggests leadership can also contribute specific negative behaviours, such as bullying (Rayner & McIvor, 2006), undermining (Duffy, Ganster & Pagon, 2002), and behaviours that can be characterized as 'health-endangering' (Kile, 1990), tyrannical (Einarsen, Aasland & Skogstad, 2007), destructive (Einarsen et al., 2007), hostile (Schaubroeck, Walumbwa, Ganster & Kepes, 2007) and abusive (Tepper, 2000). Amongst the range of conceptualizations, abusive supervision is probably the best-studied. It is defined as 'the sustained display of hostile verbal and non-verbal behaviours, excluding physical contact' (Tepper, 2000, p. 178). Research has demonstrated links between abusive supervision and a range of stress- and well-being-related outcomes, including anxiety (Harris & Kacmar, 2005; Tepper, 2000), depression (Tepper, 2000), burnout (Tepper, 2000; Yagil, 2006) and somatic health complaints (Duffy et al., 2002).

Evidence (Yagil, 2006) suggests that the effect of negative leadership on well-being and stress-related outcomes is independent of the effect of the absence of positive leadership. Further, Duffy et al. (2002) found that managers that combine both positive and negative behaviours produce more deleterious outcomes than those who show negative behaviours alone, perhaps due to their inconsistency.

Supportive Leadership

Much of the research investigating the link between leadership and employee well-being has been focused upon the level of support provided by leaders and managers. Numerous studies have shown positive consequences of supportive leadership, with higher levels of support being associated with reductions in employee stress and burnout (e.g. Lee & Ashforth, 1996; Schaufeli & Enzmann, 1998), higher employee well-being and job satisfaction (e.g. Amick & Celantano, 1991; Baker, Israel & Schurman, 1996; Moyle & Parkes, 1999; Offermann & Hellmann, 1996) and lower turnover intentions (e.g. Thomas & Ganster, 1995). However, the majority of this research has been cross-sectional, with only a few longitudinal studies: despite the positive findings from the former, the latter show limited and inconclusive evidence of these positive links (Van Dierendonck, Haynes, Borrill & Stride, 2004). A small number have explored manager support as a moderator of the stressor–strain relationship (e.g. Dekker & Schaufeli, 1995; Moyle & Parkes, 1999; Stephens & Long, 2000), though with mixed results.

Task- and Relationship-Focused Leadership

Relationship- (or consideration-)based leader behaviours include supporting employees, showing respect for employees' ideas, increasing cohesiveness, developing and mentoring, looking out for employees' welfare, managing conflict, and team building (e.g. Levy, 2003; Nyberg, Bernin & Theorell, 2005; Seltzer & Numerof, 1988; Sosik & Godshalk, 2000). In contrast, task-based (or initiating structure) leader behaviours include planning and organizing, assigning people to tasks, communicating information, monitoring performance, defining and solving work-related problems, and clarifying roles and objectives. A number of studies have investigated the relations between these two distinct types of leadership behaviour and employee stress or well-being (e.g. Duxbury, Armstrong, Drew & Henly, 1984; Selzer & Numerof, 1988; Sheridan & Vredenburgh, 1978). Overall, this research suggests that consideration/relationship behaviours have a positive impact on employee well-being but that the impact of leaders' initiating structure/task behaviours on employees' health may be more complex (e.g. Duxbury et al., 1984; Kuoppala et al., 2008; Landweerd & Boumans, 1994). High levels of initiating-structure behaviours can have a detrimental effect on employee well-being, but this negative impact may be reduced if the same manager also exhibits a range of more consideration-based behaviours.

While the evidence from research clearly suggests that leadership behaviours are important for well-being, there is an argument that, by adopting an existing leadership model (which is likely to have been conceptualized to reflect employee performance outcomes) rather than creating a model that is specific to well-being outcomes, we may leave out some leadership behaviours that are important in this context, and so the impact of leadership behaviour on employee well-being may not have been fully realized. This point was recently supported by Kelloway, Weigand, McKee and Das (2013), who found that positive leadership (defined as behaviours performed by leaders that result in an increase in followers' experience of positive emotions) not only was a different construct to transformational leadership, but resulted in different employee outcomes to those of transformational leadership behaviours.

In order to explore the full range of leadership behaviour that is important in the context of employee health and well-being, between 2005 and 2011 the authors and their colleagues conducted a four-phase research programme that looked at the specific behaviours managers need to adopt in order to prevent and reduce stress in those they manage; it was entitled 'Management competencies for preventing and reducing stress at work' (MCPARS).

Phase 1 of the MCPARS programme used interviews and written exercises conducted with 216 employees and 166 managers from a range of organizations (drawn from finance, education, healthcare, local government and central government) to develop a framework of management behaviours (Yarker, Donaldson-Feilder, Lewis & Flaxman, 2007). Phase 2 revised the framework, designed an indicator tool questionnaire and examined the usability of the framework: over 1000 managers and employees tested the measure and the data were used to develop a refined and validated version of the MCPARS framework, which consists of four competencies, divided into 12 sub-competencies for ease of understanding (Yarker, Donaldson-Feilder & Lewis, 2008). A summary of the refined and validated MCPARS framework is provided in Table 11.1.

Leadership and Employee Engagement

Although it is generally accepted by both academics and practitioners that employee engagement is important because of its significant and positive impacts on both organizational and individual outcomes of performance and well-being (see Schaufeli & Bakker, 2010), there is yet to be a consensus on the conceptualization of employee engagement. A review of the literature (Lewis, Donaldson-Feilder, Tharani & Pangallo, 2011) noted that practitioner definitions place a strong emphasis on engagement with the organization, whereas academic definitions tend to place more emphasis on engagement with roles and tasks. For example, practitioners tend to define employee engagement in terms of organizational commitment (a desire to stay with the organization in the future) and employees' willingness to 'go the extra mile', which includes extra-role behaviour and discretionary effort that promotes the effective functioning of the organization (Schaufeli & Bakker, 2010). In contrast, academics have defined engagement as a psychological state. Schaufeli and Bakker's (2004) is the definition most widely used in recent academic literature. They view employee engagement as the antithesis of burnout, characterized by vigour (high levels of energy and investing effort into one's work), dedication (work involvement and experiencing a sense of pride and enthusiasm about one's work) and absorption (fully concentrated and engrossed in one's work). Lewis et al. (2011) presented a definition which aimed to encompass both academic and practitioner definitions, and it is this definition that is used in their work in this area: 'Being focused in what you

Table 11.1 Management competencies for preventing and reducing stress at work.

Management competency	Sub-competency	Description of sub-competency
Respectful and responsible: Managing emotions and having integrity	Integrity	Is respectful and honest to employees
	Managing emotions	Behaves consistently and calmly
	Considerate approach	Is thoughtful in managing others and delegating
Managing and communicating existing and future work	Proactive work management	Monitors and reviews existing work, allowing future prioritization and planning
	Problem solving	Deals with problems promptly, rationally and responsibly
	Participative and empowering	Listens to and consults with team, provides direction, autonomy and development opportunities to individuals
Reasoning, and managing difficult situations	Managing conflict	Deals with conflicts fairly and promptly
	Use of organizational resources	Seeks advice when necessary from managers, HR and occupational health
	Taking responsibility for resolving issues	Has a supportive and responsible approach to issues
Managing the individual within the team	Personally accessible	Is available to talk to personally
	Sociable	Has a relaxed approach, e.g. socializes and uses humour
	Empathetic engagement	Seeks to understand the individual in terms of their motivation, point of view and life outside work

do (thinking), feeling good about yourself in your role and the organization (feeling), and acting in a way that demonstrates commitment to the organizational values and objectives (acting).'

Practitioner literature consistently reports significant associations between leader and manager behaviour and the engagement of employees. For example, in the Chartered Institute of Personnel and Development's (CIPD) Shaping the Future project, managers were highlighted as one of the most important influences on engagement (Miller, McCartney, Baron, McGurk & Robinson, 2011); and other practitioner literature, such as the MacLeod Report (MacLeod & Clarke, 2009) and the Towers Watson Global Workforce Study (Towers Watson, 2014), also identifies a relationship between effective leadership and management and employee engagement.

Although academic literature has been slower to provide evidence of the leadership–engagement link, a consistent body of research now exists that demonstrates a link between employee engagement and various leadership approaches, such as leader–member exchange (Breevart, Bakker, Demerouti & van den Heuvel, 2015), transformational leadership (Breevaart, Bakker, Hetland et al.,

2014; Strom, Sears & Kelly, 2014; Tims, Bakker & Xanthopoulou, 2011), authentic leadership (Bamford, Wong & Laschinger, 2013; Walumbwa, Gardner, Wersing & Peterson, 2008) and supportive leadership (Thomas & Xu, 2011).

Further research conducted by the authors (Lewis, Donaldson-Feilder, Tharani & Pangallo, 2011) aimed to identify the specific manager behaviours required to engender employee engagement (as opposed to increasing well-being and preventing stress as described in Table 11.1). A qualitative research methodology was used to identify specific management behaviours important for employee engagement. Interviews were conducted with employees to explore individuals' views on aspects of their line manager's behaviour that were important to their own engagement. The interviews were transcribed and analysed using content analysis: both positive and negative behaviours were identified, and 11 competencies emerged. For ease of comprehension, the 11 competencies were then grouped into the following three themes: supporting employee growth (which includes behaviours such as giving feedback and praise, providing autonomy and empowerment); interpersonal style and integrity (which includes behaviours such as being available to employees and role-modelling positive behaviours); and monitoring direction (which involves managers following processes, clarifying expectations and managing time and workload for employees). The competency framework emerging from this work is shown in Table 11.2.

Table 11.2 Management competencies for enhancing employee engagement.

Theme	Management competency	Description
Supporting employee growth	Autonomy and empowerment	Has trust in employee capabilities, involving them in problem solving and decision making
	Development	Helps employees in their career development and progression
	Feedback, praise and recognition	Gives positive and constructive feedback, offers praise and rewards good work
	Individual Interest	Shows genuine care and concern for employees
Interpersonal style and integrity	Availability	Holds regular one to one meetings with employees and is available when needed
	Personal manner	Demonstrates a positive approach to work, leading by example
	Ethics	Respects confidentiality and treats employees fairly
Monitoring direction	Reviewing and guiding	Offers help and advice to employees responding effectively to employee requests for guidance.
	Clarifying expectations	Sets clear goals and objectives giving clear explanations of what is expected
	Managing time and resources	Is aware of the team's workload, arranges for extra resources or re-distributes workload when necessary
	Following processes and Procedures	Effectively understands, explains and follows work processes and procedures

What is 'Positive Leadership' – the Kind of Leadership that Enhances *Both* Employee Well-Being and Engagement?

Exploring the relationship between employee well-being and engagement, a body of research supports the proposal that employee engagement is positively linked with well-being outcomes, including psychological well-being (Matz-Costa, Besen, Boone James & Pitt-Catsouphes, 2012; Shuck & Reio, 2014), a reduction in depressive symptoms (Hakanen & Schaufeli, 2012), and life satisfaction (Hakanen & Schaufeli, 2012; Shimazu, Schaufeli, Kamiyama & Kawakami, 2015; Shimazu, Schaufeli, Kubota & Kawakami, 2012).

However, there is a suggestion that the relationship between these two constructs is curvilinear, that maybe ever-higher levels of engagement are not associated with ever-greater well-being. It may be that both disengagement (or low levels of engagement) and over-engagement (or very high levels of engagement) could be detrimental to well-being. Although research has recently suggested that engagement and burnout are different constructs (see Hakanen & Schaufeli, 2012; Shimazu, Schaufeli, Kamiyama & Kawakami, 2015; Shimazu, Schaufeli, Kubota & Kawakami, 2012), not simply opposites of one another, it could be that too much engagement might be linked over time to risk of burnout or have negative impacts on employee well-being. For example, Halbesleben, Harvey & Bolino (2009) found that there was a positive relationship between state engagement and three types of work–family interference (time-based, strain-based and behaviour-based).

The practitioner literature (for instance Fairhurst & O'Connor, 2010) has extended the exploration of this relationship, by looking at the interaction between employee engagement and well-being. This work found that highly engaged individuals with high levels of well-being were the most productive and happiest employees. Highly engaged employees with low levels of well-being were more likely to leave their organization and, although they tended towards high levels of productivity, they also were more likely to experience high levels of burnout. Employees with low levels of engagement but high levels of well-being were more likely to stay with the organization, but were less committed to its goals. Employees who both were disengaged and had low levels of well-being contributed the least to the organization: in a weak employment market, this group might also be reluctant to move organizations.

Meanwhile, Robertson and Birch (2010) found preliminary evidence of the importance of psychological well-being for sustaining employee engagement. Their study found that psychological well-being enhanced the relationship between employee engagement and productivity. They suggested that if organizations only focus on initiatives that target commitment and discretionary effort, without nurturing employee psychological well-being, these initiatives will be limited in the impact they can achieve. Robertson and Birch (2010) therefore suggest it is feasible that the combined impact of engagement and well-being may be greater than each one alone.

In order to achieve sustainable positive employee and organizational outcomes, therefore, managers need to show leadership behaviours that simultaneously protect and enhance employee well-being *and* engender employee engagement. To understand what behaviours would be involved in 'managing for sustainable

Table 11.3 'Managing for sustainable employee engagement' framework.

Competency	Brief description
Open, fair and consistent	Managing with integrity and consistency, managing emotions/personal issues and taking a positive approach in interpersonal interactions
Handling conflict and problems	Dealing with employee conflicts (including bullying and abuse) and using appropriate organizational resources
Knowledge, clarity and guidance	Clear communication, advice and guidance, demonstrates understanding of roles and responsible decision making
Building and sustaining relationships	Personal interaction with employees involving empathy and consideration
Supporting development	Supporting and arranging employee career progression and development

well-being and engagement', the authors conducted research to bring together the two frameworks described in the previous sections: management competencies for preventing and reducing stress on the one hand and management competencies for enhancing employee engagement on the other hand (Lewis, Donaldson-Feilder & Tharani, 2012). This was a three-stage research programme. The first two phases involved the piloting (qualitative ($n = 17$) and quantitative ($n = 127$)) of the managing engagement questionnaire and then subsequent testing and development (506 employees and 126 managers). The third phase of the research combined the managing engagement and MCPARS questionnaires in a longitudinal research phase involving 378 employees and 108 managers. The result of this study is a behaviour framework that sets out how managers can manage for both engagement and well-being, made up of five broad themes of manager behaviour as shown in Table 11.3.

Although all the 'Managing for sustainable employee engagement' competencies (with the exception of 'handling conflict and problems') are included in some form in both of the original frameworks, there is a difference in emphasis between the three frameworks. For instance, the 'Managing for sustainable engagement' framework has a greater emphasis on developing and progressing individuals and on role requirements than the MCPARS framework, and it has a greater emphasis on personal interaction and consideration and managing one's own emotions than the 'Managing engagement' framework. This suggests that although broad behavioural themes may be common across all three frameworks, particular manager behaviours may differ in importance depending on the employee outcome sought: engagement, well-being or sustainable engagement.

Can Positive Leadership be Developed?

Once the positive leadership behaviours that are important for engendering employee engagement and well-being are identified, the challenge becomes one of supporting leaders to develop and use these behaviours in their interactions with followers. The question is how to undertake effective leadership development and ensure that the skills leaders develop are applied in the workplace.

A recent CIPD survey on learning and development (CIPD, 2015) showed that 80 per cent of the organizations questioned reported that they would be carrying out leadership development over the following 12 months. Meanwhile, the plethora of commercial and other organizations providing leadership and management development suggests that this is a significant market: organizations are spending large sums on developing managers and leaders. However, ensuring that such development activities are evidence-based and effective over the long term is not always easy.

While there is an enormous literature about models of leadership, the focus until recently was on identifying the relevant skills, behaviours and approaches for leadership. Little literature had explored how to develop leaders. A special issue of the journal *Leadership Quarterly* in 2011 focused on longitudinal studies of leadership development: it showed that, although there are a number of frameworks for how and why leaders develop over time, the majority have not been empirically tested. This is now beginning to change, with authors such as Day, Fleenor, Atwater, Sturm and McKee (2014), in their review of 25 years of leadership development research, suggesting a focus change from leadership research to the processes underpinning leadership development. Day and colleagues, however, concluded from this review that there remains a lack of strong theory or focus to this literature and that much more research is needed.

There appears to be an implicit belief that establishing the 'right' leadership theory will lead to better leaders through a learning and development intervention based on that theory, but little recognition that developing these skills is a process that unfolds over time, not in a one-off workshop or training. This quotation from Day et al. (2014, p. 80) highlights this perfectly: 'It generally takes 10 years or 10,000 hours of dedicated practice to become an expert in a given field .... For this reason, it is highly unlikely that anyone would be able to develop fully as a leader merely through participation in a series of programs, workshops, or seminars.'

The authors' own research has shown that managers can be equipped with behaviours that are important for employee well-being through provision of upward feedback and learning and development activities (Donaldson-Feilder, Lewis & Yarker, 2009). However, it also showed that carrying out management development of this type in organizations is hard, that maintaining change is even harder, and that the organizational context in which the management development takes place has a key impact on outcomes (Donaldson-Feilder & Lewis, 2011; Donaldson-Feilder, Lewis & Yarker, 2009). Others in the field have also acknowledged that the context in which management development takes place is important to its success (Day et al., 2014) and explored some of the relevant contextual factors (e.g. Garavan, Watson, Carbery & O'Brien, 2015; Greco, Spence Laschinger & Wong, 2006). This means that investment in leadership development may be wasted if organizations do not create an appropriate context in which to support and develop managers and leaders and ensure that interventions are as effective as possible.

Although the academic literature around leadership and management development is in its infancy, it does have some useful pointers about intervention formats and contextual issues to support practitioners. However, until the authors' recent research, there was no unifying model that practitioners could use to guide their thinking and activities to support leaders in their developmental process towards effectively managing in such a way as to engender health, well-being and engagement in their team followers.

Success Factors for Positive Leadership Development

In order to meet the need for a unifying model to help practitioners to understand the evidence about leadership development, the authors (Lewis, Donaldson-Feilder, Jones & Johal, 2014) used an evidence-based practice model (Briner, Denyer & Rousseau, 2009) to identify and synthesize the range of evidence available. This enabled collation of evidence from numerous sources to develop a unifying framework. The sources included academic research, practitioner research, expert views, and stakeholder and contextual perspectives.

The research focused on three main areas:

- What factors will affect the success of a development programme aimed at changing manager behaviour?
- What factors will support transfer and sustainability of learning from management development programmes into the workplace?
- What contextual factors are likely to impact on the relationship between manager behaviour and employee engagement, health and well-being outcomes?

With these three research questions as a basis, literature reviews were conducted that explored published academic and practitioner literature (including organizational case studies) to understand both the evaluated external evidence, and practitioner expertise and judgement. In order to understand the contextual, local evidence, stakeholders' preferences and also further practitioner expertise and judgement, interviews with key stakeholders in four organizations were conducted along with two focus groups with the Affinity Health at Work (AHAW) research consortium.

The evidence gathered from all these data sources was collated and screened using exclusion criteria, then synthesized into a model for each of the three research questions. The findings from each of the three research questions are summarized below, along with their explanatory models. For each of the models, a summary of the results from the particular research question is included, listing the relevant factors in each category. In the brackets after each factor the source of the data is clarified (whether from the academic literature review, the practitioner literature review or stakeholder interviews and focus groups).

Research Question 1: What factors will affect the success of a development programme aimed at changing manager behaviour?
With regard to this question, it was notable how the data from the three different evidence sources varied in focus when the success factors for management

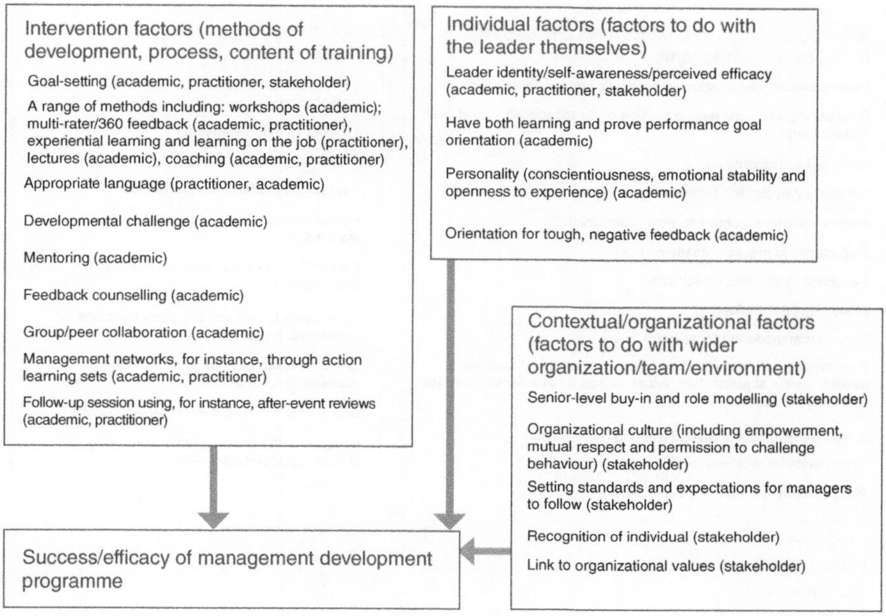

Figure 11.1 Summary of evidence responding to the research question: What factors will affect the success of a development programme aimed at changing manager behaviour?

development programmes were considered. The academic literature focused mainly on individual differences among the trainees and the managers themselves (for instance, it looked at their goal orientations and leader identity) and on the intervention methodologies (such as literature that supported the need for a range of long-term interventions). The practitioner literature was focused more on the content and methodology of the development programme (again finding support for the need for a range of long-term interventions), and the stakeholder literature on the contextual factors within the organization itself (in particular the type of culture in which management development would be successful). This difference highlights the importance of the evidence-based approach taken to develop a more rounded answer to the research questions. (See Figure 11.1.)

Research Question 2: What factors will support transfer and sustainability of learning from management development programmes into the workplace?
As found for Research Question 1, the academic literature is the only one of the three literature sources to focus upon individual differences between managers that will affect training transfer. Much of the evidence for the academic review came from two papers, an integrative literature review by Burke and Hutchins in 2007, and a meta-analysis by Blume, Ford, Baldwin and Huang (2010) which related individual factors predictive of successful training transfer to cognitive ability, personality, and motivational and attitudinal characteristics. That said, across both intervention and contextual and organizational characteristics, it is encouraging to see similar factors emerge from all three sources of evidence,

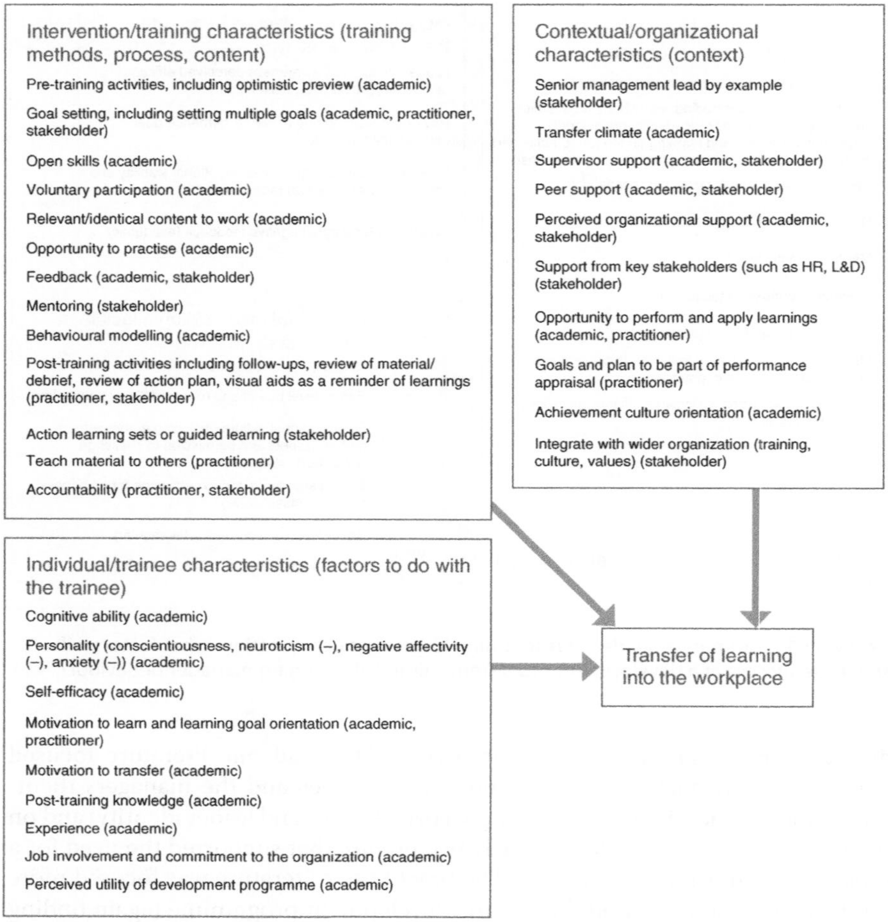

Figure 11.2 Summary of evidence responding to the research question: What factors will support transfer and sustainability of learning from management development programmes into the workplace?

with goal setting being key in the design together with a supportive organizational culture and working relationships. (See Figure 11.2.)

Research Question 3: What contextual factors are likely to impact on the relationship between manager behaviour and employee engagement, health and well-being outcomes?

With this final research question, the aim was to explore and identify the contextual factors that had been found to impact upon the relationship between manager behaviour on the one hand and employee engagement, health and well-being outcomes on the other hand. This evidence falls into different categories to the preceding two questions, where the individual, intervention and contextual or organizational factors could be identified, all of which directly impact on the area of interest (success of management development and transfer of learning respectively). For this third question, the interactions were more complex and indirect, so we explored mediators (factors that management behaviour affects and creates, which subsequently impact upon employee outcomes), moderators (factors that affect the impact of management behaviour on employee outcomes, making the behaviour of the manager more or less impactful), and barriers and facilitators (factors that have an impact on one or more parts of the relationship between management behaviour and employee outcomes).

The contribution from the academic literature in this area is very different to the practitioner and stakeholder evidence. The results from the academic literature provide good evidence for factors that are mediators and some limited evidence on moderators; the literature does not consider the broader concepts of barriers and facilitators at all. By contrast, in the practitioner literature and the stakeholder interviews and focus groups there was little or no consideration of mediators, and relevant factors tended to be explored in terms of barriers and facilitators that influence the relationship between manager behaviour and employee outcomes in a range of ways, rather than strictly moderating that relationship. (See Figure 11.3.)

For a full review of the literature contributing to each of these three models, see Lewis, Donaldson-Feilder, Jones and Johal (2014).

The models that resulted from collating the various sources of evidence were used to develop checklists designed to support organizations and practitioners in a real-world setting. The aim was to create tools that meet organizational and practitioner needs and have utility. To ensure the usability of the checklists, they were organized into three chronological stages:

- Stage 1: Before the development programme – a checklist for those considering conducting a development programme.
- Stage 2: During the development programme – a checklist for those designing and implementing a development programme.
- Stage 3: After the development programme – a checklist for those embedding learning into the workplace.

Within each stage, the data were categorized into three areas of consideration:

- Methodology (relating to the intervention factors category).
- Manager (relating to the individual factors category).
- Organization (relating to the organizational and contextual characteristics category).

The initial checklists developed were subjected to a validation process: first they were qualitatively reviewed by Affinity Health at Work (AHAW) research consortium members and six academic and practitioner experts, then they were tested in practice by four organizations to test usability and usefulness. The checklists were revised in response to these validation exercises and final versions developed. See Boxes 11.1, 11.2 and 11.3 for at-a-glance summary views of the three checklists that emerged from this research process.

Organizations and practitioners can use the checklists to support them as they design, develop and implement leadership development programmes. Working through the checklist can help them reflect on the factors that could enhance or

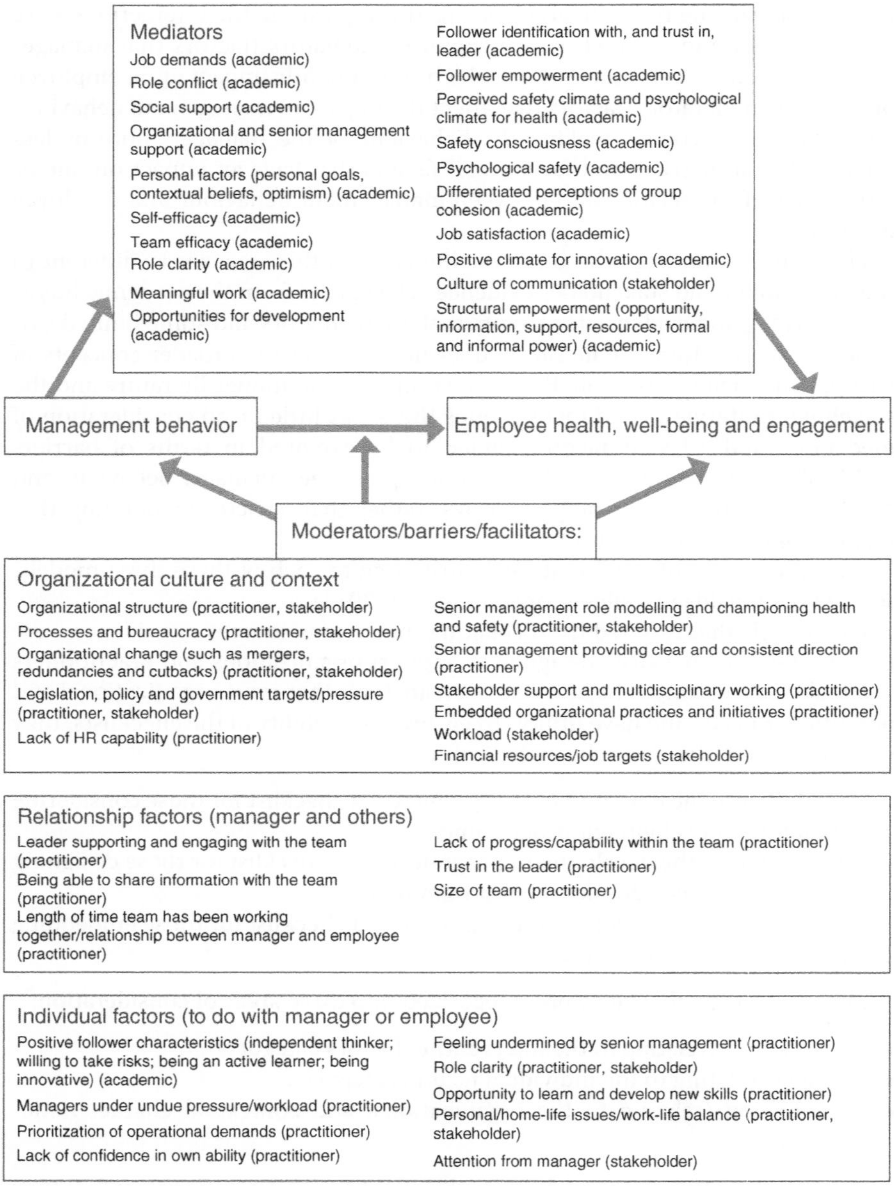

Figure 11.3 Summary of evidence responding to the research question: What contextual factors are likely to impact on the relationship between manager behaviour and employee engagement, health and well-being outcomes?

reduce the programme's effectiveness: essentially, the checklist enables them to conduct a gap analysis to establish what they already have in place and what they might need to put in place to achieve successful leadership development. The hope is that the process of conducting this gap analysis will also facilitate

Box 11.1 At-a-glance view of checklist for stage 1: before the leadership development programme

Methodology	Manager	Organization
Considerations for planning, design and format of the programme that support success	**Characteristics of manager participants that support programme success**	**Characteristics of the organizational environment that support programme success**
• MAKE the programme useful, beneficial and important to all. • MAKE programme goals SMART. • CONSIDER the resources available. • CHOOSE a good, organizationally relevant name for the programme. • INTEGRATE the programme into organizational strategy. • ENSURE shared departmental responsibility for the programme. • MAKE participants accountable for their success on the programme. • SET multiple aligned goals for participants. • USE a series of interventions over time. • USE a range of different delivery formats. • GET senior management support • ENSURE opportunities for participants to apply their learning.	• INVOLVE those participants most likely to learn. • BUILD self-awareness in managers and recognition of themselves as leaders. • ENCOURAGE managers to value learning and development. • PROVIDE support and feedback to managers to increase their management skills.	• HAVE a supportive culture with open dialogue, mutual respect and recognition. • SHOW support and recognition of, and commitment to, health and safety. • DEMONSTRATE support for innovation and initiative. • BUILD a culture where employees feel empowered. • ENSURE organizational policies and processes are accessible and helpful. • GET senior managers to engage with others. • ENSURE managers are supportive of others' learning. • LEAD by example. • ENSURE managers focus on both task and people. • SET clear standards and expectations for managers. • LET managers know what their role is. • PROVIDE meaningful work for all. • ENSURE opportunities for development.

Box 11.2 At-a-glance view of checklist for stage 2: during the leadership development programme

Methodology	Manager	Organization
Considerations for planning, design and format of the programme that support success	**Characteristics of manager participants that support programme success**	**Characteristics of the organizational environment that support programme success**
• DEVELOP a range of pre-training activities. • PROVIDE mentors, coaching and feedback support for participants. • CONSIDER ways to build collaborative working in the participant group. • USE a series of interventions over time. • USE a range of different delivery formats. • CONSIDER ways to ensure the group facilitator builds and develops trust. • SET multiple aligned goals for participants. • MAKE programme goals SMART. • MAKE the programme useful, beneficial and important to all. • ENSURE the programme content is relevant to, and reflective of, manager participants' job roles. • INTEGRATE the programme into organizational strategy. • CHOOSE the right programme name. • PROVIDE opportunities to practise, and get feedback on, their learning. • USE after-event reviews. • ENSURE opportunities to apply new learning. • CONSIDER ongoing availability of resources. • ENSURE programme goals and actions are integrated into performance appraisal or review system. • BUILD participants' confidence. • HOLD participants accountable. • GET leadership support for the programme.	• VOLUNTARY participation. • BUILD self-awareness in managers and recognition of themselves as leaders. • INVOLVE those participants most likely to learn. • ENCOURAGE managers to value the learning and development opportunity. • ENSURE managers feel they can succeed. • HELP managers see the programme as beneficial and important. • ALIGN manager and organizational values. • ENSURE managers are satisfied in their work and see it as meaningful. • MAKE sure managers are not in roles with conflicting goals and priorities.	• HAVE a supportive culture with open dialogue, mutual respect and recognition. • SHOW support and recognition of, and commitment to, health and safety. • DEMONSTRATE support for innovation and initiative. • BUILD a culture where employees feel empowered. • ENSURE organizational policies and processes are accessible and helpful. • GET senior managers to engage with others. • ENSURE managers are supportive of others' learning. • LEAD by example. • ENSURE managers focus on both task and people. • MAKE sure priorities don't conflict for managers. • SET clear standards and expectations for managers. • LET managers know what their role is. • PROVIDE meaningful work for all. • ENSURE opportunities for development. • ENSURE peer, team and social support for managers. • ENCOURAGE good-quality team relationships. • ENCOURAGE teams to trust in, and identify with, their manager. • BUILD cohesive working teams.

Methodology	Manager	Organization
Considerations for planning, design and format of the programme that support success	**Characteristics of manager participants that support programme success**	**Characteristics of the organizational environment that support programme success**
• CONTINUE to use a series of interventions. • INTEGRATE the programme into organizational strategy. • CONSIDER ongoing availability of resources. • ENSURE continued shared departmental responsibility for the programme. • KEEP senior management support. • SET multiple aligned goals for participants. • ENSURE programme goals and actions are integrated into performance appraisal or review systems. • CONSIDER a range of post-training activities. • USE after-event reviews. • CONDUCT follow-ups with participants. • MAINTAIN opportunities for participants to practise, and get feedback on, their learning. • ENCOURAGE participants to seek out opportunities to apply new learnings. • MAKE participants accountable for applying their learning. • USE a mentor, peer or colleague to hold participants accountable for applying learning. • CREATE opportunities for participants to teach others what they have learned. • USE visual aid reminders to practise learning. • EMBED learning using action learning sets or guided learning sets.	• ENSURE that participants have been equipped with the required knowledge and skills. • HELP managers see the programme as beneficial and important. • ENCOURAGE managers to value the learning and development opportunity they have been given. • BUILD optimism and confidence for managers to use their learning. • FOCUS on managers who show the behaviour characteristic of success. • ALIGN manager and organizational values. • ENSURE managers are satisfied in, and committed to, their work and see it as meaningful. • CHECK that managers are not under undue pressure and work–life conflict. • MAKE sure managers are in roles with minimal conflicting goals and priorities.	• HAVE a supportive culture with open dialogue, mutual respect and recognition. • SHOW support and recognition of, and commitment to, health and safety. • DEMONSTRATE support for initiative. • BUILD a culture where employees are empowered. • ENSURE organizational policies and processes are accessible and helpful. • CONSIDER if any significant organizational change could have affected integration of learning. • CONSIDER if political or legislative influences could be used to raise programme priority. • ENSURE HR and other stakeholders are capable of providing ongoing support. • GET senior managers to engage with others. • LEAD by example. • ENSURE managers focus on both tasks and people. • MAKE sure priorities don't conflict for managers. • SET clear standards and expectations for managers. • LET managers know what their role is. • PROVIDE meaningful work for all. • ENSURE opportunities for development. • ENSURE peer, team and social support. • ENCOURAGE good-quality team relationships. • ENCOURAGE teams to trust in their manager. • BUILD cohesive working teams. • ENSURE team members are empowered and equipped with relevant knowledge, skills and abilities.

collaboration between all relevant parties within the organization, including learning and development, HR, occupational health, well-being and health and safety, senior leadership and management, the leaders to be developed and perhaps employees or their representatives and, if appropriate, external providers; it can thereby support cross-functional and collaborative working to address any gaps identified.

The development of this framework also provides openings for further research on this topic. There is a need to test and validate the model and identify which factors are predictive, or most predictive, of success in leadership development. In addition, some of the factors identified from the practitioner evidence have not been explored within academic literature, so could provide an avenue for expanding academic enquiry.

Conclusion

The evidence for links between leadership and employee well-being and engagement is now sufficiently strong to point to leadership development as an appropriate intervention to use when aiming to improve these employee outcomes. Research has elucidated the positive leadership behaviours needed to enhance employee well-being and engagement, and there is evidence that leadership can be developed. However, developing leadership competence is not always easy; it depends on the context in which the leader works. The authors' recent research has created a synthesized model of the factors that are important for supporting the success of leadership development. The aim is that this model will support practitioners to implement effective leadership development within organizations and thereby improve employee well-being and engagement.

References

Alimo-Metcalfe, B. & Alban-Metcalfe, R. J. (2001). The development of a new transformational leadership questionnaire. *Journal of Occupational and Organizational Psychology*, 74, 1–27.

Amick, B. C. & Celantano, D. D. (1991). Structural determinants of the psychosocial work environment: Introducing technology in the work stress framework. *Ergonomics*, 34, 625–46.

Arnold, K. A. & Connelly, C. E. (2013). Transformational leadership and psychological well-being: Effects on followers and leaders. In H. Skipton Leonard, R. Lewis, A. M. Freedman & J. Passmore (eds.), *The Wiley-Blackwell Handbook of Psychology of Leadership, Change and Organizational Development*. Chichester, UK: John Wiley & Sons, pp. 175–94.

Arnold, K., Turner, N., Barling, J., Kelloway, E. K. & McKee, M. C. (2007). Transformational leadership and psychological well-being: The mediating role of meaningful work. *Journal of Occupational Health Psychology*, 12, 193–203.

Baker, E., Israel, B. & Schurman, S. (1996). Role of control and support in occupational stress: An integrated model. *Social Science and Medicine*, 43, 1145–59.

Bamford, M., Wong, C. A. & Laschinger, H. (2013). The influence of authentic leadership and areas of worklife on work engagement of registered nurses. *Journal of Nursing Management*, 21, 529–40. doi: 10.1111/j.1365-2834.2012.01399.x.

Bass, B. (1985). *Leadership and Performance Beyond Expectations*. New York: Free Press.

Bass, B. M. (1998). *Transformational Leadership: Industrial, Military, and Educational Impact*. Hillsdale, NJ: Erlbaum.

Bass, B. M. (1999). Two decades of research and development in transformational leadership. *European Journal of Work and Organizational Psychology*, 8, 9–32.

Blume, B. D., Ford, J. K., Baldwin, T. T & Huang, J. L. (2010). Transfer of training: A meta-analytic review. *Journal of Management*, 36(4), 1065–1105.

Bono, J. E., Foldes, H. J., Vinson, G. & Muros, J. P. (2007). Workplace emotions: The role of supervision and leadership. *Journal of Applied Psychology*, 92, 1357–67.

Breevaart, K., Bakker, A. B., Demerouti, E. & van den Heuvel, M. (2015). Leader–member exchange, work engagement and job performance. *Journal of Managerial Psychology*, 30(7), 754–70. 10.1108/JMP-03-2013-0088.

Breevaart, K., Bakker, A., Hetland, J., Demerouti, E., Olsen, O. K. & Espevik, R. (2014). Daily transactional and transformational leadership and daily employee engagement. *Journal of Occupational and Organisational Psychology*, 87, 138–57. doi: 10.1111/joop.12041.

Briner, R. B., Denyer, D. & Rousseau, D. M. (2009). Evidence-based management: Concept clean up time? *Academy of Management Perspectives*, 23, 19–32.

Brossoit, K. B. (2001). Understanding employee empowerment in the workplace: Exploring the relationships between transformational leadership, employee perceptions of employment and key work outcomes. Doctoral dissertation, Claremont Graduate University.

Burke, L. A. & Hutchins, H. M. (2007). Training transfer: An integrative literature review. *Human Resource Development Review*, 6(3), 263–96.

CIPD (2015). Learning and talent development. Annual survey report. London: CIPD.

Day, D. V., Fleenor, J. W., Atwater, L. E., Sturm, R. E. & McKee, R. A. (2014). Advances in leader and leadership development: A review of 25 years of research and theory. *Leadership Quarterly*, 25, 63–82. 10.1016/j.leaqua.2013.11.004.

Dekker, S. W. A. & Schaufeli, W. B. (1995). The effects of job insecurity on psychological health and withdrawal: A longitudinal study. *Australian Psychologist*, 30, 57–63.

Donaldson-Feilder, E. & Lewis, R. (2011). Preventing stress: Promoting positive manager behaviour. Phase 4: How do organisations implement the findings in practice? Research insight. London: CIPD Publications. http://www.cipd.co.uk/hr-resources/research/preventing-stress-promoting-positive-manager-behaviour-phase-4.aspx.

Donaldson-Feilder, E. J., Lewis, R. & Yarker, J. (2009). Preventing stress: Promoting positive manager behaviour. CIPD Insight Report.

Donaldson-Feilder, E., Munir, F. & Lewis, R. (2013) Leadership and employee well-being. In H. Skipton Leonard, R. Lewis, A. Freedman, and J. Passmore (eds), *The Wiley-Blackwell Handbook of Psychology of Leadership, Change and Organizational Development*. Chichester, UK: John Wiley & Sons, pp. 155–73.

Duffy, M. K., Ganster, D. C. & Pagon, M. (2002). Social undermining in the workplace. *Academy of Management Journal*, 45, 331–51.

Duxbury, M. L., Armstrong, G. D., Drew, D. J. & Henly, S. J. (1984). Head nurse leadership style with staff nurse burnout and job satisfaction in neonatal intensive care units. *Nursing Research*, 33, 97–101.

Einarsen, S., Aasland, M. S. & Skogstad, A. (2007). Destructive leadership behaviour: A definition and conceptual model. *Leadership Quarterly*, 18, 207–16.

Fairhurst, D. & O'Conner, J. (2010). Employee well-being: Taking engagement and performance to the next level. Towers Watson. https://www.towerswatson.com/en-GB/Insights/IC-Types/Ad-hoc-Point-of-View/2010/Employee-Well-Being-Taking-Engagement-and-Performance-to-the-Next-Level. Accessed 3 August 2016.

Garavan, G., Watson, S., Carbery, R. & O'Brien, F. (2015). The antecedents of leadership development practices in SMEs: The influence of HRM strategy and practice. *International Small Business Journal*. 21 pp. doi: 10.1177/0266242615594215.

Gardner, W. L., Lowe, K. B., Moss, T. W., Mahoney, K. T. & Cogliser, C. C. (2010). Scholarly leadership of the study of leadership: A review of *The Leadership Quarterly*'s second decade, 2000–2009. *Leadership Quarterly*, 21, 922–58.

Greco, P., Spence Laschinger, H. K. & Wong, C. (2006). Leader empowering behaviours, staff nurse empowerment and work engagement/burnout. *Nursing Leadership*, 19(4), 41–56.

Hakanen, J. J. & Schaufeli, W. B. (2012). Do burnout and work engagement predict depressive symptoms and life satisfaction? A three-wave seven-year prospective study. *Journal of Affective Disorders*, 141, 415–24.

Halbesleben, J. R. B., Harvey, J. & Bolino, M. C. (2009). Too engaged? A conservation of resources view of the relationship between work engagement and work interference with family. *Journal of Applied Psychology*, 94(6), 1452–65. doi: 10.1037/a0017595.

Harris, K. J. & Kacmar, K. M. (2005). Easing the strain: The buffering role of supervisors in the perceptions of politics–strain relationship. *Journal of Occupational and Organizational Psychology*, 78, 337–54.

Hauge, L. J., Skogstad, A. & Einarsen, S. (2007). Relationships between stressful work environments and bullying: Results of a large representative study. *Work and Stress*, 21, 220–42.

Hetland, H., Sandal, G. M., & Johnsen, T. B. (2007). Burnout in the information technology sector: Does leadership matter? *European Journal of Work and Organizational Psychology*, 16(1), 58–75.

Kelloway, E. K. & Barling, J. (2010). Leadership development as an intervention in occupational health psychology. *Work & Stress*, 24, 260–79.

Kelloway, E. K., Weigand, H., McKee, M. C. & Das, H. (2013). Positive leadership and employee well-being. *Journal of Leadership and Organizational Studies*, 20(1), 107–17. doi: 10.1177/1548051812465892.

Kile, S. M. (1990). Helsefarleg leierskap [Health-endangering leadership]. Doctoral dissertation, Universitetet i Bergen.

Kuoppala, J., Lamminpaa, A., Liira, J. & Vainio, H. (2008). Leadership, job well-being, and health effects: A systematic review and a meta-analysis. *Journal of Occupational and Environmental Medicine*, 50, 904–15.

Landeweerd, J. A. & Boumans, N. P. G. (1994). The effect of work dimensions and need for autonomy on nurses' work satisfaction and health. *Journal of Occupational and Organizational Psychology*, 67, 207–17.

Lee, R. T. & Ashforth, B. E. (1996). A meta-analytic examination of the correlates of the three dimensions of burnout. *Journal of Applied Psychology*, 81, 123–33.

Levy, P. E. (2003). *Industrial/Organizational Psychology: Understanding the Workplace*. Boston, MA: Houghton Mifflin.

Lewis, R., Donaldson-Feilder, E., Jones, B. & Johal, M. (2014). Developing managers to manage sustainable employee engagement, health and well-being. London: CIPD Publications. http://www.cipd.co.uk/hr-resources/research/developing-managers.aspx. Accessed 3 August 2016.

Lewis, R., Donaldson-Feilder, E. & Tharani, T. (2012). Managing for sustainable employee engagement: Developing a behavioural framework. London: CIPD Publications. http://www.cipd.co.uk/publicpolicy/policy-reports/engagement-behavioural-framework.aspx. Accessed 3 August 2016.

Lewis, R., Donaldson-Feilder, E., Tharani, T. & Pangallo, A. (2011). Management competencies for enhancing employee engagement. Research Insight. London: CIPD Publications. www.cipd.co.uk/hr-resources/research/management-competencies-for-engagement.aspx. Accessed 3 August 2016.

Lowe, K. B. & Gardner, W. L. (2000). Ten years of *The Leadership Quarterly*: Contributions and challenges for the future. *Leadership Quarterly*, 11, 459–14.

MacLeod, D. & Clarke, N. (2009). Engaging for success: Enhancing performance through employee engagement. London: Office of Public Sector Information. http://webarchive.nationalarchives.gov.uk/20090609003228/http://www.berr.gov.uk/files/file52215.pdf. Accessed 3 August 2016.

Matz-Costa, C., Besen, E., Boone James, J. & Pitt-Catsouphes, M. (2012). Differential impact of multiple levels of productive activity engagement on psychological well-being in middle and later life. *The Gerontologist*, 54(2), 277–89.

Miller, J., McCartney, C., Baron, A., McGurk, J. & Robinson, V. (2011). Sustainable organisation performance: What really makes the difference? Shaping The Future, Final Report. London: Chartered Institute of Personnel and Development.

Moyle, P. & Parkes, K. (1999). The effects of transition stress: A relocation study. *Journal of Organizational Behavior*, 20, 625–46.

Nielsen, K., Randall, R., Yarker, J. & Brenner, S. (2008). The effects of transformational leadership on followers' perceived work characteristics and psychological well-being: A longitudinal study. *Work & Stress*, 22(1), 16–32.

Nyberg, A., Bernin, P. & Theorell, T. (2005). The impact of leadership on the health of subordinates. Report No. 1:2005. National Institute for Working Life.

Offermann, L. R. & Hellmann, P. S. (1996). Leadership behavior and subordinate stress: A 360 degrees view. *Journal of Occupational Health Psychology*, 1(4), 382–90.

Rayner, C. & McIvor, K. (2006). *Report to the Dignity at Work Project Steering Committee*. Dignity at Work Report. Portsmouth University.
Robertson, I. & Birch, A. J. (2010). The role of psychological well-being in employee engagement. Paper presented at the British Psychological Society Occupational Psychology conference, Brighton, January.
Schaubroeck, J., Walumbwa, F. O., Ganster, D. C. & Kepes, S. (2007). Destructive leadership traits and the neutralising influence of an 'enriched' job. *Leadership Quarterly*, 18, 236–51.
Schaufeli, W. B. & Bakker, A. B. (2004). UWES: Utrecht Work Engagement Scale preliminary manual [version 1.1, December]. Unpublished manuscript, Utrecht University. http://www.wilmarschaufeli.nl/publications/Schaufeli/Test%20Manuals/Test_manual_UWES_English.pdf. Accessed 17 August 2016
Schaufeli, W. B. & Bakker, A. B. (2010). The conceptualization and measurement of work engagement. In A. B. Bakker & M. P. Leiter (eds), *Work Engagement: A Handbook of Essential Theory and Research*. New York: Psychology Press, pp. 10–24.
Schaufeli, W. B. & Enzmann, D. (1998). *The Burnout Companion to Study and Research*. London: Taylor & Francis.
Seltzer, J. & Numerof, R. E. (1988). Supervisory leadership and subordinate burnout. *Academy of Management Journal*, 31, 439–46.
Sheridan, J. E. & Vredenburgh, D. J. (1978). Usefulness of leadership behavior and social power variables in predicting job tension, performance, and turnover of nursing employees. *Journal of Applied Psychology*, 63, 89–95.
Shimazu, A., Schaufeli, W. B., Kamiyama, K. & Kawakami, N. (2015). Workaholism vs. work engagement: The two different predictors of future well-being and performance. *International Journal of Behavioral Medicine*, 22, 18–23.
Shimazu, A., Schaufeli, W. B., Kubota, K. & Kawakami, N. (2012). Do workaholism and work engagement predict employee well-being and performance in opposite directions? *Industrial Health*, 50, 316–21.
Shuck, B. & Reio, T. G., Jr. (2014). Employee engagement and well-being: A moderation model and implications for practice. *Journal of Leadership & Organizational Studies*, 21(1), 43–58.
Skakon, J., Nielsen, K., Borg, V. & Guzman, J. (2010). Are leaders' wellbeing, behaviours and style associated with the wellbeing of employees? A systematic review of three decades of empirical research. *Work and Stress*, 24, 107–39.
Skogstad, A., Einarsen, S., Torsheim, T., Aasland, M. S. & Hetland, H. (2007). The destructiveness of laissez-faire leadership behaviour. *Journal of Occupational Health Psychology*, 12, 80–92.
Sosik, J. J. & Godshalk, V. M. (2000). Leadership styles, mentoring functions received, and job-related stress: A conceptual model and preliminary study. *Journal of Organizational Behavior*, 21, 365–90.
Stephens, C. & Long, N. (2000). Communication with police supervisors and peers as a buffer of work related traumatic stress. *Journal of Organizational Behavior*, 21, 407–24.
Strom, D. L., Sears, K. L. & Kelly, K. M. (2014). Work engagement: The roles of organizational justice and leadership style in predicting engagement among employees. *Journal of Leadership & Organizational Studies*, 21(1), 71–82. doi: 10.1177/1548051813485437.

Tepper, B. J. (2000). Consequences of abusive supervision. *Academy of Management Journal*, 43, 178–90.
Thomas, H. C. & Xu, J. (2011). How can leaders achieve high employee engagement? *Leadership and Organisation Development Journal*, 32(4), 399–416.
Thomas, L. T. & Ganster, D. C. (1995). Impact of family-supportive work variables on work–family conflict and strain: A control perspective. *Journal of Applied Psychology*, 80, 6–15.
Tims, M., Bakker, A. B. & Xanthopoulou, D. (2011). Do transformational leaders enhance their followers' daily work engagement? *Leadership Quarterly*, 22, 121–31.
Towers Watson (2014). *2014 Global Workforce Study: At a glance*. London: Towers Watson.
Van Dierendonck, D., Haynes, C., Borrill, C. & Stride, C. (2004). Leadership behavior and subordinate well-being. *Journal of Occupational Health Psychology*, 9, 165–75.
Walumbwa, F. O., Gardner, W. L., Wersing, T. S. & Peterson, S. J. (2008). Authentic leadership: Development and validation of a theory-based measure. *Journal of Management*, 34, 89–126.
Yagil, D. (2006). The relationship of abusive and supportive workplace supervision to employee burnout and upward influence tactics. *Journal of Emotional Abuse*, 6, 49–65.
Yarker, J., Donaldson-Feilder, E. & Lewis, R. (2008). Management competencies for preventing and reducing stress at work: Identifying and developing the management behaviours necessary to implement the HSE Management Standards: Phase Two. London: HSE Books.
Yarker, J., Donaldson-Feilder, E., Lewis, R. & Flaxman, P. E. (2007). Management competencies for preventing and reducing stress at work: Identifying and developing the management behaviours necessary to implement the HSE Management Standards. London: HSE Books.

12

Mindful Leadership and Employee Well-Being

The Mediating Role of Leader Behaviours

Megan M. Walsh and Kara A. Arnold

Introduction

Employee well-being is a central concern for organizational research and practice, as there have been many studies that demonstrate the potential for the workplace to affect employees' psychological health (e.g., Lawson, Noblet & Rodwell, 2009). Following Wright and Huang (2012) we define well-being as a subjective, global judgement of positive affect. Research has identified many outcomes of employee well-being, such as reduced turnover and higher levels of job performance (Wright & Huang, 2012), that underscore its importance for healthy, productive workplaces. Moreover, studies have sought to identify antecedents to employee well-being to understand factors that contribute to healthier workplaces (Scott, Colquitt, Paddock & Judge, 2010). Leadership has been identified as an important antecedent to employee well-being, as leaders often help employees cope with workplace stressors and find meaning in their work (e.g., Arnold, Turner, Barling, Kelloway & McKee, 2007).

One aspect of leadership that has recently been identified as important to employee well-being is leader mindfulness. Although definitions vary, mindfulness is often defined as 'an awareness that arises through paying attention in a particular way: on purpose, in the present moment, and non-judgmentally' (Kabat-Zinn, 1994, p. 4). Reb, Narayanan and Chaturvedi (2012), positing that a leader's quality of attention and awareness influences employee well-being, found that leaders' trait mindfulness predicted facets of employee well-being such as job and need satisfaction. This study raises many important questions for future research, such as: What are the mechanisms linking leader mindfulness and employee well-being? And does leader mindfulness predict certain types of leader behaviours that contribute to employee well-being? The purpose of this chapter is to conceptually explore how leader mindfulness relates to employee well-being, using conservation of resources (COR) theory (Hobfoll, 1989) as a guiding framework.

This chapter will unfold as follows: first, we outline COR theory and discuss how leader mindfulness has the potential to create multiple positive resources for

Leading to Occupational Health and Safety: How Leadership Behaviours Impact Organizational Safety and Well-Being, First Edition.
Edited by E. Kevin Kelloway, Karina Nielsen and Jennifer K. Dimoff.

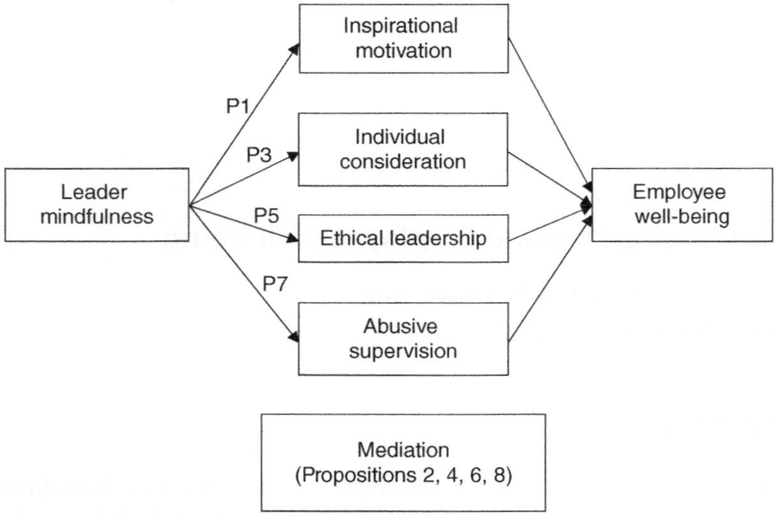

Figure 12.1 Framework outlining proposed indirect relationship between leader mindfulness and employee well-being.

followers and simultaneously reduce the likelihood of employee resource loss. Next, we suggest three key categories of leader behaviour that help explain these resource trajectories in light of COR theory: transformational behaviours, ethical leadership and abusive supervision. We will draw on theory and past empirical work to delineate a model that shows how and why leader mindfulness is associated with employee well-being. Throughout this discussion we offer propositions that explain how leader behaviours mediate the relationship between leader mindfulness and employee well-being (see Figure 12.1 for a visual summary of these relationships). Finally, we conclude by discussing the practical implications of our model for organizations in addition to theoretical implications for research.

Leader Mindfulness Through a COR Framework

Conservation of resources (COR) theory suggests that individuals are motivated to protect current resources and acquire new resources, and that many kinds of behaviours can be explained in relation to how we think about and manage our resources. Resources are defined as 'anything perceived by an individual to help attain his or her goals' (Halbesleben, Neveu, Paustian-Underdahl & Westman, 2014, p. 1138) and generally fall within four broad categories: objects, personal characteristics, conditions and energies. Objects have value because of their physical purpose (e.g. house or car), conditions are situations or states which are valued and sought after (e.g. marriage), personal characteristics are related to individuals' orientation to the world and influence how they interpret events (e.g. optimism), and energies are means through which resources are gained or that have value on their own (e.g. time, knowledge, money, attention).

In relation to employee well-being, COR theory has been used to explain and understand stress and employees' interactions with stressors. For example, many studies have found that resource depletion predicts burnout (e.g., Alarcon, 2011), while others have found that employees are motivated to avoid resource-depleting events such as interaction with an abusive supervisor (Whitman, Halbesleben & Holmes, 2014).

There are several core principles within COR theory that we draw upon to explain the mechanisms linking leader mindfulness to employee well-being. First, COR theory suggests that resource loss is psychologically harmful, and much more salient than resource gain. Second, COR theory proposes that people must invest their current resources to gain more resources in return. Given that resource gain requires some level of resource investment, COR theory also suggests that there are various trajectories that can occur, depending on individual resource reservoirs. A corollary of COR theory is that individuals can experience positive or negative resource spirals according to what they have to invest. When people lose resources (i.e., become resource-depleted) they are likely to continue to lose resources because (1) they have fewer resources to invest, and (2) they will engage in defensive behaviours to conserve their remaining resources. In contrast, when individuals gain valued resources they are likely to continue on a positive resource spiral where they can freely invest resources from their reservoir into other resource-gaining activities (Halbesleben et al., 2014).

In relation to employee well-being, COR theory has also identified *key resources* as specific subtypes that are central to selecting, altering and implementing other resources. For example, self-efficacy has been argued to be a key resource because it helps individuals utilize an abundance of other resources more effectively, such as time and knowledge (ten Brummelhuis & Bakker, 2012). Similarly, optimism is considered a key resource because it promotes a more effective response to stress (i.e., the individual is more likely to use a problem-focused coping style) and facilitates the use of other resources such as social support (ten Brummelhuis & Bakker, 2012).

Mindfulness is likely to be a key resource as its dimensions can mobilize positive resources and constrain resource-depleting activities from the leader's and their employees' points of view. Although conceptualizations of mindfulness vary, for the purposes of this chapter we define mindfulness as a dimensional human capacity that can have natural levels of variation and that can be strengthened through ongoing practice (i.e., meditation). Mindfulness as we conceptualize it has four main dimensions: present moment attention (being fully 'in the moment' and focusing on the present), intentionality (purposely focusing on the present moment), self-compassion (accepting the present moment without self-criticism) and witnessing awareness (having a non-judgemental orientation to the present moment by noticing instead of attempting to change thoughts and sensations) (Brown, Creswell & Ryan, 2015).

Research in clinical psychology demonstrates the potential for mindfulness to promote resource gain. Mindfulness has been shown to have both direct and indirect impacts on well-being, and has also promoted positive resource spirals in resource-depleted individuals with specific diagnoses. For example, in a sample of individuals with depression and anxiety (who in terms of COR theory could be considered resource-depleted), those who received mindfulness-based treatment were found to have improved mood, functionality and quality of life in comparison to waiting-list control groups who did not receive the treatment (Keng, Smoski & Robins, 2011). It is likely that such effects can be attributed to the ability of mindfulness (whether as a trait or as a resource that is experimentally induced) to be central to the activation of other resources such as adaptive emotion regulation (Farb, Anderson, Irving & Segal, 2014). Overall research suggests mindfulness is a valued resource in its own right, and is also a key resource because it helps activate other resources to create positive resource spirals.

Although most research on mindfulness has taken place in a psychological context and considered it as a form of therapy, there has recently been a growing interest in mindfulness from a business perspective. The workplace is a unique context where individuals are potentially vulnerable to resource depletion on a daily basis because of their continued resource investment at work. Therefore, the extension of research on mindfulness as a key resource in the workplace is a worthy area of investigation. From an employee perspective, Hülsheger, Alberts, Feinholdt and Lang (2013) found that employees' mindfulness predicted lower levels of emotional exhaustion, which was mediated by lower levels of employee surface acting (i.e., faking emotions). In relation to COR theory this would suggest that even in organizations, where emotional display requirements can be strong, mindfulness is a key resource that allows employees to improve well-being through a presumably more genuine form of emotion expression.

Evidently, mindfulness is a key resource for employees because it predicts primarily positive outcomes at work (e.g. Hülsheger et al., 2013). We extend this idea by suggesting that individuals in leadership positions will similarly benefit from the positive outcomes of mindfulness. Specifically, we propose that leader mindfulness will mobilize related resources for leaders, which will create positive resource spirals and enable them to enact positive leadership styles. Roche, Haar and Luthans (2014) showed that the relationship between leader mindfulness and leader well-being is mediated by increased levels of leader's psychological capital. Although there are fewer studies on mindfulness from a leader's perspective, findings such as this suggest that mindfulness may enable leaders to build strong resource reservoirs (through psychological capital and other resources), which promote psychological health.

Furthermore, related studies suggest that part of mindfulness's impact on leader well-being may be due to the positive resource spirals it can create in these types of positions. For example, Byrne, Dionisi, Barling et al. (2014) have shown that leaders who are resource-depleted are likely to enact ineffective leadership, whereas leaders with less depletion are more likely to be transformational. Leadership style itself can also be a source of resource drain or gain for leaders. In one study, leaders who were transformational were more likely to report reduced burnout; and this relationship was indirect through the use of genuine emotion (in contrast to faking or suppressing their feelings; Arnold, Connelly, Walsh & Martin Ginis, 2015). Taken together, these studies show the potential importance of positive resource spirals in leadership: leaders who have many resources are likely to invest in positive leadership behaviours, which further promotes resource gain through adaptive emotion regulation and lower stress levels. Given that mindfulness is one route to resource abundance for leaders (e.g. Roche et al., 2014), research suggests that mindfulness will promote a positive spiral of leader well-being and positive leadership behaviours that ultimately trickle down to create positive resources for employees as well.

Leadership Styles and Behaviours

We focus primarily on three styles of leadership and related behaviours (transformational, ethical and abusive) as mediators of the leader mindfulness/employee well-being relationship. There are several reasons for this focus. First, transformational leadership is of interest given that it has been one of the most widely researched leadership styles since the beginning of the new millennium (Dinh, Lord, Gardner et al., 2014). Furthermore, transformational leadership has been the subject of research relating to resource spirals within COR theory, which makes it central to our discussion of mindfulness as a contributor to positive resource spirals within leadership (Arnold, Connelly et al., 2015). Second, ethical leadership is characterized by a strong commitment to, and demonstration of, morally appropriate behaviour on the part of leaders (Brown & Treviño, 2006). We propose that communicating and consistently aligning with ethical values requires a significant resource investment on the part of a leader. As we will discuss, mindfulness is a particularly useful resource for attending and responding to ethical dilemmas from a leader's perspective. Finally, we contrast these positive leadership styles with abusive supervision to demonstrate how, even for leaders who we conceptualize as significantly resource-depleted, mindfulness can be a resource that helps form the beginnings of a positive resource spiral and lower the likelihood that leaders will enact abusive behaviour. For each leader behaviour we will begin by linking mindfulness to the leader behaviour of interest, and will then explain how these behaviours will mediate the relationship between leader mindfulness and employee well-being.

Mindfulness and Transformational Leadership

Transformational leaders are those who inspire followers to perform beyond expectations and achieve extraordinary outcomes (Bass, 1985). This leadership style is characterized by four dimensions: (1) idealized influence (acting as a role model for followers to identify with), (2) inspirational motivation (motivating followers by communicating an inspiring vision for the future), (3) intellectual stimulation (encouraging creativity and innovation), and (4) individual consideration (giving special attention to each follower's needs for development and support) (e.g., Bass & Riggio, 2006). Mindfulness has been shown to correlate with transformational leadership in one previous study of university academic chairs and supervisors (Gieseke, 2014). We build upon this finding and argue that a focus on specific transformational behaviours as they relate to mindfulness, and a greater focus on mindfulness as distinct from other constructs in Gieseke's (2014) study (e.g., leader spirituality), will have greater theoretical and practical implications.

Van Knippenberg and Sitkin (2013), in a critical assessment of the transformational leadership literature, suggest that there are challenges with transformational leadership theory that warrant a research focus on its separate dimensions. First, they suggest that transformational leadership theory does not fully capture how the specific dimensions of transformational leadership combine. Second, the theory does not effectively explain how each dimension contributes to its mediating processes. In this chapter we respond to these criticisms by focusing on two behaviours within the transformational model that are conceptually closely related to mindfulness: inspirational motivation and individual consideration. While the overall constellation of transformational behaviours may correlate with mindfulness, we posit that these two specific dimensions warrant closer attention as these behaviours have the potential to be influenced by mindfulness to a greater degree.

Mindfulness and Inspirational Motivation

The key activity within inspirational motivation is communicating a positive vision for the future of the organization. Vision can be defined as 'a set of beliefs about how people should act, and interact, to attain some idealized future state' (Strange & Mumford, 2002, p. 344). Although research has tended to focus on the outcomes of vision, some research has identified factors that contribute to the likelihood that leaders will develop and communicate an inspiring vision. Emotional expressivity on the part of leaders has been shown to predict visionary leadership (Groves, 2006). Furthermore, Strange and Mumford (2002) have shown that creating a vision requires reflection on the part of the leader, in addition to the ability to extract key goals and purpose in relation to personal experience and knowledge of business operations. Taken together, these findings suggest that developing and communicating a vision is closely tied to emotions, reflection and a deep understanding of the operations and needs of the organization.

We propose that the ability to enact visionary behaviour is impacted by mindfulness as a key leader resource. The dimensions of mindfulness will promote a leader's ability to both develop and communicate a vision in a compelling way. In terms of developing a vision, mindfulness is a unique leader resource that enables the leader to combine awareness and reflection to clearly understand the strategic goals within their organization or departmental unit. As discussed above, it is unlikely that a leader will be able to develop a vision without thoroughly understanding the inner and outer workings of their work group. With higher levels of mindfulness, leaders should be more likely to be present and to focus their attention more fully on how the organization is currently operating and what their next strategic moves should be. Empirical studies showing the positive relationship between mindfulness and working memory (Jha, Stanley, Kiyonaga, Wong & Gelfand, 2010), for example, support the idea that being in the present moment allows individuals to quickly integrate information and hold onto ideas and concepts more effectively than when they are on autopilot.

Interestingly, Reb, Sim, Chintakananda and Bhave (2015) suggest that being mindful could be detrimental to leadership as it may not allow for future-oriented planning. We argue, however, that being mindfully aware does not necessarily mean being static or unchanging. Instead, mindfulness promotes a stronger present-moment focus that allows leaders to fully absorb and remember their external environment and to truly understand the organization's needs. In addition, the self-compassion and witnessing awareness dimensions of mindfulness are likely to promote the level of reflection needed to integrate information in a visionary way. By having an attitude of acceptance and allowing thoughts to drift periodically when needed, leaders who are mindful will be likely to have enough flexibility to think creatively and long-term about strategic goals, while simultaneously having a higher level of focus than leaders who are less mindful.

Mindfulness further presents itself as a key resource that helps leaders to communicate a vision. As discussed above, a key aspect of communicating a vision successfully is the level of emotional expressivity that is shown by the leader who relays the vision. As Humphrey, Pollack and Hawver (2008) have noted, there are broad ranges of emotions that need to be expressed in leadership positions, and communicating a vision requires emotional expression to spur interest and dedication from followers. For example, leaders may need to express hope and optimism to promote their strategic goals, but may also need to express anger as part of a vision if there is something that must be overcome or improved upon in the organization.

A mindful leader's ability to communicate a vision is likely to rest on his or her ability to be in tune with the emotional needs of a situation or an individual, and to express vision in a genuinely emotional way. For example, Schutte and Malouff (2011) found that mindfulness predicts high levels of emotional intelligence, which is an individual ability to express, manage and perceive emotions (Brotheridge, 2006). Thus, a leader who is mindful is more likely to understand what types of emotions followers are feeling, and what emotional expressions would make a vision more impactful for them. Despite the fact that mindfulness has been linked with lower levels of faking emotions (Hülsheger et al., 2013), research has also shown that transformational leadership, of which vision is a key component, is related to higher levels of genuine emotion in comparison to surface acting (Arnold, Connelly et al., 2015). If these are taken together, theory suggests that mindful leaders are more likely to communicate a vision effectively because they have the resources to understand and manage the emotional climate to promote vision effectively. Although this could require some emotional regulation, as leaders will not always feel the emotions needed in a given situation, there is evidence to suggest that a key aspect of being visionary is expressing emotions as genuinely as possible, which mindful leaders are well equipped to do. Thus, we make the following proposition:

Proposition 1: Leader mindfulness will positively predict inspirational motivation.

Inspirational Motivation and Employee Well-Being

As we have outlined, COR theory and accumulating research evidence suggest that leader mindfulness will act as a resource that mobilizes the transformational dimension of inspirational motivation. We propose that, in turn, investment on the part of mindful leaders in these transformational behaviours will promote resource gain for employees in the form of improved well-being. First, there are theoretical arguments and empirical evidence to support the idea that activities mindful leaders engage in could create positive resource spirals for employees that result in higher levels of employee well-being. Transformational leadership as a whole has been empirically linked to higher performance, satisfaction, organizational commitment, and lower levels of stress on the part of followers (Judge & Piccolo, 2004). This suggests that its dimensions, two of which are discussed in this chapter, are important resources for followers that facilitate various positive outcomes; it is clear that followers who have a transformational leader will have an abundance of resources either to avoid resource loss when facing stressors (Arnold & Walsh, 2015) or to capitalize on resource-gaining activities such as experiencing a positive challenge as a team (Zhang, LePine, Buckman & Wei, 2013). Research has also linked transformational leadership to employee well-being through mediating resources, further supporting the idea of a spiralling relationship (e.g., Arnold, Turner et al., 2007; Nielsen, Randall, Yarker & Brenner, 2008).

Looking more closely at inspirational motivation, empirical studies similarly support the idea that mindful leadership relates to employee well-being through this leader behaviour. One study showed that visionary leadership predicted lower employee burnout (Densten, 2005). This suggests that mindful leaders use vision to promote resource gain for followers. Having a vision gives employees something to work towards and clarifies their goals, promoting resource gain in the form of confidence and increased motivation.

Stam, van Knippenberg and Wisse (2009) showed that the content of visions interacted with followers' own orientation to the future (i.e., whether they were motivated to avoid fearful situations or to promote positive situations). Prevention-related visions promoted higher performance for followers who were also prevention-focused, and the reverse was true for promotion-focused followers. To some extent, this suggests that the motivating effects of vision depend on how well the vision content matches the motivation of followers. As discussed above, mindful leaders are expected to have higher emotional intelligence, so it is likely that they could promote resource gain through a better ability to perceive and match their visions to their followers' needs and motivations. In turn, this could relate to higher employee well-being, as a mindful leader's ability to accommodate a vision to situations could promote higher levels of employee resources. Taking the above evidence and theoretical arguments into account,

Proposition 2: The relationship between leader mindfulness and employee well-being will be mediated by inspirational motivation.

Mindfulness and Individual Consideration

Individual consideration is a positive leader behaviour that is characterized by two distinct components: developmental and supportive behaviours (Rafferty & Griffin, 2006). Supportive behaviours are characterized by a leader's 'concern for, and [taking] account of, followers' needs and preferences when making decisions' (Rafferty & Griffin, 2006, p. 39). Developmental behaviours encompass activities such as coaching, identifying developmental opportunities for followers, and encouraging follower development.

Taking individual consideration as a whole, constructs such as an internal locus of control and self-acceptance have been shown to predict this specific aspect of transformational leadership (Bass & Riggio, 2006). Mindfulness, as a key leader resource, is likely to promote high levels of individual consideration when these correlates are taken into account. First, a key dimension of mindfulness is ongoing self-compassion, which is closely related to the self-acceptance necessary to enact individual consideration. This dimension of mindfulness requires individuals to accept what is happening in the present moment without rumination or worry about future events. Leaders who are mindful are thus more likely to be individually considerate, as they are able to accept what is happening in their own position and fully focus on the needs of followers. Furthermore, St. Charles (2010) has empirically shown that internal locus of control is strongly correlated with mindfulness. This further supports the idea that mindful leaders will be likely to enact individual consideration; with a sense that they are key influencers in the environment, and a strong focus on accepting and absorbing the present moment, leaders who are mindful have the resources to recognize followers' needs and also to act on them by offering support and guidance.

Mindfulness is also linked to individual consideration when the dimensions of support and development are considered on their own. Although not related specifically to leadership, factors such as social embeddedness predict socially supportive behaviours (Langford, Bowsher, Maloney & Lillis, 1997), which are conceptually similar to the supportive component of individual consideration. In terms of the developmental aspect of individual consideration, various antecedents of developmental activities have been identified, such as low work–life conflict and psychological need satisfaction on the part of leaders (Stebbings, Taylor, Spray & Ntoumanis, 2012). Overall, leaders' individual consideration is highly related to perceptions of control, social connection, acceptance, and the balance between work, home life and personal needs.

If we break down individual consideration into its supportive and developmental components, mindfulness can further be identified as a predictor of each of these distinct types of behaviours. In relation to supportive behaviour, mindfulness has shown the potential to create positive resource spirals in terms of social networks. For example, mindfulness has been related in clinical studies to improved interpersonal relationships, which has been explained by an improved ability to respond constructively in relationships (Barnes, Brown, Krusemark, Campbell & Rogge, 2007). As mentioned above, social embeddedness can predict supportive behaviours, so it is likely that mindfulness, as a key resource that facilitates positive relationships, will subsequently predict supportive behaviour on the part of leaders. In other words, leaders who are mindful are more likely to develop positive relationships with followers and to be securely embedded within their work groups. In terms of development, other research has similarly shown the ability of mindfulness to activate resources related to investment in developmental behaviours. For example, having greater mindfulness predicts work–family balance, and need satisfaction (Allen & Kiburz, 2012; Schultz, Ryan, Niemiec, Legate & Williams, 2015), which are complementary resources that predict developmental behaviours. It is likely that leader mindfulness will similarly mobilize leaders' resources to promote individual consideration. Thus, we propose the following:

Proposition 3: Leader mindfulness will positively predict individual consideration.

Individual Consideration and Employee Well-Being

As with the discussion of inspirational motivation, research similarly suggests that mindful leaders who enact individual consideration will instil positive resources in their followers to promote well-being. Rafferty and Griffin (2006) showed that individual consideration is associated with various positive outcomes such as job satisfaction, affective commitment, self-efficacy and career certainty. Many of these outcomes are closely related to employee well-being. Some studies, for example, use job satisfaction as an indication of work-related well-being (Kooij, Guest, Clinton et al., 2013). Thus, Rafferty and Griffin's (2006) findings suggest that individual consideration also predicts employee well-being on a broader scale, as we have conceptualized it.

We propose that the relationship between leader mindfulness and employee well-being will hinge on the individual consideration behaviours that leader mindfulness promotes. As discussed previously, leader mindfulness is closely related to individual consideration in a number of ways (e.g. through locus of control and predicting supportive behaviours). According to COR theory, the relationship of mindfulness to key correlates of individual consideration suggests that it is a key resource for leaders that helps facilitate supportive and developmental aspects of individual consideration. In turn, this positive behaviour from a leader will be an important resource for employee well-being; having a mindful leader who provides both developmental opportunities and support is an important resource that helps employees to thrive in the workplace. A leader's support will help followers avoid resource loss. In addition, having a considerate leader who invests in follower development gives followers the recognition they need to engage in their own resource investment, such as accepting training opportunities offered by their mindful leader. In turn, this will create positive resource spirals for employees. On the basis of this review we propose:

Proposition 4: The relationship between leader mindfulness and employee well-being will be mediated by individual consideration.

Ethical Leadership

Ethical leadership is defined as 'the demonstration of normatively appropriate conduct and the promotion of such conduct to followers' (Brown, Treviño & Harrison, 2005, p. 120). This leadership style is composed of two key concepts: being a moral manager (acting as an ethical example through actions and actively managing morality by encouraging ethical behaviour and discouraging unethical behaviour), and being a moral person (having ethical characteristics such as trustworthiness and fairness). As it is a newer leadership construct, research is only beginning to identify the factors that encourage ethical behaviour on the part of leaders. Mayer, Aquino, Greenbaum and Kuenzi (2012) found that having a moral identity internalization (internalizing notions of right and wrong) and having a moral identity symbolization (actively expressing and engaging in ethical behaviour) both predicted leaders' degree of ethical leadership. Other studies have found that factors such as leaders' honesty and interactional fairness were closely related to ethical behaviours (Brown, Treviño & Harrison, 2005). Taken together, these findings suggest that ethical leadership rests upon a foundation of having a moral identity, in addition to having personality traits and characteristics that promote the expression of ethical behaviour.

In relation to ethical leadership, mindfulness presents itself as a key resource that can facilitate leaders' resource investment in ethical behaviours. Giluk (2009), in a meta-analysis of mindfulness and personality traits, found that mindfulness is most strongly related to conscientiousness. COR theory would suggest that mindfulness is a resource that allows leaders to be responsible and detail-oriented in organizations. Mindful leaders, given their related resource of conscientiousness, will be more likely to enact ethical behaviours because they will be more likely to be vigilant and careful when ethical dilemmas arise. For example, given the level of conscientiousness-related mindfulness, a mindful leader will examine all ethical dimensions of a situation to demonstrate to followers, and to themselves, that ethical issues must be considered thoroughly.

In addition to personality traits, mindfulness has been shown to promote a greater sensitivity to ethical issues in followers (Eisenbeiss & van Knippenberg, 2015) and increased ethical decision making in student samples (Shapiro, Jazaieri & Goldin, 2012). It is likely that this ethical sensitivity would translate to leadership as well. Leaders who are mindful, given their heightened awareness and non-judgemental orientation, will be more likely to translate a greater sensitivity to ethical issues into ethical leadership behaviours. A mindful leader will be able to both identify ethical issues and act in ways that are fair and appropriate. For example, having an intentional focus on the present moment will help leaders fully absorb information from the environment that will help them pinpoint situations where attention needs to be paid to values of what is right and wrong within the organization. Furthermore, having a mindful, non-judgemental perspective will help leaders to communicate ethical issues in way that is fair and compelling from followers' points of view. Hence, we propose:

Proposition 5: Leader mindfulness will positively predict ethical leadership.

Ethical Leadership and Employee Well-Being

Evidently, leader mindfulness may promote greater resource investment in ethical behaviours. We propose that leader mindfulness, through this mobilization of positive leader behaviours, will relate to higher levels of employee well-being. Although research on ethical leadership is relatively new, some studies are beginning to uncover its relationship with employee well-being and related resources. The resource of ethical leadership has been shown to trickle down to employees; Mayer, Kuenzi, Greenbaum, Bardes and Salvador (2009) found that ethical leadership from the top of the organization predicted supervisory ethical leadership, lower group-level deviance, and higher levels of group organizational citizenship behaviours (OCBs). This study illustrates how leader mindfulness creates positive resource spirals for both leaders and employees: leaders who are mindful are able to activate related resources such as ethical leadership, and having this ethical orientation is an important resource for leaders at lower levels, as well as for their employee work groups. Having the resource of an ethical leader, and consequently an ethical supervisor, gives employees the support and guidance they need to enact OCBs at a greater level, and to mitigate potential resource drains such as group deviance. In turn, the resources that are cultivated at the lowest level in this example (OCBs) promote positive resource spirals because OCBs are likely to make employees feel good about themselves, while simultaneously acting as an instrumental resource to their peers. A team whose members support each other and go above and beyond their job descriptions build resources for one other, and this allows each individual on the team to further invest valued resources in their individual well-being.

More directly, research has also demonstrated the potential for ethical leadership to directly predict employee well-being, which further supports the idea that resources related to leader mindfulness promote resource gain at the follower level. Chughtai, Byrne and Flood (2015) found that ethical leadership predicted employee well-being as measured by work engagement and low levels of emotional exhaustion. Furthermore, Kalshoven and Boon (2012) found using a COR framework that ethical leadership predicted employee well-being, which subsequently related to higher levels of helping on behalf of employees. This suggests that ethical leadership is an important resource for employees in terms of well-being and that followers who have ethical leaders are likely to experience positive resource spirals. In other words, Kalshoven and Boon's (2012) findings highlight the potential for resource-abundant employees to further invest in other resource-gaining behaviours, such as helping, when they have an ethical leader. Taking empirical and theoretical arguments into account, we propose the following:

Proposition 6: The relationship between leader mindfulness and employee well-being will be mediated by ethical leadership.

Mindfulness and Abusive Supervision

Abusive supervision is defined as 'subordinates' perceptions of the extent to which supervisors engage in the sustained display of hostile verbal and nonverbal behaviors, excluding physical contact' (Tepper, 2000, p. 178). Not surprisingly, most outcomes of abusive supervision are negative, such as workplace deviance (Mackey, Frieder, Brees & Martinko, 2015). A recent meta-analysis also identified predictors of abusive supervision, such as neuroticism and leaders' perceptions of injustice (Mackey et al., 2015). According to COR theory, these findings suggest that abusive leaders are resource-depleted, which makes it difficult for them to invest in positive behaviour and more likely to engage in defensive, hostile tactics to conserve the few resources they have. An illustrative study by Burton, Hoobler and Scheuer (2012) showed that leader resource depletion predicted abusive supervision.

We propose that mindfulness would help decrease leaders' levels of abusive supervision by lowering the likelihood that a leader would waste resources on hostile behaviours, and by subsequently improving their ability to deal with resource-depleting events in a positive way. First, mindfulness is a strong predictor of psychological well-being, and implementing mindfulness training has been proved to be an effective stress management strategy (Keng et al., 2011). This is in direct contrast with abusive supervision, which is predicted by resource depletion. A mindful leader, who has a high level of resources such as intentionality and self-compassion, will not feel the need to hold onto resources defensively (i.e., behave in a hostile manner). Instead, even when experiencing potentially resource-depleting situations, they will be more likely to accept their current resource state. In terms of leader behaviours, this acceptance means that mindful leaders are less likely to be abusive, since they are not focusing on their potential losses. Instead, a mindful leader is likely to remain neutral in resource-depleting situations instead of wasting resources on hostile behaviours.

Second, an important resource-depleting event for leaders which predicts abusive supervision is the experience of injustice (Mackey et al., 2015), and empirical work on mindfulness demonstrates its potential to reduce this specific source of depletion for leaders. In an experimental study, Long and Christian (2015) found that mindfulness buffered the relationships between injustice and ruminative thought and negative emotion, thereby reducing the likelihood that people will retaliate against workplace injustice. Although this was not explored with a sample of leaders, it is likely that mindfulness could similarly help leaders overcome this source of resource depletion if abusive supervision is a form of retaliation. A mindful leader would be more likely to keep their thoughts focused in the current moment when experiencing injustice, and instead of ruminating and subsequently lashing out at followers (and thus further draining their resources) they would remain focused in the current moment and recognize that retaliating with hostility would not be a productive reaction.

Other research similarly suggests that mindfulness reduces emotional reactivity (see Shapiro, Wang & Peltason, 2015 for a review). This further supports the idea that mindful leaders would be more likely to stop and think about their behaviours before enacting abusive supervision. Overall, the non-judgemental and focused awareness of mindfulness would allow leaders to deal more effectively with injustice and other stressors at work, instead of taking it out on followers in the form of abusive supervision. Taken together, the arguments above bring forward the following proposition:

Proposition 7: Leader mindfulness will negatively predict abusive supervision.

Abusive Supervision and Employee Well-Being

As outlined above, virtually every study of abusive supervision has found its outcomes to be negative regarding employee well-being. For example, studies have found that abusive supervision directly predicted lower levels of employee well-being and higher levels of stress, strain, and negative interpersonal relationships at work (Kernan, Watson, Chen & Kim, 2011; Lian, Ferris & Brown, 2012; Wheeler, Halbesleben & Whitman, 2013). Overall, COR theory would suggest that abusive supervision creates a negative spiral of resource depletion for followers, as they experience personal stress and are less likely to have the positive relationships needed to build other resources, such as social support.

Mindfulness reduces the likelihood of leaders enacting abusive behaviour; this is another factor that helps explain the relationship between leader mindfulness and employee well-being. With mindfulness as a key resource, leaders have an abundance of resources, are less likely to suffer from the resource depletion that predicts abusive supervision, and are better able to handle resource-depleting events. Although the relationship between leaders' mindfulness and employee well-being depends on the potential for mindfulness to encourage positive leadership behaviours, it is also important to take into account that these relationships may also hinge on the ability of leader mindfulness to prevent negative behaviours. Thus, our final proposition makes the point that leader mindfulness may predict simultaneous processes in relation to employee well-being:

Proposition 8: The relationship between leader mindfulness and employee well-being will be mediated by abusive supervision.

Practical Implications

Many organizations are beginning to recognize the positive outcomes of mindfulness at various levels in organizations. Companies such as Google have trained executives in mindfulness techniques (Shachtman, 2013). Taking a COR perspective, however, allows organizations to understand exactly *why* leader mindfulness predicts higher levels of employee well-being. This understanding can help practitioners to implement leader mindfulness programmes that are based on their benefits for both leaders and followers. In an organization that is aiming to improve employee well-being, it may be more cost-effective, for example, to promote mindfulness training at the leader level instead of throughout the whole organization, as our chapter has highlighted the potential for the benefits of leader mindfulness to trickle down to the follower level. In addition, training leaders to be mindful has the added benefit of improving leader behaviours, which further helps to justify the focus on cultivating mindfulness at the top of the organization. The relationship of leader mindfulness to inspirational motivation, for example, is significant given that having a strategic vision is an important skill that many top-level leaders lack (Ibarra & Obodaru, 2009). Thus, training leaders to be more mindful can have the simultaneous benefits of improving the organization's direction and performance and improving the well-being of its employees.

Although some mindfulness programmes are costly in terms of time and money (for example, the most popular mindfulness training programmes take eight weeks), some experimental research does suggest that implementing shorter interventions can have positive impacts. In one study, having participants take part in ten-minute mindfulness exercises was enough to help them perform better on a task (Daniel, 2014), whereas other studies have shown effects from three- or four-day versions of mindfulness training (Brown, Creswell et al., 2015). This chapter further highlights the benefits of considering mindfulness and its resource-building potential at the leadership level. For leaders who are under tight time pressures and have high levels of stress, having the option to do a short mindfulness training programme can be one realistic change to make towards improving employee well-being.

Research Implications

By outlining the processes potentially linking leader mindfulness to employee well-being, we contribute to COR theory and bring forward avenues for future empirical work. First, we contribute to COR theory by discussing in detail the concept of mindfulness as a key resource in the specific context of leadership. One challenge in COR theory has been defining and categorizing resources (Halbesleben et al., 2014), so the conceptual discussion in this chapter is a useful exercise for pinpointing the benefits of mindfulness on its own and its relationship to other resources. We contribute to theory by suggesting that mindfulness, particularly in a leadership context, has the ability to mobilize other resources that are central from a contextual point of view; leaders who are mindful are more likely to alter any tendency to abusive behaviours and also to display positive behaviours such as individual consideration and ethical leadership.

In addition to inspiring empirical studies to test the propositions discussed in this chapter, we wish to outline two other avenues for future study. One important direction would be for researchers to consider the impact of mindfulness on other resources related to leadership, and its subsequent relationship with employee well-being. Organizational culture, for example, is one construct that can have important relationships with employee well-being (Beauregard, 2011), and could be another potential mediator between leader mindfulness and employee well-being. It would be helpful to understand whether leader mindfulness would be far-reaching enough to influence employee well-being through this type of group-level construct, or whether it influences employee well-being primarily through leader behaviours that impact employees individually. Second, researchers might also consider investigating how certain components of mindfulness differentially impact employee well-being. For example, it may be the case that present-moment attention is the most important dimension of mindfulness for leaders to focus on to promote follower well-being. This type of finding would have important implications for research and practice. Mindfulness training programmes, for example, could be streamlined to focus on certain aspects of mindfulness instead of others to make the most of leaders' limited time. From a theoretical point of view, these types of studies could bring forward whether the dimensions of leader mindfulness can be considered as an important group of resources that predict employee well-being, instead of considering the concept of mindfulness broadly as a singular key resource.

Conclusion

Given the promising relationship between leader mindfulness and employee well-being, this chapter has conceptually explored the mediating processes of this relationship in more detail using COR theory as a guiding framework. We have provided a conceptual model based on theory and past empirical work that shows why leader mindfulness is associated with employee well-being. Mindfulness has the potential to act as a key resource that alters other resources specific to a leadership context, and which ultimately trickles down to promote resource gain at the follower level.

References

Alarcon, G. M. (2011). A meta-analysis of burnout with job demands, resources, and attitudes. *Journal of Vocational Behavior*, 79(2), 549–62. doi: 10.1016/j.jvb.2011.03.007.

Allen, T. D. & Kiburz, K. M. (2012). Trait mindfulness and work–family balance among working parents: The mediating effects of vitality and sleep quality. *Journal of Vocational Behavior*, 80, 372–79.

Arnold, K. A., Connelly, C. E., Walsh, M. M. & Martin Ginis, K. A. (2015). Leadership styles, emotion regulation, and burnout. *Journal of Occupational Health Psychology*, 20(4): 481–90. doi: 10.1037/a0039045.

Arnold, K. A., Turner, N., Barling, J., Kelloway, E. K. & McKee, M. C. (2007). Transformational leadership and psychological well-being: The mediating role of meaningful work. *Journal of Occupational Health Psychology*, 12(3), 193–203. doi: 10.1037/1076-8998.12.3.193.

Arnold, K. A. & Walsh, M. M. (2015). Customer incivility and employee well-being: Testing the moderating effects of meaning, perspective taking and transformational leadership. *Work & Stress*, 29(4), 362–78. doi: 10.1080/02678373.2015.1075234.

Barnes, S., Brown, K. W., Krusemark, E., Campbell, W. K. & Rogge, R. D. (2007). The role of mindfulness in romantic relationship satisfaction and responses to relationship stress. *Journal of Marital and Family Therapy*, 33(4), 482–500.
Bass, B. (1985). *Leadership and Performance Beyond Expectations*. New York: Free Press.
Bass, B. & Riggio, R. (2006). *Transformational Leadership*. 2nd edn. Mahwah, NJ: Lawrence Erlbaum Associates.
Beauregard, T. A. (2011). Direct and indirect links between organizational work–home culture and employee well-being. *British Journal of Management*, 22(2), 218–37. doi: 10.1111/j.1467-8551.2010.00723.x.
Brotheridge, C. M. (2006). The role of emotional intelligence and other individual difference variables in predicting emotional labor relative to situational demands. *Psicothema*, 18, 139–44.
Brown, K. W., Creswell, J. D. & Ryan, R. M. (eds). (2015). *Handbook of Mindfulness*. New York: Guilford Press.
Brown, M. E. & Treviño, L. K. (2006). Ethical leadership: A review and future directions. *Leadership Quarterly*, 17(6), 595–616. doi: 10.1016/j.leaqua.2006.10.004.
Brown, M. E., Treviño, L. K. & Harrison, D. A. (2005). Ethical leadership: A social learning perspective for construct development and testing. *Organizational Behavior and Human Decision Processes*, 97, 117–34.
Burton, J. P., Hoobler, J. M. & Scheuer, M. L. (2012). Supervisory workplace stress and abusive supervision: The buffering effect of exercise. *Journal of Business and Psychology*, 27, 271–79.
Byrne, A., Dionisi, A. M., Barling, J., Akers, A., Robertson, J., Lys, R., Wylie, J. & Dupré, K. (2014). The depleted leader: The influence of leaders' diminished psychological resources on leadership behaviors. *Leadership Quarterly*, 25(2), 344–57. doi: 10.1016/j.leaqua.2013.09.003.
Chughtai, A., Byrne, M. & Flood, B. (2015). Linking ethical leadership to employee well-being: The role of trust in supervisor. *Journal of Business Ethics*, 128, 653–63.
Daniel, C. J. Z. (2014). Mindfulness and test performance after stereotype activation: A randomized experiment. B.Sc. thesis, Portland State University.
Densten, I. L. (2005). The relationship between visioning behaviours of leaders and follower burnout. *British Journal of Management*, 16(2), 105–18. doi: 10.1111/j.1467-8551.2005.00428.x.
Dinh, J. E., Lord, R. G., Gardner, W. L., Meuser, J. D., Liden, R. C. & Hu, J. (2014). Leadership theory and research in the new millennium: Current theoretical trends and changing perspectives. *Leadership Quarterly*, 25(1), 36–62. doi: 10.1016/j.leaqua.2013.11.005.
Eisenbeiss, S. A. & van Knippenberg, D. (2015). On ethical leadership impact: The role of follower mindfulness and moral emotions. *Journal of Organizational Behavior*, 36(2), 182–95. doi: 10.1002/job.1968.
Farb, N., Anderson, A. K., Irving, J. A. & Segal, Z. V. (2014). Mindfulness interventions and emotion regulation. In J. J. Gross (ed.), *Handbook of Emotion Regulation*. New York: Guilford Press.
Gieseke, A. R. (2014). The relationship between spiritual intelligence, mindfulness, and transformational leadership among public higher education leaders. Doctoral dissertation, Northeastern University.

Giluk, T. (2009). Mindfulness, big five personality, and affect: A meta-analysis. *Personality and Individual Differences*, 47(8), 805–11.

Groves, K. S. (2006). Leader emotional expressivity, visionary leadership, and organizational change. *Leadership & Organization Development Journal*, 27(7), 566–83. doi: 10.1108/01437730610692425.

Halbesleben, J. R. B., Neveu, J. P., Paustian-Underdahl, S. C. & Westman, M. (2014). Getting to the 'COR': Understanding the role of resources in conservation of resources theory. *Journal of Management*, 40(5), 1334–64. doi: 10.1177/0149206314527130.

Hobfoll, S. E. (1989). Conservation of resources: A new attempt at conceptualizing stress. *American Psychologist*, 44(3), 513–24.

Hülsheger, U., Alberts, H., Feinholdt, A. & Lang, J. W. B. (2013). Benefits of mindfulness at work: The role of mindfulness in emotion regulation, emotional exhaustion, and job satisfaction. *Journal of Applied Psychology*, 98(2), 310–25.

Humphrey, R. H., Pollack, J. M. & Hawver, T. (2008). Leading with emotional labor. *Journal of Managerial Psychology*, 23(2), 151–68. doi: 10.1108/02683940810850790.

Ibarra, H. & Obodaru, O. (2009). *Women and the vision thing*. Harvard Business Review, January, 62–70.

Jha, A. P., Stanley, E. A., Kiyonaga, A., Wong, L. & Gelfand, L. (2010). Examining the protective effects of mindfulness training on working memory capacity and affective experience. *Emotion*, 10(1), 54–64. doi: 10.1037/a0018438.

Judge, T. A. & Piccolo, R. F. (2004). Transformational and transactional leadership: A meta-analytic test of their relative validity. *Journal of Applied Psychology*, 89(5), 755–68. doi: 10.1037/0021-9010.89.5.755.

Kabat-Zinn, J. (1994). *Wherever You Go There You Are: Mindfulness Meditation in Everyday Life*. New York: Hyperion.

Kalshoven, K. & Boon, C. (2012). Ethical leadership, employee well-being, and helping: The moderating role of human resource management. *Journal of Personnel Psychology*, 11(1), 60–8.

Keng, S. L., Smoski, M. J. & Robins, C. J. (2011). Effects of mindfulness on psychological health: A review of empirical studies. *Clinical Psychology Review*, 31(6), 1041–56. doi: 10.1016/j.cpr.2011.04.006.

Kernan, M., Watson, S., Chen, F. F. & Kim, T. G. (2011). How cultural values affect the impact of abusive supervision on worker attitudes. *Cross Cultural Management*, 18, 464–84.

Kooij, D. T. A. M., Guest, D. E., Clinton, M., Knight, T., Jansen, P. G. W. & Dikkers, J. S. E. (2013). How the impact of HR practices on employee well-being and performance changes with age. *Human Resource Management Journal*, 23(1), 18–35. doi: 10.1111/1748-8583.12000.

Langford, C., Bowsher, J., Maloney, J. & Lillis, P. (1997). Social support: A conceptual analysis. *Journal of Advanced Nursing*, 25, 95–100.

Lawson, K. J., Noblet, A. J. & Rodwell, J. J. (2009). Promoting employee wellbeing: The relevance of work characteristics and organizational justice. *Health Promotion International*, 24(3), 223–33. doi: 10.1093/heapro/dap025.

Lian, H., Ferris, D. & Brown, D. J. (2012). Does taking the good with the bad make things worse? How abusive supervision and leader–member exchange interact to impact need satisfaction and organizational deviance. *Organizational Behavior and Human Decision Processes*, 117, 41–52.

Long, E. C. & Christian, M. S. (2015). Mindfulness buffers retaliatory responses to injustice: A regulatory approach. *Journal of Applied Psychology*, 100(5), 1409–22. doi: 10.1037/apl0000019.

Mackey, J. D., Frieder, R. E., Brees, J. R. & Martinko, M. J. (2015). Abusive supervision: A meta-analysis and empirical review. *Journal of Management*. doi: 10.1177/0149206315573997.

Mayer, D. M., Aquino, K., Greenbaum, R. L. & Kuenzi, M. (2012). Who displays ethical leadership, and why does it matter? An examination of antecedents and consequences of ethical leadership. *Academy of Management Journal*, 55(1), 151–71. doi: 10.5465/amj.2008.0276.

Mayer, D. M., Kuenzi, M., Greenbaum, R., Bardes, M. & Salvador, R. (2009). How low does ethical leadership flow? Test of a trickle-down model. *Organizational Behavior and Human Decision Processes*, 108(1), 1–13. doi: 10.1016/j.obhdp.2008.04.002.

Nielsen, K., Randall, R., Yarker, J. & Brenner, S. O. (2008). The effects of transformational leadership on followers' perceived work characteristics and psychological well-being: A longitudinal study. *Work & Stress*, 22, 16–32.

Rafferty, A. E. & Griffin, M. A. (2006). Refining individualized consideration: Distinguishing developmental leadership and supportive leadership. *Journal of Occupational and Organizational Psychology*, 79(1), 37–61. doi: 10.1348/096317905x36731.

Reb, J., Narayanan, J. & Chaturvedi, S. (2012). Leading mindfully: Two studies on the influence of supervisor trait mindfulness on employee well-being and performance. *Mindfulness*, 5(1), 36–45. doi: 10.1007/s12671-012-0144-z.

Reb. J., Sim, K., Chintakananda, K. & Bhave, D. P. (2015). Leading with mindfulness: Exploring the relation of mindfulness with leadership behaviors, styles, and development. In J. Reb & P. W. B. Atkins (eds), *Mindfulness in Organizations*. Cambridge: Cambridge University Press.

Roche, M., Haar, J. M. & Luthans, F. (2014). The role of mindfulness and psychological capital on the well-being of leaders. *Journal of Occupational Health Psychology*, 19(4), 476–89. doi: 10.1037/a0037183.

Schultz, P., Ryan, R. M., Niemiec, C. P., Legate, N. & Williams, G. C. (2015). Mindfulness, work climate, and psychological need satisfaction in employee well-being. *Mindfulness*, 6(5), 971–85.

Schutte, N. S. & Malouff, J. M. (2011). Emotional intelligence mediates the relationship between mindfulness and subjective well-being. *Personality and Individual Differences*, 50(7), 1116–19. doi: 10.1016/j.paid.2011.01.037.

Scott, B. A., Colquitt, J. A., Paddock, E. L. & Judge, T. A. (2010). A daily investigation of the role of manager empathy on employee well-being. *Organizational Behavior and Human Decision Processes*, 113(2), 127–40. doi: 10.1016/j.obhdp.2010.08.001.

Shachtman, N. (2013). In silicon valley, meditation is no fad. It could make your career. *Wired*. 18 June. http://www.wired.com/2013/06/meditation-mindfulness-silicon-valley/. Accessed 4 August 2016.

Shapiro, S. L., Jazaieri, H. & Goldin, P. R. (2012). Mindfulness-based stress reduction effects on moral reasoning and decision making. *Journal of Positive Psychology*, 7(6), 504–15.

Shapiro, S. L., Wang., M. C. & Peltason, E. H. (2015). What is mindfulness, and why should organizations care about it? In J. Reb & P. W. B. Atkins (eds), *Mindfulness in Organizations*. Cambridge: Cambridge University Press.

Stam, D. A., van Knippenberg, D. & Wisse, B. (2009). The role of regulatory fit in visionary leadership. *Journal of Organizational Behavior*, 31(4), 499–518. doi: 10.1002/job.624.

St. Charles, L. (2010). Mindfulness, self-compassion, self-efficacy, and locus of control: Examining relationships between four distinct but theoretically related concepts. MSc thesis, Pacific University.

Stebbings, J., Taylor, I., Spray, C. & Ntoumanis, N. (2012). Antecedents of perceived coach interpersonal behaviors: The coaching environment and coach psychological well- and ill-being. *Journal of Sport & Exercise Psychology*, 34(4), 481–502.

Strange, J. & Mumford, M. D. (2002). The origins on vision: Charismatic versus ideological leadership. *Leadership Quarterly*, 13(4), 343–77.

ten Brummelhuis, L. L. & Bakker, A. B. (2012). A resource perspective on the work–home interface: The work–home resources model. *American Psychologist*, 67(7), 545–56. doi: 10.1037/a0027974.

Tepper, B. J. (2000). Consequences of abusive supervision. *Academy of Management Journal*, 43(2), 178–90.

Van Knippenberg, D. & Sitkin, S. B. (2013). A critical assessment of charismatic–transformational leadership research: Back to the drawing board? *Academy of Management Annals*, 7(1), 1–60. doi: 10.1080/19416520.2013.759433.

Wheeler, A. R., Halbesleben, J. R. & Whitman, M. V. (2013). The interactive effects of abusive supervision and entitlement on emotional exhaustion and co-worker abuse. *Journal of Occupational and Organizational Psychology*, 86, 477–96.

Whitman, M. V., Halbesleben, J. R. & Holmes, O. (2014). Abusive supervision and feedback avoidance: The mediating role of emotional exhaustion. *Journal of Organizational Behavior*, 35, 38–53.

Wright, T. A. & Huang, C. C. (2012). The many benefits of employee well-being in organizational research. *Journal of Organizational Behavior*, 33(8), 1188–92. doi: 10.1002/job.1828.

Zhang, Y., LePine, J. A., Buckman, B. R. & Wei, F. (2013). It's not fair...or is it? The role of justice and leadership in explaining work stressor–job performance relationships. *Academy of Management Journal*, 57(3), 675–97. doi: 10.5465/amj.2011.1110.

13

Leading and Developing Health and Safety through Collective Psychological Capital

Julie Dyrdek Broad and Fred Luthans

Few would argue with the proposition that caring and positive leaders play an important role in health and safety in the workplace. Considerable research over the years has established that leadership behaviours are highly malleable and open to development and are associated with desirable organizational outcomes (e.g., Barling, Weber & Kelloway, 1996; Dvir, Eden, Avolio & Shamir, 2002; Kelloway, Barling & Helleur, 2000; Mullen & Kelloway, 2009). Additionally, a growing body of literature suggests that organizational leadership is linked to a wide variety of employee outcomes, both positive and negative, relevant to occupational health and safety (Kelloway & Barling, 2010). Specifically, there is growing evidence that improving organizational leadership results in improved safety outcomes (Mullen & Kelloway, 2009; Zohar, 2002) and enhanced employee well-being (McKee & Kelloway, 2009).

Despite this growing evidence of the apparent linkage between leadership and safety and health, it is surprising to learn that few leadership interventions have been designed and studied to increase occupational health and safety in the workplace. The purpose of this chapter is to address this need. We first provide an overview of the paradigm shift within psychology that has impacted management and organizational sciences in general and leadership in particular. Next, we provide an overview of psychological capital, or PsyCap, to include the theoretical underpinnings and summary of the supporting research. This is followed by an overview of how leadership can leverage the science of PsyCap to positively impact health and safety in today's workplace. Lastly, we'll introduce a new collective Psychological Capital Intervention (*c*PCI) that provides specific, day-to-day, operational guidance that leaders can utilize to enhance the health and safety of their team.

Paradigm Shift to Positivity

Over the last 15 years, a new paradigm perspective of human and organizational behaviour has emerged, represented by the fields of positive psychology and positive organizational behaviour (POB). The focus is on positive, strength-based

Leading to Occupational Health and Safety: How Leadership Behaviours Impact Organizational Safety and Well-Being, First Edition.
Edited by E. Kevin Kelloway, Karina Nielsen and Jennifer K. Dimoff.

human assets rather than just on the deficits and human weaknesses that have largely consumed the attention of scholarly inquiry in psychology following World War II. This positive psychology was initially led by Martin Seligman (Seligman, 1998; Seligman & Csikszentmihalyi, 2000), and then a bit later taken to the workplace with the launch of POB (Luthans, 2002a, 2002b).

In 1998, Martin Seligman, then President of the American Psychological Association, used his presidential address to challenge the field with 'Building Human Strengths: Psychology's Forgotten Mission.' This was a call to refocus on positive constructs such as courage, optimism, hope, interpersonal skills, honesty, virtue and perseverance. He importantly noted that before World War II psychology had three core missions: (1) curing mental illness, (2) making the lives of people more fulfilling, and (3) identifying and nurturing high talent.

The trauma surrounding World War II led a number of US federal organizations and their associated economic forces to become focused on treating mental illness. For example, the Department of Veterans Affairs and the National Institute of Mental Health grant funding was aimed at mental illness. Psychologists realized that livelihoods could be made by treating mental illnesses in clinical practices, and also drew professional attention to grant opportunities for research on mental health. While these efforts certainly addressed psychology's important mission of helping to cure mental illness, the science of making the lives of people more fulfilling and identifying and nurturing high talent was badly neglected. Seligman reminded psychologists in his 1998 speech and subsequent writing that their discipline had been side-tracked, and that a renewed focus on strength and virtue was needed to help restore some balance. However, 50 years of working in a medical model on personal weaknesses and dysfunctional behaviour left psychology ill-equipped to do effective work on prevention, to include a new paradigm perspective of positivity, strength and resilience.

In 2000, Seligman and Csikszentmihalyi published the seminal piece 'Positive Psychology: An Introduction.' They noted that prevention researchers had discovered that there are human strengths that can act as buffers against mental illness, providing a barrier of protection around mental health and well-being. They identified the importance to human flourishing of positive constructs such as contentment, hope, optimism, flow, happiness, love, courage, interpersonal skills, aesthetic sensibility, perseverance, forgiveness, originality, future-mindedness, spirituality, high talent and wisdom (Seligman & Csikszentmihalyi, 2000).

After attending and being stimulated by the first Positive Psychology Summit in 1999 while working with Gallup, Luthans (2002a, 2002b) noted the absence and evaluated the implications for organizational behaviour, to include leadership (Luthans & Avolio, 2003; Luthans, Luthans, Hodgetts & Luthans, 2002), and termed it Positive Organizational Behaviour (POB). Luthans defined micro-level, state-like POB as 'the study and application of positively oriented human resource strengths and psychological capacities that can be measured and make a contribution to performance improvement in the workplace' (Luthans, 2002a, p. 698).

From the beginning, being from the field of organizational behaviour in a business school Luthans realized that the constructs to be included in POB must demonstrate performance impact to gain respect within the field of management and organizations. Therefore, he identified three criteria that must be met for a positive construct to be considered for inclusion in POB; it must be (1) theory- and research-supported and validly measurable, (2) related to performance improvement, and (3) state-like and thus open to learning, development, change and management (Luthans, 2002a). As important as performance impact was that the POB constructs must be based on a scientific foundation and state-like, and thus be open to development through training programmes or on-the-job leadership, or self-developed. Just as Seligman had done with the field of psychology, Luthans launched a call for organizational behaviour scholars to focus on the positives: what makes individuals, teams and organizations perform at their highest capability, and how positive state-like psychological resource development could contribute to improvements in desired attitudes, behaviours and performance in the workplace broadly defined (Luthans, 2002a, 2002b).

Psychological Capital as Outgrowth of POB

Luthans and colleagues' efforts in POB led to the identification of a second-order multidimensional psychological resource construct, termed psychological capital (PsyCap), which is comprised of four first-order constructs that meet the inclusion criteria (that is, they are scientifically based and validly measurable, state-like and open to development, and related to desired attitudes, behaviours and performance in the workplace). These were determined to be: (1) hope, (2) efficacy, (3) resilience, and (4) optimism. Often referred to with the acronym of HERO or 'finding the HERO within', PsyCap has been demonstrated both theoretically (Luthans, Youssef & Avolio, 2007; Luthans, Youssef-Morgan & Avolio, 2015) and empirically (Luthans, Avolio, Avey & Norman, 2007; also see reviews by Dawkins, Martin, Scott & Sanderson, 2013 and Avey, Reichard, Luthans & Mahatre, 2011) to be a second-order construct that accounts for more variance in employee performance and satisfaction than the four individual positive constructs that make it up. As a result, PsyCap provides an additive value above and beyond hope, efficacy, resilience, and optimism. In keeping with POB inclusion requirements, PsyCap as a core construct is also open to development and has desirable impact on attitudes, behaviours and performance in the workplace.

PsyCap is defined as 'an individual's positive psychological state of development and is characterized by: (1) having confidence (self-efficacy) to take on and put in the necessary effort to succeed at challenging tasks; (2) making a positive attribution (optimism) about succeeding now and in the future, (3) persevering toward goals and, when necessary, redirecting paths to goals (hope) in order to succeed; and (4) when beset by problems and adversity, sustaining and bouncing back and even beyond (resilience) to attain success' (Luthans, Youssef & Avolio, 2007, p. 3). Although the use of the concept of 'capital' is commonplace (e.g., traditionally recognized economic capital or 'what you have', human capital or 'what you know', and social capital or 'who you know'), psychological capital represents a form of capital that focuses on 'who you are' and, most importantly, represents a type of competitive capital that is open to development and management, thereby improving both individual and organizational performance (Luthans, Luthans & Luthans, 2004; Luthans & Youssef, 2004).

Hope within PsyCap

Although hope has not traditionally been recognized or discussed within the workplace, or within the academic field of organizational behaviour, it was determined to strongly meet the PsyCap inclusion criteria to become a vital component. PsyCap hope primarily draws from the theoretical and research work of Snyder, Irving and Anderson (1991) and is defined as 'a positive motivational state that is based on an interactively derived sense of successful (1) agency (goal-oriented energy), and (2) pathways (planning to meet goals)' (p. 287). While there is considerable evidence that the construct of hope has a positive impact on academic and athletic performance, the study of hope in the workplace is still nascent. However, hope is gaining recognition through the extensive research of PsyCap and its inclusion in the development of hope within the workplace.

Efficacy within PsyCap

What is commonly called self-efficacy in the academic literature is, simply put, confidence. Basing their work on Albert Bandura's (1997) considerable theory and research, Stajkovic and Luthans (1998) define confidence, or self-efficacy, as the individual's conviction about his or her ability to mobilize the motivation, cognitive resources and courses of action needed to execute a specific task within a given context. Their meta-analysis demonstrated a strong relationship between efficacy and work-related performance, and also provided clear guidelines of how it can be developed.

Resilience within PsyCap

While most of the resilience literature is derived from developmental and clinical psychology, the application of resilience in the workplace is growing rapidly. Resilience is the ability to bounce back from adversity or even from dramatic positive changes (Luthans, 2002a; Masten, 2001). Coutu (2002) describes resilience in the workplace as including a staunch acceptance of reality, a deep belief, often buttressed by strongly held values, that life is meaningful, and an uncanny ability to improvise and adapt to significant change. Early developmental psychologists' recognized that strengths and assets can provide valuable 'buffering' effects when stress or adversity arises; similarly, organizational behaviourists find that this same concept of buffering effects can be developed in the workplace through mindful attention on assets, weaknesses and influencers.

Focusing on assets provides clear identification of human strengths that can be leveraged during difficult times or setbacks, while understanding weaknesses provides early guidance on what individual vulnerabilities or deficits introduce risk. Influencers include evaluation of those areas where employees have some sense of control, or directional influence, which may assist efforts to bounce back following adversity. In today's fast-paced, global, high-technology work environments, building resilience has become essential in developing employee flexibility and adaptability.

Optimism within PsyCap

Optimism draws from positive psychologists such as Scheier and Carver (1985) on positive future expectations that are open to development, and from Seligman (2002), which largely draws from attribution theory related to how events are interpreted. According to Seligman's research, optimists interpret bad events as being only temporary, while pessimists interpret bad events as being permanent, touching on two critical dimensions of optimism: permanence and pervasiveness. The opposite is true for good events. Optimists tend to make permanent attributions ('I'm good at what I do'), whereas pessimists make temporary attributions ('I tried hard on this particular task'). Seligman's work with Metropolitan Life Insurance sales people (1998) provides evidence of the positive impact of optimism in the workplace. He found that salespersons' optimism led to higher performance than their less optimistic, or pessimistic, counterparts, as measured through sales revenue.

As it turns out, optimism not only sets expectancies about our past and future events, it also has important implications around individual strategies of coping (Scheier, Weintraub & Carver, 1986), acting as a buffer against stress. 'Optimists and pessimists spontaneously employ quite different coping strategies when confronted by stressful situations. Optimism was positively correlated with indications of active coping, with elaboration or complexity of coping strategies, and with the seeking of social support. Optimism was inversely correlated with focus on emotion and emotional expression, and with disengagement from the goal' (Scheier & Carver, 1985, p. 241). Thus, optimism impacts how individuals perceive stress and perhaps, more importantly, how they cope with stress. Optimism also determines how individuals problem-solve with complexity or adversity when obstacles are encountered. Optimists tend to employ an approach to coping that in many life circumstances is the most adaptive, and the least dysfunctional, which has important implications for the workplace.

Theoretical Foundations for PsyCap

Each of the above four constructs comprising PsyCap has deep theoretical and psychometrically validated measures derived from extant research in clinical and developmental psychology on hope (Snyder, 2000) and resilience (Masten, 2001), from attribution and expectancy theories as related to optimism (Scheier & Carver, 1985; Seligman, 1998), and from Bandura's extensive work on efficacy and its sources of development (Bandura, 1997, 2000). As referenced earlier, Luthans (2002a, 2002b) ensured that PsyCap, under the umbrella of POB, met the requirement of being theoretically based.

As a second-order construct, PsyCap's theoretical foundation can draw from Hobfoll's (2002) psychological resources theory, which itself encompasses several stress theories. Of particular interest in Hobfoll's psychological resources theories is the conservation of resources (COR) theory, which suggests that individuals seek to acquire and maintain resources (objects, social status, social connections, time, knowledge). Stress occurs when there is a loss of resources, or a threat of loss, or when individuals fail to gain resources after substantive resource investment, which can result in increases in stress or anxiety (Hobfoll, 2002). COR also stands out in the workplace as it emphasizes means for positive adaptation under circumstances of loss, highlighting the importance of how employees acquire, maintain and foster the necessary resources to both meet their current work demands and help guard against further resource depletion (Wright & Hobfoll, 2004). Thus, 'one's ability to acquire and maintain resources is both a means and an end – a means for achieving success and ends that include adaptation, coping, and well-being. Furthermore, secondary work-related resources such as high levels of cognitive and emotional attachment to one's occupation (Wright & Hobfoll, 2004) are important for influencing people's primary resources such as their well-being' (Avey, Luthans, Smith & Palmer, 2010, p. 19). Hobfoll's psychological resource theories also speak to conflict at home (e.g. work–family conflict), and how conflict in one area of life (at home) can impact another (work) when resources are drawn down.

Bakker, Demerouti and Euwema (2005) argue that, holding job and personal resources constant, job demands will create distress in employees, leading to psychological exhaustion, anxiety and impaired health. Simultaneously, positive psychological resources, such as hope, efficacy, resilience and optimism (compromising PsyCap), counteract the distress from these demands, acting as a suppressor of stress and anxiety. In psychological resource theory, hope, optimism, efficacy and resilience are presented in the theoretical understanding of PsyCap as having shared mechanisms. There is more in common (e.g., persistence) between these discrete, discriminate constructs comprising PsyCap than there is difference (Luthans, Avolio et al., 2007).

PsyCap can also draw from Fredrickson's (2001) broaden-and-build theory of positive emotions in that when hope, efficacy, resilience and optimism are developed, not only are positive emotions increased, but there can also be upward spirals of the four positive resources. These upward spirals promote the development of overall PsyCap. The broadened thought–action repertoires can contribute to the explanation of the synergistic nature of PsyCap beyond the four positive psychological resources that make it up.

PsyCap Research to Date

Since the introduction of POB (Luthans, 2002a, 2002b) and PsyCap (Luthans, Luthans & Luthans, 2004; Luthans & Youssef, 2004; Luthans, Youssef & Avolio, 2007), the scientific work on PsyCap as a second-order construct has greatly expanded. In 2011, a meta-analysis of PsyCap 'indicated the expected significant positive relationships between PsyCap and desirable employee attitudes (job satisfaction, organizational commitment, psychological well-being), desirable employee behaviours (citizenship), and multiple measures of performance (self, supervisor evaluations, and objective). There was also a significant negative relationship between PsyCap and undesirable employee attitudes (cynicism, turnover intentions, job stress, and anxiety) and undesirable employee behaviors (deviance)' (Avey, Reichard et al., 2011, p. 127). More recent comprehensive reviews have also verified that PsyCap has a strong and consistent positive impact on desired workplace outcomes (Newman, Ucbasaran, Zhu & Hirst, 2014).

PsyCap research quickly identified it as a new robust type of capital applicable to a wide variety of occupations, organizations and outcomes. For example, PsyCap has been linked to commitment to organizational mission and intentions to stay in a study of nurses (Luthans & Jensen, 2005), improvements in performance and satisfaction among management students and high-tech manufacturing employees (Luthans, Avolio et al., 2007), improvements in individual performance, organizational performance, job satisfaction, work happiness and organizational commitment in a sample of employees from a wide range of positions in manufacturing, services, public sector and non-governmental organizations (NGOs) (Youssef & Luthans, 2007), and performance improvements in Chinese manufacturing workers (Luthans, Avey, Clapp-Smith & Li, 2008).

This research was followed by refinements of PsyCap. For example, PsyCap was found to mediate the relationship between organizational climate and employee performance (Luthans, Norman, Avolio & Avey, 2008). PsyCap has also been associated with organizational change by showing that it increases employees' positive emotions and related attitudes towards change (Avey, Wernsing & Luthans, 2008). An important study demonstrated that employees' PsyCap added value over and above established trait-like positive constructs in organizational behaviour such as self-evaluations, personality, and person–organization and person–job fit in predicting organizational citizenship behaviours (OCBs) and counterproductive work behaviours (CWB) and attitudes (Avey, Luthans & Youssef, 2010). Recently, utilizing the latest research methodologies, such as latent growth modelling, in a large financial services firm, research has demonstrated that, over time, employee PsyCap was related to changes in performance outcomes (supervisor-rated and judged according to financial performance related to individual sales revenue) (Peterson, Luthans, Avolio, Walumbwa & Zhang, 2011).

PsyCap research has also led to the development of computer-aided text analysis to elevate individual PsyCap to organizational PsyCap (McKenny, Short & Payne, 2013), and identified and empirically tested the value of domain-specific Relationship PsyCap and Health PsyCap (Luthans, Youssef, Sweetman & Harms, 2013). Specifically, this study found that Health PsyCap was related to satisfaction with overall health and to objective measures of body mass index (BMI) and cholesterol level. Other studies have found relationships between employees' PsyCap and their health and well-being over time (Avey, Luthans, Smith & Palmer, 2010). For example, the mental well-being of leaders was found to be based upon the direct effect of mindfulness (heightened awareness) and the mediating effect of their PsyCap (Roche, Haar & Luthans, 2014). Importantly, the PsyCap of deployed soldiers was found to be related to their mental health and substance abuse (Krasikova, Lester & Harms, 2015), and in the private sector the higher employees' PsyCap the lower their stress and turnover (Avey, Luthans & Jensen, 2009).

Finally, PsyCap has been clearly demonstrated to be open to development through short face-to-face PsyCap training interventions lasting 1–3 hours (Luthans, Avey, Avolio, Norman & Combs, 2006; Luthans, Avey, Avolio &

Peterson, 2010) and in web-based training interventions (Luthans, Avey & Patera, 2008). The efficacy of a PsyCap development intervention has even been demonstrated through the rigorous Solomon four-group design (Ertosun, Erdil, Deniz & Lutfihak, 2015).

Group, Team or Collective Psychological Capital (cPsyCap)

Although the research above has been at the individual level of PsyCap, scholars have recently directed their attention towards multilevel analysis. This includes PsyCap at the group and team (or collective) level of analysis (Clapp-Smith, Vogelgesang & Avey, 2009; Dawkins, Martin, Scott & Sanderson, 2015; Peterson et al., 2011; Vanno, Kaemkate & Wongwanich, 2014; West, Patera & Carsten, 2009) and the organizational level of analysis (McKenny et al., 2013; Memili, Welsh & Kaciak, 2014; Memili, Welsh & Luthans, 2013). Given the embeddedness of work teams within organizations, this level of analysis is providing promising results, which shows that the emergence of PsyCap can provide valuable team resources throughout the team lifecycle. The Center for Creative Leadership (2006) estimates that an overwhelming 83 per cent of respondents identify teams as a key ingredient in organizational success.

Individuals working in teams often forgo their individual identities to adopt the identity of their team (Terrion & Ashforth, 2002). Given this tendency to strongly identify with the team, it becomes plausible that a team's PsyCap may hold the potential to influence team mates and their interactions towards the completion of a task, and this is particularly true when work outcomes are team-level products (West et al., 2009). Research on measuring PsyCap within teams has demonstrated positive relationships with team cohesion, cooperation, coordination, conflict and team satisfaction (West et al., 2009), as well as demonstrating positive relationships between team-level PsyCap and team performance (Clapp-Smith et al., 2009; Peterson et al., 2011; Vanno et al., 2014). Peterson et al. (2011) define collective PsyCap as a team's shared positive appraisal of their circumstances and their probability of success based on their combined effort and perseverance.

Dawkins et al. (2015) draw upon social contagion theory to understand collective PsyCap. This refers to the process of communicating and exchanging information among members of a collective, resulting in a shared perception regarding some aspect pertinent to the team (Degoey, 2000). As indicated, this is also consistent with Terrion and Ashforth's (2002) findings that individuals working in teams often forgo their individual identities to adopt the identity of their team.

As well as in the health field, PsyCap has been recognized and analysed within the context of safety critical organizations (SCOs), albeit as yet to quite a limited extent. Conceptually, Eid, Mearns, Larsson, Laberg and Johnsen (2012) have initiated a theory-driven literature review examining how leadership and certain aspects of POB may affect safety outcomes in SCOs. They suggest that theoretical and conceptual advances in authentic leadership theory and PsyCap can inform potential mechanisms that affect safety outcomes. Bergheim, Nielsen, Mearns and Eid (2015) demonstrated that PsyCap was positively associated with, and explained between 10 and 12 per cent of variance in perceptions of safety climate after adjusting for socially desirable responding (i.e., answering as society thinks they should). This work identified an indirect (mediating) relationship with perceptions of safety climate through job satisfaction. Collectively, PsyCap and job satisfaction explained 21% of the variance in safety climate, defined as a 'coherent set of perceptions and expectations that workers have regarding safety in their organization' (Gyekye, 2005, p. 29).

The Role of Leadership in Collective Psychological Capital Development for Occupational Health and Safety

Kelloway and Barling (2010, pp. 262–3) provide considerable evidence that leaders play a critical role in the occupational health and safety of their followers. They state: 'Data linking the quality of leadership to other individuals' well-being has been available for over 50 years (e.g., Day & Hamblin, 1964), and evidence linking poor leadership to impaired well-being in followers is particularly well-established (for a review see Kelloway, Sivanathan, Francis & Barling, 2005). Skakon, Nielsen, Borg, and Guzman (2010) found support for their hypothesis that leader behaviours, specific leadership styles and the relationship between leaders and their employees were all associated with employee stress and affective well-being.' As indicated in the introductory comments, we know that the role of leadership has long been recognized in the occupational health and safety literature (e.g., Hofmann, Morgeson & Gerras, 2003; Hofmann & Stetzer, 1996; Kelloway, Mullen & Francis, 2006; Mullen & Kelloway, 2009; Mullen, Kelloway & Teed, 2011; Zohar, 2000; Zohar & Luria, 2005). This body of knowledge has led to the general academic consensus that when it comes to health and safety, leaders significantly influence followers.

There seems little question that leaders have a significant opportunity to either actively shape and support climates of occupational health and safety, or detract from such prescribed and desirable climates. The effects of leadership style have academic links to both mental (Bono, Foldes, Vinson & Muros, 2007) and physical health. As an example, having a supportive supervisor has been associated with lower systolic blood pressure among a sample of New York City traffic enforcement officers (Karlin, Brondolo & Schwartz, 2003), and Nyberg, Alfredsson, Theorell, Westerlund, Vahtera, and Kivimäki (2009) found that good leadership (defined as 'consideration for individual employees, provision of clarity in goals and role expectations, supplying information and feedback, ability to carry out changes at work successfully, and promotion of employee participation and control', p. 51) was negatively related to subsequent ischaemic heart disease in employees. Specifically, higher scores on leadership were associated with reduced risk of heart disease.

Unfortunately, the flip side of this coin, which is deficit-focused, informs us that supervisory injustice leads to a wide range of health-related outcomes that are undesirable, including heavy drinking (Väänänen, Kouvonen, Kivimäki et al., 2009), impaired cardiac regulation (Elovonio, Kivimäki, Puttonen et al., 2006) and questionable use of sick time (Kivimäki, Elovainio, Vahtera & Ferrie, 2003). This body of literature is valuable because it transposes the findings of supportive leadership presented above. It provides further confirmation of the research findings, and of the underlying importance of leadership to occupational health.

There is considerable evidence that leadership relates to safety climate as well as to health. Data consistently support the relationship between transformational leadership behaviours and perceived safety climate within organizations (Barling, Loughlin & Kelloway, 2002; Hofmann & Morgeson, 1999; Kelloway, Mullen & Francis, 2006; Mullen & Kelloway, 2009; Zohar, 1980; Zohar, 2002, Zohar & Tenne-Gazit, 2008). Furthermore, perceptions of management were the most common dimension assessed in measures of safety climate (Flin, Mearns, O'Connor & Bryden, 2000).

In relation to leadership and PsyCap research, we know that there is a contagion effect of global leaders' positive PsyCap on followers, and that distance and relationship quality mediate this effect (Story, Youssef, Luthans, Barbuto & Bovaird, 2013). This can be explained by the fact that the theoretical mechanisms proposed for the leader-to-follower PsyCap contagion process are social learning, observation and modelling, even though these mechanisms may be at a physical distance, with infrequent face-to-face interaction. PsyCap resources can be transferred to followers through progressive independent mastery of cognitions, affect and behaviours. Followers may find these psychological attributes desirable in their leader, or even amongst their team mates. Leaders may also provide intentional guided mastery modelling of cognitive skills and behavioural norms and expectations (Wood & Bandura, 1989). Also, and importantly, high-PsyCap leaders are more effective at buffering the potential negative effects associated with infrequent interactions on the quality of their relationships with their followers (Story et al., 2013). Under globalization, this provides a significant benefit to leaders whose employees are widely dispersed.

Positive leaders who are high on PsyCap can not only elevate follower PsyCap through the mechanisms above, they can also directly build their followers' PsyCap. Over time, followers become less dependent on their leader's PsyCap, and the associated contagion effect, because of the development of their own individual PsyCap within the workplace. As noted by Youssef and Luthans (2012, p. 543) : 'Over time, distant followers (physically distant, structurally distant, or psychologically/socially distant) may reach an elevated point in their development and maturity where their needs for proximity or psychological closeness to the leader may diminish, as they independently explore and refine their own psychological capital resources such as confidence in their abilities, hope and optimism, and resilience when faced with obstacles and setbacks. The relationship then may evolve into one of collegiality, camaraderie, and mutual appreciation, rather than dependence and mentorship.'

Leaders should also understand the importance of follower PsyCap in the relationships they invest in for developmental purposes. As it turns out, a higher level of incremental follower performance was achieved when a lack of positive PsyCap was complemented with a more authentic leadership approach than when followers had high levels of PsyCap (Wang, Sui, Luthans, Wang & Wu, 2014). This relationship was mediated by leader–member exchange (LMX) relationships, in such a way that complementary congruity between leadership behaviours and follower psychological resources contributed to follower performance, and that a higher level of incremental follower performance was achieved when a lack of positive PsyCap was complemented with a more authentic leadership approach then when followers had high levels of PsyCap. As a result, understanding follower PsyCap can provide valuable guidance on the most effective leadership style to leverage, and also allows leaders to tailor their attention and style to those followers who are in the most need of their support.

Eid et al. (2012) propose a theoretically based model whereby PsyCap mediates the relationship between authentic leadership, safety climate and safety outcomes for high-risk organizations. Authentic leadership theory emphasizes leader self-awareness and self-regulation processes as vital mechanisms in the leader–follower exchange (Luthans & Avolio, 2003). Liu (2013) found that employees who perceived higher levels of supervisor support had higher levels of PsyCap, which in turn predicted higher levels of performance, and Luthans, Norman et al. (2008) found that PsyCap fully mediated the relationship between a supportive organizational climate and employees' job performance.

Dawkins et al. (2015) argue that leadership style may be an important influencer in the development of collective PsyCap, and that authentic leaders foster follower potential by developing their strengths, including resilience and self-efficacy (Gardner & Schermerhorn, 2004), thereby enhancing performance and functioning. Dawkins et al. (2015) also suggest that PsyCap and organizational climate (flexibility, reflexivity, effort, clarity of organizational goals) may share a bidirectional relationship. For example, teams demonstrating high PsyCap may be more likely to perceive their organization as more flexible and reflexive. At the same time, organizations that foster flexibility, reflexivity, effort and clarity of organizational goals may promote greater PsyCap among teams. As a result, 'there may be potential opportunity to develop training interventions aimed at bolstering team PsyCap. This type of intervention could adapt the goals and training exercises from the individual level PsyCap interventions (Luthans et al., 2010) so as to encompass a team rather than an individual focus and thereby aim to bolster team PsyCap' (Dawkins et al., 2015, p. 21). Avolio and Gardner (2005) argue further that leader development, including authentic leadership, that enhances employee PsyCap, will pay dividends in increasing individual, collective and organizational PsyCap.

Similar to the paradigm shift within psychology and management and organizational sciences described at the beginning of this chapter, the extensive academic literature on leadership and follower behaviours has also experienced a critical shift, focusing on human strengths and opportunities, rather than deficits. As a result, constructs such as transformational leadership, leader–member exchange, authentic leadership and positive global leadership have continued to expand since the turn of the century. In fact, transformational leadership theory was noted by Barling and colleagues (Barling, Christie & Hoption, 2011) as the single most widely studied leadership theory (Barling, Christie & Hoption, 2011).

Even so, most managerial decisions are made in response to crises or performance gaps, rather than for the purpose of elevating and optimizing performance through leveraging inherent individual and team strengths (see Youssef-Morgan & Luthans, 2013a).

Rather than advocating a particular leadership style in our prescribed Collective Psychological Capital Intervention (*c*PCI) that follows, we opt to discuss operationally how a leader can build domain-specific collective PsyCap within the teams they lead to promote occupational health and safety climates and outcomes. Although there is literature integrating PsyCap with mental and physical health, as well as with safety climates in high-risk organizations, the use of a *c*PCI that builds collective health and safety is novel. We also believe that this intervention appropriately focuses attention not only on the leader, but on the followers as well, showing that when groups and teams interact, social learning theory is activated. In a sense, this *c*PCI targets health and safety at a collective level (group and team) from both a follower and a leader perspective. Unequivocally, the leader has a critical role to play in developing healthy and safe teams.

The Conceptual Framework of Collective Health PsyCap and Safety PsyCap with Authentic Leadership

We propose a new conceptual framework based upon the emergence of leadership PsyCap, and a new domain-specific focus on collective Health PsyCap and Safety PsyCap development. We further propose that this conceptual framework on collective Health PsyCap and Safety PsyCap can be developed through short, targeted interventions within intact groups and teams that can be facilitated and coached, and sustained day by day, by the leader, in support of Health PsyCap and Safety PsyCap.

Figure 13.1 outlines the approach we recommend for increasing individual and collective Health PsyCap and Safety PsyCap. At this stage, both Health PsyCap

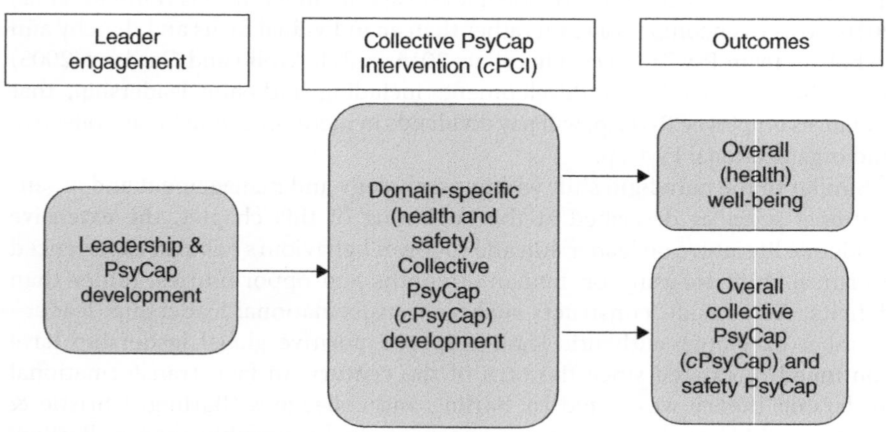

Figure 13.1 Conceptual Framework of Health PsyCap and Safety PsyCap.

(Luthans, Youssef, Sweetman & Harms, 2013; Youssef-Morgan & Luthans, 2015) and Safety PsyCap (Eid et al., 2012) have been conceptualized. However, future research needs to be conducted in order to determine if Safety PsyCap can indeed provide organizational advantage for high-risk organizations.

Health Psycap and Well-Being

Well-being has been found to be related to a variety of outcomes, including physical and psychological health (Ryff & Singer, 2003), personal striving and coping with stress (Diener & Fujita, 1995; Emmons, 1992; Folkman, 1997) and satisfaction with important life domains (Diener, 2000; Diener & Suh, 1999). Research in positive psychology on the sources of happiness and well-being have indicated them to be due to heredity and nurturing (about 50%), intentional activity (about 40%), and circumstances, including age, income, location (only about 10%) (Lyubomirsky, 2007). Youssef-Morgan and Luthans (2013b) support conceptually that PsyCap resides in the 40% of positivity that can be drawn through intentional activity. 'PsyCap is proposed to trigger cognitive, affective, conative, and social mechanisms leading to happiness and well-being' (Youssef-Morgan & Luthans, 2015, p. 184).

Youssef-Morgan and Luthans (2015) propose that PsyCap is theoretically linked to well-being because: (1) well-being is primarily shaped by cognitive and affective appraisals of life, and PsyCap develops the formation of positive appraisals of past, present and future events; (2) satisfaction with important life domains represents an integral component of well-being; PsyCap has been shown to predict satisfaction with work, relationships, and health (Luthans, Youssef, Sweetman & Harms, 2013); (3) well-being is shaped by retained memories of various life events, and these retained memories have been demonstrated to be both qualitatively and quantitatively different from real-time experiences. PsyCap can facilitate attention, interpretation, and memory retention processes, which all contribute to domain-specific experiences and satisfaction to deliver a lasting impact on well-being (Diener & Biswas-Diener, 2008; Lyubomirsky, 2001); (4) since PsyCap is considered a psychological resource to be drawn upon when needed, it serves as a buffer when adversity is encountered (see Wright & Hobfoll, 2004), and also as a means to increase perceptions of well-being (Cameron, 2008); and (5) PsyCap can help mitigate the negativity bias (Baumeister, Bratslavsky, Finkenauer & Vohs, 2001; Cameron, 2008) and hedonic adaptation.

Collective PsyCap and Safety PsyCap

We know from emerging collective PsyCap literature that social contagion theory may play an active role between leaders and followers (Dawkins et al., 2015), and we argue that social contagion theory also plays an important role within the intact team, who are specifically training on domain-specific Health PsyCap and Safety PsyCap. As a result, we propose that the leadership development directed towards leader PsyCap development may also result in increases in follower PsyCap. Simultaneously, by building a Collective PsyCap Intervention, or *c*PCI, focused on building domain-specific Health PsyCap and Safety PsyCap within intact groups and teams, additional influences of social contagion will take hold within the collective.

Development Guidelines for Collective Health PsyCap and Safety PsyCap

The development of Collective Health PsyCap and Safety PsyCap through the *c*PCI leverages a referent shift to the group and team level of engagement of the original PCI intervention targeting individuals (Luthans, Avey, Avolio, Norman & Combs, 2006; Luthans, Avey, Avolio & Peterson, 2010), as well as the inclusion of new content targeting the development of leader PsyCap skills to promote Health PsyCap and Safety PsyCap. Also, the *c*PCI that we have developed includes time spent up front building what we call 'team self-awareness', which provides the team with a snapshot of relatively stable personality traits and core self-evaluations (CSEs) of each member, in a consolidated team view.

The following intervention guidelines are designed for leaders' implementation of *c*PCI in their workplaces. The review above of academic literature associated with leadership in general, as it relates to health and safety, provides solid background to leaders for *why* their role is mission-critical to health and safety attitudes, behaviours and performance outcomes. Now the task at hand is to actively engage followers to expand their knowledge of *c*PCI and how it can create a healthier, safer work environment. Leaders should understand and explain that PsyCap can be viewed at individual, collective, organizational and even country levels of analysis. Leaders should also emphasize the power of the malleability of PsyCap (it is open to development) and its domain-specificity (Health PsyCap and Safety PsyCap). A good primer for preparing leaders for knowledge about PsyCap can be found in Luthans, Youssef-Morgan, and Avolio (2015).

Leaders should also be informed about the impact of social contagion: how their leader attitudes and behaviours can be contagious to their followers, and how followers experience social contagion from one another's attitudes and behaviours. It should be pointed out that leaders, and the intact group and team members they manage, heavily influence one another's perceptions of PsyCap and of domain-specific Health PsyCap and Safety PsyCap.

Following the *c*PCI, outlined below, we recommend that leaders are reminded of the mission-critical role that they play in keeping *c*PCI alive in the workplace, targeting domain-specific Health PsyCap and Safety PsyCap. We know from Vanhove, Herian, Perez, Harms and Lester (2015) that resilience intervention programme effects diminish over time; however, serving blended learning strategies (intact group and team classroom settings, online engagement, leader engagement, and even serious gaming solutions) and systematic periodic coaching can assist in retaining and enhancing skills that are learned during the *c*PCI. As a result, the role of the leader equipped with knowledge of domain-specific Healthy PsyCap and Safety PsyCap is an essential component in keeping this training alive and sustainable in the workplace.

cPCI for Health PsyCap and Safety PsyCap: Hope

Similarly to the original PCI (Luthans, Avey, Avolio, Norman & Combs, 2006; Luthans, Avey, Avolio & Peterson, 2010), the *c*PCI uses the same three-pronged strategy in a goal-oriented framework, which includes goal design, pathway generation and overcoming obstacles. Leaders should gather participants, organized into intact groups and teams, and begin with identifying a valuable collective safety goal that they will use throughout the session. Leaders should instruct participants on the ideal design for goals, including (1) concrete end points to measure success, (2) an approach (rather than an avoidance) framework, which allows team participants to move positively towards goal accomplishment instead of away from desired goals (e.g., to work towards safety performance targets instead of avoiding accidents), and (3) the identification of sub-goals in order to reap the benefits of even small 'wins', which Snyder, Irving and Anderson (1991) call 'stepping'.

After a team safety goal is determined, pathways should be developed. First, team members, working individually, should be asked to generate multiple pathways to this goal. They are encouraged to think of as many alternative pathways as possible, regardless of practicality of implementation. Then the team works together to brainstorm these multiple pathways. The second step is to inventory pathways, which entails considering the resources required to pursue each pathway. After careful team deliberation, the unrealistic safety goal pathways are discarded and a smaller number of realistic safety goal pathways are identified. This may also pose a good opportunity for the leader to openly discuss the competing pressures of meeting safety goals *and* performance goals.

Obstacles can act as goal blockers that lead to negative reactions and disengagement from pursuing the goal. The final stage in the *c*PCI hope development is to build collective goal-setting processes and anticipatory abilities in such a way as to anticipate, plan for, and overcome obstacles. Teams are instructed by their leaders to take a few minutes to consider the potential obstacles, or 'What can stop you from accomplishing your safety goal?' After time for self-reflection, the intact groups and teams again gather to hear alternative perspectives on potential obstacles and strategies to overcome them. The leaders should focus on utilizing this process to identify obstacles in advance, and choose an alternative pathway or pathways to avoid blockage.

At the completion of this hope dimension of the *c*PCI, teams have defined a collective valuable safety goal in such a way as to take ownership, be prepared for obstacles, and be ready to implement multiple pathways as contingency plans. Throughout this *c*PCI development process, the leader should acknowledge and encourage positive 'self and team talk'. The leader maintains focus on goal setting, pathway generation and overcoming obstacles as a process that can and should be applied to an array of participants' and team goals in the workplace. Transferability back to the job should be constantly emphasized. In other words, this part of the *c*PCI focuses on how to increase participants' level of hope in the collective PsyCap (our newly introduced *c*PsyCap) developmental process.

*c*PCI for Health PsyCap and Safety PsyCap: Efficacy

As indicated above, Albert Bandura is widely recognized for his establishment of the theoretical foundation and developmental process for building efficacy or confidence (the term commonly used when applied to the workplace), and efficacy is arguably the most extensive and accepted term. The efficacy input into our *c*PCI largely draws from his taxonomy of sources of efficacy, and from the extensive academic literature that evolves efficacy from an individual asset, to the collective, through collective efficacy development. These include task mastery of success, modelling or vicarious learning, social persuasion and positive feedback, and physiological and/or psychological arousal.

In our *c*PCI, following Bandura's emphasis on the role that goal orientation and framing play in building efficacy, we integrate our previously described goal exercise with the four sources of efficacy, while also reflecting on what we know about the relatively stable personality traits and CSEs that have been identified and composed as a snapshot of the team. For example, leaders should encourage teams to reflect back on the personality and CSE exercise composing a team view of personalities, and then encourage team members to evaluate where there may be natural talents and where personality factors match efficacy requirements (for example, they might choose an extravert to deliver an executive brief on team safety goals). During this time, the leader should engage team members by allowing them to experience and model success, and, through social persuasion and arousal, make sure they are all aimed at accomplishing the team goals set earlier in the session. This efficacy-building process elicits positive emotions and builds the participants' confidence, and also collectively the team's confidence, to generate and implement plans to attain goals.

The leaders and followers serve as role models for each other in this efficacy-building process. Bandura asserts that the perceived expertise and the relevance of models are the key to determining the magnitude of influence. As described in the subsection on the hope input into the *c*PCI, when participants generate pathways, inventory resources required for goal accomplishment, and identify sub-goals as milestones or mini-goals to accomplishment, they create an imaginal successful experience. This success in turn is modelled by participants for each other. Participants are able to visualize the accomplishment of each step towards their goal. In other words, in this input into the *c*PCI, participants and intact groups and teams (the collective) gain imaginal task mastery and experience success to enhance their individual and collective efficacy in the PsyCap development process. Additionally, the detailed work of composing a view of the collective personality dimensions and CSEs deepens knowledge about inherent personality dimensions among team members, fostering an environment in which inherent personality dimensions combined with individual skills and abilities can be matched to tasks that build individual and collective efficacy.

*c*PCI for Health PsyCap and Safety PsyCap: Resilience

Consistent with individuals' development in the PCI are the three major recognized components of resilience attributed to the work of positive psychologist Ann Masten (2001): asset factors, risk factors and influence processes.

These components are adapted to the collective level of discussion and analysis. Assets are factors that increase team resilience (e.g., examples of team cooperation, leadership support). Typically, both assets and risks are present within any team. Masten's (2001) work, as well as that of others, has found that resilience factors can be managed, developed and accelerated, and that the most effective development strategies are based upon enhancing assets, and proactively avoiding risky, potentially adverse events.

The resilience input into our *c*PCI draws mainly from Masten's work and focuses on developing and changing team members' perception of influence through cognitive, emotional and behavioural processes. Coutu (2002) noted that highly resilient people are characterized by a staunch view of reality. Thus, as the resilience input into our *c*PCI strategy, team member participants identify a recent team setback within their domain. This can be major (the firm is downsizing) or minor (we have two managers who want different things on project X, and some of these may directly compete with safety goals). Team members are instructed to write down their immediate reactions to the identified setback. The leader can then elaborate on examples of a staunch view of reality and an ideally resilient process for mentally framing a setback: what is within the team's control, what is out of the team's control, and various options for taking collective action.

To affect the perception of influence in building resiliency, cognitive processes are employed to frame team setbacks in terms of impact, control, and options associated with safety goals. Leaders should request that participants repeat these new processes on additional team-relevant setbacks at work in order to reinforce learned cognitive processes which perpetuate the development of not only resiliency, but also 'realistic' optimism. Participants are encouraged to practise anticipating and addressing setbacks associated with team safety goals in the hope-building process or in other team events at work. When participants frame a team setback more accurately in terms of true impact, control and options, they not only are more apt to bounce back from a setback, but may be able to attain levels even above where the team started. Thus, going beyond the original level of team performance after a setback is central to the collective resilience input in the *c*PsyCap development process.

*c*PCI for Health PsyCap and Safety PsyCap: Optimism

For the input of optimism into the *c*PCI, we draw from expectancy-value orientation and positive attributional, explanatory style, realistic optimism being the ideal. Again we leverage the existing knowledge we have from the individual-level PCI in order to complete a referent shift to the *c*PCI. Once again, we focus on team-level optimism rather than individual optimism (although we believe that individual optimism will also increase through this intervention). The leader should ask the team to complete an exercise in which each member writes down three things they are thankful for as they relate to team safety performance. Each team member shares their three things within the group, and then they collectively build a list of team attributes they currently possess that contribute towards meeting safety goals and strengthening the team.

The leader should next provide information to the teams about how hope, efficacy and resilience can also provide value by building team optimism. In addition, the leader should address how optimism can impact decision making under stress, the so-called threat rigidity cycle (Staw, 1981), and common reactions to stress in the workplace. Once again, the team reflects on the outcomes of a collective personality and CSE view of the team. They identify who on the team may be naturally optimistic, and who naturally pessimistic. Critical in this phase of the intervention is that there is no one gold standard; in fact, a naturally optimistic team member may gain great value by spending time with a pessimistic counterpart in identifying obstacles to goals, and finding that level of optimism that is rooted in a staunch sense of reality. The leader should describe tendencies of optimists and pessimists. For example, in preparing for obstacles, pessimists lose more options by expecting bad things to happen. In the collective hope development portion of this *c*PCI, the worst-case scenarios are anticipated and preparations are proactively put in place for the team to move ahead and succeed. This process counteracts pessimism and supports the development of realistic, yet optimistic, expectations, and is reinforced by positive 'self and team talk'.

Conclusions and Recommendations

While the development of the *c*PCI model in creating domain-specific Health PsyCap and Safety PsyCap is just emerging, we believe this multilevel approach to developing PsyCap will lead to results of which the whole is greater than the sum of the individual parts. Moreover, we believe that our approach of levering a *c*PCI, engaging intact groups and teams, and leveraging leader engagement to develop knowledge of domain-specific Health PsyCap and Safety PsyCap, will serve a significant role in the collective Health PsyCap and Safety PsyCap. We believe, and the scientific research supports this, that leaders play an essential role in collective Health PsyCap and Safety PsyCap, from a social contagion and modelling perspective. They also serve an important role in keeping Health PsyCap and Safety PsyCap alive and sustainable within the team. We know from extant research that passive leadership styles are not effective in promoting safety climates (Kelloway, Mullen & Francis, 2006), and that group-level climates are critical to safety climate (Zohar & Luria, 2005). Therefore we believe that our *c*PCI focused on Health PsyCap and Safety PsyCap provides a potential solution to make individuals, and the groups and teams they work within, safer. It is also a solution that addresses both intact group and team members, simultaneously with leadership engagement, providing a bottom-up and top-down approach to occupational health and safety.

Future research should include the testing of this proposed *c*PCI for Health PsyCap and Safety PsyCap in a multitude of occupations and domains. In addition, there is opportunity to conduct empirical studies evaluating the gains that can accrue to and from Health PsyCap and Safety PsyCap as a result of different leadership styles, such as transformational and authentic.

Research evaluating the impact of personality traits and core self-evaluations (CSEs) on PsyCap is also nascent. This work provides an opportunity to begin to evaluate these relatively stable personality traits and CSEs in relationship to PsyCap. Future work may explore how different personality types and CSEs interact with PsyCap interventions and with inherent levels of PsyCap at baselines.

Lastly, the academic research on intact group and team, or collective, levels of PsyCap intervention has not been explored significantly, and this work provides specific guidance on how our *c*PCI can be approached, building upon the seminal research on interventions focused on individual PsyCap development (Ertosun et al., 2015; Luthans, Avery, Avolio, Norman & Combs, 2006; Luthans, Avey, Avolio & Peterson, 2010). We believe this area of academic inquiry will provide rich results in future domain-specific uses of PsyCap as a second-order construct, operating at multiple levels: individual, group or team, organizational and eventually community and even country.

References

Avey, J. B., Luthans, F. & Jensen, S.M. (2009). Psychological capital: A positive resource for combating employee stress and turnover. *Human Resource Management*, 48(5), 677–93.

Avey, J. B., Luthans, F., Smith, R. M. & Palmer, N. F. (2010). Impact of positive psychological capital on employee well-being over time. *Journal of Occupational Health Psychology*, 15(1), 17–28.

Avey, J. B., Luthans, F. & Youssef, C. M. (2010). The additive value of positive psychological capital in predicting work attitudes and behaviors. *Journal of Management*, 36(2), 430–52.

Avey, J. B, Reichard, R. J., Luthans, F. & Mahatre, K. H. (2011). Meta-analysis of the impact of positive psychological capital on employee attitudes, behaviors, and performance. *Human Resource Development Quarterly*, 22(2), 127–52.

Avey, J. B., Wernsing, T. S. & Luthans, F. (2008). Can positive employees help positive organizational change? Impact of psychological capital and emotions on relevant attitudes and behaviors. *Journal of Applied Behavioral Science*, 44(1), 48–70.

Avolio, B. J. & Gardner, W. L. (2005). Authentic leadership development: Getting to the root of positive forms of leadership. *Leadership Quarterly*, 16(3), 315–38.

Avolio, B. J., Zhu, W., Koh, W. & Bhatia, P. (2004). Transformational leadership and organizational commitment: Mediating role of psychological empowerment and moderating role of structural distance. *Journal of Organizational Behavior*, 25(8), 951–68.

Bakker, A. B., Demerouti, E. & Euwema, M. C. (2005). Job resources buffer the impact of job demands on burnout. *Journal of Occupational Health Psychology*, 10(2), 170–80.

Bandura, A. (1997). *Self-Efficacy: The Exercise of Control*. New York: Freeman.

Bandura, A. (2000). Cultivate self-efficacy for personal and organizational effectiveness. In E. A. Locke (ed.). *The Blackwell Handbook of Principles of Organizational Behavior*. Oxford: Blackwell, pp. 120–36.

Barling, J., Loughlin, C. & Kelloway, E. (2002). Development and test of a model linking safety-specific transformational leadership and occupational safety. *Journal of Applied Psychology*, 87, 488–96.

Barling, J., Christie, A. & Hoption, A. (2011). Leadership. In S. Zedeck (ed.), *APA Handbook of Industrial and Organizational Psychology. Volume 1: Building and Developing the Organization*. Washington, DC: American Psychological Association, pp. 183–240.

Barling, J., Weber, T. & Kelloway, E. K. (1996). Effects of transformational leadership training on attitudinal and financial outcomes: A field experiment. *Journal of Applied Psychology*, 81(6), 827–32.

Bergheim, K., Nielsen, M. B., Mearns, K. & Eid, J. (2015). The relationship between psychological capital, job satisfaction, and safety perceptions in the maritime industry. *Safety Science*, 74, 27–36.

Baumeister, R. F., Bratslavsky, E., Finkenauer, C. & Vohs, K. D. (2001). Bad is stronger than good. *Review of General Psychology*, 5(4), 323–70.

Bono, J. E., Foldes, H., Vinson, G. & Muros, J. P. (2007). Workplace emotions: The role of supervisor and leadership. *Journal of Applied Psychology*, 92(5), 1357–67.

Cameron, K. S. (2008). Paradox in positive organizational change. *Journal of Applied Behavioral Science*, 44(1), 7–24.

Center for Creative Leadership (2006). CCL poll: Teams in organizations. *Leading Effectively* e-newsletter, August. http://www.ccl.org/leadership/enewsletter/2006/AUGissue.aspx?pageId=1721. Accessed 23 June 2015.

Clapp-Smith, R., Vogelgesang, G. R. & Avey, J. B. (2009). Authentic leadership and positive psychological capital: The mediating role of trust at the group level of analysis. *Journal of Leadership & Organizational Studies*, 15(3), 227–40.

Coutu, D. L. (2002). How resilience works. *Harvard Business Review*; 80(5), 46–55

Dawkins, S., Martin, A., Scott, J. & Sanderson, K. (2013). Building on the positives: A psychometric review and critical analysis of the construct of psychological capital. *Journal of Occupational and Organizational Psychology*, 86(3), 348–70.

Dawkins, S., Martin, A., Scott, J. & Sanderson, K. (2015). Advancing conceptualization and measurement of psychological capital as a collective construct. *Human Relations*, 68(6), 925–49.

Day, R. C. & Hamblin, R. L. (1964). Some effects of close and punitive styles of supervision. *American Journal of Sociology*, 69, 499–510.

Degoey, P. (2000). Contagious justice: Exploring the social construction of justice in organizations. *Research in Organizational Behavior*, 22, 51–102.

Diener, E. (2000). Subjective well-being: The science of happiness and a proposal for a national index. *American Psychologist*, 55(1), 34–43.

Diener, E. & Biswas-Diener, R. (2008). *Rethinking Happiness: The Science of Psychological Wealth*. Malden, MA: Blackwell Publishing.

Diener, E. & Fujita, F. (1995). Resources, personal strivings, and subjective well-being: A nomothetic and idiographic approach. *Journal of Personality and Social Psychology*, 68(5), 926–35.

Diener, E. & Suh, E. M. (1999). National differences in subjective well-being. In D. Kahneman, E. Diener & N. Schwarz (eds.), *Well-Being: Foundations of Hedonic Psychology*. New York: Russell Sage Foundation, pp. 434–50.

Dvir, T., Eden, D., Avolio, B. J. & Shamir, B. (2002). Impact of transformational leadership on follower development and performance: A field experiment. *Academy of Management Journal*, 45(4), 735–44.

Eid, J., Mearns, K., Larsson, G., Laberg, J. C. & Johnsen, B. H. (2012). Leadership, psychological capital and safety research: Conceptual issues and future research questions. *Safety Science*, 50(1), 55–61.

Elovainio, M., Kivimäki, M., Puttonen, S., Lindholm, H., Pohjonen, T. & Sinvervo, T. (2006). Organizational injustice and impaired cardiac regulation among female employees. *Occupational and Environmental Medicine*, 63, 141–4.

Emmons, R. A. (1992). Abstract versus concrete goals: Personal striving level, physical illness, and psychological well-being. *Journal of Personality and Social Psychology*, 62(2), 292–300.

Ertosun, Ö. G., Erdil, O., Deniz, N. & Lütfihak, A. (2015). Positive psychological capital development: A field study by the Solomon four group design. *International Business Research*, 8(10), 102–11.

Flin, R., Mearns, K., O'Connor, P. & Bryden, R. (2000). Measuring safety climate: Identifying the common features. *Safety Science*, 34(1), 177–92.

Folkman, S. (1997). Positive psychological states and coping with severe stress. *Social Science & Medicine*, 45(8), 1207–21.

Fredrickson, B. L. (2001). The role of positive emotions in positive psychology: The broaden-and-build theory of positive emotions. *American Psychologist*, 56(3), 218–26.

Gardner, W. L. & Schermerhorn, J. R. (2004). Unleashing individual potential: Performance gains through positive organizational behavior and authentic leadership. *Organizational Dynamics*, 33(3), 270–81.

Gyekye, S. A. (2005). Workers' perceptions of workplace safety and job satisfaction. *International Journal of Occupational Safety & Ergonomics*, 11, 291–302.

Hobfoll, S. (2002). Social and psychological resources and adaptation. *Review of General Psychology*, 6, 307–24.

Hofmann, D. A. & Morgeson, F. P. (1999). Safety-related behavior as a social exchange: The role of perceived organizational support and leader–member exchange. *Journal of Applied Psychology*, 84(2), 286–96.

Hofmann, D. A., Morgeson, F. P. & Gerras, S. (2003). Climate as a moderator of the relationship between leader–member exchange and content specific citizenship: Safety climate as an exemplar. *Journal of Applied Psychology*, 88, 170–8.

Hofmann, D. & Stetzer, A. (1996). A cross-level investigation of factors influencing unsafe behaviors and accidents. *Personnel Psychology*, 49(2), 307–39.

Karlin, W. A., Brondolo, E. & Schwartz, J. (2003). Workplace social support and ambulatory cardiovascular activity in New York City traffic agents. *Psychosomatic Medicine*, 65(2), 167–76.

Kelloway, E. K. & Barling, J. (2010). Leadership development as an intervention in occupational health psychology. *Work & Stress*, 24, 260–79.

Kelloway, E. K., Barling, J. & Helleur, J. (2000). Enhancing transformational leadership: The roles of training and feedback. *Leadership & Organization Development Journal*, 21(3), 145–9.

Kelloway, E. K., Mullen, J. E & Francis, L. (2006). Injuring your leadership: How passive leadership affects employee safety. *Journal of Occupational Health Psychology*, 11(1), 76–86.

Kelloway, E. K., Sivanathan, N., Francis, L. & Barling, J. (2005). Poor leadership. In J. Barling, E. K. Kelloway & M. R. Frone (eds.), *Handbook of Work Stress*. Thousand Oaks, CA: Sage, pp. 89–112.

Kivimäki, M., Elovainio, M., Vahtera, J. & Ferrie, J. E. (2003). Organisational justice and health of employees: Prospective cohort study. *Occupational and Environmental Medicine*, 60, 27–34.

Krasikova, D. V., Lester, P. B. & Harms, P. D. (2015). Effects of psychological capital on mental health and substance abuse. *Journal of Leadership & Organizational Studies*, 22, 280–91.

Liu, Y. (2013). Mediating effect of positive psychological capital in Taiwan's life insurance industry. *Social Behavior and Personality*, 41(1), 109–11.

Luthans, F. (2002a). The need for and meaning of positive organizational behavior. *Journal of Organizational Behavior*, 23, 695–706.

Luthans, F. (2002b). Positive organizational behavior: Developing and managing psychological strengths. *Academy of Management Executive*, 16(1), 57–72.

Luthans, F., Avey, J. B., Avolio, B. J., Norman, S. M. & Combs, G. M. (2006). Psychological capital development: Toward a micro-intervention. *Journal of Organizational Behavior*, 27(3), 387–93.

Luthans, F., Avey, J. B., Avolio, B. J. & Peterson, S. J. (2010). The development and resulting performance impact of positive psychological capital. *Human Resource Development Quarterly*, 21(1), 41–67.

Luthans, F., Avey, J. B., Clapp-Smith, R. & Li, W. X. (2008). More evidence on the value of Chinese workers' psychological capital: A potentially unlimited competitive resource? *International Journal of Human Resource Management*, 19(5), 818–27.

Luthans, F., Avey, J. B. & Patera, J. L. (2008). Experimental analysis of a web-based training intervention to develop positive psychological capital. *Academy of Management Learning & Education*, 7(2), 209–21.

Luthans, F. & Avolio, B. (2003). Authentic leadership: A positive development approach. In K. S. Cameron, J. E. Dutton & R. E. Quinn (eds), *PositiveOrganizational Scholarship*. San Francisco, CA: Berrett-Koehler, pp. 241–58.

Luthans, F., Avolio, B. J., Avey, J. B. & Norman, S. M. (2007). Positive psychological capital: Measurement and relationship with performance and satisfaction. *Personnel Psychology*, 60, 541–72.

Luthans, K. W. & Jensen, S. M. (2005). The linkage between psychological capital and commitment to organizational mission: A study of nurses. *Journal of Nursing Administration*, 35(6), 304–10.

Luthans, F., Luthans, K. W., Hodgetts, R. M. & Luthans, B. C. (2002). Positive approach to leadership (PAL): Implications for today's organizations. *Journal of Leadership Studies*, 8, 3–20.

Luthans, F., Luthans, K. W. & Luthans, B. C. (2004). Positive psychological capital: Beyond human and social capital. *Business Horizons*, 47(1), 45–50.

Luthans, F., Norman, S. M., Avolio, B. J. & Avey, J. B. (2008). The mediating role of psychological capital in the supportive organizational climate–employee performance relationship. *Journal of Organizational Behavior*, 29(2), 219–38.
Luthans, F. & Youssef, C. M. (2004). Human, social, and now positive psychological capital management. *Organizational Dynamics*, 33, 143–60.
Luthans, F., Youssef, C. M. & Avolio, B. J. (2007). *Psychological Capital*. Oxford: Oxford University Press.
Luthans, F., Youssef-Morgan, C. & Avolio, B. J. (2015). *Psychological Capital and Beyond*. Oxford: Oxford University Press.
Luthans, F., Youssef, C. M., Sweetman, D. S. & Harms, P. D. (2013). Meeting the leadership challenge of employee well-being through relationship PsyCap and Health PsyCap. *Journal of Leadership & Organizational Studies*, 20, 118–33.
Lyubomirsky, S. (2001). Why are some people happier than others? The role of cognitive and motivational processes in well-being. *American Psychologist*, 56(3), 239–49.
Lyubomirsky, S. (2007). *The How of Happiness: A New Approach to Getting the Life You Want*. New York: Penguin.
Masten, A. S. (2001). Ordinary magic: Resilience processes in development. *American Psychologist*, 56, 227–39.
McKee, M. & Kelloway, E. K. (2009). Leading to wellbeing. In *Annual meeting of the European Academy of Work and Organizational Psychology, Santiago de Compostella*, Spain.
McKenny, A. F., Short, J. C. & Payne, G. T. (2013). Using computer-aided text analysis to elevate constructs: An illustration using psychological capital. *Organizational Research Methods*, 16(1), 152–84.
Memili, E., Welsh, D. H. B. & Kaciak, E. (2014). Organizational psychological capital of family franchise firms through the lens of the leader–member exchange theory. *Journal of Leadership & Organizational Studies*, 21(2; SI), 200–9.
Memili, E., Welsh, D. H. B. & Luthans, F. (2013). Going beyond research on goal setting: A proposed role for organizational psychological capital of family firms. *Entrepreneurship Theory and Practice*, 37(6), 1289–96.
Mullen, J. & Kelloway, E. K. (2009). Safety leadership: A longitudinal study of the effects of transformational leadership on safety outcomes. *Journal of Occupational and Organizational Psychology*, 82(2), 253–72.
Mullen, J., Kelloway, E. K. & Teed, M. (2011). Inconsistent style of leadership as a predictor of safety behaviour. *Work & Stress*, 25(1), 41–54.
Newman, A., Ucbasaran, D., Zhu, F. & Hirst, G. (2014). Psychological capital: A review and synthesis. *Journal of Organizational Behavior*, 35, 120–38.
Nyberg, A., Alfredsson, L., Theorell, T., Westerlund, H., Vahtera, J. & Kivimäki, M. (2009). Managerial leadership and ischaemic heart disease among employees: The Swedish WOLF study. *Occupational and Environmental Medicine*, 66, 51–5.
Peterson, S. J., Luthans, F., Avolio, B. J, Walumbwa, F. O. & Zhang, Z. (2011). Psychological capital and employee performance: A latent growth modeling approach. *Personnel Psychology*, 64(2), 427–50.
Roche, M., Haar, J. M. & Luthans, F. (2014). The role of mindfulness and psychological capital on the well-being of leaders. *Journal of Occupational Health Psychology*, 19(4), 476–89.

Ryff, C. D. & Singer, B. (2003). Flourishing under fire: Resilience as a prototype of challenged thriving. In C. L. M. Keyes, & J. Haidt (eds), *Flourishing: Positive Psychology and the Life Well-Lived*, Washington, DC: American Psychological Association, pp. 15–36.
Scheier, M. F. & Carver, C. S. (1985). Optimism, coping, and health: Assessment and implications of generalized outcome expectancies. *Health Psychology*, 4(3), 219–47.
Scheier, M. F., Weintraub, J. K. & Carver, C. S. (1986). Coping with stress: Divergent strategies of optimists and pessimists. *Journal of Personality and Social Psychology*, 51(6), 1257–64.
Seligman, M. (1998). *Learned Optimism*. New York: Pocket.
Seligman, M. (2002). *Authentic Happiness*. New York: Free Press.
Seligman, M. E. & Csikszentmihalyi, M. (2000). Positive psychology: An introduction. *American Psychologist*, 55(1), 5–14.
Skakon, J., Nielsen, K., Borg, V. & Guzman, J. (2010). Are leaders' wellbeing, behaviours and style associated with the affective wellbeing of their employees? A systematic review of three decades of research. *Work & Stress*, 24(2), 107–39.
Snyder, C. R. (2000). *Handbook of Hope*. San Diego: Academic Press.
Snyder, C. R., Irving, L. M. & Anderson, J. R. (1991). Hope and health: Measuring the will and the ways. In C. R. Snyder & D. R. Forsyth (eds), *Handbook of Social and Clinical Psychology: The Health Perspective*. Oxford: Pergamon Press, pp. 285–305.
Stajkovic, A. & Luthans. F. (1998). Self-efficacy and work-related performance: A meta-analysis. *Psychological Bulletin*, 124, 240–61.
Staw, B. (1981). Threat-rigidity effects in organizational behavior: A multilevel analysis. *Administrative Science Quarterly*, 26(4), 501–24.
Story, J. S., Youssef, C. M., Luthans, F., Barbuto, J. E. & Bovaird, J. (2013). Contagion effect of global leaders' positive psychological capital on followers: Does distance and quality of relationship matter? *International Journal of Human Resource Management*, 24(13), 2534–53.
Terrion, J. L. & Ashforth, B. E. (2002). From 'I' to 'we': The role of putdown humor and identity in the development of a temporary group. *Human Relations*, 55(1), 55–88.
Väänänen, A., Kouvonen, A., Kivimäki, M., Oksanen, T., Elovainio, M., Virtanen, M., Pentti, J. & Vahtera, J. (2009). Workplace social capital and co-occurrence of lifestyle risk factors: The Finnish public sector study. *Occupational and Environmental Medicine*, 66(7), 432–7.
Vanhove, A. J., Herian, M. N., Perez, A. L., Harms, P. D. & Lester, P. B. (2015). Can resilience be developed at work? A meta-analytic review of resilience-building programme effectiveness. *Journal of Occupational and Organizational Psychology*, 89(2), 278–307.
Vanno, V., Kaemkate, W. & Wongwanich, S. (2014). Relationships between academic performance, perceived group psychological capital, and positive psychological capital of Thai undergraduate students. *Procedia – Social and Behavioral Sciences*, 116, 3226–30.
Wang, H., Sui, Y., Luthans, F., Wang, D. & Wu, Y. (2014). Impact of authentic leadership on performance: Role of followers' positive psychological capital and relational processes. *Journal of Organizational Behavior*, 35(1), 5–21.

West, B. J., Patera, J. L. & Carsten, M. K. (2009). Team level positivity: Investigating positive psychological capacities and team level outcomes. *Journal of Organizational Behavior*, 30(2), 249–67.
Wood, R. and Bandura, A. (1989). Social cognitive theory of organizational management. *Academy of Management Review*, 14, 361–84.
Wright, T. A. & Hobfoll, S. E. (2004). Commitment, psychological well-being and job performance: An examination of conservation of resources (COR) theory and job burnout. *Journal of Business and Management*, 9, 389–406.
Youssef, C. M. & Luthans, F. (2007). Positive organizational behavior in the workplace: The impact of hope, optimism, and resilience. *Journal of Management*, 33(5), 774–800.
Youssef, C. M. & Luthans, F. (2012). Positive global leadership. *Journal of World Business*, 47(4), 539–47.
Youssef-Morgan, C. M. & Luthans, F. (2013a). Positive leadership. *Organizational Dynamics*, 42(3; SI), 198–208.
Youssef-Morgan, C. M. & Luthans, F. (2013b). Psychological capital theory: Toward a positive holistic model. In A. B. Bakker (ed.), *Advances in positive organizational psychology*. Bingley, UK: Emerald, pp. 145–66.
Youssef-Morgan, C. M. & Luthans, F. (2015). Psychological capital and well-being. *Stress & Health*, 31(3), 180–8.
Zohar, D. (1980). Safety climate in industrial organizations: Theoretical and applied implications. *Journal of Applied Psychology*, 65, 96–102.
Zohar, D. (2000). A group-level model of safety climate: Testing the effect of group climate on microaccidents in manufacturing jobs. *Journal of Applied Psychology*, 85(4), 587–96.
Zohar, D. (2002). Modifying supervisor practices to improve submit safety: A leadership-based intervention model. *Journal of Applied Psychology*, 87(1), 156–163.
Zohar, D. & Luria, G. (2005). A multilevel model of safety climate: Cross-level relationships between organization and group-level climates. *Journal of Applied Psychology*, 90(4), 616–28.
Zohar, D. & Tenne-Gazit, O. (2008). Transformational leadership and group interaction as climate antecedents: A social network analysis. *Journal of Applied Psychology*, 93(4), 744–57.

14

'Choose a Job You Love, and You Will Never Have to Work a Day in your Life'

A Strengths-based Leadership Approach to Optimal Functioning at Work

Philippe Dubreuil and Jacques Forest

Positive Psychology and the Strengths Movement

Positive psychology (Seligman & Csikszentmihalyi, 2000) is the scientific study of positive subjective experiences and individual traits (at the person level), and civic virtue as well as positive institutions (at the group level), for the purpose of decreasing negative experiences (e.g., depression, negative emotions) and increasing positive experiences (e.g., states of flow, positive emotions and optimal functioning). The application of positive psychology in the workplace, which is named either positive organizational scholarship (Cameron, Dutton & Quinn, 2003) or positive organizational behaviour (Luthans, 2002), is the scientific effort to find an answer to the question 'How can people's work make their life most worth living?' (Forest, 2004).

Work is a sphere of life where we spend almost half of our waking time (Vallerand & Houlfort, 2003), and it is a worthy endeavour to make sure that this daily period, sustained every weekday for several decades, is mainly positive and productive. In positive psychology, there is a general agreement that well-being can (broadly) be outlined on five different levels, namely positive emotions (experiencing happiness and life satisfaction), engagement (being deeply involved and absorbed in one's actions), positive relations (cultivating positive and meaningful relationships), meaning (belonging to or serving something that you believe is greater than yourself) and accomplishment (pursuing achievement and mastery for their own sakes). These together are also known as the PERMA model of well-being (Seligman, 2011).

Be it in work or general life, one main way to achieve well-being and optimal functioning through increased positive emotions, engagement, relationships, meaning and accomplishment is to identify and use one's personal strengths (Seligman, 2011). In this chapter, we will outline how leaders can use their own strengths and optimize their followers' strengths to ensure a healthy and productive workplace. We will first present a brief explanation of the strengths movement and its three main schools of thoughts, in order to clearly define the concept of 'strength' and to provide a general overview of the main research results in the

Leading to Occupational Health and Safety: How Leadership Behaviours Impact Organizational Safety and Well-Being, First Edition.
Edited by E. Kevin Kelloway, Karina Nielsen and Jennifer K. Dimoff.

field. Then, we will redirect our focus onto an applied perspective and discuss how leaders can identify strengths, their own or their subordinates', and increase their daily use in the workplace. Lastly, we will describe some of the main managerial practices that can be implemented by leaders to support the development of a strengths-based culture among their teams.

Three Streams of Research on Strengths

We can confidently say that in the scientific literature there are three main sources of thought and research on strengths: (1) the Gallup Organization, (2) the Positive Psychology Center (PPC) and (3) the Centre of Applied Positive Psychology (CAPP). While each source has its own specificities, they also share some significant similarities, as they influenced each other during their development process.

The Gallup Organization

The Gallup Organization's strengths model is based on Donald Clifton's original work in which he and his collaborators interviewed, over a period spanning almost 30 years, more than 2,000,000 individuals in search of excellence patterns (Asplund, Lopez, Hodges & Harter, 2007). Their view is that high-performance individuals have talents, which are further developed or emancipated through the use of knowledge (facts, information, education, etc.) and skills (steps of a process, technical abilities, etc.). These three elements combined (talents, knowledge and skills) create a strength, which is ultimately defined as 'the ability to provide consistent, near-perfect performance in an activity' (Buckingham & Clifton, 2001, p. 25). Using their large database of millions of interviews, Clifton and his collaborators at the Gallup Organization were able to isolate, define and measure 34 specific (what they called) themes of talents (see Box 14.1).

Research using this conceptualization has led to many applications at the individual (e.g., coaching), group (e.g., team development) and organizational (e.g., career management, training, and performance evaluation) levels, as described in their popular books *First, Break All the Rules* (Buckingham & Coffman, 1999), *Now, Discover Your Strengths* (Buckingham & Clifton, 2001), *Go Put Your Strengths to Work* (Buckingham, 2007) and *Strengths-based Leadership* (Rath & Conchie, 2009). Subsequent research on strengths also showed that talent identification and strengths development initiatives in the workplace were associated with increases in employee engagement, customer satisfaction, profit and productivity, as well as decreases in turnover and safety incidents (Asplund & Blacksmith, 2012; Clifton & Harter, 2003; Harter, Schmidt & Hayes, 2002; Hodges & Asplund, 2010). Thus, there is evidence, with this conceptualization, that developing one's strengths at work leads not only to personal benefits (more engagement, competence and performance) but also to organizational benefits (profits). Leaders or persons in leadership positions are thus well advised, in order to have a performing and healthy workforce, to identify and use their strengths and their employees' strengths.

The Positive Psychology Center

The Positive Psychology Center's (PPC) strengths model is part of the birth of the positive psychology movement, in 1999, under the impetus of the then APA president Martin Seligman. With private funding and the help of 55 well-known researchers, it was decided to create an 'Anti DSM-V (diagnostic and statistical manual of mental disorders)', or what they called a manual of the sanities. This thorough process involved brainstorming sessions with partners, consultations at international congresses and an exhaustive literature review of scientific, philosophical and religious writings. This extensive review process generated a long list of potential candidates as strengths, which was narrowed down to 24 'character strengths' using ten discriminant criteria (Peterson & Seligman, 2004). Examples of such criteria are that a strength must contribute to fulfilment and self-actualization (using this strength leads to satisfaction and well-being), must be ubiquitous (it is recognized and celebrated across cultures) and must be valued by institutions and organizations.

In this conceptualization, strengths are 'the psychological ingredients – processes or mechanisms – that define the virtues' (Peterson & Seligman, 2004, p. 13), and the 24 strengths are separated into six broad virtues (see Box 14.1), namely (1) wisdom and knowledge (5 strengths), (2) courage (4 strengths), (3) humanity (3 strengths), (4) justice (3 strengths), (5) temperance (4 strengths) and (6) transcendence (5 strengths). Research allowed the verification of the fact that these character strengths are recognized and valued universally in the world (Biswas-Diener, 2006; Park, Peterson & Seligman, 2006), while there have been efforts to study strengths' presence and distribution at different ages (e.g., children, teenagers, adults) (Park, Peterson & Seligman, 2004; Steen, Kachorek & Peterson, 2003), in different populations (e.g., military, work) (Peterson, Stephens, Park, Lee & Seligman, 2010; Reivich, Seligman & McBride, 2011), in different cities (e.g., in the USA) (Park & Peterson, 2010) and in multiple countries (Linley et al., 2007; Park et al., 2006). Research on character strengths has also demonstrated that the identification and use of strengths can not only increase happiness in general life, but also decrease depressive symptoms (Gander, Proyer, Ruch & Wyss 2013; Seligman, Steen, Park & Peterson, 2005) and, in the work context, increase well-being (Forest et al., 2012) and performance (Dubreuil et al., 2016). This second stream of research again emphasize the importance, at all levels (employees, leaders, organizations), of knowing and using everyone's strengths.

The Centre of Applied Positive Psychology

This British centre is led by psychologist Alex Linley and his team and has a research programme on strengths but also a strong inclination towards applied interventions (as its name implies). The Centre of Applied Positive Psychology's (CAPP) strengths model was forged through discussions, research and interventions with their expert staff (Linley & Dovey, 2015). For them, a strength is 'a pre-existing capacity for a particular way of behaving, thinking or feeling that is authentic and energizing to the user, and enables optimal functioning, development and performance' (Linley, 2008). A strength is thus a trait that is natural (it seems always to have been there, it feels natural and authentic), energizing (it makes the person feel particularly 'alive') and leads to tangible results (performance, proactivity, development, adaptation, etc.).

The CAPP classification of 60 strengths (see Box 14.1) is not categorized by themes of virtues, but rather placed in four different possible scenarios when you fill in their questionnaire: (1) realized strengths (you use your strengths, you perform well and you should have a higher use of these), (2) unrealized strengths (you perform well while using these strengths but you underuse them), (3) learned behaviours (you perform adequately while using these strengths but it is de-energizing to do so and you should moderate their use), (4) weaknesses (you perform poorly with these, it is de-energizing to do so and you should minimize their use).

According to this intervention model, the goal is to marshal the use of realized strengths, maximize unrealized strengths, moderate learned behaviours and minimize weaknesses. These actions can be initiated by individuals but will be more impactful and thorough if done by persons in a leadership or influence role, hence the importance of strengths identification and its use as a management tool for optimal functioning. Using this general template, their research has shown that strengths use leads to greater well-being, vitality, confidence and self-esteem (Govindji & Linley, 2007; Proctor, Maltby & Linley, 2011; Wood, Linley, Maltby, Kashdan & Hurling, 2011). They also provided the scientific and practitioners' communities with numerous publications of tools and intervention models mainly rooted in their consulting practice (Biswas-Diener, 2010; Linley, 2008; Linley, Harrington & Garcea, 2010).

Strengths Identification

As stated earlier, we now turn to a more applied perspective and will first examine how leaders can identify strengths, be it their own or their subordinates', as this is the first step in any strengths development initiative. In this regard, a wide array of methods are available to help individuals identify their main areas of strengths, and the most common methods used by scientists and human resources professionals will be described in the following lines as they will be useful for leaders. That is, the use of psychometric instruments, the observation of strengths and the collection of feedback on strengths will be presented as management practices. It must be noted that although each method on its own can provide very useful information and insights regarding one's particular strengths, the combination of these different methods can yield an even more accurate and complete picture.

Psychometric Instruments

A first identification method involves the use of psychometric instruments. This method offers the advantages of being simple, brief, and grounded in solid empirical research evidence. However, its main disadvantage is that the results provided are based on general classifications which sometimes fail to capture the specificity of each individual. Still, these psychometric instruments remain excellent starting points that appropriately introduce the strengths philosophy, deliver powerful insights and motivate individuals to apply and better understand their strengths. So far, three main strengths identification instruments have been developed: the StrengthsFinder® (Asplund et al., 2007), the VIA Survey (Peterson & Seligman, 2004) and the R2 Strengths Profiler® (Linley & Dovey, 2015).

Developed by the Gallup Organization on the basis of decades of research and interviews conducted in the workplace to better understand the most natural thoughts, feelings and behaviours of successful people (Hodges & Asplund, 2010), the StrengthsFinder® is an online instrument that identifies individuals' main areas of talent (see Box 14.1). It is available in 24 languages and takes approximately 30 minutes to complete, and results are provided instantly online under the form of a personalized report. This report presents the individual's top five themes of talents and includes supporting material that helps build these talents into strengths.

Similarly, the VIA Survey is an online strengths identification instrument that was developed by Peterson and Seligman (2004) at the PPC (in a venture funded by the VIA Institute on Character) following the birth of positive psychology. It is based on the Character Strengths and Virtues Classification, which comprises 24 strengths categorized under six broad virtues (see Box 14.1). As stated earlier, this classification was based on an impressive research effort aiming to identify universal strengths and virtues that consistently emerged across history and culture (Dahlsgaard, Peterson & Seligman, 2005; Peterson & Seligman, 2004). The VIA Survey is available in 14 languages, takes approximately 15 minutes to complete and provides results instantly online in the form of a report which ranks in order the individual's 24 strengths; the first five are termed 'signature strengths'.

Finally, the R2 Strengths Profiler® is an online strengths assessment and development tool created by Linley and his colleagues at the CAPP (Linley & Dovey, 2015). This instrument is based on a classification of 60 strengths (see Box 14.1), which was developed on the basis of the CAPP team's expertise regarding strengths interventions. The R2 Strengths Profiler® comprises 60 different attributes, which the individual must rate according to the dimensions of performance, energy and use. This assessment takes approximately 20 minutes to complete and results are provided instantly online in the form of a personalized report in which the main attributes are classified under realized strengths (perform well, energizing, use often), unrealized strengths (perform well, energizing, don't use often), learned behaviours (perform well, not energizing) or weaknesses (hard to do well, draining). The report also includes additional material that helps the individual to fully take advantage of this slightly different model and put strengths into action.

Self-Observation and Introspection

A second identification method involves the observation of specific indicators of strengths before, during or after an activity. This method is referred to as *Strengthspotting* by some researchers and authors (Linley & Burns, 2010; Linley, Garcea, Hill, Minhas, Trenier & Willars, 2010) and can be useful for leaders, both

Box 14.1 Strengths identification instruments

Instrument	StrengthsFinder®	VIA Survey	R2 Strengths Profiler®	
Definition of a strength	Ability to consistently provide near-perfect performance on a task (Buckingham & Clifton, 2001)	The psychological ingredients – processes or mechanisms – that define the virtues (Peterson & Seligman, 2004)	A pre-existing capacity for a particular way of behaving, thinking or feeling that is authentic and energizing to the user, and enables optimal functioning, development and performance (Linley, 2008)	
Number of strengths	34	24	60	
Strengths list	1) Achiever	**Wisdom and knowledge**	1) Action	32) Innovation
	2) Activator	1) Creativity	2) Adherence	33) Judgement
	3) Adaptability	2) Curiosity	3) Adventure	34) Legacy
	4) Analytical	3) Judgement	4) Authenticity	35) Listener
	5) Arranger	4) Love of learning	5) Bounceback	36) Mission
	6) Belief	5) Perspective	6) Catalyst	37) Moral compass
	7) Command	**Courage**	7) Centred	38) Narrator
	8) Communication	6) Bravery	8) Change agent	39) Optimism
	9) Competition	7) Perseverance	9) Compassion	40) Order
	10) Connectedness	8) Honesty	10) Competitive	41) Persistence
	11) Consistency/Fairness	9) Zest	11) Connector	42) Personal responsibility
	12) Context	**Humanity**	12) Counterpoint	
	13) Deliberative	10) Love	13) Courage	43) Personalization
	14) Developer	11) Kindness	14) Creativity	44) Persuasion
	15) Discipline	12) Social intelligence	15) Curiosity	45) Planful

	16) Empathy 17) Focus 18) Futuristic 19) Harmony 20) Ideation 21) Inclusiveness/Includer 22) Individualization 23) Input 24) Intellection 25) Learner 26) Maximizer 27) Positivity 28) Relator 29) Responsibility 30) Restorative 31) Self-assurance 32) Significance 33) Strategic 34) Woo	**Justice** 13) Teamwork 14) Fairness 15) Leadership **Temperance** 16) Forgiveness 17) Humility 18) Prudence 19) Self-regulation **Transcendence** 20) Appreciation of beauty and excellence 21) Gratitude 22) Hope 23) Humour 24) Spirituality	16) Detail 17) Drive 18) Efficacy 19) Emotional awareness 20) Empathic connection 21) Enabler 22) Equality 23) Esteem builder 24) Explainer 25) Feedback 26) Gratitude 27) Growth 28) Humility 29) Humour 30) Improver 31) Incubator	46) Prevention 47) Pride 48) Rapport builder 49) Reconfiguration 50) Relationship deepener 51) Resilience 52) Resolver 53) Scribe 54) Self-awareness 55) Service 56) Spotlight 57) Strategic awareness 58) Time optimizer 59) Unconditionality 60) Work ethic
Information	www.gallupstrengthscenter.com	www.viacharacter.org	www.cappeu.com/R2StrengthsProfiler	

in relation to themselves and to manage their subordinates. It implies the careful observation of signs of strengths present in particular activities or behaviours, and can be conducted by the individual through self-observation or through a strengths discussion with another person. While the use of psychometric instruments provides people with a ready framework and language for strengths, this open-ended method is more flexible and offers the possibility to explore, discover and name singular strengths. It can be used in itself to discover strengths from the ground up, but can also be a useful complement to psychometric instruments.

Most scholars agree that the main signs of a strength are authenticity, energy, flow and performance (Buckingham, 2007; Hodges & Clifton, 2004; Linley, 2008; Peterson & Seligman, 2004). 'Authenticity' means that when people use their strengths, they feel they are being 'the real me'; they are being true to themselves and they feel they are doing what is right for them (Linley, 2008; Peterson & Seligman, 2004). 'Energy' means that when people use their strengths, they feel energized and vitalized. The activity or behaviour is not draining them; on the contrary, it seems to provide them with even more energy (Linley, 2008; Peterson & Seligman, 2004). The flow component is the feeling people report having, when they use their strengths, of being deeply absorbed in the activity and losing all sense of time (Buckingham, 2007; Linley, 2008). This particular experience of deep engagement is well known as the state of flow (Nakamura & Csikszentmihalyi, 2002). Finally, 'performance' signifies that when people use their strengths, they usually display impressive performances in that particular activity, such as rapid learning and development, constant success, innovation and remarkable task efficiency (Hodges & Clifton, 2004; Linley, 2008; Peterson & Seligman, 2004).

Therefore, it is possible for leaders to be particularly attentive to these signs and identify an activity or a behaviour as a strength when it meets all these criteria. This can be done through careful self-observation, either at the time or retrospectively, or through a discussion with another person. For example, leaders can use this technique as an introspective self-observation tool to identify their own strengths. They can also use it in the form of a one-to-one discussion with a colleague or a mentor that specifically aims at better understanding and identification of their personal strengths. Similarly, they can apply this technique with their employees, by observing and identifying their strengths in action or in a coaching perspective through conversations that aim to reveal more about their strengths. In this regard, many authors have developed lists of indicators and questions that can help individuals observe themselves, and discuss and identify their personal strengths (Biswas-Diener, 2010; Buckingham, 2007; Linley, 2008; Linley & Burns, 2010; Peterson & Seligman, 2004). Box 14.2 presents some indicators and questions that can help start a personal reflection (or a managerial discussion) of this kind.

Feedback on Personal Strengths

A third identification method involves the collection and organization of feedback from peers about one's strengths. Also known as the Reflected Best Self exercise (Roberts, Dutton, Spreitzer, Heaphy & Quinn, 2005; Roberts, Spreitzer,

Box 14.2 Indicators and questions for strengths identification

	Authenticity
Indicators	• A sense of being genuine and particularly true to yourself during an activity • A sentiment of doing something that fits with who you really are • A feeling of deep personal satisfaction after an activity
Questions	• What makes you feel particularly connected with yourself? • What kind of activities provide you a sense of being who you really are?
	Energy
Indicators	• Being energized and vitalized rather than drained by an activity • Feeling alive and seeming to continuously have energy for a particular activity • Being irrevocably drawn to a particular activity
Questions	• What kind of activities do you find particularly energizing? • What sort of activities or tasks do you always end up looking forward to? • What do you enjoy doing on a daily basis?
	Flow
Indicators	• Being intensively focused and concentrated during an activity • Being deeply involved and doing things almost automatically • Losing track of time during an activity
Questions	• In what kind of activities do you find yourself deeply concentrated and engaged? • When do you lose sense of time because you are so absorbed in what you do?
	Performance
Indicators	• Quickly learning new information, skills and techniques in a particular activity or domain • Receiving praise, recognition and compliments in a specific activity • A feeling that this behaviour or activity seems almost natural to you
Questions	• When you are at your very best, what are you doing? • What sort of activities do you pick up quickly? • What seems somehow easier for you than for others? • In what kind of activities have you always been successful? • Do other people compliment you or tell you that you are gifted in particular activities?

Dutton, Quinn, Heaphy & Barker, 2005; Spreitzer, Stephens & Sweetman, 2009), this method comprises three main steps: (1) gathering feedback from peers, (2) summarizing the information collected and (3) composing a self-portrait representing oneself at one's best. This method requires more time and effort; however, as it is based on a collection of first-hand observations it also provides more precise and compelling information regarding one's personal strengths.

In the first step the individual collects feedback from significant people around him or her. These can be past and present colleagues, supervisors, clients, mentors, friends or family members, as long as they know the person well and the individual feels comfortable asking them for positive feedback. It is recommended that a diverse group of about ten people is selected who come from various contexts in which the person is involved. Once these people are identified, the individual asks them to provide information about his or her strengths, accompanied by specific examples. This can be done in person, by phone or by email; however, emails are generally preferred as they constitute a fast and convenient method, and they facilitate the subsequent analysis of the information.

The second step consists of analysing and summarizing the information collected. After all the feedback is gathered, the individual searches for common themes and patterns in the examples provided and organizes the information. A table including separate columns for common themes, examples and personal notes can be a helpful tool in making sense of the feedback (see Box 14.3). For some people, the result will be a confirmation of what they already knew about themselves, reaffirming their strengths with even more conviction. For others, it will be a true revelation, exposing behaviours they were not aware had such an impact. For others again, the feedback provided will shed a more nuanced light on particular strengths, giving them useful information on what exactly constitutes an edge in their behaviours and how to make the most of it.

In the third step the person writes a brief description of him- or herself at his or her best. This description should capture the themes, examples and observations from the previous step and weave them together in a short paragraph. This paragraph should begin with the phrase 'When I am at my best ...' and be about ten sentences long. The final result must constitute a powerful and inspiring image of the individual at his or her best and serve as a guide for future action (see Box 14.3). This introspective process can be quite hard and time-consuming; however, it is very important as it allows one to carefully examine one's strengths, make even more connections and consolidate this information in one's identity.

Strengths Use and Development

As a leader, it is important to know how to make the most of your strengths and how to help others fully take advantage of theirs. This section will present the main strategies proposed in the strengths development literature. Again, the following methods and advice are applicable to leaders in the development of their own careers, as well as in coaching or development processes intended for their employees.

Strengths-Based Job Crafting

While strengths identification is essential, it is only the first step in a strengths development process. In order to fully harness the benefits of this approach, one must make a conscious effort to find and develop new opportunities to apply one's strengths at work. This active process, through which people gradually shape their jobs around their areas of interest and specialities, is also known as job crafting. More precisely, job crafting is defined as 'the physical and cognitive changes that individuals make in the task or relational boundaries of their work' (Wrzesniewski & Dutton, 2001, p. 179). Job crafting can therefore be either

Box 14.3 Example of steps 2 and 3 of the Reflected Best Self exercise

Step 2 Feedback analysis

Common themes	Examples	Personal notes
Justice and fairness	As a sales assistant, I stood up to a supervisor who asked me to sell damaged merchandise. I publicly defended my colleague who was wrongly accused, even though it meant trouble for me.	Justice is a fundamental value for me and I am willing to sacrifice my own good for it.
Connection	I organized a successful mentoring programme in my organization from the ground up. I started a running club in my community just a few weeks after we moved in.	I love to remove barriers and help new people meet, team up and develop projects together.
Listener	Somehow, people always end up in my office to discuss personal matters. Many people tell me that I always find the right words to explain what they are trying to say.	People deeply appreciate it when I listen to them and genuinely try to understand how they feel.
[…]	[…]	[…]

Step 3 – Self description

When I am at my best, I stand up in front of injustice. I deeply believe it is a common value that must be respected and I am ready to sacrifice my own good for it. I expect fairness from others and I also act accordingly. By setting an example, I gain trust and respect from people around me. At my best, I easily envision new possibilities, projects and structures that bring people together. It gives me meaning, because I help people grow, team up and start new ventures that would not have come to life otherwise. When I am at my best, I take my time and carefully listen to what others are saying. It is a sign of respect, consideration and engagement that others appreciate and […]

physical (changing the form, scope or number of tasks), cognitive (changing how one sees the job) or relational (changing the people with whom one interacts). Research on this topic has shown that job crafting is predictive of work engagement (Bakker, Tims & Derk, 2012; Chen, Yen & Tsai, 2014), well-being (Slemp & Vella-Brodrick, 2014) and work performance (Bakker et al., 2012). However, it must remain aligned with organizational objectives and respect other colleagues'

Box 14.4 Questions about strengths-based job crafting
How can you use your personal margin to gradually carve and shape your role so you can spend more time working from your strengths? Given the current objectives of your team and organization, where do you think you could make your greatest contribution? Are there any projects that would particularly benefit from your strengths? How can you volunteer or offer your help on those projects? Can you start new projects that would play to your strengths and be useful for your organization? How can you free up your time and make better use of your strengths? Can you delegate specific tasks? Is it possible to team up with someone? Do you need to rearrange your work schedule? In what new situations can you put yourself in order to use your strengths more and make them known to others? Are there any of your strengths that remain underused in your work? If so, how can you change this situation? What new skills and techniques can you learn in order to develop and hone your strengths even more? Who can help you achieve this? Can any of your strengths help you overcome any of your weaknesses?

workloads and preferences; otherwise it can quickly become detrimental to the organization (Tims, Bakker & Derks, 2015).

From a strengths development perspective, this means gradually steering your job towards your main areas of strength, while staying focused on priorities and organizational objectives. Strengths-based job crafting involves using the flexibility provided around your core tasks carefully and finding new opportunities to use your strengths, develop them and make them known in the organization. By doing so, individuals gain as their strengths become more and more used, known and demanded by their peers, and the organization also gains from the performance and innovation that follows. In order to help individuals craft their jobs around their strengths, authors and scholars have developed a series of specific questions regarding strengths positioning and deployment in the workplace (Buckingham, 2007; Linley, 2008; Linley, Willars & Biswas-Diener, 2010). Box 14.4 presents a sample of such questions, which can be used by leaders in a self-development perspective, or in the development of their followers' strengths.

The 'Me at My Best' Exercise

The 'me at my best' exercise was developed and tested by Seligman et al. (2005). In this activity, participants are asked to write about and discuss a time when they are functioning optimally and to think about how their strengths contributed to this episode. We applied it to the work context (Forest et al., 2012) and expanded it to a three-hour format where this basic idea of optimal functioning using one's signature strength is broken down into several different sub-questions (see Box 14.5). This exercise can be done as an individual (to foster one's own optimal functioning) or with a group of employees by a leader who wants to foster the team's optimal functioning.

Box 14.5 Examples of questions for the three-hour version of the 'me at my best' exercise

1) Take a few minutes to think about something that you did, a decision that you made or a project you accomplished, for which you feel a great sense of pride and satisfaction. Briefly describe this situation. Which strengths allowed you to be successful in this situation?
2) What kind of compliments do you usually receive from your colleagues/friends/family/partner? To which strength(s) do these compliments refer to?
3) What kind of circumstances would you say allow you to be at your best? To which strengths do these circumstances refer to?
4) When you think about the future (next week, next month), what motivates and stimulates you? What are you looking forward to? Which strengths are implicated in your anticipations about the future?
5) Are there any strengths that are underused in the context of your work? In which context could they be used? Which strategy could you adopt to concretize their application?
6) Do you think there are any downsides to your strengths? In which contexts do you need to be especially careful about this?
7) Can certain strengths be used to compensate for your weaknesses? If so, how?

The first questions are aimed at helping the participants understand the idea that to function optimally we need to use our signature strengths often, intensely, and for long periods of time (see question 1 in Box 14.5). To get another point of view on this same idea, we ask participants to ask each other what significant others (colleagues, friends, family, partner) appreciate about them, for example what compliments they receive from them (see question 2 in Box 14.5). Once this idea has been grasped, the intervention brings the participants to think about the circumstances which allow them to be at their best (see question 3 in Box 14.5). We specifically ask participants to enumerate and describe in detail the ingredients, elements, components or type of colleagues they need in order to be able to use each of their top five strengths. Participants have often called the answer to this question their 'operating manual', meaning that a colleague reading this list should know how to make the best use of them.

Having thought about and discussed a past event that displayed our optimal functioning and qualities and strengths in the eyes of other people, we turn to the anticipation of a future event (see question 4 in Box 14.5). This question is specifically aimed at the energization component of a strength. Then, to jolt the use of unrealized strengths, we try to devise and put in place strategies to use them more intensively and frequently (see question 5 in Box 14.5). Finally, in this extended version of the exercise, we also devote time and energy to the 'dark' side of strengths use (see questions 6 and 7 in Box 14.5). We force participants to think about situations where combinations of strengths or strengths overuse might be problematic or even negative (question 6 in Box 14.5), and also about how someone's strengths can be put to use in buffering or neutralizing weaknesses (question 7 of Box 14.5). For this latter question, we can imagine the example of someone who has difficulty in being organized but has a love of learning: they might put this latter strength to use by taking courses and reading books about classification and organizing systems.

As mentioned earlier, we want to emphasize the idea that this exercise can be conducted by leaders on an individual basis (for their own development or with individual employees), but is especially well suited for medium to large teams or groups. In such settings, after strengths have been identified with the use of psychometric instruments, a first hour is devoted to the introduction of positive psychology and strengths (what is positive psychology, what is a strength, definitions of all the different strengths, etc.). The questions are then presented and explained to the group and participants are asked to write down, individually, their answers to the questions. The leader moves from person to person (or from table to table) to facilitate individual progress and take note of some good examples, which are then shared in plenary with the whole group. This is done for each question and usually takes two hours. This process allows participants to gain a deeper knowledge about their strengths, share their ideas with their colleagues and find new and exciting ways to optimize the workplace as well as the use of their strengths.

Using Signature Strengths in a New Way

Another short and very simple intervention that can be employed by leaders to increase the use of strengths is to ask people to use one (or two) of their top five signature strengths in a new way, every day, for a whole week (Forest et al., 2012; Seligman et al., 2005). To help with this task, there is a free online list which offers 340 new ways to use signature strengths (Rashid, 2014). This list has suggestions of specific actions to do, books to read, songs to listen to and films to watch in order to practise (or hear or see) the use of signature strengths (for movies specifically, see Niemiec & Wedding, 2014). In the work context (Forest et al., 2012), we used this activity (in complement with others) by asking participants to write and sign a 'contract' in which they engaged themselves, in order to try to use their signature strengths in new ways. This is an intervention that requires a low investment of time and effort, and which helps increase the use of strengths in various domains.

Card Games on Strengths

While there have been a host of scientifically tested interventions to increase strengths' identification and use, this positive movement also encouraged numerous initiatives. One such initiative is a Canadian-based personal development tool called 'Totem: The feel good game' (www.totemteam.com/en). Their goal is to propose an activity to help people become aware of their own strengths and qualities while having fun with colleagues. This exercise can be used by a leader if employees have doubts about and an unfavourable perception of psychometric instruments, or if a more playful intervention is necessary. While making no scientific claims for their game, they tried to take into account the research showing that people who know their strengths, and use them more often, over longer periods of time and more intensively, have a stronger feeling of general well-being. This company developed something that people would want to use on social or professional occasions. It is a card game which comes with 80 'strengths' cards, each associated with a different animal (an example is 'Caribou: You fearlessly explore new trails'), and 80 'quality' cards (e.g., 'Organized'). The goal of the game is to make a 'Totem' representing the individual, which is composed of an animal (a strength) and a complementary quality. This idea was taken from different social movements, such as the boy scouts in Canada, where participants are 'totemized' after a certain period of time (for example, 'Optimistic Fox' is the TOTEM name of the second author of this chapter).

In a game, when it is your turn to get your Totem, you randomly distribute to each other player seven strength cards (in the first round) and seven quality cards (in the second round). Each player then selects from their cards the one that they see the most in you, and places it face down on the table. When you uncover these cards one by one, the player who selected the card identifies themselves and tells you why they selected it, when they saw that strength or quality in action, and how it positively affected them and those who surround you. At the end of the process, the group selects the most representative cards (one strength card and one quality card) and creates a Totem for the person. This simple game creates a rare occasion when colleagues are gathered to tell, one after the other, the strengths and qualities that they see in the target individual. It has been used in corporate and academic settings as a team-building tool, and we are now in the midst of testing its effects scientifically through a web-based platform. While the game has an end-product (the Totem) which may sound peculiar, it is the process (hearing others talk about one's strengths and qualities and having them aggregated in two words) that leads to this end-result which is positive. This is but one initiative in the public arena which was fostered by the positive psychology movement and we can expect several others in the years to come.

Strengths Overuse and Misuse

Although most scholars adopt an approach in which they simply encourage people to 'use their strengths more', practical experience shows that a certain amount of caution must be exercised regarding this advice. It is important to remember that more is not always better and that all strengths can become weaknesses if they are overused (Biswas-Diener, Kashdan & Minhas, 2011; Kaplan & Kaiser, 2009). For example, an individual whose strength is 'analytical ability' may tend to stick too much to details during meetings, slowing down processes and irritating his colleagues. Likewise, strengths can be of great value in one context but harmful in another (Biswas-Diener et al., 2011; Linley, Willars et al., 2010). For instance, a manager whose strength is 'persistence' may be particularly appreciated by his customers because he puts a lot of time and effort into meeting their expectations, but at the same time he may ruin the climate in his work unit if he applies the same strength without discernment and is uncompromising towards his staff. Finally, one must also be aware that putting too much emphasis on one area at work may also cause one to neglect an opposing but necessary area (Kaiser & Overfield, 2011). For example, an overly assertive manager will not only be firm, but will also lack the capacity to delegate, empower and collaborate. Similarly, an analytical individual who pushes her strength too far will not only be trapped and slowed down by details, but will also lack the vision and perspective needed for her projects.

Therefore, it is important to remain aware of and sensitive to the context and situational demands in order to use one's strengths wisely. In other words, after identifying your strengths, instead of simply trying to 'use your strengths more', the right approach is to learn to use the right strength, at the right time and with the right intensity – what some authors call the 'golden mean' of strengths (Biswas-Diener, 2010; Linley, 2008). It involves having the sensitivity and judgement to read your environment, select the appropriate strength and use it with the intensity that is required in the situation. A first step to preventing strengths overuse can be to identify, one by one, the potential downsides of your strengths and plan how you can avoid them. A helpful tool in this regard can be found in *The Strengths Book* (Linley, Willars et al., 2010), in which the authors provide a list of pitfalls and mistakes to avoid for each strength of their classification. Another helpful way to stay facing the right direction and prevent strengths overuse is to proactively ask for feedback from trusted colleagues about your use of your strengths (e.g., 'Am I sometimes excessive regarding [a representative aspect of your strength]? If so, under what circumstances? What consequences does it have?'). Finally, a more formal way can be to include in individual evaluation surveys (e.g., performance appraisal surveys, 360-degrees surveys) specific questions regarding the person's main areas of strength, whether any of those strengths are sometimes overused and, if so, in what contexts (Kaiser & Overfield, 2011).

Managerial Practices

The holy grail of management is to increase performance while maintaining and developing well-being (Cropanzano & Wright, 2001), and it seems that strengths use is an efficient way to attain both of these aims. The presence of well-being and the absence of ill-being are also important outcomes as, according to the World Health Organization, psychological health in the workplace is closely associated with individuals' physical, mental and social health and is a key public health concern with clear implications for society at large (Leka & Jain, 2010). Since strengths use has been shown to be effective in decreasing ill-being (Gander, Proyer, Ruch & Wyss 2013) and increasing well-being (Forest et al., 2012), it can be considered an efficient way to create a healthy workplace (Kelloway & Day, 2005a, 2005b). Regarding performance, a study conducted by the Corporate Leadership Council (2002) of 19,187 employees from 34 organizations in 29 different countries revealed that a strengths-based management approach led to a 36.4% increase in performance while, in contrast, a weakness- or deficit-based management approach led to a 26.8 per cent decrease. In the same line of thought, Hodges and Asplund (2010) have presented the results of a study conducted with 469 work units, in which managers trained to use a strengths-based management approach produced an 8.9 per cent greater increase in net profits than those who didn't receive such training.

Strengths-based managerial practices can be used in a variety of moments of a career (e.g., attraction of talents, recruitment and selection, onboarding and induction; Linley, Garcea, Harrington, Trenier & Minhas, 2011; Linley & Page, 2007) to increase performance and create a long-term healthy workplace. We will, however, concentrate in the following paragraphs on two of the main strategies, namely strengths-based performance appraisal and strengths-based team development.

Strengths-Based Performance Appraisal

While performance reviews and appraisals are often the most feared events of the year, that is mainly because most leaders adopt a deficit-based approach or a competency-based approach to them (Boyatzis, 1982). That is, we identify the level of competence an individual should have and the gap there is to cover, and then try to find ways for people to attain it, *regardless of whether it plays to their strengths or not.* This is typical of a fixed-mindset or a mechanistic approach to performance management. Moving towards a strengths-based type of performance appraisal needs some changes to be made to the 'traditional' approach; we completely endorse Linley and Page's (2007) recommendations, which chime with our experience.

First, feedback needs to be given often, not just once a year. The good news is, it is slightly easier to say what is right and increase it than to say what is wrong and change it. This positive feedback needs to be given in a timely fashion and in a trustworthy way, and if it is sustained in the long run it will help create a strengths-based culture in which giving a compliment to a colleague or a boss is seen as a normal daily act rather than as a manipulative political action to gain access to more resources.

Second, the time frame is changed. While traditional deficit-based performance appraisals adopt a past-time orientation and evaluate development areas (a more neutral expression to designate weaknesses), a strengths-based approach implies a future-time orientation and a focus on what people are good at. In other words, the questions shifts from 'What are you not good at, and how can we help you be ordinary at it?' to 'What are you good at and could do more? What are your aspirations?' Rather than spending time, energy and resources in trying to fill the gaps and 'fix' weaknesses which can hardly shift significantly, it is much easier and more productive to facilitate what is already natural, energizing and performant for an individual.

Third, weaknesses should be tolerated if they are not performance killers. This is not to say that weakness management must stop, but this new mindset puts a different perspective on weaknesses, which everyone has (plentifully). A weakness is a lack of capacity or a fault, so by definition the best we can expect from weakness management is the absence of a fault, not the presence of something more. To use an analogy, weakness management is like expecting someone with a sprained ankle to run as fast with crutches as he would normally do with a healthy leg. The absence of a fully functioning leg can be alleviated or facilitated with the help of crutches, but never can we expect fast runs in these conditions. To sum it up, strengths-based performance appraisal shifts from past (lack of) performance and weaknesses to future (high) performance and strengths.

We have two specific examples (among dozens of others) from our experience following these recommendations. The first is the Centre de Réadaptation Estrie [Eastern townships physical re-adaptation centre], a physical rehabilitation centre which is part of the Québec health system. The second is Normandin Beaudry consulting actuaries, a consultation firm specializing in pensions, group benefits, compensation and health.

In the Centre de Réadaptation de l'Estrie, the objective of the performance appraisal has been changed to 'create a space and time to help generate what is best in the employee'. Two main points are now pursued: (1) recognize and emphasize strengths; make sure to optimize their use and development by aligning them with individual, group and/or organizational objectives, and (2) reframe areas of improvement and translate them into learning objectives; make sure that the employee sees the benefits that can realistically be expected from these learning achievements. We can thus see that the spotlight and emphasis are clearly on the knowledge and use of strengths, while fixing weaknesses remains an important but secondary objective. In that same document, the employees are asked to write down their five signature strengths (from the VIA survey) and a section is reserved for discussion of the employee's dreams, hopes, wishes and career aspirations. This positive outlook has been well received by the supervisors, who are happy to discuss positive things with their employees, as well as by the employees themselves, who now look forward to the performance appraisal as it entails having a positive developmental discussion with their supervisor. Anecdotally, managers and employees have told us that this shift towards the positive has improved the institution's work climate and helped them provide even better care for their patients.

At Normandin Beaudry consulting actuaries, strengths-based management was jolted into existence with a kick-off conference which was held during the lunch break, with all the employees in the same room. Before the conference they had been invited to complete the VIA Survey, and then asked to bring their results with them to the conference, at which all the different strengths were presented and the research results on the positive effects of strengths use discussed. Then, on demand, teams could ask an organizational psychologist to help them implement strengths-based management by identifying synergies between strengths portfolios and by allocating tasks according to strengths. To make sure that these self-regulated initiatives by different teams percolated through and sank into the organization's culture, we changed a few questions in their performance review. For example, questions which were added for the employees are: 'To what extent is my immediate supervisor knowledgeable about my strengths?' and 'To what extent does my immediate supervisor give me tasks which are aligned with my strengths?' This simple change gave a stronger voice to the employees and initiated many conversations on strengths, mostly regarding how they could be better known and used in the workplace. It took about a year to develop a common language and to answer all the concerns, questions and preoccupations about strengths-based management, but it is now part of the culture. The main outcome associated with strengths-based management is that it has become part of the vocabulary and reflexes of the organization. Any decisions about mandates, roles, clients or services are now addressed with strengths. They have a matrix of different levels of responsibilities (e.g., junior or senior employees, leaders and partners) with different tasks, and all their decisions are aligned with the employees' strengths, which are known to everyone. According to Normandin Beaudry, the keyword that describes this whole process is 'propelling'. It propels employees to give their best, moves leaders forward so that they energize themselves and their team to help clients, and also helps clients to be at

Table 14.1 Results of the *Normandin Beaudry consulting actuaries* engagement survey before (2012) and after (2015) the implementation of strengths-based management.

	Results (%)	
Engagement survey questions	**2012**	**2015**
I clearly understand what is expected in my role at work.	85	90
My talent manager gives me enough information (instructions, tips) so I can do my job.	70	85
The work I do is important to the success of my team.	83	99
My colleagues and I are demonstrating solidarity and cooperation at work to achieve our goals.	86	91
When possible, I am entrusted tasks/responsibilities that match my strengths and my interests.	88	88
For managers: When possible, I try to assign tasks/responsibilities in line with the specific strengths and interests of the members of my team.	84	86

their best and create healthy workplaces. To prove this point, the internal engagement survey compared results from 2012 (before strengths-based management was introduced) and 2015 (after the implementation; see Table 14.1). Results show that Normandin Beaudry were able to maintain or increase their engagement survey scores, which they had thought would be hard, if not impossible.

This company implemented strengths-based management inside its own walls, but they also started educating their 150 client companies about the added value of strengths identification and use in their non-monetary rewards. Along with their direct compensation and benefits recommendations, strengths-based advice was given concerning indirect compensation, that is, elements which motivate employees but cannot be easily quantified in dollars.

These examples (among many others that we could have given) reinforce the idea that strengths-based performance appraisal can lead to positive outcomes for employees as well as for organizations, and can be implemented in different economic sectors (e.g., health, consultation firms), with employees of all ages (we had employees who were 18 to 68 years of age) and with varied backgrounds and training (e.g., accountant, nurse, actuary, physiotherapist).

Strengths-based Team Development

One of the most effective ways to fully harness the potential of the strengths approach in the workplace is through strengths-based team development, a task perfectly suited to leaders or persons in a position of influence. A wide array of interventions and processes are available to help teams develop their knowledge and use of their strengths and increase their performance (Buckingham, 2007; Linley, 2008; Linley, Willars et al., 2010). Generally, these processes revolve around three fundamental steps, which can be managed by the leader: (1) strengths identification, (2) strengths affirmation, and (3) strengths

Box 14.6 Strengths identification debriefing questions

1) What do you think about your results? Are you surprised? Or does it confirm what you already knew about yourself?
2) Which strengths do you think best represent you? Why?
3) Are there any words or sentences that particularly stand out to you in these descriptions? Why?
4) In what kind of activities would you say you are at your best at work? Does it refer to any strengths in your results?
5) Are there any other strengths or talents you feel are not represented adequately in these results? Which ones?

optimization. In the following paragraphs, these steps will be described and examples will be given to show how they can be conducted.

The first step in any strengths-based team development initiative is to identify each team member's strengths. The preferred method is usually the use of psychometric instruments, as it is a simple, quick and motivating first step, and it can be further complemented by colleagues' comments afterwards. In this first step, the team leader invites all members to complete the chosen online assessment and asks them not to share their results with each other. In the following days, she meets each team member for a discussion about the latter's strengths. The objective of this discussion is to conduct a small debriefing with the member regarding his results on the strengths assessment, to gain a deeper knowledge of his strengths in general and to prepare for the next step (which will involve sharing his strengths with the other members). In order to do so, questions such as those provided in Box 14.6 can be asked. These one-to-one meetings are usually very much appreciated by team members, as they are eager to talk about their results and find the overall process interesting and stimulating. The positive mood that ensues sets the tone for the following step.

The second step consists in the affirmation of strengths in the team. This step involves the presentation of each team member's strengths, followed by a discussion in which the objective is to acknowledge these strengths and make them better known and understood in the team. In order to do so, the team leader can facilitate the discussion by going around the room and asking each member to present his results on the strengths assessment and to comment on them (e.g., Does he agree with the assessment results? Is he surprised? Which strengths represent him particularly well? Are there any nuances to be made? How do these different strengths relate to his work? Can he provide some examples?). During this process, the person is also free to present any other strengths or talents that were not included in the original assessment and the other members are encouraged to complete the explanations provided by the person. This active presentation, discussion and validation of each other's strengths is a very powerful team process, as it allows the individuals to present their areas of expertise in a humble way, to gain an external confirmation of their strengths from their peers and to explain, with the help of examples and answers to questions, where their maximal contribution to the team resides. At the end of this discussion, a team chart representing all the strengths present in the team can be made and distributed to every member. This affirmation step allows the team to appreciate each other's strengths and to have a significant and constructive discussion on this important topic, a process which is rarely done.

The third and final step is to optimize the use of strengths in the team. At this stage, it is up to the team to determine how they can maximize the use of each member's strengths and to devise tailored strategies for that purpose. A good way to start is to review the teams' current objectives and projects, and to try to see how the different strengths could be better used to achieve team goals. Some teams will find they can rearrange the way tasks and responsibilities are allocated and create a better alignment between individual strengths, roles and responsibilities. Some teams will find they can develop complementary partnerships, where some members' strengths are used to help other members' weaknesses. Other teams will find new projects they can develop on the basis of their particular configuration of strengths. In all cases, many opportunities for strengths optimization will be found and it will be essential to structure them appropriately so that they can be taken full advantage of. It is important at this step to keep in mind that a strength is not only about performance, but also about energy and interest. Therefore, tasks must be allocated in consideration of this; otherwise the team risks draining its members in the long run. Furthermore, particular care must be taken to make sure that any new work configuration is not unfair (e.g., imposing a higher workload on a member, assigning all the enjoyable tasks to some members and all the boring ones to others) and that it allows members who need to develop different competencies opportunities to do so (that is, it must avoid the situation in which a member cannot develop a particular competency because it is always assigned to a specific person).

In order to keep this approach active, it will be important afterwards to conduct regular meetings in which team members will have the opportunity to discuss the advantages, disadvantages and adjustments to be made that relate to this initiative. In such meetings, a particular attention can be directed towards strengths overuse and underuse, fairness, and professional development opportunities. As new projects and tasks develop, it will be important to keep these habits alive, by allocating responsibilities according to strengths, encouraging complementary partnership, giving positive feedback about strengths and making strengths visible (for example, in some companies employees display their top five strengths on their office door, others include them in their email signature). With time, strengths will become an integral part of the team's culture, as members will develop a strengths vocabulary, collaborate more fluidly based on their strengths and become used to a strengths-based management style.

A Healthy and Performant Workplace is One in which Strengths are Identified and Used

By now, we hope that reading this chapter has convinced you that the combination of strength identification, use and development – in all their varieties and possibilities – forms a winning approach to both performance and well-being and that it is a new paradigm which would benefit today's and tomorrow's workplaces.

Many books (e.g, Buckingham, 2007; Rath & Conchie, 2009) and articles (e.g., Linley & Harrington, 2006; Kaiser & Overfield, 2011) have been written on how to be a strengths-based leader, but the main takeaway message at any level of intervention is that individuals, leaders, teams and organizations who operate at their best know their strengths and use them wisely, intensely and for long periods of time. To exemplify this idea, research has shown that highly engaged staff report using their strengths 70 per cent of the time (Biswas-Deiner & Garcea, 2009) and that strengths use is something which can be increased through relatively short but structured interventions (Dubreuil et al., 2016; Forest et al., 2012). Thus, not only does it lead to positive results but it can be increased as well. It seems feasible that using this path will create happy-productive workers and companies, as strength use is an active ingredient which has been linked to well-being and performance (Clifton & Harter, 2003; Dubreuil, Forest & Courcy, 2014; Harter et al., 2002; Harzer & Ruch, 2013, 2014).

Giving training on strength-spotting and strength use to a growing number of workers and companies (see the example of *IBM Australia* on the VIA Institute for Character website) will hopefully bring to the general public the benefits of the cutting-edge research positive psychology is presently doing. While doing so, we might simultaneously get rid of the century-long paradigm of fixing deficiencies and move on to a new paradigm of creating abundance. It is our hope that strength identification, use and development become the new normal, in leadership roles specifically and the workplace more generally, so that this popular saying applies to (almost) everyone: 'Choose a job you love, and you will never have to work a day in your life.'

References

Asplund, J. & Blacksmith, N. (2012). Leveraging strengths. In K. S. Cameron, G. M. Spreitzer (eds), *The Oxford Handbook of Positive Organizational Scholarship.* New York: Oxford University Press, pp. 353–65.

Asplund, J., Lopez, S. J., Hodges, T. & Harter, J. (2007). *The Clifton StrengthsFinder 2.0 Technical Report: Development and Validation.* Princeton, NJ: Gallup Press.

Bakker, A. B., Tims, M. & Derks, D. (2012). Proactive personality and job performance: The role of job crafting and work engagement. *Human Relations,* 65(10), 1359–78. doi: 10.1177/0018726712453471.

Biswas-Diener, R. (2006). From the equator to the North Pole: A study of character strengths. *Journal of Happiness Studies,* 7(3), 293–310. doi: 10.1007/s10902-005-3646-8.

Biswas-Diener, R. (2010). *Practicing Positive Psychology Coaching: Assessment, Activities, and Strategies for Success.* Hoboken, NJ: John Wiley & Sons. doi: 10.1002/9781118269633.

Biswas-Diener, R. & Garcea, N. (2009). Strengths-based performance management. *Human Capital Review,* July.

Biswas-Diener, R., Kashdan, T. B. & Minhas, G. (2011). A dynamic approach to psychological strength development and intervention. *Journal of Positive Psychology,* 6(2), 106–18. doi: 10.1080/17439760.2010.545429.

Boyatzis, R. E. (1982). *The Competent Manager: A Model for Effective Performance*. New York: John Wiley & Sons.

Buckingham, M. (2007). *Go Put Your Strengths to Work*. New York: Gallup Press.

Buckingham, M. & Clifton, D. (2001). *Now, Discover Your Strengths*. New York: Gallup Press.

Buckingham, M. & Coffman, C. (1999). *First, Break All the Rules*. New York: Gallup Press.

Cameron, K. S., Dutton, J. E. & Quinn, R. E. (2003). *Positive Organizational Scholarship: Foundations of a New Discipline*. San Francisco, CA: Berrett-Koehler.

Chen, C., Yen, C. & Tsai, F. C. (2014). Job crafting and job engagement: The mediating role of person–job fit. *International Journal of Hospitality Management*, 37, 21–8. doi: 10.1016/j.ijhm.2013.10.006.

Clifton, D. & Harter, J. K. (2003). Investing in strengths. In K. S. Cameron, J. Dutton & R. Quinn (eds), *Positive Organizational Scholarship*. San Francisco, CA: Berrett-Koehler, pp. 111–21.

Corporate Leadership Council (2002). *Performance Management Survey*. Washington, DC: Author.

Cropanzano, R. & Wright, T. A. (2001). When a 'happy' worker is really a 'productive' worker: A review and further refinement of the happy-productive worker thesis. *Consulting Psychology Journal: Practice And Research*, 53(3), 182–99. doi: 10.1037/1061-4087.53.3.182.

Dahlsgaard, K., Peterson, C. & Seligman, M. P. (2005). Shared virtue: The convergence of valued human strengths across culture and history. *Review of General Psychology*, 9(3), 203–13. doi: 10.1037/1089-2680.9.3.203.

Dubreuil, P., Forest, J. & Courcy, F. (2014). From strengths use to work performance: The role of harmonious passion, subjective vitality, and concentration. *Journal of Positive Psychology*, 9(4), 335–49. doi: 10.1080/17439760.2014.898318.

Dubreuil, P., Forest, J., Gillet, N., Fernet, C., Thibault-Landry, A., Crevier-Braud, L. & Girouard, S. (in press). Facilitating well-being and performance through the development of strengths at work: Results from an intervention program.

Forest, J. (2004). How can people's work make their life most worth living? Poster presented at the Third International Positive Psychology Summit, Washington, DC, October.

Forest, J., Mageau, G. A., Crevier-Braud, L., Bergeron, É., Dubreuil, P. & Lavigne, G. L. (2012). Harmonious passion as an explanation of the relation between signature strengths' use and well-being at work: Test of an intervention program. *Human Relations*, 65(9), 1233–52. doi: 10.1177/0018726711433134.

Gander, F., Proyer, R. T., Ruch, W. & Wyss, T. (2013). Strength-based positive interventions: Further evidence for their potential in enhancing well-being and alleviating depression. *Journal of Happiness Studies*, 14(4), 1241–59. doi: 10.1007/s10902-012-9380-0.

Govindji, R. & Linley, A. (2007). Strengths use, self-concordance and well-being: Implications for strengths coaching and coaching psychologists. *International Coaching Psychology Review*, 2(2), 143–53.

Harter, J. K., Schmidt, F. L. & Hayes, T. L. (2002). Business-unit-level relationship between employee satisfaction, employee engagement, and business outcomes: A meta-analysis. *Journal of Applied Psychology*, 87(2), 268–79. doi: 10.1037/0021-9010.87.2.268.

Harzer, C. & Ruch, W. (2013). The application of signature character strengths and positive experiences at work. *Journal of Happiness Studies*, 14(3), 965–83. doi: 10.1007/s10902-012-9364-0.

Harzer, C. & Ruch, W. (2014). The role of character strengths for task performance, job dedication, interpersonal facilitation, and organizational support. *Human Performance*, 27(3), 183–205. doi: 10.1080/08959285.2014.913592.

Hodges, T. D. & Asplund, J. (2010). Strengths development in the workplace. In P. Linley, S. Harrington & N. Garcea (eds), *Oxford Handbook of Positive Psychology and Work*. New York: Oxford University Press, pp. 213–20.

Hodges, T. D. & Clifton, D. O. (2004). Strengths-based development in practice. In A. Linley & S. Joseph (eds), *Positive Psychology in Practice*. Hoboken, NJ: John Wiley & Sons, pp. 256–68.

Kaiser, R. B. & Overfield, D. V. (2011). Strengths, strengths overused, and lopsided leadership. *Consulting Psychology Journal: Practice and Research*, 63(2), 89–109. doi: 10.1037/a0024470.

Kaplan, R. E. & Kaiser, R. B. (2009). Stop overdoing your strengths. *Harvard Business Review*, 87, 100–3.

Kelloway, E. K. & Day, A. (2005a). Building healthy workplaces: What we know so far. *Canadian Journal of Behavioural Sciences/Revue Canadienne des Sciences du Comportement*, 37, 223–35.

Kelloway, E. K. & Day, A. (2005b). Building healthy workplaces: Where we need to be. *Canadian Journal of Behavioural Sciences/Revue Canadienne des Sciences du Comportement*, 37, 309–12.

Leka, S. & Jain, A. (2010). *Health Impact of Psychological Hazards at Work: An Overview*. Geneva: World Health Organization.

Linley, P. A. (2008). *Average to A+: Realising Strengths in Yourself and Others*. Coventry, UK: CAPP Press.

Linley, P. A. & Burns, G. W. (2010). Strengthspotting: Finding and developing client resources in the management of intense anger. In G. W. Burns (ed.), *Happiness, Healing, Enhancement: Your Casebook Collection for Applying Positive Psychology in Therapy*. Hoboken, NJ: John Wiley & Sons, pp. 3–14.

Linley, P. A. & Dovey, H. (2015). Technical Manual and Statistical Properties for R2 Strengths Profiler (version 1.4, July 2015). http://www.cappeu.com/downloads/R2%20Technical%20Manual_2015.pdf. Accessed 6 August 2016.

Linley, P. A., Garcea, N., Harrington, S., Trenier, E. & Minhas, G. (2011). Organizational applications of positive psychology: Taking stock and a research/practice roadmap for the future. In K. M. Sheldon, T. B. Kashdan & M. F. Steger (eds), *Designing Positive Psychology: Taking Stock and Moving Forward*. New York: Oxford University Press, pp. 365–81. doi: 10.1093/acprof:oso/9780195373585.003.0024.

Linley, P. A., Garcea, N., Hill, J., Minhas, G., Trenier, E. & Willars, J. (2010). Strengthspotting in coaching: Conceptualisation and development of the Strengthspotting Scale. *International Coaching Psychology Review*, 5(2), 165–76.

Linley, P. A. & Harrington, S. (2006). Playing to your strengths. *The Psychologist*, 19(2), 86–9.

Linley, P. A., Harrington, S. & Garcea, N. (2010). *Oxford Handbook of Positive Psychology and Work*. New York: Oxford University Press.

Linley, P. A., Maltby, J., Wood, A. M., Joseph, S., Harrington, S., Peterson, C., Park, N. & Seligman, M. P. (2007). Character strengths in the United Kingdom: The VIA Inventory of Strengths. *Personality and Individual Differences*, 43(2), 341–51. doi: 10.1016/j.paid.2006.12.004.

Linley, P. A. & Page, N. (2007). Positive approaches to human resources management: Outlines of a strengths-based organization. *PersonalFührung*, 10, 22–30.

Linley, P. A., Willars, J. & Biswas-Diener, R. (2010). *The Strengths Book: Be Confident, Be Successful, and Enjoy Better Relationships by Realising the Best of You*. Coventry, UK: CAPP Press.

Luthans, F. (2002). The need for and meaning of positive organization behavior. *Journal of Organizational Behavior*, 23(6), 695–706. doi: 10.1002/job.165.

Nakamura, J. & Csikszentmihalyi, M. (2002). The concept of flow. In C. R. Snyder & S. J. Lopez (eds), *Handbook of Positive Psychology*. New York: Oxford University Press, pp. 89–105.

Niemiec, R. M. & Wedding, D. (2014). *Positive Psychology at the Movies: Using Films to Build Character Strengths and Well-Being*. 2nd edn. Cambridge, MA: Hogrefe.

Park, N. & Peterson, C. (2010). Does it matter where we live? The urban psychology of character strengths. *American Psychologist*, 65(6), 535–47. doi: 10.1037/a0019621.

Park, N., Peterson, C. & Seligman, M. P. (2004). Strengths of character and well-being. *Journal of Social and Clinical Psychology*, 23(5), 603–19. doi: 10.1521/jscp.23.5.603.50748.

Park, N., Peterson, C. & Seligman, M. P. (2006). Character strengths in fifty-four nations and the fifty US states. *Journal of Positive Psychology*, 1(3), 118–29. doi: 10.1080/17439760600619567.

Peterson, C. & Seligman, M. E. P. (2004). *Character Strengths and Virtues: AHandbook and Classification*. Washington, DC: American Psychological Association.

Peterson, C., Stephens, J. P., Park, N., Lee, F. & Seligman, M. P. (2010). Strengths of character and work. In P. A. Linley, S. Harrington, N. Garcea, P. A. Linley, S. Harrington & N. Garcea (eds), *Oxford Handbook of Positive Psychology and Work*. New York: Oxford University Press, pp. 221–31.

Proctor, C., Maltby, J. & Linley, P. A. (2011). Strengths use as a predictor of well-being and health-related quality of life. *Journal of Happiness Studies*, 12(1), 153–69. doi: 10.1007/s10902-009-9181-2.

Rashid, T. (2014). Ways to use VIA character strengths. VIA Institute on Character. http://www.viacharacter.org/resources/ways-to-use-via-character-strengths/. Accessed 6 August 2016.

Rath, T. & Conchie, B. (2009). *Strengths-Based Leadership*. New York: Gallup Press.

Reivich, K. J., Seligman, M. P. & McBride, S. (2011). Master resilience training in the U.S. Army. *American Psychologist*, 66(1), 25–34. doi: 10.1037/a0021897.

Roberts, L. M., Dutton, J. E., Spreitzer, G. M., Heaphy, E. D. & Quinn, R. E. (2005). Composing the Reflected Best-Self portrait: Building pathways for becoming extraordinary in work organizations. *Academy of Management Review*, 30(4), 712–36. doi: 10.2307/20159164.

Roberts, L. M., Spreitzer, G., Dutton, J., Quinn, R., Heaphy, E. & Barker, B. (2005). How to play to your strengths. *Harvard Business Review*, 83(1), 74–80.

Seligman, M. E. P. (2011). *Flourish*. New York: Free Press.

Seligman, M. E. P. & Csikszentmihalyi, M. (2000). Positive psychology: An introduction. *American Psychologist*, 55(1), 5–14. doi: 10.1037/0003-066X.55.1.5.

Seligman, M. P., Steen, T. A., Park, N. & Peterson, C. (2005). Positive psychology progress: Empirical validation of interventions. *American Psychologist*, 60(5), 410–21. doi: 10.1037/0003-066X.60.5.410.

Slemp, G. R. & Vella-Brodrick, D. A. (2014). Optimising employee mental health: The relationship between intrinsic need satisfaction, job crafting, and employee well-being. *Journal of Happiness Studies*, 15(4), 957–77. doi: 10.1007/s10902-013-9458-3.

Spreitzer, G., Stephens, J. P. & Sweetman, D. (2009). The Reflected Best-Self field experiment with adolescent leaders: Exploring the psychological resources associated with feedback source and valence. *Journal of Positive Psychology*, 4(5), 331–48. doi: 10.1080/17439760902992340.

Steen, T. A., Kachorek, L. V. & Peterson, C. (2003). Character strengths among youth. *Journal of Youth and Adolescence*, 32(1), 5–16. doi: 10.1023/A:1021024205483.

Tims, M., Bakker, A. B. & Derks, D. (2015). Examining job crafting from an interpersonal perspective: Is employee job crafting related to the well-being of colleagues? *Applied Psychology: An International Review*, 64(4), 727–53. doi: 10.1111/apps.12043.

Vallerand, R. J. & Houlfort, N. (2003). Passion at work: Toward a new conceptualization. In S. W. Gilliland, D. D. Steiner & D. P. Skarlicki (eds), *Emerging Perspectives on Values in Organizations*. Greenwich, CT: Information Age Publishing, pp. 175–204.

Wood, A. M., Linley, P., Maltby, J., Kashdan, T. B. & Hurling, R. (2011). Using personal and psychological strengths leads to increases in well-being over time: A longitudinal study and the development of the strengths use questionnaire. *Personality and Individual Differences*, 50(1), 15–19. doi: 10.1016/j.paid.2010.08.004.

Wrzesniewski, A. & Dutton, J. E. (2001). Crafting a job: Revisioning employees as active crafters of their work. *Academy of Management Review*, 25(2), 179–201.

15

Leadership and Mental Illness

Realities and New Directions

Erica L. Carleton and Julian Barling

Much is known about how leaders influence the mental health and well-being of their employees at work (see Chapter 9), but at the same time precious little is known about how leaders' own mental health or illness affects their own leadership. Indeed, there are probably few other topics in organizational psychology or behaviour about which so little is known.

The absence of research on how leaders' own mental health affects their leadership behaviour could be based on several assumptions: (1) that leaders do not experience mental illness and so no research is needed in this area, (2) that leaders do experience mental illness, but their mental illness does not affect their leadership, i.e. it has no negative consequences for their employees, or their organizations, and (3) that even if leaders did experience mental health issues, there is nothing that could be done. All these assumptions are unsatisfactory as there is research that suggests that employees with personality disorders are likely to find themselves in leadership roles (e.g., Hogan, 2007) and that mental illness negatively affects their leadership behaviours (e.g., Westerlaken & Woods, 2013).

'Mental illness' refers to a wide range of conditions and disorders that affect individual mood, thinking and behaviour and are associated with significant distress and impaired functioning over an extended period of time (Health Canada, 2002; Mayo Foundation for Medical Education and Research, 2015b). The economic burden of mental illness is immense. This includes health care costs, lost productivity, and reductions in health-related quality of life (Lim, Sanderson & Andrews, 2000; Smetanin, Stiff, Briante et al., 2011).

The goal of this chapter is to outline what is known about mental illness and its relationship to leadership through the examination of personality disorders (specifically, narcissism and psychopathy), depression and anxiety. We also consider three factors (stress, alcohol use, sleep) that could cause or exacerbate any effects of mental illness on leadership.

Leading to Occupational Health and Safety: How Leadership Behaviours Impact Organizational Safety and Well-Being, First Edition.
Edited by E. Kevin Kelloway, Karina Nielsen and Jennifer K. Dimoff.

Why Should Organizational Behaviour Researchers Care about Mental Illness?

There are many good reasons for organizations to be concerned with mental illness, such as social and financial considerations (Knapp, 2003; Stuart, 2006). In this chapter we focus our concern on the implications of mental health issues for leaders in the organization, and specifically on what is known about mental health and leadership. This is important as, before any interventions can be effective, we need to understand how mental illness affects all employees, including leaders.

Personality Disorders

Personality disorders cause enduring patterns of inner experience and behaviour that deviate from the expectations of society, are pervasive, intractable and stable over time, and lead to distress or impairment (Health Canada, 2002). Some deviations may be quite mild and interfere very little with home or work life; others may cause great disruption to family and work. In general, individuals with personality disorders find it difficult to get along with others and may be irritable, demanding, hostile, fearful or manipulative (Mayo Foundation for Medical Education and Research, 2014). Estimates of the prevalence of personality disorders in the US range from 6 to 9 per cent (Lenzenweger, Lane, Loranger & Kessler, 2007). While there are many types of personality disorders, we will focus specifically on psychopathy and neuroticism and what they mean for leaders' own behaviours.

Psychopathy

Psychopathy is a 'socially devastating disorder defined by a constellation of affective, interpersonal, and behavioural characteristics, including egocentricity; impulsivity; irresponsibility; shallow emotions; lack of empathy, guilt, or remorse; pathological lying; manipulativeness; and the persistent violation of social norms and expectations' (Hare, 1996, p. 25). Estimates from the US suggest that as many as three million employees and employers could be classified as fully expressing psychopathy (Babiak & Hare, 2006; Babiak, Neumann & Hare, 2010). Psychopathy in the workplace is of importance: irrespective of whether it was the leader or the follower who scored highly on psychopathy, meta-analytic findings show it is associated with lower levels of employees' job performance and a higher level of counterproductive workplace behaviours (O'Boyle, Forsyth, Banks & McDaniel, 2012).

Media portrayals suggest a disproportionately higher rate of psychopathy among those holding leadership positions (e.g., Babiak & Hare, 2006). However, with few exceptions, research on psychopathy in the corporate world remains limited (Babiak, 1995, 2000; Babiak & Hare, 2006). In one exception, Babiak and Hare's (2006) extensive analysis of psychopathology in the workplace suggested that 3.5 per cent of top executives score very highly on standard measures of psychopathy, significantly higher than the typical range (.5–3.0%) in the general population.

To understand why leaders score higher on measures of psychopathy than the general population, researchers have recently turned to the adaptive side of psychopathy to understand where psychopathy may be advantageous. As one example, Furnham (2010) details cases where high levels of psychopathy, when combined with other factors such as intelligence and physical attractiveness, can help individuals acquire leadership positions.

A separate line of research has focused on the link between leaders' psychopathy and their success or failure. In one study, psychopathy was positively associated with ratings of charisma but negatively associated with ratings of responsibility and individual and team performance (Babiak et al., 2010). Lilienfeld et al. (2012) examined the 43 US presidents up to and including George W. Bush using estimates of psychopathy derived from personality data completed by historical experts on each president, and objective indicators of presidential performance. Fearless Dominance, which reflects the boldness inherent in psychopathy, was associated with more positive presidential characteristics, namely leadership, persuasiveness and crisis management, and with being viewed as a world figure. In contrast, the Impulsive Antisociality component of psychopathy was not associated with rated presidential performance, but did predict negative presidential outcomes such as congressional impeachment resolutions and tolerating unethical behaviour in subordinates.

While there is research on psychopathy in famous leaders, less is known about how psychopathy affects everyday leadership behaviours. An exception to this is a study focusing on 115 student leaders (Westerlaken & Woods, 2013). Psychopathic traits among these student leaders was associated with lower levels of transformational leadership, and higher levels of passive leadership behaviours (Westerlaken & Woods, 2013). Research has also shown that leaders' psychopathy is associated with followers' job dissatisfaction, involvement in counterproductive workplace behaviours, and higher levels of work–family conflict (Mathieu, Neumann, Hare & Babiak, 2014). Meta-analytic results (O'Boyle et al., 2012) demonstrate that, in general, the dark triad traits (psychopathy, narcissism and Machiavellianism) are negatively related to job performance and positively related to counterproductive work (CWB) behaviours across 186 articles.

To conclude this discussion, the charismatic interpersonal skills associated with psychopathy help these individuals get hired and possibly even promoted to leadership positions, irrespective of their actual performance (Babiak, 1995; Babiak & Hare, 2006; Babiak et al., 2010). Organizations need to do what they can to avoid falling into this trap, as some of the traits associated with psychopathy (e.g., impulsive antisociality) negatively affect the quality of leadership behaviours and employee outcomes.

Narcissism

Like psychopathy, narcissism is a clinical personality disorder (American Psychiatric Association, 2013, p. 717) reflected in 'a grandiose sense of self-importance', needing 'excessive admiration', 'a sense of entitlement', 'a lack of empathy', and a tendency towards being 'exploitative, manipulative, and arrogant'. Not surprisingly, narcissists elicit negative responses from those with whom they interact (e.g., Leary, Bednarski, Hammon & Duncan, 1997).

An important point that must be made, however, is that organizational researchers focus on subclinical levels of narcissism.

Narcissism in the workplace has been linked to a variety of important outcomes, including unsatisfactory task performance (Judge, LePine & Rich, 2006). This might be important for our focus, as leadership behaviours can be seen as one specific form of task performance.

Narcissism has often been viewed as a key ingredient of leadership emergence and success (Grijalva, Harms, Newman, Gaddis & Fraley, 2015), perhaps because narcissists engage in more self-promotion (De Vries & Miller, 1986), impression management (Vohs, Baumeister & Ciarocco, 2005) and organizational politicking (Vredenburgh & Shea-VanFossen, 2010), which ultimately enables them to get noticed by, and gain favour with, their superiors. Multiple studies support this phenomenon (e.g., Galvin, Waldman & Balthazard, 2010; Harms, Spain & Hannah, 2011; Judge, LePine & Rich, 2006). As well, in a longitudinal study of military school cadets, narcissism positively predicted leadership development and performance (Harms et al., 2011). However, caution needs to be exercised in interpreting these findings: Judge et al. (2006) showed that narcissism was positively related only to self-ratings of transformational leadership (even after controlling for the Big Five personality traits). Narcissism is positively related to charismatic leadership as rated by subordinates, through the visionary boldness component of charisma – the component representing the tendency to take risks and be inspirational and exciting (Galvin et al., 2010). Nonetheless, the meaning of these findings is cast into question, because Judge et al. (2006) also showed that leaders' narcissism was negatively associated with subordinates' ratings of transformational leadership.

Chatterjee and Hambrick's (2007) research may be most persuasive as they used unobtrusive measures of the narcissism of 111 CEOs in the computer hardware and software industries, creatively avoiding the need for self-ratings of narcissism. They showed that, as expected, CEOs' narcissism was positively related to strategic dynamism and grandiosity. However, higher levels of narcissism were also linked to a greater number and size of acquisitions, and engendered extreme and fluctuating organizational performance. In general, their findings suggest that narcissistic CEOs favour bold actions that attract attention to themselves (for example, the media would be most interested in higher-value mergers and acquisitions), resulting in big wins or big losses. At the same time, the performance of firms with narcissistic CEOs is neither better nor worse than that of firms with non-narcissistic CEOs.

Along with the research showing positive effects of leader narcissism, several studies point to potential negative effects of narcissism on leaders' behaviours and effectiveness. In one study, narcissism was negatively and indirectly related to charismatic leadership, with narcissism being associated with lower levels of altruism, which it turn were linked with lower levels of charisma (Galvin et al., 2010). A separate study focused on CEOs of Major League Baseball (Resick, Whitman, Weingarden & Hiller, 2009), and showed that CEO narcissism was negatively related to the contingent reward component of transformational leadership, and indirectly associated with higher levels of managerial turnover. Last, having a narcissistic leader is associated with reduced group-level information exchange, which is detrimental to team performance (Nevicka, Ten Velden, De Hoogh & Van Vianen, 2011).

Thus, findings concerning narcissistic leaders seem to be inconsistent. One possible reason for this is that narcissism affects different aspects or phases of leadership. For example, research shows that, like psychopaths, narcissists generally make a positive first impression, as others initially perceive them to be charming and self-confident (Grijalva et al., 2015), and thus it is no surprise that narcissistic leaders have an advantage regarding leadership emergence. Over time, however, more negative behaviours associated with narcissism become apparent (e.g., arrogance, exploitativeness, self-centredness) which are associated with diminished effectiveness (Back, Schmukle & Egloff, 2010; Paulhus, 1998; Robins & Beer, 2001). This is confirmed in a recent meta-analysis (Grijalva et al., 2015) showing that narcissists are more likely to emerge as leaders, which was explained by the overlap of narcissism with extraversion. At the same time narcissistic leaders were no more or less likely to be effective (Grijalva et al., 2015). Grijalva et al. (2015) then extended their analyses, and isolated a curvilinear relationship between narcissism and leadership effectiveness which showed that moderate levels of narcissism predicted leadership effectiveness, beyond which narcissism becomes detrimental to leadership effectiveness.

Thus, both narcissists and psychopaths possess traits that tend to help them to emerge as leaders. These two personality disorders then diverge in terms of their effects on leadership behaviours and employee outcomes, with psychopathy seemingly having worse effects. It remains for research, however, to investigate whether leader psychopathy is also associated in a curvilinear fashion with follower outcomes. In any case, leader personality disorders tend to be problematic for employees and the organization. Moving away from personality disorders, we will now examine a mood disorder (depression) and anxiety disorders.

Mood Disorders

Individuals with mood disorders suffer significant distress and impairment in all areas of life, including social, occupational and educational. Mood disorders include major depression, bipolar disorder (combining episodes of mania and depression) and dysthymia (Health Canada, 2002). In this chapter, we focusing on the most common mood disorder, depression.

Depression

Depression is the leading cause of years lived with disability in adults (Gilmour & Patten, 2007). In North America, approximately 11–13 per cent of adults will experience major depression at some time in their lives, and 6.6 per cent of adults in the USA have experienced a major depressive disorder in the last 12-month period (Pearson, Janz & Ali, 2013). Individuals with diagnosed depression suffer significant distress and impairment with symptoms that include problems with sleep, feelings of sadness, loss of interest in activities, difficulty making decisions, trouble thinking or concentrating, feelings of worthlessness, and having a pessimistic outlook about the future (Mayo Foundation for Medical Education and Research, 2015a). As well, individuals with depressive symptoms report significantly more health service usage (e.g., Johnson, Weissman & Klerman, 1992), need for social assistance (e.g., Judd, Akiskal & Paulus, 1997), and higher levels of household and financial strain (e.g., Judd, Paulus, Wells & Rapaport, 1996). Depressive symptoms have also been linked with job-related problems such as poorer job performance (Judd, Paulus et al., 1996). Indeed, the impact of depression on job performance is estimated to be greater than that of chronic conditions such as arthritis, hypertension, back problems and diabetes (Goetzel et al., 2004).

One report found that 79 per cent of workers who had experienced depression stated that the symptoms had interfered with their ability to work (Gilmour & Patten, 2007). On average, depressed workers reported 32 days in the past year during which the symptoms had resulted in their being totally unable to work or carry out normal activities (Gilmour & Patten, 2007). The marked degree to which depression interfered with functioning at work is not surprising, as a number of crucial elements of job performance are particularly vulnerable to these symptoms, such as time management, concentration and teamwork (Burton, Pransky, Conti, Chen & Edington, 2004).

However, while much is known about how depression impacts work generally, there is virtually no research on whether and how depression affects leaders and their leadership behaviours specifically. This is important, as there are no conceptual reasons why leaders would be immune from either suffering from depression or its adverse effects. Supporting this, there have been numerous accounts of famous leaders throughout history, both in public life (e.g., Eleanor Roosevelt) and in the private sector (e.g., media mogul Ted Turner), who have suffered from depression.

Outside of the organizational behaviour area, the book *A First-Rate Madness* (Ghaemi, 2011) examined the link between mental illness and leadership using retrospective analyses of major leaders. Ghaemi, a professor of psychiatry, examined the connections between mood disorders and leadership in some of history's greatest leaders. He posited that many leaders did suffer from mood disorders, and that the very symptoms of either depression or bipolar disorder are what made these leaders great in times of crisis.

For example, one key finding from psychology is that in contrast to mentally healthy individuals, who use optimism to make themselves happier but by doing so cloud their ability to make realistic judgements, depressed individuals make more realistic assessments of the control that they have over their environment (Alloy & Abramson, 1979). This 'depressive realism,' Ghaemi (2011) suggests, enables leaders to make better decisions during a crisis. He cites Winston Churchill as an example of a leader who had a more realistic view of the Nazi threat than others in power in England (Ghaemi, 2011), which contributed to his emergence and success as a leader.

Empathy is also an outcome of depression (O'Connor, Berry, Weiss & Gilbert, 2002), and Ghaemi (2011) posits that this too could help depressed individuals' leadership behaviour. Ghaemi cites Gandhi as an example of a leader whose radical empathy enhanced his leadership behaviours in his goal of preserving a united India.

One exception to the lack of empirical studies in this area is a study by Byrne et al. (2014) that examined how leaders' mental health affected leadership behaviour. These authors showed that leaders' depressive symptoms predicted lower transformational leadership behaviours and higher abusive supervision across 172 leader–subordinate dyads. Importantly, Byrne et al.'s findings run counter to Ghaemi's (2011) assertion that mental illness is productive for leadership, clearly indicating the need for more research on this important topic.

In conclusion Ghaemi (2011) argues that during crises, mental illness enhances leadership behaviours and effectiveness. This is a bold claim based on a restricted group of historical leaders that awaits empirical replication on a broad range of leaders. As shown, the relationship between depression and leadership is sorely lacking research and this area is ripe with research opportunity.

Anxiety Disorders

Another common mental illness among the general population is anxiety disorders. There are a number of types or forms of anxiety disorders, including generalized anxiety disorder, post-traumatic stress disorder, social anxiety, panic disorder and obsessive compulsive disorder. Pooled one-year and lifetime prevalence rates in the general population for anxiety disorders are estimated to be 10.6 per cent (Somers, Goldner, Waraich & Hsu, 2006), with anxiety being less common among adults than depression (Pearson et al., 2013). A common feature of anxiety disorders, however, is its comorbidity with other mental illnesses such as depression. For example, 80 per cent of individuals with lifetime generalized anxiety disorder also experienced a comorbid mood disorder during their lifetime (Judd et al., 1998).

Individuals with anxiety disorders experience severe anxiety on a chronic basis, that is, it lasts at least six months, and although each anxiety disorder has different symptoms, all the symptoms cluster around excessive and irrational fear and dread (National Institute of Mental Health, 2016). Left untreated, anxiety can worsen (American Psychiatric Association, 2013). Everyone feels anxious in response to specific events, but individuals with an anxiety disorder have excessive and unrealistic feelings that interfere with their lives, including their relationships, school and work performance, social activities and recreation (Health Canada, 2002). Anxiety disorders also have major economic and personal costs (Hollifield, Katon, Skipper et al., 1997; Kessler, Chiu, Demler & Walters, 2005), and contribute to lowered work performance (Waghorn, Chant, White & Whiteford, 2005) and lost productivity due to time away from work (Katerndahl & Realini, 1997). As well, anxiety disorders are associated with high unemployment and low health-related quality of life (Ettigi, Meyerhoff, Chirban, Jacobs & Wilson, 1997; Hollifield et al., 1997; Katerndahl & Realini, 1997).

Research on the effects of anxiety on work performance has a relatively long history (e.g. Cherry, 1978; Doby & Caplan 1995). One study showed that individuals who reported higher anxiety also reported greater work impairment (Erickson et al., 2009). Kessler and Frank (1997) used the US National Comorbidity Survey data, and showed that, compared with persons without anxiety, individuals with anxiety disorders experienced significantly higher rates of work impairment, with panic disorders causing the greatest number of days in which productivity was reduced (*mean* = 4.87 days per month). In addition, the effects of anxiety go beyond work performance. Frone (2000) showed that along with being related to work performance and productivity, anxiety is related to work–family conflict. This study found that individuals who experience more work–family conflict were 2.46 times more likely to have an anxiety disorder than those who report never experiencing work–family conflict.

Thus, while research has examined anxiety disorders and work, much less is known about the impact of anxiety disorders on leaders and leadership behaviours. Some reports in the popular press suggest that anxiety might be good for leadership (Porter, 2014), as, without anxiety, little would be accomplished. Similarly, Robert Rosen (2008) suggests in his book *Just Enough Anxiety: The Hidden Driver of Business Success* that anxiety helps leaders to concentrate, learn, relate to people, think more creatively, and deliver better results. Empirical research, however, refutes these notions. Byrne et al. (2014) showed that leaders' anxiety was associated with lower levels of transformational leadership behaviours, and higher levels of abusive supervisory behaviours. As was the case with leaders' depression, there is a disconnect between speculation about and findings from empirical research on leaders' anxiety; and clearly, more research is warranted.

Thus, it would be premature to think that we have an adequate understanding of the effects of mental illness on leaders, or on their leadership behaviours. This is an important omission for organizations, made more complex by the social stigma and discrimination experienced by those suffering from mental illness. Nonetheless, under supportive conditions and with proper treatment and support, mental illness in no way precludes people from appropriate work performance, whether as leaders or employees. Work is often a very positive experience for individuals recovering from mental illness. The development of social networks and a sense of purpose and accomplishment make employment a key part of many people's recovery (Gilmour & Patten, 2007). The challenge is to develop a more complete understanding of the links between mental illness and leadership, so that organizations and mental health providers can create the conditions under which all people can thrive in the workplace.

Mental Health Challenges

Aside from the formal mental illness issues experienced by some leaders, all leaders face daily problems of living that, while not formally classifiable as mental illness, challenge their mental health. In this section, we deal with three such issues, namely work stress, alcohol use and sleep problems.

Work Stress

Work stressors are pervasive, and when they exceed individual resources and ability to cope they can threaten mental health (Partnership for Workplace Mental Health, 2016). Indeed, it is not uncommon to find that diverse work stressors are associated with mental health problems such as anxiety and depression. For example, one study found that employees who considered most of their days to be 'quite a bit' or 'extremely' stressful were more than three times as likely to suffer a major depressive episode than those who reported low levels of general stress (Szeto & Dobson, 2013). A separate study of 3,707 employees found that high psychological job demands increased the risk of both subsequent anxiety and depression (Andrea, Bültmann, van Amelsvoort & Kant, 2009). Moreover, work stress can exacerbate an already present mental illness (Partnership for Workplace Mental Health, 2016).

Considerable research has been devoted to *employee* stress and health, including how leadership behaviours affect employee stress and well-being (e.g., Kelloway, Turner, Barling & Loughlin, 2012). The time has come for work stress research to focus on the stress and well-being of leaders, who are not immune from experiencing work stress or its negative effects. A report by the Center for Creative Leadership examined 240 upper-middle-management or executive-level leaders' work stress (Campbell, Baltes, Martin & Meddings, 2007). Fully 88 per cent of the leaders examined reported that work was their primary source of stress, and that having a leadership role increased the level of stress they were under. Moreover, 60 per cent of these leaders also believed that their organizations failed to provide them with the tools to manage stress, and more than two-thirds reported that their stress had been increasing across the last five years. Intriguingly, what stressed the leaders most was a lack of resources and time (Campbell et al., 2007), the same stressors often reported by employees. All this might become worse, as Roche, Haar and Luthans (2014) suggest that leaders are under ever-increasing pressure because of the competitiveness and complexity of the global economy.

Alcohol Use

While there is a very substantial body of knowledge on alcohol use and abuse, a separate line of research has focused on workplace alcohol consumption. Many of the predictors of context-free alcohol consumption also predict workplace alcohol consumption, such as (job) stress, negative affectivity and impulsivity (Cooper, Frone, Russell & Mudar, 1995; Frone, 2003). Workplace alcohol use is of unique importance to an understanding of leaders' mental health for several reasons. First, a survey using a nationally representative sample of 2,805 employed adults in the US showed significantly higher levels of alcohol consumption at work among organizational managers and leaders than among those lower in the organizational hierarchy (Frone, 2006). Second, there is some evidence that workplace alcohol use impacts leader and managerial performance. An earlier study (Streufert, Pogash, Roache et al., 1994) that explored alcohol use among managers found that strategy and planning were negatively affected in a management simulation task at both .05 and .10 blood alcohol levels. Third, and more recently, a survey showed that even moderate levels of workplace alcohol consumption by leaders were associated with lower levels of transformational leadership and higher levels of abusive supervision (Byrne et al., 2014). This same study showed that leaders' depressive symptoms mostly hurt their transformational leadership behaviours when workplace alcohol consumption was medium or high. Taken together, these two studies (Byrne et al., 2014; Streufert et al., 1994) point to the negative effects of leaders' workplace alcohol consumption; and the former study also suggests that leaders' alcohol consumption interacts with other indicators of mental illness. Clearly, more research is needed on leaders' workplace alcohol consumption, and its effects on the quality of leadership behaviours. For example, it is not far-fetched to posit that higher levels of workplace alcohol consumption may predispose leaders to engage in more passive leadership behaviours.

Sleep

Researchers have recently turned their attention to the workplace antecedents and consequences of sleep problems (Barling, Barnes, Carleton & Wagner, 2016), and we now know that poor sleep affects a variety of work-related outcomes (e.g., Åkerstedt, Fredlund, Gillberg & Jansson, 2002; Barnes, Wagner & Ghumman, 2012). For example, problems with sleep quantity and quality lead to poor task performance (Kessler et al., 2011) and concentration at work (Wagner, Barnes, Lim & Ferris, 2012), as well as workplace deviance (Christian & Ellis, 2011). By depleting individuals' psychological resources, sleep problems can even result in unethical behaviour (Barnes, Schaubroeck, Huth & Ghumman, 2011).

There are now good reasons to believe that sleep problems might also affect the quality of leadership behaviours. In general, lack of sleep results in poorer interpersonal functioning, including reduced empathy towards others and diminished interpersonal relationships, poorer stress management skills (reduced impulse control and difficulty with delay of gratification), and poorer coping (Killgore, Kahn-Greene, Lipizzi et al., 2008). In addition, sleep problems reduce an individual's willingness to behave in ways that facilitate effective social interaction (Kahn-Greene, Lipizzi, Conrad, Kamimori & Killgore, 2006), and increases the propensity to make risky choices (e.g., Killgore, Kamimori & Balkin, 2011).

One study examining sleep and leadership supported this general notion. Barnes, Lucianetti, Bhave and Christian (2014) demonstrated that daily sleep quality indirectly affected daily abusive supervisory behaviours; moreover, their findings also showed that ego depletion mediated this link: specifically, sleep problems predicted lower levels of ego depletion, which in turn were associated with higher levels of abusive supervision. Underscoring the need for research on the effects of sleep on leadership behaviours, Barnes et al. also showed that leaders' sleep problems had a distal and negative effect on their teams' work unit engagement, and this effect was mediated by abusive supervision.

Moving Forward

Neither leadership nor mental health can be construed as new issues in the workplace; instead, there is a very vibrant body of research on each of these two areas, enabling separate but substantial bodies of knowledge on leadership (Barling, 2014) and mental health (Harder, Wagner & Rash, 2014) in the workplace. Leaders' mental health can no longer be taken for granted, and probably has substantial and complex effects on the quality of their leadership behaviours, and, in turn, on their employees' performance and well-being. While there is a long tradition of speculating about the mental health of our political and military leaders (e.g., L'Etang, 1969; Owen, 2008), the time has come to replace speculation with knowledge.

References

Åkerstedt, T., Fredlund, P., Gillberg, M. & Jansson, B. (2002). Work load and work hours in relation to disturbed sleep and fatigue in a large representative sample. *Journal of Psychosomatic Research*, 53, 585–88.

Alloy, L. B. & Abramson, L. Y. (1979). Judgment of contingency in depressed and nondepressed students: Sadder but wiser?. *Journal of Experimental Psychology: General*, 108, 441–85.

American Psychiatric Association (2013). *Diagnostic and Statistical Manual of Mental Disorders*. Arlington, VA: American Psychiatric Publishing.

Andrea, H., Bültmann, U., van Amelsvoort, L. G. & Kant, Y. (2009). The incidence of anxiety and depression among employees: The role of psychosocial work characteristics. *Depression and Anxiety*, 26, 1040–8.

Babiak, P. (1995). When psychopaths go to work: A case study of an industrial psychopath. *Applied Psychology*, 44, 17–188.

Babiak, P. (2000). Psychopathic manipulation at work. In C. B. Gacono (ed.), *The Clinical and Forensic Assessment of Psychopathy: A Practitioner's Guide*. London: Routledge, pp. 287–311.

Babiak, P. & Hare, R. D. (2006). *Snakes in Suits: When Psychopaths Go to Work*. New York: Regan Books/HarperCollins.

Babiak, P., Neumann, C. S. & Hare, R. D. (2010). Corporate psychopathy: Talking the walk. *Behavioral Sciences & the Law*, 28, 174–93.

Back, M. D., Schmukle, S. C. & Egloff, B. (2010). Why are narcissists so charming at first sight? Decoding the narcissism–popularity link at zero acquaintance. *Journal of Personality and Social Psychology*, 98, 132–45.

Barling, J. (2014). *The Science of Leadership: Lessons from Research for Organizational Leaders*. New York: Oxford University Press.

Barling, J., Barnes, C., Carleton, E. L., Wagner, D. (eds) (2016). *Sleep and Work: Research Insights for the Workplace*. New York: Oxford University Press.

Barnes, C., Lucianetti, L., Bhave, D. & Christian, M. (2014). You wouldn't like me when I'm sleepy: Leader sleep, daily abusive supervision, and work unit engagement. *Academy of Management Journal*, 58, 1419–37.

Barnes, C. M., Schaubroeck, J. M., Huth, M. & Ghumman, S. (2011). Lack of sleep and unethical behavior. *Organizational Behavior and Human Decision Processes*, 115, 169–80.

Barnes, C. M., Wagner, D. T. & Ghumman, S. (2012). Borrowing from sleep to pay work and family: Expanding time-based conflict to the broader non-work domain. *Personnel Psychology*, 65, 789–819.

Burton, W. N., Pransky, G., Conti, D. J., Chen, C. Y. & Edington, D. W. (2004). The association of medical conditions and presenteeism. *Journal of Occupational and Environmental Medicine*, 46, S38–S45.

Byrne, A., Dionisi, A. M., Barling, J., Akers, A., Robertson, J., Lys, R., ... & Dupré, K. (2014). The depleted leader: The influence of leaders' diminished psychological resources on leadership behaviors. *Leadership Quarterly*, 25, 344–57.

Campbell, M., Baltes, J. I., Martin, A. & Meddings, K. (2007). The stress of leadership. CCL Research White Paper. Center for Creative Leadership. http://media.ccl.org/wp-content/uploads/2015/04/StressofLeadership.pdf. Accessed 7 August 2016.

Chatterjee, A. & Hambrick, D. C. (2007). It's all about me: Narcissistic chief executive officers and their effects on company strategy and performance. *Administrative Science Quarterly*, 52, 351–86.

Cherry, N. (1978). Stress, anxiety and work: A longitudinal study. *Journal of Occupational Psychology*, 51, 259–70.

Christian, M. S. & Ellis, A. P. (2011). Examining the effects of sleep deprivation on workplace deviance: A self-regulatory perspective. *Academy of Management Journal*, 54, 913–34.

Cooper, M. L., Frone, M. R., Russell, M. & Mudar, P. (1995). Drinking to regulate positive and negative emotions: A motivational model of alcohol use. *Journal of Personality and Social Psychology*, 69, 990–1005.

De Vries, M. F. K. & Miller, D. (1986). Personality, culture, and organization. *Academy of Management Review*, 11, 266–79.

Doby, V. J. & Caplan, R. D. (1995). Organizational stress as threat to reputation: Effects on anxiety at work and at home. *Academy of Management Journal*, 38, 1105–23.

Erickson, S. R., Guthrie, S., VanEtten-Lee, M., Himle, J., Hoffman, J., Santos, S. F., ... & Abelson, J. L. (2009). Severity of anxiety and work-related outcomes of patients with anxiety disorders. *Depression and Anxiety*, 26, 1165–71.

Ettigi, P., Meyerhoff, A. S., Chirban, J. T., Jacobs, R. J. & Wilson, R. R. (1997). The quality of life and employment in panic disorder. *Journal of Nervous and Mental Disease*, 185, 368–72.

Frone, M. R. (2000). Work–family conflict and employee psychiatric disorders: The national comorbidity survey. *Journal of Applied Psychology*, 85, 888–95.

Frone, M. R. (2003). Predictors of overall and on-the-job substance use among young workers. *Journal of Occupational Health Psychology*, 8, 39–54.

Frone, M. R. (2006). Prevalence and distribution of alcohol use and impairment in the workplace: A U.S. National Survey. *Journal of Studies on Alcohol*, 67, 147–56.

Furnham, A. (2010). *The Elephant in the Boardroom: Speaking the Unspoken about Pastoral Transitions.* Basingstoke, UK: Palgrave Macmillan.

Galvin, B. M., Waldman, D. A. & Balthazard, P. (2010). Visionary communication qualities as mediators of the relationship between narcissism and attributions of leader charisma. *Personnel Psychology*. 63. 509–37.

Ghaemi, N. (2011). *A First-Rate Madness: Uncovering the Links between Leadership and Mental Illness.* New York: Penguin.

Gilmour, H. & Patten, S. B (2007). Depression and work impairment. *Health Reports.* (Statistics Canada, Catalogue no. 82-003), 18(1), 9–22.

Goetzel, R. Z., Long, S. R., Ozminkowski, R. J., Hawkins, K., Wang, S. & Lynch, W. (2004). Health, absence, disability, and presenteeism cost estimates of certain physical and mental health conditions affecting US employers. *Journal of Occupational and Environmental Medicine*, 46, 398–412.

Grijalva, E., Harms, P. D., Newman, D. A., Gaddis, B. H. & Fraley, R. C. (2015). Narcissism and leadership: A meta-analytic review of linear and nonlinear relationships. *Personnel Psychology*, 68, 1–47.

Harder, H. G., Wagner, S. & Rash, M. J. (2014). *Mental Illness in the Workplace: Psychological Disability Management*. Farnham, UK: Gower.

Hare, R. D. (1996). Psychopathy: A clinical construct whose time has come. *Criminal Justice and Behavior*, 23(1), 25–54.

Harms, P. D., Spain, S. M. & Hannah, S. T. (2011). Leader development and the dark side of personality. *Leadership Quarterly*, 22, 495–509.

Health Canada (2002). *A Report on Mental Illnesses in Canada*. Ottawa: Health Canada.

Hogan, R. (2007). *Personality and the Fate of Organizations*. Mahwah, NJ: Lawrence Erlbaum Associates.

Hollifield, M., Katon, W., Skipper, B., Chapman, T., Ballenger, J. C., Mannuzza, S. & Fyer, A. J. (1997). Panic disorder and quality of life: Variables predictive of functional impairment. *American Journal of Psychiatry*, 154, 766–72.

Johnson, J., Weissman, M. M. & Klerman, G. L. (1992). Service utilization and social morbidity associated with depressive symptoms in the community. *Journal of the American Medical Association*, 267, 1478–83.

Judd, L. L., Akiskal, H. S. & Paulus, M. P. (1997). The role and clinical significance of subsyndromal depressive symptoms (SSD) in unipolar major depressive disorder. *Journal of Affective Disorders*, 45, 5–18.

Judd, L. L., Kessler, R. C., Paulus, M. P., Zeller, P. V., Wittchen, H. U. & Kunovac, J. L. (1998). Comorbidity as a fundamental feature of generalized anxiety disorders: Results from the National Comorbidity Study (NCS). *Acta Psychiatrica Scandinavica*, 98, 6–11.

Judd, L. L., Paulus, M. P., Wells, K. B. & Rapaport, M. H. (1996). Socioeconomic burden of subsyndromal depressive symptoms and major depression in a sample of the general population. *American Journal of Psychiatry*, 153, 1411–17.

Judge, T. A., LePine, J. A. & Rich, B. L. (2006). Loving yourself abundantly: Relationship of the narcissistic personality to self- and other perceptions of workplace deviance, leadership, and task and contextual performance. *Journal of Applied Psychology*, 91, 762–76.

Kahn-Greene, E. T., Lipizzi, E. L., Conrad, A. K., Kamimori, G. H. & Killgore, W. D. (2006). Sleep deprivation adversely affects interpersonal responses to frustration. *Personality and Individual Differences*, 41, 1433–43.

Katerndahl, D. A. & Realini, J. P. (1997). Quality of life and panic-related work disability in subjects with infrequent panic and panic disorder. *Journal of Clinical Psychiatry*, 58, 1–478.

Kelloway, E. K., Turner, N., Barling, J. & Loughlin, C. (2012). Transformational leadership and employee psychological well-being: The mediating role of employee trust in leadership. *Work & Stress*, 26, 39–55.

Kessler, R. C., Berglund, P. A., Coulouvrat, C., Hajak, G., Roth, T., Shahly, V. & Walsh, J. K. (2011). Insomnia and the performance of US workers: Results from the America Insomnia Survey. *Sleep*, 34, 1161–71.

Kessler, R. C., Chiu, W. T., Demler, O. & Walters, E. E. (2005). Prevalence, severity, and comorbidity of 12-month DSM-IV disorders in the National Comorbidity Survey Replication. *Archives of General Psychiatry*, 62, 617–27.

Kessler, R. C. & Frank, R. G. (1997). The impact of psychiatric disorders on work loss days. *Psychological Medicine*, 27, 861–73.
Killgore, W. D. S., Kahn-Greene, E. T., Lipizzi, E. L., Newman, R. A., Kamimori, G. H. & Balkin, T. J. (2008). Sleep deprivation reduces perceived emotional intelligence and constructive thinking skills. *Sleep Medicine*, 9, 517–26.
Killgore, W. D., Kamimori, G. H. & Balkin, T. J. (2011). Caffeine protects against increased risk-taking propensity during severe sleep deprivation. *Journal of Sleep Research*, 20, 395–403.
Knapp, M. (2003). Hidden costs of mental illness. *British Journal of Psychiatry*, 183(6), 477–8.
Leary, M. R., Bednarski, R., Hammon, D. & Duncan, T. (1997). Blowhards, snobs, and narcissists. In R. M. Kowalski (ed.), *Aversive Interpersonal Behaviors*. New York: Springer, pp. 111–31.
Lenzenweger, M. F., Lane, M. C., Loranger, A. W. & Kessler, R. C. (2007). DSM-IV personality disorders in the National Comorbidity Survey Replication. *Biological Psychiatry*, 62, 553–64.
L'Etang, H. (1969). *The Pathology of Leadership: Old Diseases and New Treatments*. London: William Heinemann Medical Books.
Lilienfeld, S. O., Waldman, I. D., Landfield, K., Watts, A. L., Rubenzer, S. & Faschingbauer, T. R. (2012). Fearless dominance and the US presidency: Implications of psychopathic personality traits for successful and unsuccessful political leadership. *Journal of Personality and Social Psychology*, 103, 489–505.
Lim, D., Sanderson, K., Andrews, G. (2000). Lost productivity among full-time workers with mental disorders. *Journal of Mental Health Policy and Economics*, 3, 139–46.
Mathieu, C., Neumann, C. S., Hare, R. D. & Babiak, P. (2014). A dark side of leadership: Corporate psychopathy and its influence on employee well-being and job satisfaction. *Personality and Individual Differences*, 59, 83–8.
Mayo Foundation for Medical Education and Research. (2014). Diseases and conditions: Personality disorders. January 31. http://www.mayoclinic.org/diseases-conditions/personality-disorders/basics/definition/con-20030111. Accessed 7 August 2016.
Mayo Foundation for Medical Education and Research (2015a). Diseases and conditions: Depression (major depressive disorder). July 22. http://www.mayoclinic.org/diseases-conditions/depression/basics/definition/con-20032977. Accessed 7 August 2016.
Mayo Foundation for Medical Education and Research (2015b). Diseases and conditions: Mental illness. October 13. http://www.mayoclinic.org/diseases-conditions/mental-illness/basics/definition/con-20033813. Accessed 7 August 2016.
National Institute of Mental Health (2016). Anxiety disorders. National Institutes of Health. March. http://www.nimh.nih.gov/health/topics/anxiety-disorders/index.shtml.
Nevicka, B., Ten Velden, F. S., De Hoogh, A. H. & Van Vianen, A. E. (2011). Reality at odds with perceptions: Narcissistic leaders and group performance. *Psychological Science*, 22(10), 1259–64.
O'Boyle, E. H., Forsyth, D. R., Banks, G. C. & McDaniel, M. A. (2012). A meta-analysis of the Dark Triad and work behavior: A social exchange perspective. *Journal of Applied Psychology*, 97, 557–79.

O'Connor, L. E., Berry, J. W., Weiss, J. & Gilbert, P. (2002). Guilt, fear, submission, and empathy in depression. *Journal of Affective Disorders*, 71, 19–27.
Owen, D. (2008). *In Sickness and in Power: Illness in Heads of Government in the Last 100 Years*. London: Methuen.
Partnership for Workplace Mental Health (2016). Stress. American Psychiatric Association Foundation. http://www.workplacementalhealth.org/Topics/Stress-at-Work.aspx.
Paulhus, D. L. (1998). Interpersonal and intrapsychic adaptiveness of trait self-enhancement. *Journal of Personality and Social Psychology*, 74, 197–208.
Pearson, C., Janz, T. & Ali, J. (2013). Mental and substance use disorders in Canada. *Health at a Glance*, September (Statistics Canada, Catalogue no. 82-624-X).
Porter, J. (2014). Relax, being anxious makes you a good leader. *Fast Company*. 28 January. http://www.fastcompany.com/3025488/how-to-be-a-success-at-everything/relax-being-anxious-makes-you-a-good-leader.
Resick, C. J., Whitman, D. S., Weingarden, S. M. & Hiller, N. J. (2009). The bright-side and the dark-side of CEO personality: Examining core self-evaluations, narcissism, transformational leadership, and strategic influence. *Journal of Applied Psychology*, 94, 1365–81.
Robins, R. W. & Beer, J. S. (2001). Positive illusions about the self: Short-term benefits and long-term costs. *Journal of Personality and Social Psychology*, 80, 340–52.
Roche, M., Haar, J. M. & Luthans, F. (2014). The role of mindfulness and psychological capital on the well-being of leaders. *Journal of Occupational Health Psychology*, 19(4), 476–89.
Rosen, R. H. (2008). *Just Enough Anxiety: The Hidden Driver of Business Success*. New York: Penguin.
Smetanin, P., Stiff, D., Briante, C., Adair, C. E., Ahmad, S. & Khan, M. (2011). *The Life and Economic Impact of Major Mental Illnesses in Canada: 2011 to 2041*. Toronto: RiskAnalytica, on behalf of the Mental Health Commission of Canada.
Somers, J. M., Goldner, E. M., Waraich, P. & Hsu, L. (2006). Prevalence and incidence studies of anxiety disorders: A systematic review of the literature. *Canadian Journal of Psychiatry*, 51, 100–13.
Streufert, S., Pogash, R., Roache, J., Severs, W., Gingrich, D., Landis, R., Lonardi, I. & Kantner, A. (1994). Alcohol and managerial performance. *Journal of Studies on Alcohol and Drugs*, 55(2), 230–38.
Stuart, H. (2006). Mental illness and employment discrimination. *Current Opinion in Psychiatry*, 19, 522–6.
Szeto, A. C. & Dobson, K. S. (2013). Mental disorders and their association with perceived work stress: An investigation of the 2010 Canadian Community Health Survey. *Journal of Occupational Health Psychology*, 18, 191–7.
Vohs, K. D., Baumeister, R. F. & Ciarocco, N. J. (2005). Self-regulation and self-presentation: Regulatory resource depletion impairs impression management and effortful self-presentation depletes regulatory resources. *Journal of Personality and Social Psychology*, 88, 632–57.
Vredenburgh, D. & Shea-VanFossen, R. (2010). Human nature, organizational politics, and human resource development. *Human Resource Development Review*, 9, 26–47.

Waghorn, G., Chant, D., White, P. & Whiteford, H. (2005). Disability, employment and work performance among people with ICD-10 anxiety disorders. *Australian and New Zealand Journal of Psychiatry*, 39, 55–66.

Wagner, D. T., Barnes, C. M., Lim, V. K. & Ferris, D. L. (2012). Lost sleep and cyberloafing: Evidence from the laboratory and a daylight saving time quasi-experiment. *Journal of Applied Psychology*, 97, 1068–76.

Westerlaken, K. M. & Woods, P. R. (2013). The relationship between psychopathy and the Full Range Leadership Model. *Personality and Individual Differences*, 54(1), 41–6.

Index

Page numbers in *italics* refer to figures; those in **bold** refer to tables and boxes.

Leading to Occupational Health and Safety: How Leadership Behaviours Impact Organizational Safety and Well-Being, First Edition.
Edited by E. Kevin Kelloway, Karina Nielsen and Jennifer K. Dimoff.

Printed and bound by CPI Group (UK) Ltd, Croydon, CR0 4YY
16/04/2025
14658557-0001